THE STATE OF THE
EUROPEAN UNION

Vol. 4

 *A biennial project of the*
European Community
Studies Association

THE STATE OF THE EUROPEAN UNION

Vol. 4

Deepening and Widening

edited by

Pierre-Henri Laurent
Marc Maresceau

LYNNE
RIENNER
PUBLISHERS

BOULDER
LONDON

Published in the United States of America in 1998 by
Lynne Rienner Publishers, Inc.
1800 30th Street, Boulder, Colorado 80301

and in the United Kingdom by
Lynne Rienner Publishers, Inc.
3 Henrietta Street, Covent Garden, London WC2E 8LU

Library of Congress Cataloging-in-Publication Data
The state of the European Union: Deepening and widening / edited by
  Pierre-Henri Laurent and Marc Maresceau.
      p.   cm.—(State of the European Union ; vol. 4)
    Includes bibliographical references and index.
    ISBN 1-55587-720-6 (alk. paper)
    1. European Union. I. Laurent, Pierre-Henri, 1933–
  II. Maresceau, Marc. III. Series.
  JN30.D39 1998
  341.242'2—dc21   97-36618
                                                        CIP

British Cataloguing in Publication Data
A Cataloguing in Publication record for this book
is available from the British Library.

Printed and bound in the United States of America

      The paper used in this publication meets the requirements
 ∞   of the American National Standard for Permanence of
      Paper for Printed Library Materials Z39.48-1984.

      5 4 3 2 1

Contents

Tables and Figures

Tables

Figures

Preface

This is the fourth volume in a series, sponsored by the European Community Studies Association (ECSA), that combines a short- and a longer-term glance back at Europe's regional integration process and also evaluates and assesses its direction and momentum.

As one of several projects of ECSA, this series is directed at a growing number of people throughout the world interested in the European integration experiment of nearly half a century. The goals of ECSA include promoting the study of the EU by aiding research projects and other collaborative work among its members and other EU students; ameliorating connections between ECSA and its organizational working parts, especially in Europe; publishing the *ECSA Review;* holding workshops and conferences and organizing sessions and panels at both its own biennial conferences and other professional gatherings; and funding teaching and research on the EU. The overall objective is to develop a closely knit community of teachers, scholars, and policy practitioners that raises the level of knowledge about European integration.

This volume was prepared and edited on the eve of and during the early months of the 1996 Intergovernmental Conference (IGC). The purpose of the IGC was to make an evaluation of the functioning of the EU since the enforcement on 1 November 1993 of the Treaty on European Union (TEU), signed at Maastricht, and to examine how the EU can be consolidated and strengthened. Articles B and N of the TEU make explicit reference to the 1996 IGC—in particular, Article B is formulated in broad terms and refers to "policies and forms of cooperation introduced by this Treaty" that may need to be revised in an IGC that "shall be convened in 1996." The 1995 Reflection Group established for that purpose and chaired by Carlos Westendorp suggested that the 1996 IGC should pursue three main goals: bring Europe closer to its citizens, allow the Union to function better in order to prepare for enlargement, and give the Union greater capacity for external action. At the Turin European Council of 29 March 1996, the European Council endorsed this approach.

The contents and structure of this volume are to a large extent but not exclusively determined by both the official and informal agendas of the 1996 IGC. The leading EU issues and institutional reforms at the end of this century, such as enlargement, security, and monetary union, are extensively covered in this book, but so are those issues tangential to or disconnected from the 1996 IGC—e.g., relations with the United States, Russia, and the new World Trade Organization (WTO). The articles were completed in the winter of 1996–1997.

The editors extend their gratitude to Mary-Ann Kazanjian, Annette Lazzara Dawson, and Miriam Seltzer at Tufts, to Linda De Lange at Ghent, and to Sally Glover at Lynne Rienner Publishers.

Pierre-Henri Laurent
Marc Maresceau

1

Introduction: Moving to a Multispeed Europe

Pierre-Henri Laurent & Marc Maresceau

The adaptation to the Maastricht Treaty by the Fifteen of the European Union intensified in 1995–1996 as it prepared for and entered into its fourth IGC since 1985. The IGC that ended with the Single European Act (SEA) was followed legally by two IGCs, one on monetary union and another on political union. The task of reforming the institutions and preparing for further enlargement became imperatives that were at the heart of the IGC begun at Turin in March 1996. This introductory essay focuses on the major goals that diplomatic exercise confronted, specifically, monetary union, the construction of security and foreign policy, institutional adjustments, and the deepening of a truly EU society in policy areas such as social and environmental concerns.

In exposing the central IGC objectives and problems, the chapter reviews the contributions in this volume and attempts to both add to them and assess them collectively. What emerges are the recurrent competing and conflicting visions of European unity ("federalist" and "confederalist"; "Atlanticist" and "Europeanist"), the institutional challenges associated with expansion in terms of EU voting procedures and numbers of Commission decisionmakers, and the pros and cons of a two- or maybe multispeed Europe that appears to be breaking forth in the Union.

The IGC in Historical Perspective

Historical perspectives on EU development and the integration process in general, particularly in this decade, have been increasingly skeptical of the chances for significant progress.[1] In the case of this newest IGC, there is evidence that the timing may be wrong, the impetus weak, and the chosen mechanism incorrect.

The employment of the IGC for integration diplomacy is, in fact, chal-

lenged in the case of 1996–1997 by Desmond Dinan (Chapter 2). A historical and comparative study of the 1985 and 1991 IGCs leads him to conclude that IGCs are cumbersome, unwieldy, and controversial tools for
change. If his argument and evidence that the IGC is at best a questionable
mechanism to deepen and prepare to widen, and furthermore that IGCs
ought not to be employed to negotiate, then the Maastricht II process is
flawed and its real success questionable. Certainly, the recent increase in
public skepticism about the EU and the lingering recession, with the stagnant productivity and high unemployment it has brought, make bold initiatives and actual transfers of sovereignty in transnational deals more difficult. One might argue that member states' refusal to subordinate their own
sectional interests are increased in times of economic downturn, and any
lack of public enthusiasm for integration ventures further circumscribes
power transfers away from the nation-state. Dinan maintains that the commitment to both transparency and democratization in this current exercise
will be examined closely by the EU voters, who now seek a "people's
Europe," not one driven by technocratic logic.

Seen through the prism of recent history, the construction of the EU
appears to have reached a stage where much political control devolves to a
minority of member states who seek little more than a European marketplace—an EU-wide free market with free movement of labor, capital,
goods and services.[2] But there are differing views, both in Europe and
among outside observers, about the EU's evolution, and some of our
authors contradict this assessment of the EU as just a marketplace.

This volume looks first at the post–Cold War necessity for EU widening because of the numerous problems posed for all other EU enterprises.
This means examining both the challenges of absorbing the Central and
Eastern European Countries (CEECs) themselves and the necessary institutional adjustments required of the larger EU. It also brings up the entire EU
attempt to construct a Common Foreign and Security Policy (CFSP) within
the 1990s context of a new European security order. A particular effort
must go into forging with Europe's main ally, the United States, a regional
relationship that encompasses the former Soviet satellites and does not
alienate Russia. After considering other IGC goals of increased common
policy coherence, this volume surveys the cardinal EU issue of monetary
union and a single currency and reviews and assesses the EU's major external relations.

Enlargement and Relations with Eastern Europe

Enlargement is perhaps the most challenging issue the EU currently faces.
No fewer than ten CEECs have now applied for EU membership. On the
applications already introduced by Turkey, Cyprus, and Malta, the

European Commission has formulated its opinion, stating that negotiations for membership with Turkey could not be opened but handing down a positive decision on Cyprus and Malta in 1993. Moreover, the 1995 Cannes European Council reiterated the view that negotiations for membership with Cyprus and Malta would start six months after the conclusion of the IGC. At the 1995 Madrid European Council, the Commission was asked to expedite preparation of its opinion on the applications by the CEECs and to embark upon preparation of a composite paper on enlargement. All applicant countries would be treated on an equal basis. The European Council expressed the hope that the initial phase of the negotiations for membership would coincide with the start of negotiations with Cyprus and Malta. All of this has led some critics to assert that the EU has become obsessed with the Eastern movement to the point of twisting the Maastricht agenda items out of shape, if not putting them completely out of sight.[3]

In its economic and geographic dimensions, Eastern enlargement projects more threateningly the potential imbalances between the stable and prosperous "core" and the dependent and needy "periphery" territories on the Continent. The possible political tensions (previously North-South, now East-West) that could result have not diminished EU ardor. The rationale for bringing the EU to the CEEC was powerfully and cogently put forth at the December 1995 Madrid summit and throughout 1996. Extending the club of fifteen to perhaps twenty-five was "both a political necessity and historic opportunity." Thus the IGC's work has a primary connection to the preparation for negotiations with Cyprus and Malta and at least the Visegrád Three, the projected "first wave" of Poland, the Czech Republic, and Hungary.

If enlargement is a key EU strategy to preserve and promote economic and political stability in Europe, it undeniably forces the Fifteen into far-reaching internal reforms. The most difficult problems in terms of EU change would revolve around money, for the poor CEEC applicants could be an enormous burden on the Common Agricultural Policy (CAP) subsidies funding and structural funds benefits. These two EU accounts are almost 80 percent of the entire EU budget. As potentially large net beneficiaries (they put less into the budget than they get back), the CEECs worry both large EU contributor members (Germany, Britain, France, the Netherlands) and current net "winners" (the Mediterranean-rim states, Ireland) whose handouts will most likely diminish. Policies must be changed, or a frightening 60 percent budget increase will accompany even the entry of the 1997 group from the East.[4]

CAP reform and stricter allocation controls may alleviate what appear to be unacceptable costs, but the EU will require accommodation from the Eastern newcomers, too. Subsidies and development funds will probably be lowered by IGC decisions, now or later in the 1990s, which will suggest use of the now famous mechanism of slow transition phases into benefits to absorb the financial blow on the EU. The difficulty in this solution is the perception that a two-tier member state system will evolve, with alienated second-class states getting lesser rewards.[5]

These chapters examine and analyze the previous and the next enlargement and the implications of both. The contribution by Péter Balázs (Chapter 4) examines the various possible strategies and theoretical models for the Eastern enlargement of the European Union. One of the fundamental questions raised is whether a classical enlargement scenario can be applied to the accession requests from the Central and Eastern European countries. Balázs, after having noted "a surprising discrepancy . . . between the integration ambitions and integration abilities of the CEECs," is of the opinion that Eastern enlargement cannot take place "as long as the EU defines itself as a homogeneous organization and regards the CEECs as a homogeneous bloc." Federalist homogeneity should be set aside, for only a multispeed approach to integration can bring a viable and successful solution. This differentiation would also, according to Balázs, more easily allow differentiation among the applicants. John Peterson and Elizabeth Bomberg (Chapter 3) evaluate the effect of the most recent northern enlargement on the policy and functioning of the EU. They observe that contrary to what some commentators had expected, northern enlargement did not reinforce the intergovernmental tendencies. They argue that perhaps "the most important effect of northern enlargement is that it made the next enlargement more likely to be relatively ambitious and soon." Bart Kerremans's contribution (Chapter 5) is a case study on the effects of enlargement on the institutional framework in the EU, particularly the Council. Kerremans examines how enlargement will hurt the capacity of and control in the Council. He fears that as a consequence of the increasing conflicts of interests among member states, consensus on the necessary institutional structures will be difficult, if not impossible. The probability that a compromise may be sought at the expense of the capacity of the Council shows how the EU can become the victim of its own success.

Enlargement has become a priority of the Union, but it could not be the major preoccupation in 1995–1996, given the IGC requirements in terms of internal reforms and the progress on monetary union. Since the financing system approved at the 1992 Edinburgh European Council runs only to 1999, decisions about the budgetary structure from 1999 onward need to be decided soon after completion of the 1996–1997 IGC and probably parallel with the next enlargement negotiations. These talks, projected to commence in late 1997 or early 1998, will call for reconfigurations among the Fifteen and the first-wave Eastern entrants. What will be the biggest and most historically important EU budget crunch will necessitate budget reallocation decisions that the current IGC has avoided. Broad external-relations issues that include the European security architecture, meaning not just the former Soviet bloc nations but Russia itself, in 1996–1997 became the focal point of the Euro-Atlantic states. The crowded EU agenda in the last years of the twentieth century suggests that the most critical tests in the half-century history of integration are in the immediate future. The outer fringes of Europe are to be part of this great continental experiment; the periphery is to become part of the core.

Security and Foreign Policy

This forthcoming enlargement process has developed in the last few years alongside EU foreign and security ambitions. The further development of a CFSP was mandated as a primary IGC goal after its creation in the early 1990s. By 1995–1996, its progress was in fact hindered by internal EU differences and external security decisions. Within the EU, efforts on a civilian foreign policy for the EU encountered widely divergent views, and movement on the European Union defense identity and organization was impacted by the Atlantic Alliance restructuring led by Washington.[6] The European economic conditions, mainly in terms of budget decisions that in part emanate from the European and Monetary Union (EMU) demands and are accentuated by domestic belt-tightening and austerity programs, have resulted in intensified military cutbacks and greater emphasis on interinstitutional defense approaches. The advancement of a European defense concept appears to mean a new, more flexible and inclusive North Atlantic Treaty Organization (NATO) *now* and a real but limited (in power and scope and probably influence) and subsidiary European Security and Defense Identity (ESDI) in the Western European Union (WEU) *later.*

Two interconnected problems have contributed to this redefinition of European security. European defense attitudes and policies and enlargement politics have interacted to produce a diminished possibility for a better, fuller CFSP resulting from the IGC. There will be improvement mechanisms, as Michael Smith specifies (Chapter 8), in the formation of a planning/analysis unit (without initiator powers), some budgeting for CFSP, small arms production cooperation, and possibly an EU chief spokesperson on foreign and security matters. The prospects are slight that transfers of authority to the EU by member states will occur, least of all in any qualified majority voting (QMV) application that communitarizes CFSP. Variable geometry in the defense field, as in EMU, is the most likely end result of Maastricht II.

The European governments and defense establishments have failed to prepare for a larger and independent post–Cold War regional military role. In the struggle to create a new security identity, economic considerations have resulted in huge cuts in defense and labor power. Operations at the outer limit of or beyond NATO's geographic perimeters are not possible now for any kind of a European force. The military assets of the United

States, in particular sophisticated communications equipment and sea and air troop transports, have been central and mandatory in the Bosnian peace-keeping tasks, so the truism remains that security in and for Europe comes via the Americans.[7]

This growing reliance on the United States is also based on smaller European forces, less military research and development, and numerous equipment cancellations. Given the public's marked proclivity for defense cuts over reduced social programs, national leaders have since 1990 constantly chosen to diminish their military budgets and reshape into smaller, more efficient and mobile forces.

The combination of contemporary warfare needs and the new geopolitical order illustrates the dilemma for Europe most profoundly in the question of "lift." Getting rapidly to a faraway crisis area was clearly not a European possibility in the Gulf War. In transportation and logistics, in most areas of command and control, the Europeans have simply not planned and spent their way to a point where any "out-of-region" trouble can be addressed with European force. Although it is less apparent regarding internal European trouble spots, the fact remains that for the rest of this century only modest military operations could emanate from a WEU command center. Smaller, more professional, and well-equipped elements such as the five-nation Eurocorps do have value in certain limited contexts, but a European defense identity will not result from the sharply reduced forces and military spending of the 1990s.[8]

A strong European ambivalence, among elites and general populations alike, concerning the costs behind more military autonomy from the United States played a large role in the NATO decisions in June 1996 in Berlin. The France of Jacques Chirac, as Ronald Tiersky aptly points out (Chapter 9), has slashed its military spending under the duress of strong domestic presences but has launched a new power projection capacity with an end to conscription and a reorganized armed force that will soon aim at a first-rate standing in its equipment status. Tiersky in addition asserts that France got its way in NATO's decision to address structural issues before augmenting alliance membership. Nevertheless, European leaders including Chirac were obviously pressed to accept the Berlin NATO agreements on shared assets, "coalitions of the willing," and so on. The fact will remain into the next millennium that Europe cannot have strong independent defense desires while economic malaise continues.[9] Tiersky sees the dominant significance of France in the security issues of the EU in the same manner that Dorothee Heisenberg (Chapter 14) reflects the controlling role of Germany and its domestic economic and financial orientations in the EMU arena.

EU military dependency is also the end result of fundamental disagreements that persist on weapons (three fighter aircraft—the Rafael, Grepen, and Eurofighter) and strategy (rapid-deployment force vs. long-term sustainable "total" forces). There is even a comprehensible conflict concerning the kind of military restructuring that a European force like WEU would require to answer in terms of military responses of diverse types (military juntas or popular ethnic, civil uprisings) in different parts of the Continent (again, Turkey or eastern Finland or the Baltic states).[10]

The Atlantic Alliance enlargement imperative has forced itself into EU plans with the goal of a larger role for both NATO and the United States in the new security architecture. The June and December 1996 decisions of the NATO Council outlined a revamped alliance that, with France's reentry, constituted the primary vehicle for Eastern enlargement. This 1996 facelift of NATO, deemed to be the organ best suited to address post–Cold War realities in the entire Euro-Atlantic area, was based on European solidarity, albeit with some ambivalence about alliance renovation, given the present limitations of the WEU and CFSP.[11] In essence, as Tiersky points out, with France strikingly taking the initiative, the EU states agreed that there was no real political will or capability nor the money in the immediate future to construct a distinctively European pillar or a serious defense body. They furthermore conceded that in the debate about Europe's moving east, NATO, not the EU, should most appropriately and realistically come first. The new NATO would be the alliance for all seasons and would eclipse WEU for the medium term, in terms of keeping Europe secure.

There was no agreement by early 1997 in either the EU or NATO about the specifics of taking in new members from the East. The questions concern timing, finances, and treaty commitments. In NATO's case there appeared to be strong reasons for enlarging before the EU, starting with negotiations in 1997. The cost factor appears central and is connected to the enlargement strategy, that is, decisions on whether NATO would provide for defense against Russia by means of actual presence or even cheaper "partial presence" in the former Warsaw Pact states. Money is also at the center of the overwhelming short-term problem for Europe in the *dual* enlargement of NATO and EU, which will call for huge spending increases. In the longer term (but this means into the middle and latter parts of the first decade of the twenty-first century), the defense costs will be reduced and the Eastern European economic demands will augment the EU economy.

EU Eastern enlargement appears to be on a slower pace than NATO enlargement simply because the EU has indicated in its preaccession strategy that negotiations will not begin until at least six months after the conclusion of the IGC. Even if there were swift progress in the debate on enlargement in 1997–1998, parliamentary ratifications would most likely extend into 1999, and candidate countries would not become members until 2000 or later. The major variant in the EU and NATO enlargement process is the complex and diverse amount of adaptation required in the EU case, including numerous factors on free market operations and progress in creating parliamentary democracy. Just as some U.S. leaders have negative outlooks on NATO's stretching east, there is subterranean resistance in some sectors, elite and otherwise, on whether EU expansion is urgent or even necessary, particularly when the costs are factored in.

Recent developments have demonstrated that many in the West, especially in Europe, believe the outside determinant is Russia. To Russians, an expanded NATO security blanket on the Russian western frontier several hundred kilometers east of the former iron curtain is merely Cold War containment strategy reaffirmed in *fin de siècle* Europe. For some in the West, developing a new, regionwide, comprehensive special relationship with Russia appears to be a job that is easier for Brussels South (EU) than Brussels North (NATO) in that the EU is no threat and an open Russian economy benefits the EU. It might easily be argued that the EU should make an EU-Russian agreement that ranges from financial aid to trade concessions a top priority, leading to a structured and institutionalized close economic association between Moscow and Brussels alongside a projected 1997 NATO-Russia agreement. Even though Russia's reaction to economic enlargement may be benevolent, it appears that Moscow's leery view of Western security expansion may indeed need to be addressed first to avoid a new Yalta.

If the IGC decisions on security issues deny real progress on CFSP with WEU as the European defense arm, as Joseph Coffey believes (Chapter 6), does the EU's increased dependency on the United States doom any meaningful future ESDI?[12] Again, awareness of European power limitations is at the heart of recent European (in)action, reflecting the reluctance of some states to turn over their foreign and security decisionmaking powers to a collective like the EU. The creation of an effective European CFSP is possible, but the 1996–1997 IGC will not make a reality out of the concept of using the WEU as the defense arm of the Union.

Internal Reform

Monetary union and enlargement have overshadowed the crucial institutional agenda in the IGC. If the IGC's goal was to prepare the ground for enlargement, the preponderance of evidence suggests the development of a multilayered system of states that increasingly select where and when they will participate. The universality of rules and procedures, let alone policies, appears to diminish as cracks in the integration structure become visible in IGC reform failures. The IGC review of EU procedures and structures brings up the most sensitive problems in the regional organization that range from the power balance between large and small states, majority voting, national sovereignty, bloated decision groups, and most significant, the demographic and economic weighting of member states and the related equality-efficiency controversy.

The most contentious issue in the domain of IGC institutional reform centers on the question of power sharing between large and small states in an enlarged EU. The big-small balance in the EU-15 serves everyone's interests fairly well, but the increase in small, weaker states will undeniably require institutional adjustments that favor larger countries. Most proposals that answer that demand highlight the double-majority voting system in the Council of Ministers, that is, decisions require the support of both the majority of votes cast by member states and those states voting in favor of the decision representing the majority of the EU population. Whether this double majority is a single or two-thirds majority and whether this applies as well to EP voting must also be dealt with in the IGC.[13]

Some experts believe the most painful diplomacy will be about EU operating capability and whether efficiency will win over equality or vice versa. This problem of equality, rebalancing power between large (and to some degree medium-sized) and small states, will not be solved in the simplest manner, with more federalism or supranationality; a plain, mechanical recalculation of votes has less than a scant chance of IGC support. This challenge of enlargement—the equality contradiction, as it is known—demands the double-majority solution that protects the big states but also needs to address the small countries' loss of direct power. A workable and efficient EU would not necessarily be based on absolute, across-the-board fairness, unless some way could be found to protect all member states with equal rights rather than equality. If the federal route, the one that gives true equality, is not possible now, then the double-counting method, which similarly enhances the democratic legitimacy of decisionmaking, appears to be the next best answer.

Nevertheless, more members means more difficult payoffs, logrolling, and even constitutional bargains in solving enlargement and reform problems. The concept of the equality of states and of citizens should be translated into reality with the double-country method, in that EU legitimacy that now comes from its member states would henceforth also come from its people.[14] In late 1996 the EU debated the merits of the UN Security Council as a model for a reformed EU Commission, which would set up a small permanent group of commissioners and a rotation of others, with accompanying safeguards for the small states. The reasoning was that alliances and partnerships are an EU reality that could be built on.

The EU's capacity to act will not be settled in the 1996–1997 IGC. But if the EU cannot establish a genuine federal state and bicameral legislative system, the double-majority voting process that does emerge will reflect the real balance of European economic and political power, with some respect for democratic principles. This is admittedly the best scenario possible, as it would provide for a wider Europe with an effective streamlining of institutions.

The stakes in this problem area are enormous, and the extent of differences was indicated by the 1995 Reflection Group's weak, meager, and even unclear recommendations on voting. Because QMV raised so many contentious issues in the preliminary negotiations, many observers believed IGC reweighing and rebalancing would be nearly impossible. Unless a cross-issue trade-off results in an extended QMV, especially in the Council and Pillar I and II decisions, there is a true possibility of freezing future EU development.

If the EU institutions have been the subject of intensive IGC diplomacy, so have the Pillar III topics. Actual IGC achievements appear most likely in these areas, especially those that deal with justice, human rights, and home affairs. This category was established by the TEU and is to be reviewed, evaluated, and improved, if possible, in the 1996–1997 IGC. Although there are many differences among the Fifteen on such problems as asylum policy, immigration, and judicial coordination in criminal and civil matters, there can be further commitments to cross-national cooperation. Customs and police cooperation in the transfrontier combat of drug trafficking and terrorism will probably emerge, including new measures related to the enlargement of the Europol (European Police) convention.

These will not be insignificant EU gains, but in other areas IGC prospects are dimmer. Environment does not have the highest priority in Maastricht II, but John McCormick (Chapter 10) describes and analyzes the recent development of environmental law on water, air, and noise pollution and control of biotechnological, chemical, and nuclear threats. Since the SEA made the environment an EU treaty subject, Maastricht I took large strides, for instance, with a Cohesion Fund that promised some $9 billion to environmental projects. On the questions of continued environmental cooperation and the relationship between environmentalism and future accession, McCormick believes that the divergent views of the applicant states, the recent northern entrants, the southern member states, and the original six members pose gigantic difficulties.

Social policy, the social dimension of integration, has an even lower status in the overall EU outlook. As Robert Geyer and Beverly Springer show in their treatment of the European Works Councils (EWC) directive (Chapter 11), some governments and the trade unions want more emphasis on that aspect. Geyer and Springer do believe some positive lessons can be learned from the British experience and see the recent entrants as pressing for employment and equality policy amelioration along with more coalition building on moving from social dialogue to common social policies. They foresee few positive outcomes in IGC considerations involving the social dimension. In the related area of EU efforts for women, R. Amy Elman, in her critical analysis of the gender dimension (Chapter 12), discerns a disconcertingly low interest after some minimal attention in the 1980s. She furthermore disagrees with some other contributors (e.g., McCormick) who consider the EU simply a marketplace, painting a rather depressing portrait of marginalized women in the EU.

Monetary Union

After the completion of the internal market in 1992, EMU was the next logical regional integration step. In 1990 the Commission had unequivocally observed that "a single currency [was] the natural complement of a single market" and that "the full potential of the latter [would] not be achieved without the former."[15] This conceptual linkage of the completion of the internal market on the one hand with EMU on the other led to a number of specific and detailed provisions in the Treaty of Maastricht. The TEU, signed in February 1992 and entering into force in November 1993, created a three-pillar Europe that was then to be called a European Union. The first pillar centered inter alia on the formation of an EMU that committed Europe to move from the first stage of improved economic and monetary policy convergence and removal of exchange controls in member states to two more advanced stages in the late 1990s. Article B of the TEU stipulated that a second stage beginning in 1994 would establish a European Monetary Institute (EMI) that would be the transition to a European Central Bank (ECB). The third stage set a 1 January 1999 start to the monetary union in nations that qualified (met the convergence criteria), with the irrevocable locking of exchange rates and the introduction of a single currency (later named the "Euro").

As opposed to CFSP and cooperation in the field of justice and home affairs, which became the second and third pillars outside the EC treaty, EMU policy objectives and procedures were integrated in the *EC* monetary union as one of the main objectives of the *Community*. Article 3a(2) of the EC treaty says that the establishment of EMU "shall include the irrevocable fixing of exchange rates leading to the introduction of a single currency, the ECU, and the definition and conduct of a single monetary policy and exchange-rate policy." These objectives have been further worked out in Title VI of the EC treaty on economic and monetary policy (Articles 102a–109m) and in specific protocols signed in Maastricht and declarations annexed to the Final Act of the TEU. Strictly speaking, EMU is not on the IGC agenda. The EMU has its own framework in which it operates. But if it is true that the EMU scenario does not need the 1996 IGC in order to materialize, the setting up of EMU necessarily affects any further reflection on future EU cooperation models taking place during Maastricht II.

On 1 January 1994, the second stage of EMU started, and the European Monetary Institution was established and finally located in Frankfurt. Its main tasks were to strengthen the coordination of the monetary policies of the member states and to prepare for the transition toward Stage III. The moment of starting this stage was not clearly defined in the Treaty, but the Madrid European Council (1995), reiterating the need for a high degree of economic convergence as a sine qua non to achieve the EMU objective, agreed that this would be 1 January 1999.

Stage III of EMU is therefore the crucial phase. Its commencement will mean that the exchange rates of the various currencies will be locked to each other and to the Euro, so that the EMU participant currencies and the Euro will in effect be the same currency. All monetary policy operations will be executed in Euros, meaning that financial markets will convert to this one European currency. The Euro will become legal tender only when the European Central Bank issues Euro coins and banknotes and national currencies are withdrawn from circulation, set for 2002.

The Dublin December 1996 summit showed that the prospects for achieving EMU were realistic. It had become clear by that time that the attainment of the fiscal convergence criteria by a critical mass of EU states was entirely possible, but it would not be all of them. The difficult criterion requiring budget deficits of its members not exceeding 3 percent of gross domestic product (GDP) and a gross debt not exceeding 60 percent is in many of the EU member states a top domestic political priority. Although the terms of the Treaty do not leave much scope for interpretation regarding the 3 percent criterion, with the debt ratio (60 percent of GDP) there is some flexibility, since that reference may be exceeded if "the ratio is suffi- ciently diminishing and approaching the reference value at a satisfactory pace."[16] At the end of 1996, the Dublin summit did not succumb to pres- sures on the national leaders to soften the criteria or relax the launch date. Backsliding was defeated by the Paris-Bonn concert, with Helmut Kohl and Jacques Chirac providing the political momentum, determination, and opti- mism.

If it seems likely that EMU will begin with six to nine members in 1999, it should also be made clear that EMU will not be a panacea for the unemployment problem. Daniel Gros is right when he says that the EU even with EMU is not equipped to solve this issue: "The potential to reduce structural unemployment in a major way . . . remain[s] under the responsi- bility of national governments."[17]

German EMU concerns have been paramount, and in Chapter 14 Heisenberg shows how the German Bundesbank perceptions of monetary policy and monetary union were gradually institutionalized. She goes on with an account of German preference formation and its close linkage to the development of European monetary cooperation but also some conflict. This was, as so often happens in the field of European integration, the result of a close interplay of political, economic, and legal factors. The explanation of the dominance of the Bundesbank's policy in recent EMU decisions starts in Heisenberg's analysis with the 1993 German Constitutional Court decision on the compatibility between the TEU and the German constitution. In this ruling the court stated that before Germany could be part of EMU, the Bundestag and Bundesrat had to confirm that the convergence criteria of the TEU are actually met. Consequently, since EMU without Germany is unthinkable, the Bundesbank assumes a dominant supervisory position in the European monetary integration process. The other member states, at least those interested in monetary integration, seem to have openly or implicitly accepted the leading role of Germany. In this context, the initial, almost trivial discussion around the name of the common currency is particularly revealing. Notwithstanding the fact that the TEU already explicitly qualified the common currency as "the ECU" (Article 3a[2]), the Bundesbank and German political leaders argued that the question of the name had not yet been settled. The influence of the German position in European monetary integration was clearly demonstrated in the Commission's acknowledgment, in its green paper "The Practical Arrangements for the Introduction of the Single Currency," that the question of the currency's name should not become an obstacle for the preparation of EMU and its statement that "if necessary, this requires a discussion at the political level."[18]

The other EMU topics addressed in this book largely concentrate on the external dimension of EMU. The adjective "external" perhaps needs further elucidation. It denotes first the relations with the other major international partners of the EU, particularly the United States. Peter Loedel, who focuses on the international pressures to create monetary union (Chapter 13), shows how Germany, which already has a prominent role in the formulation of European monetary strategy, has linked its policy to that of the United States. One of the unavoidable consequences of this approach is that "the EMU, as the monetary arm of the EU, does not retain an identity of its own with separate and distinct interests vis-à-vis the United States or the dollar." At this stage of the process of monetary integration, it is difficult to predict the outcome of the further evolution. Most commentators seem to agree on at least one thing: that a two-speed monetary integration is likely to occur. The analysis of recent changes in European monetary cooperation by Alison Watson (Chapter 15) asserts that in a two-speed EMU there is a strong need for specific arrangements to guarantee exchange rate stability, control currency volatility, and set up a legal framework organizing the institutional relations with those EU members unable or unwilling to join EMU. The initial two-speed monetary integration involves a magnitude of the problems and many unknown consequences that the EU will face on the road to EMU.

A particular point that must be addressed is the relationship of EMU with enlargement. At the 1993 Copenhagen European Council, agreement was reached on the principle of acceptance of the associated countries from Central and Eastern Europe who desired to become members of the

European Union, stressing that membership presupposed the candidate's ability to take on the obligations of membership *including adherence to the aims of political, economic, and monetary union.* It goes without saying that establishment of EMU will make accession of the CEECs much more difficult. It is true that most of the past enlargement experiences have shown an intricate relationship between enlargement and monetary policy, as Peterson and Bromberg demonstrate in Chapter 3. It may also be true, as Loedel argues in Chapter 13, that deepening monetary union and enlargement are not necessarily contradictory, since "deepening monetary union can stimulate the necessary reforms of the decisionmaking structure and agricultural policies of the EU." What is not debatable is that at the moment of accession, the state of achievement of EMU, whatever the monetary integration structure at that time may be, will be part of the *acquis communautaire* to which any new member state will have to adhere.[19]

Through many discordant EU debates, however, the EMU has remained on track. This may be the great EU achievement of 1995–1996. The promises and compelling attraction of greater competitiveness, increased trade, lower interest rates, and lower inflation have prevailed over the critics of monetary integration changes.

The drive to complete EMU is the recognition that without it the single internal market remains fragmented in fifteen different currencies that involve risks in exchange rate activity and unnecessary transaction costs. Given that impetus and the maintenance of Franco-German solidarity, European monetary unification *will* occur not simply because an increasing number of member states appear to be able to qualify and the timetable is realistic but because Bonn and Paris have struck a bargain. Even though Pan-European monetary policy is tied to a political union accord, testy questions in many cases remain. Will political and/or economic considerations lead to packaging the EMU together with a stability council and exchange rate bonds? Does EMU have the necessary popular support and credibility? Will the control bank have a true governmental framework with democratic accountability? Can strengthened monetary institutions and a wide EMU avert a permanent two-speed EMU?

External Relations

Two global powers and a new multilateral organization, alongside NATO, seem to be at the center of all EU external relations. The EU security and enlargement arenas are still defined by the paramount roles Washington and Moscow play.[20] Roy Ginsberg (Chapter 16) argues that the 1990 Transatlantic Declaration (TAD) and 1995 New Transatlantic Agenda (NTA) are the centerpieces of the most critical post–Cold War relationship.

And yet the transatlantic relationship has its problems, for trade spats have frequently worked themselves into full-blown crises. From the chicken war of the 1960s to the Boeing-Airbus disputes of the 1990s, brinkmanship has necessitated more and more crisis diplomacy to avoid a serious rupture. Ginsberg suggests that the stakes got larger with the Helms-Burton and D'Amato Bills concerning Cuba, Libya, and Iran, as threats led to sanctions and other retaliatory actions. European solidarity is also noteworthy in these cases, with EU claims of U.S. unilateralism resulting in heightened tensions.

Ginsberg's accent, however, is on the ties that bind the peace and prosperity in the transoceanic connection, especially with the improved closeness of communications and understanding. He does illustrate how U.S. orientations and policies contribute to Europeanist-Atlanticist divisions in the EU that are now a half century old and still vibrant, even after the Cold War. Ginsberg is convinced that the new challenges and global realignments have led the Europeans and Americans to adapt their partnership via institutional improvements and patterns of cooperation that should ameliorate their economic and security concerns.[21] The Transatlantic Dialogue of 1990 evolved from a broader dialogue to more specific goals and commitments to cooperate with more frequent multilevel contacts. By the end of 1995, the New Transatlantic Agenda launched in Madrid delineated an action program focusing on collaborative means for promoting peace, democracy, and development. It contained responses to global challenges, contributed toward expanded global trade and more open economic relations, and accelerated and deepened the possibilities for transatlantic bridge building. With EU-U.S. trade accounting for 30 percent of world trade and constituting almost 60 percent of the industrialized world's gross domestic product, this transatlantic relationship centers on trade, but it also concerns investment and peace and stability. Furthermore, the recent partnership accords call for coordination and cooperation in combating drug trafficking, terrorism, and crime as well as communicable diseases and other public health problems.

The prime example of Western coordination has been the Washington-Brussels diplomacy regarding Russia and Eastern Europe that was initiated in the case of the Bosnian crisis with the Dayton accords in late 1995. A broader East-West charter that links Russia in some fashion with NATO and is intended to ease Russian opposition to NATO expansion became the new and major Western initiative in the fall of 1996. U.S. secretary of state Warren Christopher and German chancellor Helmut Kohl both indicated that alliance enlargement would proceed in 1997 in tandem with the diplomatic negotiations for a special NATO-Russia charter that deals with standing arrangements for consultation, joint action, nuclear weapons reductions, and even combined training operations. The aim was to avoid provoking Russian (and Ukrainian and Belarusian) suspicion and fear and to resolve the dispute by gaining Russian approval for an enlarged NATO and defining Moscow's future role in European security. NATO members hoped the admission of the first wave of former Soviet states into the alliance would take place as Russia's NATO role was resolved diplomatically, averting a division of the Continent into rival Russian and Western camps.

Second thoughts about moving East have surfaced in NATO and the EU. For the United States, NATO growth means the high costs and risks of further U.S. military commitments in return for the retention of Washington's leadership position in Europe and the maintenance of European security itself. Opposition to alliance expansion and its dangers has gained new ground among some in the United States, including influential experts and politicians.[22] The security problems associated with EU enlargement therefore involve relations with Russia as much as the United States, for it cannot be denied that one of the main considerations for accession to the EU of many CEECs is the consolidation of the split from the former USSR, particularly Russia. In a rather simplistic way, the institutions of the EU take for granted that further Eastern enlargement will necessarily contribute to peace and security.[23] However, so far this geopolitical factor of enlargement does not seem to have been sufficiently addressed by the EU members and the EU itself. In other words, all the political and security implications of Eastern enlargement are not yet fully perceived. Excluding the former USSR—except maybe the Baltic states—may create a new and possibly threatening separation line in Europe, a worry that dictates the primacy of the NATO venture.

The EU will need to be very imaginative, certainly be more creative than with its "partnership formula" as expressed in the partnership and cooperation agreements with Russia, Ukraine, Belarus, and Moldova. Although it contains some potential for development, the partnership agreement is considered by some to be an inadequate response to Russia's political and economic needs. Therefore, parallel and simultaneously to the enlargement debate with the CEECs, there is compelling evidence that a far-reaching, workable, and mutually acceptable security *and* trade partnership framework with Russia should be the highest priority for the Fifteen and the United States. The developments of late 1996 and early 1997 show that Washington, Brussels, and Moscow are aware of this need, but many worry about the low priority in the West, as Russia's complex economic and military sensitivities continue to exist.

Given the expanding importance of global trade, one of the major multilateral achievements of the 1990s in which the EU was a main actor was undoubtedly the creation of the WTO. The multilevel negotiations that finally led to the signing of the Marrakesh agreement on 15 April 1994 were made difficult not only because of the complexity of EU-U.S. relations but also because of the tridimensional distribution conflict among the

Commission, Council, and member states.[24] A striking feature of these basically political and economic conflicts is that they were expressed in terms of a legal issue. The "judiciability" of the political and economic debate proved to be feasible with the rendering of the significant opinion of the Court of Justice of the European Communities of 15 November 1994.[25] At the same time, the Court's ruling indicates where the delimitation of competence in the field of trade negotiations and diplomacy have to be drawn. Mary Footer (Chapter 17) explains the underlying legal and political rationale behind the Court's decision and analyzes the issues of mixed EC and member state participation in the WTO. She furthermore elaborates on the Helms-Burton and D'Amato legislation controversies and complaints and how they will test the credibility of the WTO as the new centerpiece of the global trading system. She is convinced that there may be more tests for Washington than Europe. Incorporating the criteria and "guidelines" provided by the Court, Footer concludes with an analysis of the main commercial relations of the EU, emphasizing, as does Ginsberg, the necessity of both EU and U.S. commitments to the multilateral forum to settle the inevitable disputes that will continue to arise.

Conclusion

The rewriting of the TEU, with a generalized first draft at the December 1996 Dublin summit and a final accord resulting from the summer 1997 Amsterdam summit, was accomplished but with many incomplete answers to the EU's future. Critics will question the document's thoroughness and its contribution to answering queries about European integration. Once again a giant effort yielded only modest incremental results because of the wariness of some states to commit to the further building of truly common policies. Human and civil rights, environmental protection, and employment security got unanimous backing, but the possibility of permanent changes involving a shift from unanimous voting to qualified majority and the Commission size were less certain.

There will be those who hypothesize that EU internal reform failed in the IGC because the prerequisite solidarity was needed for EMU first and Euro-Atlantic strategic consensus second. The priorities of monetary union and NATO enlargement were and are undeniable, but they did exact a price at the IGC. Monetary and currency union will probably be advanced, although some minor calendar slowdown might reflect member state worries. The introduction of a European Central Bank and the Euro itself will require institutions capable of action, and these must be constructed at the IGC. Framing more specifics of a European-wide defense policy and moving from European Political Cooperation (EPC) to an EU foreign-policy-making scheme and structure will remain sketchy, fragmentary, and very intergovernmental. Cooperation agreements in Pillar III are likely to increase in number but probably also to remain intergovernmental. The outlook for internal reforms on democratizing procedure and increasing accountability, let alone making EU voting less complex, more flexible, and efficient, is not sanguine. Solutions that indicate in any decisive manner what kind of European polity and integration may be forthcoming are not to come from the 1996–1997 IGC. In sum, as a preenlargement conference, there are indicators that numerous decisions that would facilitate both a more unified and efficient Union of twenty or more may not emerge in Maastricht II.

In the concluding chapter, Anthony Forster and William Wallace write about the limited prospects for success but focus on the insurmountable challenges that apparently will require Europe to look to the future once again for more thorough solutions. Their forecast that the dominance of IGC divergence will require another conference soon is noteworthy in that it depicts a calendar on EU enlargement negotiations parallel in time with further EU budget and institutional reform decisions between 1998 and 2002.

They see the IGC probably producing a multispeed, even variable, geometry and slow-paced integration that is currently labeled "flexibility." What once was Europe with concentric circles, or à la carte, is presently seen as the flexible solution, or the ability for member states to pick and choose among EU policies. This opt-out alternative, however, threatens the *acquis communautaire* and may lead to a divided EU of core and periphery states if applied to policies already in existence.

The politicization of EU affairs in money and security areas indicates that achieving uniformity in this organization has become harder and that differentiation as much as solidarity often characterizes the EU. It must be remembered that policy construction, but not constitutional change, is open to *groups* of countries within the EU if they wish to advance together on *a* policy basis in *one* area. Significant precedents like the EMS, WEU, Schengen, and the TEU's famous "opt-out" clauses are—perhaps unhappily so for many members—becoming the sum of much EC diplomacy. The 1996–1997 IGC has once again brought forth the lowest-common-denominator resolutions.

Modest changes in a few telling sectors will not make the 1996–1997 IGC a turning point in integration history. The EU, this most innovative and creative twentieth-century approach to interstate cooperation and collective institution construction, will devise some necessary corrections and move forward in crablike fashion in a few domains, but beyond the notable EMU, scant progress toward political union will be visible. What should be discernible is the further development of an EU core and a periphery, with an inner core of eight to ten members who forge ahead in certain sectors and another three to five or so who exclude themselves on particular common-policy formations. The question about "flexibility" concerns the size of the gap between the inner core that are willing to integrate faster and further and those left behind. It appears that even before enlargement, which itself most surely will prompt a more multispeed EU, the Fifteen themselves are repeatedly segmenting and dividing, based on internal divergent perspectives and the resulting crises.

Forster and Wallace see the further evolution of a "core Europe" around the original member states, which aims to move beyond intergovernmentalism and is lined up frequently against a British-led divergent group that opposes further relinquishing national sovereignty to the EU. A multispeed Europe, first seen clearly in the "opt-outs" of Maastricht I, appears to Foster and Wallace as the only route that answers the contradictions between domestic and regional politics. The absence of anything like a grand design, with significant conflicts in many agenda items, implies to them that modest incrementalism will rule the final IGC decisions. They maintain that when the multiple demands and needs of the EU *and* Europe call for more radical transnational decisions and meaningful, future-oriented institutional alterations, only piecemeal answers and Band-Aid solutions appear likely. They see a further reinforcement of cooperation, coordination, and consensus formation in the IGC but not a replacement of the European nation-state. A federal EU with significant transfers of power from the national governments to EU institutions appears an unlikely outcome in this exercise and probably in the near-term future.

This kind of minimalist outcome would be based in part on the compulsory EU tendency to practice accommodative diplomacy, but also on the perceived necessity (and luxury) of postponements of decisions. There are sentiments about a better time for problem solving in the future; surely, goes one argument, with Tony Blair as prime minister in the UK, an economic upswing, further NATO reforms, and decisions vis-à-vis the East including Russia, a later meeting of possibly eighteen to twenty-one states in 2002 (Maastricht III?) might more positively face the deepening imperative.

Even if economic growth returns and the European geopolitical arena stabilizes, the internal differences will persist and mean a more diverse EU—a Europe of clubs. One need merely ask what will transpire in terms of the political will and leadership for integration when its only full-fledged and unwavering advocate, Kohl, disappears from the scene. The need for a European integration advocate with a strategic vision will become increasingly evident. One might also ask what the prospects for EU enlargement are when those next negotiations will be led by a British Council presidency in early 1998. Even the Blair government might still reflect a forceful confederalist stance on many central EU issues.

The 1996–1997 exercise on deepening in preparation for a larger Union will yield up different speeds and different interests. Whether this multispeed Europe is so divided that it cannot act together and truly be any kind of integrated Europe can be determined only when the Maastricht II revisions are put into operation, after either Amsterdam in summer 1997 or Luxembourg in December 1997. The necessity of further EU bargaining about expansion and internal problem solving will remain after the 1996–1997 IGC. The Fifteen have kept their monetary goals rolling through difficult times, but the EU diplomacy that would overhaul the fundamental system has once again run into competing and controversial visions of Europe and been diverted by the urgent security task.

Notes

1. For a full history of integration, see Desmond Dinan, *Ever Closer Union? An Introduction to the European Community* (Boulder: Lynne Rienner, 1994), pp. 99–198. For comprehensive treatments on the post–Cold War era, see John McCormick, *The European Union: Politics and Policies* (Boulder: Westview, 1996), pp. 292–302, and Michael J. Baum, *An Imperfect Union: The Maastricht Treaty and the New Politics of European Integration* (Boulder: Westview, 1996), pp. 161ff.

2. *Politique étrangère* in its spring 1996 issue entitled "L'UE á l'échéance de 1996" looked at the IGC in thirteen articles. Its overall tone was not basically positive. On the rise of European doubts about the Union, see the editors' essay in Alan W. Cafruny and Carl Lankowski (eds.), *Europe's Ambiguous Unity: Conflict and Consensus in the Post-Maastricht Era* (Boulder: Lynne Rienner, 1996).

3. See Conclusions of the Presidency, *Bulletin of the European Union,* 12-1995, 18.

4. For the evolution of the impact of enlargement on EU institutions, see Pierre-Henri Laurent, "Widening Europe: The Dilemmas of Community Success," *Annals of American Academy of Political and Social Science* 531 (January 1994): 124–140, and for the earlier thinking (of 1993–1994) and for more contemporary insights (of 1996), see the articles of W. Wessels and J. Hallaert in *Politique étrangère* 1 (1996).

5. Structural funds are made up of the TEU's Cohesion Fund on environment and infrastructure projects and the earlier European Seasonal Fund (ESF), European Regional Development Fund (ERDF), and the guidance pacts of the European Acquisitional Guidance and Guarantee Fund (EAGGF). These EU funds, totaling $17.5 billion in the 1993–1995 budgets, were aimed at cofinancing projects in lesser-developed regions or areas in economic distress or industrial decline.

6. See Simon Serfaty, "Half Before Europe, Half Past NATO," *Washington Quarterly* 18 (Spring 1995): 49–58, and "America and Europe Beyond Bosnia," *Washington Quarterly* 19 (Summer 1996), 31–44, for the evolution of Euro-American conflicts and cooperation. See also Frédéric Bozo, *Deux stratégies pour l'Europe: de Gaulle, les États Unis et l'alliance atlantique, 1958–69* (Paris: Plon, 1996), and for the post-Gaullist period, Charles G. Cogan, *Oldest Allies, Guarded Friends: The United States and France Since 1940* (Westport, CT: Praeger, 1994), *passim* on the history of power-sharing efforts. For the present era, see Kevin Featherstone and Roy H. Ginsberg, *The United States and the European Union in the 1990s* (New York: St. Martin's Press, 1996), pp. 266ff., and Simon Serfaty, *Stay the Course: European Unity and Atlantic Solidarity* (New York: Praeger, 1997).

7. Ole Waever, "European Security Identities," *Journal of Common Market Studies* 34, 1 (March 1996): 103–132. See also William Wallace, *Opening the Door: The Enlargement of NATO and the European Union* (London: Centre for European Reform, 1996).

8. Rick Atkinson and Bradley Graham, "A Misaligned Alliance," *Washington Post*, 5–11 August 1996, pp. 11–12.

9. Michael Hennes, "The Reflection Group of the European Union," *Aussenpolitik* 1 (1996): 33–42.

10. Wallace, *Opening the Door*, pp. 13–15, 23–35.

11. *Europe Magazine*, May and July/August 1996, and the *Economist*, 1 June 8 June, and 3 August 1996. Also see the articles of P. de Schoutheete, F. Cameron, M. Vopp, R. Rummel, and G. Burghardt in Elfriede Regelsberger, Philippe de Schoutheete de Tervarent, and Wolfgang Wessels (eds.), *Foreign Policy of the European Union: From EPC to CFSP and Beyond* (Boulder: Lynne Rienner, 1996).

12. For an interesting comparison with the EDC of the 1950s, see Simon Duke, "The 2nd Death (or the 2nd Coming?) of the WEU," *Journal of Common Market Studies* 34, 2 (June 1996): 167–190.

13. Anthony L. Teasdale, "The Politics of Majority Voting in Europe," *Political Quarterly* 67, 2 (April-June 1996): 101–115.

14. *In a Larger EU, Can All Member States Be Equal?* (Brussels: Philip Morris Institute for Public Policy Research, 1996).

15. Economic and Monetary Union, Communication of the Commission of 21 August 1990, Luxemburg, 11.

16. Christopher Taylor, *EMU 2000? Prospects for European Monetary Union* (London: Royal Institute of International Affairs, 1996), p. 120.

17. Daniel Gros, *Towards Economic and Monetary Union: Problems and Prospects* (Brussels: CEPS, 1996), p. 4. See also George A. Kourvetaris and Andreas Moshonas (eds.), *The Impact of European Integration: Political, Sociological and Economic Change* (Westport, CT: Praeger, 1996), primarily the articles of Holman, Van der Pijl, and Bonvincini on EMU.

18. COM (95) 333 final, 31 May 1995, 1, note 1.

19. See the conclusions of Patrick M. Crowley, "EMU, Maastricht, and the 1996 Intergovernmental Conference," *Contemporary Economic Policy* 14, 2 (April 1996): 41–55.

20. The broad analytical sweep of Michael Smith, "The EU and a Changing Europe: Establishing the Boundaries of Order," *Journal of Common Market Studies* 24, 1 (March 1996): 5–28, on the future of an enlarged Europe catches the problems of EU limits very well. For the German viewpoint, see Christian Deubner, *Deutsche Eurapolitik: von Maastricht nach Kerneuropa* (Baden-Baden: Nomos Verlagsgesellschaft, 1995), and Josef Janning (ed.), *The 1996 IGC-National Debates* (London: Royal Institute of International Affairs, 1996). See also the contributions of Stephen Sestanovich and Stanley Hoffmann in Robert Lieber (ed.), *Eagle Adrift: American Foreign Policy at the End of the Century* (New York: Longman, 1997).

21. See the essay of Bonvincini and Messas in Kourvetaris and Moshonas, *Impact of European Integration*.

22. For the most elaborate portrait on the threat and insecurity involved in NATO expanding, see Michael Mandelbaum, *The Dawn of Peace in Europe* (New York: Twentieth Century Fund, 1996).

23. See Marc Maresceau and Elisabetta Montaguti, "The Relations Between the European Union and Central and Eastern Europe: A Legal Appraisal," *Common Market Law Review* 1995, 1328. At the 1995 Madrid European Council, it was

stated that enlargement "is both a political necessity and a historic opportunity for Europe" that "will ensure the stability and security of the continent"; see also, for example, "European Commission, Enlargement, Questions and Answers," *Agence Europe*, 9 August 1996.

24. For background, see Youri Devuyst, "The European Community and the Conclusion of the Uruguay Round," in Carolyn Rhodes and Sonia Mazey (eds.), *The State of the European Union*, vol. 3: *Building a European Polity?* (Boulder: Lynne Rienner, 1995), 449–467.

25. Opinion 1/94, [1994] ECR I-5267.

2

Reflections on the IGCs

Desmond Dinan

Since the mid-1980s, intergovernmental conferences (IGCs) have dominated the history of European integration. Reflecting the increasing complexity of international political and economic life, IGCs became a forum for negotiations to revise the founding treaties in order to equip the European Community/Union with an institutional apparatus and policy competence necessary to confront the challenges its member states were unable to confront alone or could better confront together. Yet a look at the results of past IGCs calls into question whether IGCs are either inherently necessary or effective as catalysts for major reform. The unwieldy variety of issues on the table and member states' predictable refusal to subordinate their own perceived national interests to the greater European good have made it impossible for IGCs to produce clear-cut results. IGCs have thus become increasingly cumbersome and controversial, their ability to forge deeper integration more and more doubtful. The lack of enthusiasm with which member states embarked on the 1996 IGC suggests that IGCs will become less frequent and less ambitious, although the internal and external challenges facing the European Union will become no less fraught.

The 1985 IGC

Before 1985, IGCs had served the largely formal purpose of endorsing specific treaty changes already decided by the Council of Ministers. The idea of an IGC as an open-ended opportunity to negotiate wide-ranging reform emerged in the mid-1980s in response to a combination of internal and external challenges confronting the Community and its member states. During the previous five years, technological developments, economic vicissitudes, and a marked deterioration in East-West relations combined to make Western Europe even less competitive internationally and even more marginalized. European Community (EC) member states could no longer afford business as usual: a combination of national responses to international pressures and loose economic and political integration.

Confronted by new political and economic challenges, the EC responded in part with its famous single market strategy.[1] Yet given that the single market was an original objective of the Treaty of Rome, why was an IGC necessary to implement it? The reason ostensibly was that the single market could not be completed without a reform of decisionmaking procedures in the Treaty. Specifically, the political will to complete the internal market could never translate into action unless unanimity gave way to qualified majority voting in the Council of Ministers. Without reform of the legislative process, single market proposals would ultimately bog down in disputes among member states, as had happened for the past twenty years.

Not everyone agreed with that analysis. The British argued that procedural changes were possible within the existing Treaty framework. At a foreign ministers meeting in Stressa in May 1985, British foreign secretary Geoffrey Howe proposed a code of good behavior in decisionmaking, whereby member states would eschew the national veto when legislating for the single market. Margaret Thatcher made the same point at the decisive Milan summit the following month but failed to persuade a majority of her Community counterparts to accept a "Milan accord" instead of calling for an IGC.[2]

Despite the Community's dismal record of decisionmaking since the Luxembourg compromise of 1966, the British had a point. Business and political pressure to complete the single market was unprecedented, and the decisionmaking environment in the mid-1980s was far better than at any time since the mid-1960s. Moreover, the Community was already moving toward greater use of qualified majority voting, without any treaty reform (during their Council presidency in early 1982, the Belgians had succeeded in curbing use of the veto). A combination of weariness with the Luxembourg compromise, pressure to get Europe going economically, and Belgium's assertive Council presidency augured well for the relatively smooth legislative passage of single market proposals using existing Treaty provisions.

Indeed, the history of the single market program bears out Britain's point. Enough is known about the Council's record to suggest that for most single market proposals for which, under the terms of the Single European Act (SEA) majority voting was permitted, voting rarely took place. Instead, the president-in-office continued to work toward a consensus. Arguably the possibility (or the threat) of a vote helped the president to achieve consensus. But arguably also the member states' mutual interest in completing the single market, rather than treaty provisions for qualified majority voting, nudged the legislative program along. Moreover, despite the SEA's provisions for majority voting, the single market program took off only in 1988, after resolution of the Delors I budgetary battle and after an enormous increase in public and business pressure because of the persuasiveness of the Cecchini Report[3] and the catchiness of "1992."

In reality, the extension of qualified majority voting to cover single market legislation was not a compelling reason for the member states to decide in 1985 to convene an IGC to revise the Treaty of Rome. Even new Commission president Jacques Delors, in whose interest it was to hold an IGC, felt that whatever legislative changes were necessary to enable completion of the single market could be included in the accession treaties for Spain and Portugal.[4] That the member states themselves recognized the superfluity of an IGC in order to facilitate the single market program is evident in one of the conclusions of the Milan summit, in which the European Council asked the Council of Ministers to study the institutional conditions necessary to complete the single market without Treaty reform.[5] This seems contradictory, given that at the same summit the heads of state and government also decided to hold an IGC to reform the Treaty. However, the heads of state and government had no idea how long the IGC would last or whether it would succeed. In the event, it was not necessary for the Council of Ministers to act on the European Council's request.

Why, therefore, was an IGC necessary? There were two other pressures for Treaty reform in the early 1980s, one internal and the other external. First, political elites were increasingly concerned about the Community's patent lack of democratic legitimacy. Although European publics were not clamoring for greater involvement and openness, many national governments felt that Community governance was too restricted. Led by Altiero Spinelli, the veteran Eurofederalist, a group of directly elected members of the European Parliament (EP) sought not only to close the Community's democratic deficit by increasing the EP's legislative power but also to launch a constitutional revision that would transform the European Community into a European Union. Their efforts resulted in the "Draft Treaty Establishing the European Union," which the EP resoundingly endorsed in February 1984.[6]

Those governments already well disposed toward the EP took the draft treaty seriously; others dismissed it as an extravagant irrelevance. Nevertheless the first directly elected EP had at least focused more attention on the related issues of legitimacy and parliamentary power. Spinelli's indefatigable advocacy of the draft treaty obliged national governments to think about democratic accountability at a time of manifest economic and political transformation. In and of themselves, however, concerns about the Community's legitimacy and about the EP's lack of legislative power were insufficient to impel member states to revise the Treaty of Rome: Not even the most ardent national governmental champions of greater EP power would have called for an IGC only, or even largely, on that account.

Member states' obvious inability to coordinate foreign policy at a time of rising international tension was another more compelling reason to attempt Treaty reform. The onset of the "second Cold War" in the late 1970s tested member states' capacity to act in concert on the international stage. European Political Cooperation proved an inadequate instrument, especially in response to sudden crises such as the Soviet invasion of Afghanistan in December 1979 and the imposition of martial law in Poland two years later. At the same time, the Reagan administration's uncompromising policy toward the Soviet Union and tendency to see international relations exclusively through Cold War spectacles put transatlantic ties under enormous strain. Many Western European governments felt that they needed a mechanism through which they could assert themselves better not only in their dealings with Moscow but in their dealings with Washington.

Efforts in the early 1980s to strengthen EPC and give the member states a louder voice in international affairs had failed dismally.[7] There were too many differences between the member states about foreign and security policy cooperation for the outcome to have been otherwise: It was clear that member states would make little progress for some time to come on improving EPC, either procedurally or substantively. Although EPC became a subset of the 1985 IGC, member states' low expectations for more concerted foreign policy cooperation suggest that EPC reform was not the main or even a leading reason for convening the IGC.

What therefore accounts for the decision to hold an IGC in 1985? The answer lies in the eagerness of some member states to deepen European integration through a combination of new Community competences and institutional reform and the unwillingness of other member states to countenance more than a minimum of change in order to complete the single market. A wide rift had opened between the original member states, which (despite differences over policy and procedure) were developing a greater commitment to European integration, and the later arrivals, which had never subscribed to European integration in the first place. Ireland, a late arrival *and* a believer in European integration, was a notable exception.

Fundamental differences about the nature and course of European integration separated Britain and Denmark, two of the three "deviant" member states, from the original member states plus Ireland. Contrariness rather than conviction motivated Greece, the third deviant. All ten member states agreed that completion of the single market was imperative for their economic survival and development and that a degree of foreign policy cooperation was indispensable to enhance their global influence. Beyond that, the Seven and the Three disagreed strongly about Community competences and decisionmaking procedures. Bitter resentment over the British budgetary dispute compounded these differences. As a large member state with the potential either to accelerate the pace of European integration or to slow it down to a crawl, Britain was the primary focus of the Seven's ire.

The Dooge Committee's work showed the extent of the gulf.[8] Although the Seven were far from accord on every issue, the Three disagreed with most of the committee's major recommendations. Most important, whereas the Seven endorsed an IGC, the Three dissented. Given the lack of compelling procedural or policy reasons to reform the Treaty in the first place, the most plausible explanation for the Seven's call for an IGC is that they wished to send a strong signal to the Three: that the Three could either join the Seven and invest in deeper European integration or go their own way.

With the Seven eager to move ahead in the early 1980s and the Three unwilling to budge, talk of a two-speed Community—an idea circulating since the Tindemans Report of 1975[9]—inevitably increased during that time. For instance, the EP's draft treaty envisioned the establishment of an EU with fewer than the Community's existing number of member states. Similarly, in a famous speech to the EP in May 1984, François Mitterrand hinted that some member states would proceed alone down the path of deeper integration.[10] To the Seven, an IGC would present an ideal opportunity both to attract public and political attention to the desirability of deeper integration and to warn recalcitrant member states that they risked expulsion from the club.

Thus, by calling for a vote at the June 1985 Milan summit on whether to hold an IGC, President-in-office Bettino Craxi sent a clear signal to the dissenting member states. The European Council had never before (and has never since) acted on the basis of a show of hands.[11] Craxi's ploy and the ensuing vote in favor of convening an IGC were intended to warn the British especially that those in the majority were willing to press ahead on their own, if necessary.

For all their determination, however, the Seven's position before and during the IGC was surprisingly weak. First, there was a damaging lack of leadership. Although it is commonplace now to talk about the importance of Franco-German leadership for the Community's revival in the mid-1980s, even a cursory look at events during that time demonstrates that neither France and Germany collectively nor France and Germany individually provided much leadership in 1985, the crucial IGC year.

François Mitterrand had shown inspired and decisive leadership during France's Council presidency in early 1984, culminating in the Fontainebleau summit, arguably the most successful European Council in the Community's history. Soon thereafter, however, Mitterrand's involvement in Community affairs (if not his commitment to European integration) noticeably waned. For instance, Mitterrand did little to advance the Seven's agenda in the run-up to the crucial Milan summit in June. By the same token, Chancellor Kohl seemed either unable or unwilling to provide decisive leadership in the Community in 1984 and 1985. His inability to nominate a Commission president in mid-1984, when by common consent it was Germany's turn to do so, is legendary. Beset by electoral setbacks in the *Länder* and embarrassed by a German veto on cereal prices only days

before the Milan summit, Kohl was surprisingly unassertive immediately
before and during the IGC.[12]

Moreover, Mitterrand and Kohl disagreed strongly over a number of
issues at the G7 summit in Bonn in May 1985 and had an unusually unpro-
ductive bilateral summit later that month. Although France and Germany
made a joint submission on EPC shortly before the Milan summit, their
paper lacked the clarity and forcefulness that characterized similar Franco-
German initiatives later in the decade.[13]

Lack of leadership within the Seven played into the hands of the Three,
who were at an advantage in any case in the IGC process. Because of the
need for unanimity to decide treaty changes, recalcitrant member states
found it easy to ratchet ambitious proposals down to the lowest common
denominator. EPC is an obvious example, but marked differences within
the Seven, let alone between the Seven and the Three, meant that there
were few expectations at the outset of a breakthrough on foreign policy
cooperation. Differences within the Seven on a range of other issues covered in the IGC meant that as the negotiations progressed and bargaining
intensified, the distinction between the Seven and the Three became less
noticeable and relevant. What emerged at the end was a series of compromises on the single market, qualified majority voting, powers of the EP,
environmental policy, research and development, social policy, monetary
capacity, and cohesion that reflected a collective commitment in principle
to European integration but an unwillingness in practice to take a radical
new departure.[14]

The leadership void in the IGC at least had an important side effect that
proved advantageous for European integration: It gave the Commission a
degree of influence and maneuverability out of proportion to its expected
role in an avowedly intergovernmental activity. Although the Commission
had been represented on the Dooge Committee, it had not played a prominent part in the IGC's initiation or preparation, not least because of the
presidential and collegial turnover in January 1985, in the midst of the
committee's deliberations. Moreover, Jacques Delors spent his first months
in office engrossed first in the resolution of a dispute over financial transfers to Greece in return for Spanish and Portuguese accession, and later in
drafting and propagating the Commission's white paper on completing the
single market. Because he was not a head of state or government, Delors
was unable to cast a vote at the Milan summit on whether or not to hold an
IGC, but he did press Craxi to call the fateful vote.

Despite its explicitly intergovernmental nature, member states did not
object to the Commission's participation in the 1985 or subsequent IGCs.
On the contrary, national governments expected the Commission, with its
institutional memory and commitment to collective action, to play an active
role. At the 1985 conference, the Commission was well prepared to tackle

institutional and policy issues with which it was well acquainted. By going into the IGC with a number of carefully crafted demands, the Commission acquired a key agenda-setting role. During the negotiations themselves, the Commission played an important part in shaping the final outcome, notably the SEA's provisions for economic and social cohesion and for legislative cooperation between the Council and the EP.

The Commission's role in the IGC has major implications for integration theory, specifically for the debate about whether supranational institutionalism (essentially neofunctionalism) or liberal intergovernmentalism (large member state politicking) account for the EC's transformation in the late 1980s.[15] Controversy surrounds mainly the influence of supranational actors in the IGC's causes, conduct, and consequences. A liberal intergovernmentalist interpretation of the IGC seems consistent with what is, after all, primarily an intergovernmental affair. Despite the constraints imposed by a strongly intergovernmental Community system and an avowedly intergovernmental treaty reform process, however, the Commission arguably played a decisive role in shaping the SEA. Accordingly, the Commission's ability to get the ball rolling and set the terms of the subsequent negotiations does not necessarily endorse supranational institutionalism but points to a major weakness of liberal intergovernmentalism: its tendency to dismiss the contributions of nonstate actors to treaty reform and to integration acceleration.[16]

The Commission's clever exploitation of the SEA's provisions calls liberal intergovernmentalism further into question. Andrew Moravcsik, the main proponent of liberal intergovernmentalism, cites the SEA's weak provisions for cooperation in economic and monetary policy as evidence of how national governments triumphed in the IGC over the Commission, which had advocated stronger EMU language. If Moravcsik is right, then it was a Pyrrhic victory for the anti-EMU member states: Within twelve months of the SEA's implementation, the European Council not only agreed to hold an IGC on EMU but also charged Delors with chairing the decisive preparatory committee. Similarly, the SEA's provisions for economic and social cohesion may have seemed modest, but thanks largely to Delors they were translated within twelve months of the SEA's ratification into a powerful force for integration in the recently enlarged EC.

Contemporary assessments of the SEA by politicians and academics were mostly negative. Three months of intensive negotiations had failed to make much headway on EPC, had resulted in only modest legislative authority for the EP, and had not brought about a significant extension of Community competence. Nor had the IGC achieved its undeclared objective of scaring recalcitrant member states into conformity. On the contrary, Britain would become even more obstructionist in the years ahead, and a negative ratification vote in the Danish parliament almost scuttled the SEA.

Ironically in view of what would happen in 1992, the Danish electorate's approval in 1986 of the treaty changes nullified the Danish parliament's earlier rejection of them.

What saved the IGC politically, however, was the retrospective gloss it acquired as the pace of integration quickened in the late 1980s. Successful resolution of the Delors I budgetary package in February 1988, including a generous side payment to the Community's poorer member states for their acquiescence in the single market program, set the stage for rapid progress in other areas. But it was the surprising psychological impact of "1992," together with a buoyant economy, that fueled the Community's revival. Propelled by an unusually assertive German presidency during the first half of 1988, the Council began to crank out single market legislation and, in that sense, make a success of the SEA.

The 1991 IGC

The successful single market program, whose lineage stretched back thirty years, looked like the progeny of the 1985 IGC. There was no shortage of claimants to the single market's parenthood. Indeed, like mothers of adorable children whose eagerness to have another obliterates the memory of childbirth, member states were so smitten by the single market program that they were predisposed to hold another IGC in the near future. Once again, Britain and Denmark were the exceptions.

In this instance, there was a pressing reason to hold another IGC: The success of the single market program and the experience and vagaries of the European Monetary System (EMS) developed a strong momentum for EMU. In practical terms, the single market's liberalization of capital movements and full integration of financial markets fulfilled two of the three preconditions the Delors Report identified as essential for EMU. Here was a heartening example, for theorists of European integration, of functional spillover.[17] The relationship between the single market and EMU was seen as automatic and axiomatic: Not only would EMU crown the single market program, but failure to achieve EMU might jeopardize the single market's success.[18] The Werner Plan, an earlier effort to achieve EMU, had failed because no solid single market foundation existed and because EMU seemed at the time (the early 1970s) to be a quantum leap forward in European integration.[19] Fifteen years later, not only was the single market being put in place, but European integration had progressed to the point where EMU looked like a logical next step. In the aftermath of the 1992–1993 currency crises and the Maastricht ratification debacle, when public opinion turned strongly against EMU and politicians began to doubt its feasibility and wisdom, it is hard to recall most member states' enthusiasm for EMU in the late 1980s.

Clearly, EMU would require major institutional innovations in the Community. The SEA's weak reference to EMU stipulated that "insofar as further development in the field of economic and monetary cooperation necessitates institutional changes, the provision of Article 236 shall be applicable." When the SEA was being negotiated, this statement seemed like a setback for proponents of further integration. Only three years later, such was the prevailing Europhoria that the SEA's stricture about cooperation on economic and monetary policy contributed to the impetus for a new IGC.

The EMU IGC would be radically different from the 1985 IGC. There was no effort in 1988 and 1989 to exclude or threaten to exclude those member states in the minority, a strategy that had failed completely in 1985. On the contrary, the majority's concern in the run-up to and during the EMU IGC was to keep everyone on board. This does not mean that every member state would be able economically or politically willing to participate in EMU. Indeed, the prospect of a two-tier Community became more explicit as the IGC progressed. But it was imperative that no member state prevent an agreement from being reached and EMU from being launched. Although she objected strenuously to EMU, Thatcher had not attempted to block the IGC. John Major, who replaced Thatcher on the eve of the IGC, shared his predecessor's general distaste for European integration but was not opposed in principle to EMU. Early in the negotiation, Delors came up with a formula to satisfy both the British and those who were eager to press ahead: No member state would be obliged to move to the final stage of EMU; no member state could prevent others from moving to the final stage; and no member state that met the as yet unspecified convergence criteria would be excluded from the final stage.[20]

Delors's activism in the early phase of the IGC and his predominant role in the IGC's preparation cast further doubt on the validity of the liberal intergovernmentalist interpretation of European integration in the late 1980s. As well as convincing the European Council to appoint him chairman of the EMU preparatory committee, Delors recommended that the committee consist of central bank governors, thereby giving him a chance to co-opt a key EMU constituency. Delors and a small team drafted the influential committee report, while Delors himself successfully lobbied at the Madrid (June 1989) and Strasbourg (December 1989) summits for a decision on whether and when to hold an IGC. This is not to say that an IGC would not have happened without Delors. After all, the post-SEA political and economic environment favored a move in that direction. France wanted EMU, and Germany's reluctance (because of the Bundesbank's opposition) could be overcome (because of Kohl's long-standing commitment to deeper integration). Yet Delors's dogged advocacy of EMU in 1988 and 1989, when he was at the height of his power as

Commission president, greatly shaped the IGC's timing, agenda, and eventual outcome.

During the IGC itself, Germany was the most important player. Given the size of its economy, the strength of its currency, and the Community-wide influence of its central bank, this was hardly surprising. But Germany did not so much take the lead as expect other countries to defer to its wishes. On a number of key issues (the sanctity of price stability, the prerequirement of economic convergence, the independence of the European Central Bank and the importance of its inauguration only at the beginning of Stage III), Germany would have to prevail. France and Germany were often at loggerheads on these and other issues, but France recognized the need to make concessions, not least to strengthen Kohl's hand domestically. At the same time, and in accordance with the give-and-take of IGCs, France won some points, too, most notably a decision on the timetable for moving to Stage III.

The EMU deliberations seemed like a textbook example of an IGC's purpose, operation, and outcome: well planned, well run, focused on a specific topic, uncomplicated by extraneous issues (although influenced by domestic politics), and resulting in an undisputed leap forward for European integration (as long as EMU could be implemented as planned in the Treaty). The Commission and the Parliament may not have been fully satisfied with EMU's institutional architecture, but both agreed that a firm commitment to EMU was a major achievement for the Community.

Compared to the simultaneous IGC on European Political Union (EPU), the IGC on EMU was obviously well executed. Of course, the IGC on EMU was tidy precisely *because* there was a parallel IGC on political union. EMU raised important political and institutional problems, such as the Community's fragile democratic legitimacy, that went far beyond how to launch a single currency and manage monetary policy. For substantive and/or political reasons, EMU also focused attention on other policy areas (cohesion was an example of a policy issue related to EMU for substantive *and* political reasons). Had a parallel IGC on political union not taken place, some of the main issues discussed in it would have been discussed instead in the EMU IGC, thereby broadening the negotiations' scope and greatly increasing their complexity.

As it was, the heads of state and government decided to convene a parallel IGC because of developments in Central and Eastern Europe. The imminence of German unification, the need for a Community *Ostpolitik,* and the prospect of further enlargement made a compelling case for deeper integration, including especially a Common Foreign and Security Policy. As usual, Delors was far ahead of the pack with a call in January 1990 for an IGC on political union.[21] A few national politicians made similar appeals during the following weeks, but it was Kohl and Mitterrand, acting jointly, who ensured that a parallel conference would take place. In a letter to the

Council presidency in April 1990, the French and German leaders linked the need "to accelerate the political construction" of the Community to recent events in Central and Eastern Europe, as well as to moves already under way to achieve EMU. Their proposed solution was an IGC on political union not only to devise a CFSP but also to tackle issues indirectly related to EMU: democratic legitimacy; institutional efficiency; and coherence of economic, monetary, and political action.[22]

Despite having been consigned to a separate IGC, issues relating to German unification directly affected the EMU negotiations. "What the events of 1989 did," Michael Baun has written, "was to accelerate action on EMU, making it a matter of much greater geopolitical urgency . . . [that] may have contributed to an overly ambitious schedule for EMU, one that got too far ahead of both public opinion and economic conditions."[23] Yet without German unification the IGC might not have concluded successfully, however unsatisfactory the results were. After all, as Baun points out, it was a perceived need to assuage France and other EC member states about the consequences of unification that bolstered Kohl's resistance to the German central bank's and finance ministry's strong opposition to EMU.

There was a specific link also between the EMU and EPU negotiations, as distinct from a general link between EMU and German unification: Kohl threatened to veto EMU without a far-reaching agreement on EPU. The reason, quite simply, was that Germany had the most to lose from EMU and the most to gain from EPU. By agreeing to a single currency, Germany would be giving up the mark and surrendering control over European monetary policy, which it then enjoyed in the EMS. In return, Germany wanted a Community with a familiar federal system of governance in which controversial domestic issues (such as immigration and defense) might be resolved and in which a more powerful EP (with a large German contingent) would play a greater legislative role.

CFSP, including the relationship among the WEU, NATO, and the putative EU, was the only element of the political union IGC that pertained directly to German unification and the end of the Cold War. The SEA's provisions for EPC mentioned a possible revision of foreign policy cooperation five years after the SEA's implementation, but without revolution in Eastern Europe, which nobody foresaw in 1985, it is unlikely that such a revision would have amounted to an IGC. As it happened, events in Eastern Europe were so momentous that member states, including Britain and Denmark, agreed on the need for greater foreign and security policy cooperation in order to improve their international influence and enhance European stability, although neither Denmark nor Britain agreed that an IGC was necessary for such a development. Nevertheless both went along with the decision to launch an IGC on political union in tandem with the previously planned IGC on EMU.[24]

Given consensus on the need to improve foreign and security cooperation in a radically changing international environment, why was so little achieved at the IGC? The IGC's failure seems even more surprising in view of events during the negotiations themselves. Both the Gulf and Yugoslav wars broke out in 1991 while the IGC was in session and provided compelling reasons for a CFSP that would allow the Community to exert diplomatic and even military pressure commensurate with its economic weight. What emerged instead was a procedurally complicated and politically weak CFSP that confirmed the member states' unwillingness and inability to act collectively in international affairs beyond trade and development.

The failure of CFSP was not due simply to British or Danish recalcitrance: Many other countries objected as well to the communitarization of foreign and security policy. Paradoxically, Greece was not among them: A change in government had brought to power the conservative New Democracy Party, whose fervent supranationalism was based as much on hostility toward the outgoing prime minister as on enthusiasm for the EC.

The difficulties with CFSP went much deeper than British and Danish intergovernmentalism or British Atlanticism and Danish neutralism. Few member states could reconcile their security orientations and policies with a meaningful CFSP that included defense. Ireland was officially neutral, the Dutch and Portuguese were fervent Atlanticists, and Italy wavered between Atlanticism and Europeanism. France was avowedly Europeanist and would happily have brought the WEU fully into the proposed EU, regardless of the implications for NATO. Germany had considerable sympathy for France, and both countries attempted to act jointly on CFSP issues at the IGC. But Germany was not about to jeopardize NATO solidarity and operational capability for the sake of French hubris.

U.S. concern about a putative CFSP gave the question of NATO's future particular urgency. The United States feared that an independent European defense capability, or even the intention to develop such a capability, would undermine NATO at a time when its role was already being questioned because of the Cold War's end. U.S. lobbying early in the IGC was indiscreet but effective. It also provided cover for those member states who agreed with the U.S. position but projected instead a Europeanist image. Even without U.S. intervention, the IGC would probably not have endorsed a merger of the proposed EU and the WEU. With U.S. intervention, such a merger was out of the question.

Apart from defense and the WEU, institutional and procedural aspects of CFSP divided the member states. France may have wanted a Europeanist security and defense identity, but France did not want a supranational CFSP. In that regard, France was closer to Britain than to Germany. Most member states agreed that CFSP's decisionmaking apparatus could not be the same as the single market's, but the more Community-minded among them hoped for a degree of Commission and EP involvement in it and for majority voting. Yet supranationalist Luxembourg, acting in its capacity as

Council president, submitted a draft treaty early in the negotiations that consigned CFSP to an intergovernmental, extra-Community pillar. Despite a celebrated Dutch effort, supported only by Belgium and the Commission, to scrap the proposed EU's intergovernmental pillars, Luxembourg's treaty architecture endured.

Given the political sensitivity of foreign and security policy and the tortuous history of EPC, it is hardly surprising that CFSP emerged from the IGC as a weak intergovernmental process. Yet in view of the IGC's high expectations and prevailing international challenges (not least the deteriorating situation in Bosnia), the EU's procedurally impaired CFSP proved doubly disappointing. Member states are paying a high price: CFSP inefficiency and ineffectiveness has severely undermined the EU's credibility, both within and outside the EU.

The Kohl-Mitterrand letter of April 1990 had not only ensured that an IGC on political union would take place but signaled that France and Germany would take the lead during the negotiations to follow. Far from setting a steady course, however, their next major contribution—a joint letter to the Council presidency on the eve of the IGC in December 1990—foreshadowed many of the difficulties ahead. The letter advocated long-standing French and German objectives that in some cases were mutually exclusive. For instance, the intergovernmentalism of a more powerful European Council (a French goal) was fundamentally incompatible with the supranationalism of a strengthened EP (a German goal). France may have deferred to Germany in the EMU IGC, but it struck a tougher bargain in the political union talks. Indeed, one of the most striking aspects of the negotiations was that France (and other member states) balked at making the kinds of institutional reforms Kohl had espoused as a means of tying Germany firmly into the putative EU and had demanded in return for EMU. Those reforms had been long-standing German objectives, but their nonrealization at Maastricht provided further evidence that despite a supposed sense of urgency due to the Cold War's end, the TEU would not be a great leap forward.

Progress at the IGC was impaired in any case by the number and diversity of agenda items and by a lack of conference planning and preparation: There was no equivalent of the 1984–1985 Dooge Committee or the 1995 Reflection Group. More important, member states and the Commission did not have an opportunity to present carefully crafted, well thought out position papers. Because of its involvement in the EMU IGC and because of an unusual number of other heavy commitments in 1990 and 1991, the Commission was virtually marginalized during the political union negotiations. This reflected also growing member state concern about the Commission's ambition and about Delors's assertiveness. Delors made no secret of his dissatisfaction with the Luxembourg presidency and especially with its draft treaty. But his heavy-handed efforts to scrap the Luxembourg draft treaty seriously backfired. Delors may have had the intellectual support of a majority of member state negotiators, but his own and the Commission's political influence was on the wane. Far from enhancing its power as a result of the IGC, the Commission found itself on the defensive during most of the negotiations.[25] By contrast, the growing influence of the Council secretariat in the EPU negotiations (and an explicit reference to the Council secretariat in the ensuing TEU) was a significant indicator of increasing intergovernmentalism in the Community process.[26]

The 1996 IGC

The 1996 IGC was intended as a sequel to the 1991 negotiations. Disappointed with the TEU's institutional and CFSP provisions, a number of member states proposed in 1991 that a follow-up conference be held five years later to try to forge more progress in sensitive areas. The prospect of southern and Eastern enlargement, which seemed distant in 1991, added a degree of urgency in the mid-1990s to the forthcoming IGC. The EU's institutional structure, designed for six member states and creaking under the weight of fifteen, would need a major overhaul to accommodate a Union of twenty-some countries. If the IGC had not already been planned, surely it would have had to be convened because of circumstances unforeseen as recently as the early 1990s.

Yet far from being an opportunity to advance European integration, the 1996 IGC became instead an exercise in damage control. By 1993, when the TEU finally came into operation, let alone three years later when the review conference began, few member states wanted another IGC. Public reaction against Maastricht tainted not only the Treaty itself but the process by which it had been reached. To a Eurojaundiced public, IGCs connoted a malign mechanism for governing elites to advance European integration at the expense of democratic legitimacy. Although the TEU had increased the EP's legislative authority and power of appointment, had inaugurated a Committee of the Regions, and had enshrined the principle of subsidiarity, these supposed democratic refinements reinforced public skepticism about European integration and public antipathy toward the IGC process: Low voter turnout in the 1994 elections demonstrated widespread indifference, or even hostility, toward the EP; few people took the Committee of the Regions seriously; and subsidiarity seemed both an impenetrable concept and a parody of Eurospeak. At the same time, serious economic recession sapped public confidence in European integration as a panacea, and weak political leadership sapped initiative at the top.

With the 1996 IGC already scheduled, timid national governments and a chastened Commission had little choice but to make a virtue of necessity. Seizing on the pressure of impending enlargement and responding to the wake-up call of the Maastricht ratification crisis, they put forward a plethora of proposals intended primarily to make the EU more open and effective. The 1996 IGC produced more planning and position papers than the other IGCs combined. Yet the Reflection Group's deliberations and reports confirmed a dearth of original ideas and the unlikelihood of consensus on major reforms.[27] Although insufficient to resolve the Union's underlying problems, such improvements as a more comprehensible treaty, more accessible institutions, and more effective policies would at least be a step in the right direction. But fearful of rejection in ratification referenda, which are likely to be more prevalent and less predictable next time around and which will coincide with unpopular budgetary decisions having to do with EMU, national governments are shying away from bold initiatives at the IGC. Impending enlargement seems insufficient to instigate radical reform. The EU may have to muddle through, much as the EC did in the past.

Perhaps one of the most symbolic and problematical legacies of the 1991 IGC, with which the 1996 IGC cannot deal, is the name "European Union." For the 1991 IGC did not establish a European Union in any real sense. National divisions sharpened during and after the negotiations, Britain's Social Protocol opt-out formalized differentiated integration, EMU contained the seeds of serious discord, and the Treaty's single institutional structure barely disguised the supranational institutions' virtual exclusion from two of the EU's pillars. Yet the name "European Union" fueled both exaggerated concern about institutional centralization and unrealistic expectations about external capabilities. Ideally, the 1996 IGC is a chance to give the Union more coherence and unity; in practice, it is unlikely to produce more than minor reform.

Conclusion

IGCs have become decisive events in the history of European integration. But their significance is misunderstood and their achievements overrated. The assumption of the Seven in 1985 was that pressure to achieve results in an IGC would cause governments to subordinate national interest to a mutually beneficial European interest. That proved unrealistic even for the Seven themselves, let alone for the Ten as a whole. Nevertheless, mythmaking about how the 1985 IGC and the ensuing SEA produced the single market program led to excessive expectations for the 1991 IGC. Unfortunately (if predictably), the dominance of national interests was even more manifest in the 1991 IGC, despite endless harping on such key Eurowords as "union" and "common." The aftermath of the 1991 IGC has in turn limited prospects for serious reform at the 1996 IGC. In the current atmosphere of public grumpiness and political weakness, member states seemed less likely than ever to push the frontiers of European integration.

On a practical level, IGCs are inherently unwieldy; the inability of

leaders to control the scope of discussions is a major drawback. Too many
issues on the table make IGCs difficult to manage and make package deals
difficult to negotiate. The EMU IGC was an exception, but its scope was
limited only because inevitable, messy side issues were shunted into the
parallel IGC on political union. By contrast, the EPU negotiations are a
case study of what can go wrong with the IGCs, in terms of scope and participant motivation. With the Commission shoved to the sidelines, France
and Germany ostensibly acting in concert but actually competing for influence, Britain holding itself hostage to an increasingly powerful anti-
European domestic lobby, and the other member states divided by special
interests, it is hardly surprising that the outcome was so unsatisfactory.

Moreover, IGCs have become a victim of their supposed success by
encouraging leaders to believe that difficult issues of democracy and governance can be resolved in late-night deals behind closed doors. That
Maastricht was a debacle did not become clear to European leaders until
they saw the baffled and hostile public response to its results. Although the
IGCs were intended in part to redress the democratic deficit, because of
their inadequate results and because of the public dissatisfaction with the
process itself, they have ultimately succeeded only in accentuating the distance between European institutions and European voters. Maastricht and
the ensuing ratification crisis have greatly diminished the psychological
and symbolic value of IGCs: Rather than reaffirming a grand commitment
to ever closer union, the risk is that they will throw national differences
into sharper relief and, by raising the political stakes, make them harder to
resolve.

As currently construed, IGCs are unsuitable instruments to promote
deeper integration. The EU is already too large and its member states' interests too diverse to make IGCs work. The situation will become worse as the
EU expands. The solution could be to exploit the existing treaties' full
potential and return IGCs to their former role as a means of ratifying agreement already reached by the member states on specific issues. But such a
strategy depends for success on an ever elusive "political will" to confront
Europe's internal and external challenges through collective action, for
which the pomp and bustle of the IGC process has proved an ineffective
substitute. Sadly, recent developments in European integration, including
recent IGCs, suggest that the necessary political will is fast evaporating.

Notes

1. For a history of European integration in the 1980s, see Desmond Dinan,
Ever Closer Union? An Introduction to the European Community (Boulder: Lynne
Rienner, 1994), pp. 99–157.
2. Member state positions were recorded in the daily newsletter, *Agence
Europe*.

3. Commission of the European Communities, *Research on the "Cost of Non-Europe": Basic Findings,* 16 vols. (Luxembourg: Office for Official Publications of the European Communities, 1988).

4. European Communities, *Bulletin,* 1-1986.

5. Ibid., 6-1985.

6. European Communities, *Official Journal* C 77, 19 March 1984, pp. 33–48. For an academic assessment of the draft treaty, see Roland Bieber, Jean-Paul Jacque, and Joseph Weiler (eds.), *An Ever Closer Union: A Critical Analysis of the Draft Treaty Establishing the European Union* (Luxembourg: Office for Official Publications of the European Communities, 1985).

7. See Gianni Bonvincini, "The Genscher-Colombo Plan and the 'Solemn Declaration on European Union' (1981–1983)," in Roy Pryce (ed.), *The Dynamics of European Union* (London: Croom Helm, 1987), pp. 174–187.

8. Ad Hoc Committee on Institutional Affairs (Dooge Committee), *Interim Report to the European Council (Dublin, December 3–4, 1984); Report to the European Council (Brussels, March 29–30, 1985).* For an academic assessment of the Dooge Committee's work, see Patrick Keatinge and Anna Murphy, "The European Council's Ad-Hoc Committee on Institutional Affairs (1984–1985), in Pryce, *Dynamics of European Union,* pp. 217–237.

9. "Report by Mr. Leo Tindemans to the European Council," European Communities, *Bulletin,* supplement 1-1976.

10. European Communities, *Bulletin,* 5-1984.

11. Two participants in the Milan European Council, Garret FitzGerald (Ireland's prime minister) and Margaret Thatcher (Britain's prime minister), give interesting accounts of the summit in their respective memoirs. See Garret FitzGerald, *All in a Life: An Autobiography* (Dublin: Gill and Macmillan, 1991), pp. 594–595; and Margaret Thatcher, *Downing Street Years* (London: HarperCollins, 1993).

12. See Otto Schmuck and Wolfgang Wessels, "Die Mailänder Tagung des Europäischen Rates: Weder Fehlschlag noch Durchbruch zur Europäischen Union," in *Integration* 3(1985): 80–87.

13. These and other key documents relating to the IGC are reproduced in Marino Gazzo, *Towards European Union II: From the European Council in Milan to the Signing of the Single European Act* (Brussels: Agence Europe, 1986).

14. For an account of the negotiations and their outcome, see Jean de Ruyt, *L'Acte unique européen: commentaire* (Brussels: Editions de l'Université de Bruxelles, 1987).

15. The debate can be followed in Wayne Sandholtz and John Zysman, "1992: Recasting the European Bargain," *World Politics* 42 (1989): 95–128; Andrew Moravcsik, "Negotiating the Single European Act," in Robert Keohane and Stanley Hoffmann (eds.), *The New European Community* (Boulder: Westview, 1991); Andrew Moravcsik, "Preferences and Power in the European Community: A Liberal Intergovernmentalist Approach," *Journal of Common Market Studies* 31, 4 (1993): 473–524; D. Wincott, "Institutional Interaction and European Integration: Towards an Everyday Critique of Liberal Intergovernmentalism," *Journal of Common Market Studies* 33, 4 (1995): 597–609; and Andrew Moravcsik, "Liberal Intergovernmentalism and Integration: A Rejoinder," *Journal of Common Market Studies* 33): 611–628.

16. For an assessment of the Commission's role in the IGC process, see Desmond Dinan, "The Commission and the Intergovernmental Conferences," in Neill Nugent (ed.), *At the Heart of the Union: Studies of the European Commission* (London: Macmillan, 1997).

17. See Finn Laursen, "Explaining the Intergovernmental Conference on

Political Union," in Finn Laursen and Sophie Vanhoonacker, *The Intergovernmental Conference on Political Union: Institutional Reform, New Policies and International Identity of the European Community* (Maastricht: European Institute of Public Administration, 1992), pp. 229–248.

18. For the official Commission position, see European Commission, *One Market, One Money: An Evaluation of the Potential Benefits and Costs of Forming an Economic and Monetary Union* (Luxembourg: Office for Official Publications of the European Communities, 1990). For a trenchant academic analysis, see Wayne Sandholz, "Choosing Union: Monetary Politics and Maastricht," *International Organization* 47, 3 (Winter 1993): 1–40.

19. See Peter Kenen, *Economic and Monetary Union in Europe: Moving Beyond Maastricht* (Cambridge: Cambridge University Press), pp. 11–12. The Werner Plan itself can be found in European Communities, *Bulletin,* supplement 3-1970.

20. George Ross, *Jacques Delors and European Integration* (Oxford: Oxford University Press, 1995), pp. 154, 167.

21. European Communities, *Bulletin,* supplement 1-1990.

22. The Kohl-Mitterrand letter and other key documents relating to the EPU IGC are reproduced in Laursen and Vanhoonacker, *Intergovernmental Conference.*

23. Michael Baun, *An Imperfect Union: The Maastricht Treaty and the New Politics of European Integration* (Boulder: Westview, 1996), pp. 155, 156.

24. European Communities, *Bulletin,* 6-1990.

25. See Dinan, "Commission."

26. For an insider's account of the Maastricht Treaty negotiations and an analysis of their outcome, see Jim Cloos et al., *Le Traité de Maastricht: genèse, analyse, commentaire* (Brussels: Bruylant, 1993).

27. Reflection Group on the Intergovernmental Conference, *Interim Report* (Luxembourg: Office for Official Publications of the European Communities, 1995); Reflection Group on the Intergovernmental Conference, *Final Report* (Luxembourg: Office for Official Publications of the European Communities, 1996). For an assessment of the IGC's prospects, see Geoffrey Edwards and Alfred Pijpers (eds.), *The European Union: 1996 and Beyond* (London: Pinter, 1997).

PART 1

ENLARGEMENT

3

Northern Enlargement and EU Decisionmaking

John Peterson & Elizabeth Bomberg

The accession of Sweden, Austria, and Finland in 1995 made the EU a considerably different economic, demographic, linguistic, and geographic animal. After northern enlargement, the EU's economy increased in size by about 7 percent and its population grew by slightly less, to reach just over 370 million. The EU added two new official languages. Most dramatically, northern enlargement increased the EU's territory by no less than one-third and gave it a 2,300 kilometer border with Russia. This chapter considers how and how much northern enlargement made the Union a different political and institutional animal. It confronts three broad questions: What effects did northern enlargement have on EU decisionmaking? How did it change calculations and potential coalitions within the 1996–1997 IGC? Is further enlargement compatible with collective EU action without radical institutional reform?[1]

Our central argument is that northern enlargement had modest effects compared to past enlargements but still altered EU decisionmaking in four fundamental ways. First, it brought three new net contributors into the Union and thus considerably expanded the existing coalition of member states that instinctually oppose new EU expenditure. Second, northern enlargement added three small states to the EU and thus exacerbated existing anxieties among large states about the diminution of their relative power. Third, it unfolded as the EU was preparing for the IGC and thus reinforced pressure for institutional reform, particularly because all three newcomers firmly supported early, further enlargement. Fourth, northern enlargement infused the EU with a distinctive set of "social democratic" values and administrative traditions, thus giving impetus to the campaign to make the EU "cleaner," more transparent, and committed to fighting unemployment.

We examine northern enlargement from four different angles. Our first section applies different theoretical models of EU decisionmaking. The next section rates the postaccession performance of each of the newcomers. A third presents an overview of postenlargement decisionmaking in selected EU policy sectors. The fourth section considers the IGC and the positions of Austria, Sweden, and Finland within it. Our conclusion looks ahead to the EU's next enlargement.

Enlargement and Decisionmaking: The Theoretical Angle

The theoretical literature on the EU has a less than flattering reputation, especially among nonspecialists, that is not entirely undeserved.[2] Theorists often fail to specify precisely what they are trying to explain at which level of analysis in a multitiered system of decisionmaking.[3] To illustrate the point, neofunctionalism and intergovernmentalism are both essentially macrotheories of European *integration,* which seek to explain its broad pace and direction.[4] They shed considerable light on "history-making" decisions taken at the highest political level, including those taken to enlarge the EU. However, macrotheories are far less well equipped to tell us why or how enlargement may lead to change in day-to-day EU policy outcomes.

One of the fathers of neofunctionalism argues that "neither it nor any other theory of integration can explain why the Community began with six—rather than seven or nine—subsequently expanded to twelve, and may even reach twenty-five or thirty before exhausting itself somewhere on the Asian steppes."[5] A more charitable view might begin by recalling that neofunctionalism is based mainly on the idea of spillover, which supposes that integration feeds upon itself. Northern enlargement could be explained as the consequence of three different kinds of spillover. The first was *functional* spillover as the creation of the European Economic Area (EEA) between the EU and European Free Trade Area (EFTA) harmonized policies of low political salience that then led to further integration of a wider range of policies.[6] Second came *institutional* spillover: The EEA was based on a sort of imperialism whereby the EU made rules and the EFTA states adjusted to them without any institutionalized means for influencing their content. This system eventually became politically untenable,[7] leading to *political* spillover: Neofunctionalists have tended to miss the point that "political spillover will also occur from the outside in" as elites from non-EU states become acclimated to operating in a new political environment and increasingly appreciate the benefits available to insiders.[8]

From a neofunctionalist perspective, it is important that the three newcomers had political cultures and institutions broadly similar to those of existing member states. Moreover, all three possessed competent and committed civil services, as well as outward-looking political and business elites. Austrian, Swedish, and Finnish elites appeared to be more carefully

and systematically prepared for EU membership than had been their counterparts from previous applicants. Forward-looking efforts by the newcomers to try to cope with the demands of EU membership continued even after
enlargement. For example, Finland's ministry of foreign affairs held a
workshop in spring 1996 for civil servants, members of parliament, and
business leaders on preparing for the Finnish presidency, which was scheduled for the end of 1999. A veteran Brussels consultant recalled, "I had to
say to them: don't tell them in Brussels that you're preparing now because
they'll think that you don't know how the EU works!"[9]

For their part, proponents of intergovernmental theories of EU politics
would note that northern accession nearly foundered on the question of the
relative power of small and large states in an EU of fifteen. Large states
naturally feared that small states, which have always enjoyed EU representation disproportionate to their relative population, would be in a stronger
position to block decisions as the EU enlarged. Despite agreement at the
1992 Lisbon European Council that enlargement would take place on the
basis of existing institutional provisions, the United Kingdom sought to
prevent a fall in the commensurate weight of large states by blocking the
carryover of existing rules on the percentage of votes needed to constitute a
blocking minority under qualified majority voting.[10] In the event, the UK
finally gave in after a compromise was struck at a Council meeting on the
Greek island of Ioannina. The Ioannina compromise stated that if twenty-
three or more votes were cast against any proposal approved under QMV,
the measure would be suspended for three months while the Council presidency and European Commission sought to convince one or more dissi-
dents to switch their votes. The compromise may be meaningless in practice (as we argue below), but the need for it gives succor to intergovernmentalists.

More generally, intergovernmentalists insist that enlargement always
makes the EU more conflictual because it diversifies the range of national
preferences that must be accommodated. The explanatory power of neofunctionalism wanes with each successive enlargement, given that "successful spillover requires prior programmatic agreement amongst governments, which is more difficult to reach with a larger EU."[11] For example,
northern enlargement made budgetary decisionmaking more prone to intergovernmental bickering because the existing coalition of net contributors
expanded by three in 1995. Austria and Sweden in particular gave frosty
receptions to 1996 Commission proposals to earmark unused agricultural
funds for job creation.

Yet if the process of enlargement is any guide to its eventual effects, it
must be conceded that northern enlargement proceeded extremely smooth-
ly. Only thirteen months separated the opening of accession negotiations
and a final agreement.[12] Transition periods were shorter than for any previous enlargement.[13] All three newcomers became integrated into the EU

decisionmaking quickly and without fanfare. It is not clear that northern enlargement made the EU a fundamentally less unified actor. To illustrate the point, insiders at EU summits in 1995–1996 noted that proposals from the presidency tended to be accepted with little dissension, partly because time constraints frequently precluded *tours de table*. In an EU of fifteen, summits became crowded, rushed media circuses. It was easy to forget that the summits were designed as "fireside chats" for an intimate and much smaller group of European leaders.[14]

At a more mundane level, northern enlargement caused little disruption to actual policymaking. At this level of analysis, institutionalist theory sheds considerable light on decisions that set policy as opposed to those that "make history."[15] The "new institutionalism" highlights two features of EU decisionmaking: competition among different EU institutions under the "Community method" of decisionmaking (i.e., the Commission proposes, the Council disposes, etc.) and routines that are established or "institution-alized" through iterated decisionmaking.

From this perspective, interinstitutional rivalry between the Council and EP sharpened in the post-Maastricht period. However, the new codeci-sion procedure did not immediately lead to impasse or stalemate, even given the addition of three new member states and a host of inexperienced members of the European Parliament. Moreover, as a senior Swedish offi-cial explained, the shadow of the IGC hung over the Council and encour-aged compromise:

> It all works surprisingly well with rules that are obviously not constructed or designed to deal with the current situation. . . . But it is partly on the basis that everyone assumes that it is a temporary situation anyhow. . . . I have seen several cases at the Council, at the ministerial level, where peo-ple explicitly refer to this and say "listen, we are in a difficult situation here. We know these rules are not really made for this situation but we cannot address this now because that is an IGC sort of issue. So let's try to be reasonable."[16]

At the same time, northern enlargement made the Council a more hydralike institution. Coalition building in the Council became more com-plex, with forceful diplomacy by the Council more often needed to avoid isolating any delegations. Package deals probably became a more institu-tionalized (if still informal) norm of Council decisionmaking, since creative and complicated bargains were more frequently needed to achieve agree-ment among a larger number of member states. Institutionalism thus offers the insight that enlargement may have made the Council presidency a more important determinant of EU policy outcomes.

However, outcomes are only agreed after they are shaped by a complex process of interest mediation, much of which takes place before the Commission even tables a formal proposal. The difficulty of altering pro-posals after they are agreed by the Commission makes subsystemic decisionmaking and policy-shaping decisions important determinants of eventual EU policies. At this level of analysis, an increasing number of scholars have deployed the concept of "policy networks" with considerable profit.[17] A policy network may be defined as a (more or less) structured cluster of public and private actors who have interests in a specific sector of policy and effective influence over policy outcomes. EU policy networks tend to correspond to individual policy sectors. Their internal characteristics, particularly their relative stability, exclusiveness, and strength of resource dependencies among their members, are crucial determinants of how much policies are shaped by relatively informal bargaining at a subsystemic level.

For nonmember states, lack of access to EU policy networks is as potentially threatening as lack of access to the Union's formal political institutions. After the Norwegian no vote in September 1994, Helene Sjursen argued that "Norway was overnight cut off from the EU's policy networks and working groups" and thus was "politically more isolated than at any time since 1905."[18] Officials from the three member states that *did* enter in 1995 agreed that they remained outgunned at the subsystemic level long after accession. Most were still learning how policy networks were structured, and their national lobbies were still getting acclimated. Above all, they remained underrepresented in the Commission's services.[19]

Part of the problem was that much bargaining occurs informally and discreetly within policy networks. One Finnish official reflected: "From the books you might think that it is very complicated and takes a lot of time. . . . But it needs good oil and the oil is people who know and can use this machinery. That is why I now understand when people say that there is a Brussels bureaucracy, they mean that there is a group of people who know how to work in Brussels: how to use the lobbies, how to use the Commission services, etc."[20]

In sum, neofunctionalists and intergovernmentalists may disagree about the causes and effects of northern enlargement, but both offer useful insights into how it changed the Union. Institutionalists highlight a general lack of change at a systemic level of analysis due to the strength of informal cooperative norms, as well as the opportunity offered by the IGC to revamp the EU's decision rules. Meanwhile, at least initially, many EU policy networks appeared little changed by northern enlargement.

The Newcomers: A Scorecard

This section reviews the performance of the newcomers as member states seeking to influence EU decisionmaking. Before taking each in turn, we should recall speculation that enlargement would create a new, stronger "Nordic bloc" in EU decisionmaking.[21] Nordic cooperation was extensive during the accession negotiations in 1993–1994. For twenty years previous,

Denmark had acted as the lone Nordic voice in the EU. In the immediate aftermath of accession, the Swedes and Finns often sought informal advice from the Danes. Finland even chose a site for its permanent representation in Brussels across the street from Denmark's, with a shared underground parking garage.

The extent of Nordic cooperation has depended very much on the issue under discussion. New antifraud measures agreed in 1996 almost certainly would have been far less comprehensive without Sweden and Finland.[22] Shared concerns that EU membership would weaken domestic environmental and consumer standards led to considerable unity of Nordic (and Austrian) views on related issues. On questions related to the Lomé convention, the Nordics generally urged that the EU's development effort be reformed and strengthened. It is plausible to assume that cooperation among the Nordics will become more systematic as EU enlarges further and differentials among Nordic preferences become narrower in relative terms.

However, in 1995–1996 Swedish, Finnish, and Danish preferences on the Council proved to be surprisingly distinct from one another. An important factor that mitigated against the formation of a Nordic bloc was the continued (perhaps enhanced) importance of package deals in EU negotiations. Officials from the three newcomers tended to admit that they had difficulties acclimating to this practice, which usually involves striking complex bargains across sectors and securing the consent of often quite autonomous policy networks. Package deals usually arise when the Council presidency tries to "buy off" member states by offering them concessions on relatively narrow questions, which are unlikely to be equally salient for all members of any "bloc." In short, a Nordic bloc failed to materialize with any consistency after 1995.

Sweden

Because Sweden was the largest of the former EFTA states, its shift from apparently permanent rejection of EU membership to its 1991 application made northern enlargement inevitable in some form. High unemployment and economic stagnation in Sweden diminished both the perceived sanctity of the "Swedish model" and concerns that EU membership would do violence to it by lowering labor, environmental, and consumer standards. One of Sweden's only postwar nonsocialist governments, headed by Carl Bildt between 1991 and 1994, saw EU membership as a way to encourage lowered welfare spending, deregulated employment markets, and a natural evolution of Sweden's traditional neutrality after the Cold War.

Yet according to Bildt, a significant minority of Swedes continued to subscribe to a sort of "welfare isolationism" and "an unrealistic belief that the now-extinct 'Swedish model' has given us a society generally superior to those in other parts of Europe."[23] Swedish Euroskepticism was fueled by the rejection of the Maastricht Treaty by Danish voters in the 1992 referendum. It then was reflected in the narrow margin—52.2 to 46.9 percent—by which voters assented to EU membership in Sweden's own 1994 referendum, which came only a month after Finns had voted yes by a clear margin of 57 percent. Sweden's referendum (and to some extent Finland's) exposed a stark "north-south, urban-rural divide," with large majorities in sparsely populated northern provinces voting against EU membership.[24] Sweden's behavior as an EU member state was shaped by a streak of domestic Euroskepticism stronger than that of any other member state, even the UK.[25]

The onus for explaining why EU membership was a good thing for Sweden fell largely on Anita Gradin, Sweden's nominee to the Commission. A former journalist and diplomat, Gradin proved to be a capable and popular commissioner, assuming the tricky Pillar III portfolio of justice and home affairs and spearheading the Commission's antifraud campaign. Gradin sold the EU to a skeptical Swedish public with skill and imagination. As a Swedish official put it, "We have a limited experience of trying to bargain with the EU. . . . Quite a large amount of Swedish newspaper readers are not aware that the Minister for Foreign Affairs in Sweden is sitting on sort of an overall coordinating role for the Council—they have no clue. But they know what Mrs Gradin is doing. . . . She knows how to talk to the public and she is a very tough woman."[26]

Although Gradin proved to be an asset, adjusting to EU membership posed a severe challenge to Sweden's political and diplomatic classes. Other member states found the Swedes to be awkward and occasionally supercilious. One EU ambassador suggested, "The Swedes have domestic political problems which hurt them right now . . . but their basic problem is that they want the EU to be just like the UN."[27] Sweden's tradition of independent activism and "a view on everything" often translated into a general inability to prioritize. A Swedish official admitted, "Sweden always had its own little empire and we have always been very active. Our problem has been that we have had to say to our government: 'please make some priorities because we don't have a lot of political capital down here.'"[28]

One of the issues Sweden had prioritized by late 1995 was a new version of the European Monetary System that could act as a bridge between the first wave of countries who were in on a single currency and those who were still outside. As an export-oriented state with strong domestic opposition to EMU, Sweden expressed severe misgivings about the idea. However, neither Sweden nor the UK was in any position to block the creation of EMS Mark II. After the EU's Monetary Committee and the European Monetary Institute were instructed to prepare an interim report on it before the Florence summit of June 1996, the Swedish government, headed by Social Democrats, appeared to shift toward insisting that

Sweden would meet the convergence criteria for EMU, regardless of the costs, while pledging that it would seek a Treaty commitment to full employment in the current IGC as a sort of counterweight. The government's position was hardly likely to change the minds of Swedish Euroskeptics, many of whom supported the Social Democrats and fiercely opposed Swedish participation in a single currency. However, in the words of Erik Asbring, Sweden's finance minister, "There is no pleasant road for Sweden outside EMU."[29]

Austria

In contrast to Sweden, Austria quickly developed a reputation as an EU member state that normally "should belong to the integration core in Europe."[30] The Austrian schilling was sound enough to join the EMS only a week after Austria's entry into the Union. Austria's commissioner, Franz Fischler, handled the intricate agricultural portfolio with skill, maneuvering through the political minefields of enlargement and the beef crisis with most of his credibility intact. Austria's domestic anti-EU movement, stoked at times by the charismatic leader of the far right Austrian Freedom Party (FPÖ), Jörg Haider, was unable to make political gains in the 1995 Austrian general election.

Yet Austria appeared to suffer from four fundamental problems. First, the Austrians found life difficult under the shadow of the Germans. Austria sometimes took positions in EU negotiations that were different from those of Germany, even when the practice seemed contrary to Austrian interests. German officials frequently complained about the perceived Austrian "need to be different from us for political reasons."[31] In 1996, tensions broke out within Austria's coalition government, with Social Democrats attacking the foreign minister, Wolfgang Schüssel of the People's Party, for pursuing "too pro-German a policy" and creating a "Kohl-Schüssel axis."[32]

Second, despite strong support for accession among Austrian elites and a two-thirds popular vote for membership in the 1994 referendum, Austria did not seem well prepared for entry when it came. By spring 1995 Austria lacked identifiable views on a range of key IGC issues.[33] It immediately earned the dubious distinction of having the worst record of any member state in implementing internal market legislation.[34] In a high-profile 1996 case, the Commission threatened to haul Austria before the European Court of Justice (ECJ) when the region of Niederösterreich broke nearly every important EU rule on procurement in awarding contracts for the construction of extensive public buildings in Sankt Pölten, which replaced Vienna as the region's capital.[35]

A third and related problem was that Austria's positions in EU negotiations sometimes were poorly coordinated. Many civil servants in Austria's "domestic" ministries (for industry, social affairs, etc.) had no previous experience with international organizations. Officials of these and other Austrian ministries who were sent to Brussels often seemed cut off from decisionmaking, which remained highly centralized in Austria. One British diplomat observed, "A lot of them seem to have been sent to Brussels as a sort of punishment."[36]

Fourth and finally, the rising unpopularity of Austria's ruling coalition and declining support for EU membership seemed to feed upon each other. After 1995 the Austrian government instituted painful cutbacks in public spending, largely to ensure qualification for EMU, and undertook unpopular agricultural reforms to bring Austria into line with the Common Agricultural Policy. One consequence was the strongest showing ever in any election by Haider's Freedom Party in the October 1996 Austrian European Parliament election. The FPÖ polled nearly 28 percent and gained mostly at the expense of the ruling Social Democrats, who suffered their worst result in a nationwide election since 1918. Put simply, Austria's early record as an EU member state was a very mixed one.

Finland

The first two years of EU membership were far happier for Finland than for the other newcomers. Even more than Gradin or Fischler, the former Finnish finance minister, Erkki Likannen, turned out to be a star of the Santer Commission. In particular, Likannen used the budget portfolio to shake up and professionalize the Commission's internal organization.[37] Finland's first postaccession ambassador to the EU, Antti Satuli, quickly became a highly respected member of the clubby Committee of Permanent Representatives (COREPER).

By most accounts the Finns showed remarkable pragmatism and negotiating skill from the earliest days of their EU membership. A Swedish official described her Finnish counterparts as "good negotiators. They always get a good hand before they start playing. Of course, they had lots of practice with the Russians."[38] The low-key Finnish approach to its EU membership was a product both of tradition and interest. In marked contrast with Sweden, postwar Finland rarely spoke its mind on international matters. More generally, Finland's interest in appearing *communautaire* was less clouded than those of the other newcomers. The broad, strategic benefits of EU membership were more important for Finland than narrow, specific ones, such as lower food prices. In the words of one Finnish official, "People understand [now] that we are part of western democracy, even with our specific culture, heritage and everything. . . .We are not Finlandized any longer."[39]

Nevertheless, the benefits of being an EU member were illustrated clearly on several specific issues in 1995–1996. One was a proposal to limit the length of transport trucks—which often are 25 meters or longer in

Finnish lumber shipping—to 18.75 meters. After Finland (along with Sweden) obtained a derogation, Satuli claimed that "the European Commission would not have considered a compromise proposal if we had not become members of the EU and were only members of the EEA."[40]

The ledger for the Finns has not been completely positive. Finland is certainly the most frequently misunderstood member state in EU negotiations because of its language and the difficulties of translating it. The Finnish civil service lacks enough officials who can handle documents in both English and French, and the technical nature of much EU legislation often presents a double barrier.

Ultimately, however, Finland has had an easier transition to EU membership mostly because it has been less constrained by domestic political opposition compared to Sweden or Austria. Polls suggested that Finns were far more enthusiastic about both the EU and its major policies, including EMU, than their Nordic counterparts.[41] Despite the threat posed to Finland's timber industry, especially by Swedish competition, the Finnish markka joined the EMS in 1996, and Finland signaled its intention to become one of the first EMU "ins." After years of being "Finlandized," Finnish elites and ordinary citizens alike clearly had become used to making trade-offs in political life.

The Policy Angle

This section provides an overview of how and how much northern enlargement has altered patterns of decisionmaking in different EU policy sectors.[42] The newcomers joined the EU after the internal market was, in theory, complete. As members of the EEA, all three had already harmonized their domestic laws with most internal market rules. In the aftermath of northern enlargement, relatively little progress was made toward further liberalization, particularly since the EU began to focus on tricky matters related to the freeing of markets for public goods such as electricity and telecommunications. Still, the internal market remained mostly free of the bickering over competence and institutional prerogative that encumbered research, external trade, and the Common Foreign and Security Policy in 1995–1996. A Swedish official observed that "nobody is questioning the role of the Community on the internal market. . . . Everybody including Britain is on board."[43]

The addition of Sweden, Finland, and Austria acted to strengthen a northern coalition that usually supported further liberalization. For example, Finland and Sweden joined the UK in arguing that draft rules designed to ensure "universal service," or minimum telephone services at an affordable price, were too stringent and restrictive to industry. However, efforts to create an internal market in broadcasting found Sweden fighting its corner aggressively to try to maintain national restrictions on advertising aimed at minors. The Swedes also joined Belgium, Ireland, and Portugal in pushing to ensure that EU money for promoting homegrown European films was available for projects that showcased cultural and linguistic diversity, and not just "super-productions with international appeal."[44] For its part, Austria opposed several proposals to liberalize public utilities under pressure from its powerful unions and owing to fear of stiff German competition. Generally, however, northern enlargement did not have a dramatic effect on internal market policy.

Much the same might be said for external trade policy. Northern enlargement strengthened the pro–free-trade bloc on the Council, but its effect was muted by two overriding factors.[45] First, few earthshaking decisions concerning external trade were taken in the immediate post–Uruguay Round period as the new World Trade Organization was being set up. Second, northern enlargement came at a time of generally stagnant economic growth in northern Europe. A Swedish official lamented, "On free trade, we thought we would have an alliance with Germany but we don't have it anymore."[46] Austria often voted with more protectionist southern states in decisions on the use of EU trade armor, such as antidumping measures.

On research policy, all three newcomers were well integrated into the EU's technology framework program by virtue of a long-standing agreement that allowed nearly full participation by research organizations from EFTA members. Membership in the European Research Cooperation Agency (EUREKA), an intergovernmental scheme that rivaled the EU's programs in size and finance, also facilitated extensive technological links between the Union and Sweden, Austria, and (especially) Finland.[47] Major decisions on the five-year budget and priorities of the EU's Framework IV program (1994–1998) were agreed in 1993–1994 and thus accepted as faits accomplis by the newcomers. Decisionmaking concerning the actual distribution of funds between firms, projects, and technological sectors tends to be highly technocratic and routinized, and enlargement changed little at this level.[48]

However, the dynamics of decisionmaking concerning funding for EU technology programs was altered considerably by northern enlargement. Setting a budget for EU research has always been contentious, as illustrated by the need for the European Council to decide on a compromise budget for Framework IV in 1993.[49] The deal contained provisions for a "reserve" of ECU 700 million to supplement Framework IV's guaranteed budget, which could be activated only by a unanimous decision in 1996. To mobilize support for spending the reserve, the research commissioner, Edith Cresson, created task forces to draw up proposals for research needed to develop "the car of the future," new viral vaccines, and the next generation of educational software. Ultimately, however, the UK and Germany were joined by Austria and Sweden (as well as France and the Netherlands) in a coalition that blocked proposals to earmark unspent agricultural funds for research. Negotiations on the budget for Framework V (1999–2004) promised to be slow and hard fought.

Environmental policy also witnessed significant change in the balance of national preferences represented on the Council. On most issues, the newcomers lined up with an existing "green coalition" of Germany, Denmark, and the Netherlands.[50] However, important exceptions arose: Austria and Germany clashed over Alpine transit restrictions, while Sweden opposed a compromise on a carbon/energy tax supported by Finland.

Earlier the accession negotiations had been troubled by the insistence of all three newcomers that they be allowed to apply environmental standards that were stricter than many EU standards. This sticking point was resolved by allowing the applicants to apply tougher legislation for up to four years, during which they clearly hoped to encourage a ratcheting up of EU-wide standards. To some extent, their chances were helped by the influx of Nordic nationals into Directorate-General (DG) XI (environment) of the Commission, which went to considerable lengths to second officials from the environmental ministries of the newcomers prior to their accession. The effect was to empower green influences at the policy-shaping stages.

Leaving aside the beef crisis, agriculture was a relatively quiet policy sector after the conclusion of the Uruguay Round and the emergence of a laager mentality in advance of Eastern enlargement. Yet the dynamics of CAP decisionmaking changed considerably after northern enlargement, as the quite distinctive agricultural interests of the newcomers made negotiations more unpredictable and volatile. More careful inquisition often was needed on the part of the Commission and Council presidency to head off blocking minorities on the Special Committee on Agriculture (SCA). A generally consensual and powerful body before 1995, the SCA quarreled frequently and appeared to be deciding less and less as time went on.

The newcomers did not line up together on all CAP issues. Sweden and Finland agitated for more environmentally friendly farming methods and greater allowances to be made for different seed-sowing timetables in the Arctic region. However, Sweden's market-oriented agricultural tradition contrasted with Finland's policy of high support levels for farmers. Finland won rights to give state aids to its northern farmers in the accession negotiations, in part because its agricultural exports to Russia had fallen so dramatically after 1991. One effect was that Finnish exports of eggs to Sweden increased dramatically after 1995, leading to an "egg war" that consumed considerable diplomatic effort because its effects were concentrated in regions that had voted strongly against EU membership in 1994.

For its part, Austria negotiated well on agriculture in the accession negotiations.[51] Subsequently, the Austrians appeared little fazed about taking positions close or identical to those of Germany on the CAP. For example, after beef consumption fell dramatically in Austria, it voted consistently with a German-led bloc against Commission proposals to ease the export ban on British beef.

One specific episode of decisionmaking on the CAP—concerning agrimonetary aids—is worth singling out for the way it illustrated the daunting challenge posed to any newcomer by the cut and thrust of EU negotiations, as well as the apparent emptiness of the Ioannina compromise. A French-inspired proposal of aid to farmers who had suffered from exchange rate changes was opposed by the UK, Italy, and Sweden, which together wielded twenty-four votes under QMV: less than a blocking minority but enough to trigger the Ioannina compromise, at the UK's request. Italy offered to switch its vote but sought concessions on citrus fruit, which it considered too expensive. The Spanish presidency shunned British requests for changes in the actual text, and thus Sweden became the key player. In the words of one participant, "Sweden just kept asking for changes in the text, which showed that they are not used to dealing across issue-areas. In the end, they got state aids to their northern regions allowed, but it wasn't really their idea."[52] The incident showed that the Commission and Council normally would seek to deal with whichever member was the cheapest to buy off, not the one that invoked the Ioannina compromise, as the UK had intended.

Regional and social policies witnessed history-making decisions prior to northern enlargement—the creation of the social chapter at Maastricht and the 1993 structural funds round—that set clear parameters for subsequent decisionmaking. However, northern enlargement did give rise to the new "objective 6" regions in Scandinavia that qualified for EU regional funds based on low population density rather than economic criteria. The move constituted a good example of the EU's propensity for "creative adaptation"[53] of its existing rules to suit new members. In general, enlargement means more competition for limited structural funds but also more scope for partnership and cooperation of regions across member states.

On social policy, strong corporatist traditions in all three new member states led them to give strong support to the dialogue between the social partners, as mandated in the Maastricht Treaty's Social Protocol. Northern enlargement thus gave impetus to a process that brought surprising progress toward agreements on parental leave and posted workers in 1996. Similarly, Sweden, Austria, and Finland generally favored high levels of protection on consumer and health issues. All three strongly supported a proposed ban on tobacco advertising, although it proved impossible to shift a blocking minority on the issue.

The CFSP is treated at length elsewhere in this volume (see Part 2). Besides, it could be argued that little meaningful decisionmaking took place within Pillar II in 1995–1996. However, two effects of northern enlargement on the CFSP are worth noting. First, all three newcomers sought to ensure that their neutral status did not disrupt the CFSP or block EU actions. Particularly on most issues related to peacekeeping, the new-comers tended to take similarly activist views and act as allies to the UK, Germany, and the Netherlands in 1995–1996.

Second, the EU became more focused on the Baltic and Balkan regions as a consequence of northern enlargement. Sweden and Finland both pushed the Commission hard to develop its Baltic Sea Region Initiative, which culminated in an eleven-nation Baltic summit in Visby, Sweden, in May 1996. The summit yielded little besides strengthened cooperation in the fight against organized crime. Yet the Nordics along with Germany remained committed to stronger EU links with the Baltic republics, Poland, and Russia. For its part, Austria was an important ally in the Italian presidency's successful bid to secure a cooperation agreement with Slovenia.

To summarize, northern enlargement had tangible effects on policy content in several important EU sectors, but general patterns of decision-making changed very little. The addition of the three newcomers changed the EU's general policy orientation far less than had past enlargements, which had made the Community dramatically more free-trade oriented after 1973 and far more concerned with cohesion issues after 1986. It was harder to pin down precisely what was different about the EU after 1995 but also clear that the Union was generally "greener," more focused on unemployment and the status of workers, and perhaps most important, more east-ward-looking and concerned about Russian and Baltic stability. These effects were particularly evident in the IGC.

The Newcomers and the IGC

The Turin summit of 29 March 1996 formally launched the IGC. Its conclusions made it clear that no wholesale recasting of the Union was in the offing. Rather, the IGC would limit itself to three broad issues: bringing Europe closer to the citizen, reforming its institutions in advance of the next enlargement, and strengthening its position in international relations.[54]

Two factors set the 1996 IGC apart from those that produced the Single European Act in 1986 and Maastricht Treaty in 1991. First, the obstinacy of the UK convinced many delegations that no big decisions could be taken until after the British general election, which had to take place in spring 1997 at the latest.[55] Second, members of the EP had monthly meetings with both foreign ministers and the IGC's working group[56] and were briefed constantly on the state of the negotiations. The Parliament's participation gave a boost to moves to make EU decisionmaking more transparent. Increased transparency was resisted by several member states (particularly the UK), which argued that the Council simply could no longer negotiate because of its large size. More openness, so the line went, would worsen the problem. However, with strong support from Denmark, the Netherlands, and (perhaps most fervently) Sweden, the EP's delegates made the counterargument that unless EU citizens knew which individuals to blame for unpopular decisions, they would blame the Union as a whole.

An apparent similarity of Nordic views on transparency and other issues led to speculation that a systematic burden-sharing arrangement had been agreed, with the Danes pushing environmental protection, the Swedes arguing for a Treaty article on fighting unemployment, and the Finns taking the lead on transparency.[57] However, it soon became clear that no such agreement existed. For example, in contrast to Sweden, the Finns tended to argue that some secrecy was needed because otherwise "the real decisions will be taken in another corridor, in a deal struck secretly between the big member states."[58]

Nordic positions became more closely aligned toward the end of the IGC when, as a Swedish official had predicted, the Nordics had to "decide what we are ready to bleed for."[59] Less dramatically, Austria joined all three Nordics in supporting the introduction of "sustainable development" as a basic EU policy objective in Article 2 of the Treaty of Rome. All four also sought to replace the halfhearted existing Treaty pledge to "respect the environment" with a commitment to promote the "preservation, protection and improvement of the quality of the environment." More generally, northern enlargement strengthened calls for a "progressive" IGC agenda. All three new member states supported proposals for a Treaty reference to the need to combat racism and xenophobia, as well as provisions to suspend and sanction any member state found to be violating basic human or democratic rights. Despite German and British opposition, all three argued for a Treaty article committing the Union to fight unemployment, although Finnish support was muted.

On Pillar II, the Swedes and Finns went as far as to issue a joint policy paper on peacekeeping and conflict management.[60] The paper sought to draw a sharper distinction between peacekeeping and "defence" by encouraging the EU to develop a clear role in the former arena while eschewing a merger between the Union and WEU, of which neither Finland nor Sweden was a full member. The Swedish-Finnish paper was an important contribution to the IGC. It provided further evidence of the evolution of their neutrality toward an acceptance of greater responsibility for external crises while trying to influence the rest of the EU to embrace traditional Nordic foreign policy priorities.

However, Pillars II and III generally gave rise to divisions among the newcomers. Finland declared its readiness to accept more majority voting on the CFSP and even stated that giving the Union more control of the WEU was "one of the central tasks of the IGC in the CFSP area."[61] The

Swedes argued that applying QMV to Pillar II "would mean that the decisions taken would not have the full political support of member countries"
and remained coy about links with the WEU.[62] Austria took a nuanced
position, arguing that military security issues required unanimous decisions
and that anything decided by QMV required arrangements for "constructive
abstentions."[63] On Pillar III the Finns and Austrians generally supported
more majority voting and a limited right of initiative for the Commission,
while Sweden endeavored "to ensure that cooperation will continue to be
primarily an intergovernmental matter."[64]

On more general institutional issues, all three newcomers joined a
broad coalition in favor of more QMV and extension of the codecision procedure, thus isolating France and the UK. Otherwise, Sweden, Austria, and
Finland joined the other small states in seeking to preserve the status quo.
The only areas where Austria appeared to have strong views were on preserving the overrepresentation of small states under QMV and maintaining
each state's right to nominate a commissioner.[65] Finland and Sweden joined
Denmark and the Benelux countries in insisting on their right to appoint a
commissioner and scorned the idea of junior and senior commissioners in a
two-tier structure.

As for QMV, some rebalancing to more closely reflect population differentials between small and large states seemed inevitable. Meanwhile,
proposals to replace unanimity with double- or super-majority voting were
taken seriously in the IGC. With characteristic superciliousness, the
Swedish representative on the IGC working group, Gunnar Lund, complained that such proposals were "fairly provocative . . . undesirable but
also badly justified."[66] For his part, a Finnish official conceded that "the
status quo is the best possible [situation] for Finland as a small member
state in the decision-making process."[67]

The rub for the newcomers was that all firmly wanted early *further*
enlargement, which stood to expand the EU's coterie of small states, particularly to include the Baltic republics, Slovenia, and Hungary.[68] As *demandeurs* on enlargement, the newcomers' leverage on the rights of small
states, as well as other issues, was very limited. For example, Sweden
pushed hardest for a treaty commitment to the fight against unemployment
after its domestic political opinion turned decisively against the EU. With a
general election looming, several members of the Swedish Social
Democratic government even demanded a clause similar to the Maastricht
Treaty's on defence: "a common employment policy leading to common
strategies." But the proposals were watered down considerably, and Section
II of the Amsterdam Treaty precluded any major expenditure of Community resources.

The newcomers thus occupied unenviable negotiating positions. All
were forced into pushing hard on further enlargement while taking highly
defensive stances on most institutional questions. The newcomers were left

with few cards to play on unemployment, consumer protection, or the environment. Their negotiating strategies generally focused on taking maximalist positions in these areas early in the IGC, while adopting very restrictive positions on institutional reform.

To sum up, the IGC negotiations certainly were colored by the presence of the three newcomers. Generally, the difference was one of hue rather than pigment, except on two particularly crucial sets of issues. One, of course, was the balance between small and large states. The other, less tangible but even more salient set of concerns overhung the negotiations like a cold, thick fog: how to prepare the EU for further enlargement. In the absence of northern enlargement, perhaps these concerns could have been put off until well into the twenty-first century. Given northern enlargement, they simply could not be avoided in the IGC, even if they were dodged at the Amsterdam summit.

Conclusion

A reviewer of the third volume of *The State of the European Union* was struck by the "relative calm" of the post-Maastricht EU, but speculated that this state of the Union "may be temporary."[69] By mid-1996, northern enlargement appeared not to have changed things much. A sharper north-south divide had emerged in EU politics, particularly on environmental and consumer safety issues. Yet southern member states that had approached the accession negotiations with trepidation found their positions as net recipients of EU funds bolstered by northern enlargement. Longtime member states (particularly France), concerned that adding three neutral states would skew decisions on foreign and security policies, found the newcomers surprisingly active and constructive on external policy.

If northern enlargement did not disrupt the relative calm of the post-Maastricht period, it also marked the last time that the EU could expand by employing the "classical" Community method. All EU enlargements to date have been guided by five principles: no permanent opt-outs for new members, no radical EU policy innovations, no unpicking of existing agreements, no major changes to EU institutions, and no negotiating with anyone other than a bloc of applicant states with close relations to one another.[70] It is impossible to imagine that the EU could stick to these principles in the future. The Swedes, Austrians, and Finns clearly benefited from the sharp contrast between the relatively modest changes needed to accommodate their entry and the vast and fundamental reforms the EU faces in undertaking Eastern enlargement.

Still, northern enlargement changed the EU in important ways. Veterans of EU negotiations observed that when membership of the Council and its adjuncts expanded from twelve to fifteen, it often became impossible physically to see the face of the person speaking in negotiations. A Swedish official thoughtfully commented, "I fear, and especially my Benelux colleagues tell me, that something was lost [after the last enlargement] which will not be found again."

In this context, the Benelux alliance asserted itself with alacrity as the lines of debate within the IGC emerged. In a dramatic joint statement, the prime ministers of all three Benelux states insisted that they would oppose any further enlargement of the Union if EMU was not completed by 1999. They allowed that some reweighting to give big states more votes under QMV might be acceptable but only in exchange for concessions on the CFSP. They joined the Nordics in insisting that all states had to retain the right to appoint a commissioner.[71]

In short, with history-making decisions to reach on EMU, the IGC, and Eastern enlargement, the quiet, post-Maastricht chapter in the Union's history was a brief one. In particular, the agreement forged at the 1993 Copenhagen summit made Eastern enlargement inevitable, although the precise timetable remained an open question. The Copenhagen decisions promised EU membership to Eastern states that could ensure accession would not lead to an implosion of their economies, as occurred in East Germany after 1990, thus shifting the onus of adjustment onto the applicants.

However, the EU itself cannot hide from the formidable challenges it faces, especially in terms of institutional reform, as it prepares for further enlargement. During the IGC, France and the UK (joined at Amsterdam by Germany) could still fight a last stand against the extension of QMV. A halfway-meaningful debate could take place on large and small state voting weights under QMV. However, the next enlargement was set to move the Union tangibly closer to a situation in which the results of votes taken under QMV would only very rarely be different from the results under a simple majority voting rule.[72] EU decisionmaking thus was approaching a radical, monumental sea change.

In the shorter term, the assertion that northern enlargement would "probably reinforce the intergovernmental tendencies and integration dilemma within the EU" turned out to be apocryphal, or at least far too simple.[73] In their positions on transparency, social matters, environmental policy and QMV, the newcomers often "advocate[d] a strengthening of EU policies, rather than a loosening of integration."[74] Clearly, even if northern enlargement made more flexible integration likelier in the twenty-first century, particularly on defence issues, it also reinforced the importance of Brussels as a political capital with global power.

The most important effect of northern enlargement is that it made the *next* enlargement more likely to be relatively ambitious and soon. Ultimately, northern enlargement exacerbated only marginally the tensions between the two prisoner's dilemma games that Fritz Scharpf argues are played out in EU decisionmaking: between the rich countries keen to increase their productivity and the poorer ones that seek to compete on the basis of factor costs.[75] Pressures for competitive deregulation can be contained through measures such as mutual recognition that allow multiple standards to exist side-by-side and thus offer different levels of protection at different prices, as long as there is a minimum level of harmonization of process-related regulations at the EU level. However, the tensions between these two games will become far more acute and more difficult to contain after Eastern enlargement. As a senior Swedish official put it, "We were a good enlargement, we were the easy enlargement and maybe the obvious one to make."[76] It is impossible to imagine that any future enlargement could be so comfortable.

Notes

1. This chapter culls findings from a wider project into post-Maastricht EU decisionmaking. Most of the fieldwork was done in 1994–1996. We are grateful to the UK Economic and Social Research Council (grant R000235829); the European Commission; the Joseph Rowntree Foundation; and the Universities of York, Stirling, and Glasgow for research grants; to Antje Brown, Ricardo Gomez, and Clare McManus for research assistance; and to the Centre for European Policy Studies (Brussels) and Institute for Governmental Studies (Berkeley) for hosting us. For general findings, see John Peterson and Elizabeth Bomberg, *Decision-Making in the European Union* (London: Macmillan, forthcoming).

2. This section builds on the framework developed in John Peterson, "Decision-making in the European Union: Towards a Framework for Analysis," *Journal of European Public Policy* 2, 1 (March 1995): 69–93.

3. Although frustratingly vague, the idea of "multilevel governance" developed primarily by Marks and his colleagues is useful in highlighting "the existence of overlapping competencies among multiple levels of governments and the interaction of political actors across those levels." Gary Marks, François Nielsen, Leonard Ray, and Jane Salk, "Competencies, Cracks and Conflicts: Regional Mobilization in the European Union," in Gary Marks, Fritz W. Scharpf, Philippe C. Schmitter, and Wolfgang Streeck (eds.), *Governance in the European Union* (London: Sage), 41. See also Gary Marks, Liesbet Hooghe, and Kermit Blank, "European Integration from the 1980s: State-Centric vs. Multi-Level Governance," *Journal of Common Market Studies* 39, 3 (September 1996): 341–378.

4. Good examples of these contending approaches are Dorette Corbey, "Dialectical Functionalism: Stagnation as a Booster of European Integration," *International Organization* 49, 2 (1995): 253–284; Andrew Moravcsik, "Preferences and Power in the European Community: A Liberal Intergovernmentalist Approach," *Journal of Common Market Studies* 31, 4 (December 1993): 473–524.

5. Philippe C. Schmitter, "Examining the Present Euro-Policy with the Help of Past Theories," in Marks et al., *Governance in the European Union, p. 13.*

6. The EEA fell short of a customs union but offered EFTA (Sweden, Finland, Austria, Switzerland, Norway, and Iceland in 1992) an expanded free trade that gave them access to the internal market but not EU decisionmaking. The main

effect of the EEA was considerable harmonization of laws in the EFTA states with EU directives.

7. We are grateful to Jacques Pelkmans for suggesting this point to us. On the notion of "institutional spillover," see Robert Keohane and Stanley Hoffmann, "Institutional Change in the Europe in the 1980s," in Keohane and Hoffmann (eds.), *The New European Community* (Boulder: Westview, 1991), pp. 18–22.

8. Lee Miles, John Redmond, and René Schwok, "Integration Theory and the Enlargement of the European Union," in Carolyn Rhodes and Sonia Mazey (eds.), *The State of the European Union,* vol. 3: *Building a European Polity?* (Boulder: Lynne Rienner, 1995), p. 181.

9. Interview, Brussels public affairs consultant, 5 May 1996.

10. Instead of keeping the same percentage (about 30 percent) of votes needed to block a proposal (twenty-three of seventy-six votes in an EU of twelve), the UK proposed to keep unchanged the number of votes needed to block (twenty-three of ninety in an EU of sixteen), thus effectively lowering the percentage of votes (to 26 percent) constituting a blocking minority.

11. Miles et al., "Integration Theory and the Enlargement of the EU," p. 187.

12. The same terms were agreed for all three newcomers plus Norway, which ultimately declined to join after a 52 percent no vote in its November 1994 referendum.

13. Fraser Cameron, "Keynote Article: The European Union and the Fourth Enlargement," *Journal of Common Market Studies Annual Review* 33 (August 1995): 33.

14. Martin Westlake, *The Council of the European Union* (London: Cartermill, 1995), pp. 21–23.

15. Simon Bulmer, "The Governance of the European Union: A New Institutionalist Approach," *Journal of Public Policy* 13, 4 (1993): 351–380; Simon Bulmer, "Institutions and Policy Change in the European Communities: The Case of Merger Control," *Public Administration* 72, 3 (Autumn 1994): 423–444. For an institutionalist treatment of the European integration process writ large, see Paul Pierson, "The Path to European Integration: An Historical Institutionalist Perspective," *Comparative Political Studies* 29, 2 (1996): 123–163.

16. Interview, Swedish permanent representation to the EU, 2 May 1996.

17. Adrienne Héritier, ed., *Policy Analyse: Kritik und Neuorientierung* (Opladen: Westdeutscher Verlag, 1993); Keith Middlemas, *Orchestrating Europe: The Informal Politics of the European Union 1973–95* (London: Fontana Press, 1995); John Peterson, "Policy Networks and European Union Policy Making," *West European Politics* 18, 2 (1995): 389–407; Beate Kohler-Koch, "Catching Up with Change: The Transformation of Governance in the European Union," *Journal of European Public Policy* 3, 3 (1996): 359–380.

18. Helene Sjursen, "Enlarging the Union," in S. Stavridis, E. Mossialos, R. Morgan, and H. Machin (eds.), *New Challenges to the European Union* (Aldershot: Dartmouth, 1997), p. 163.

19. This problem was an especially acute one for Austria, which had far more difficulty than Finland or Sweden in placing its nationals in senior Commission posts "reserved" for the newcomers. Explanations for the low Austrian success rate included relatively better economic conditions and lower taxes in Austria compared to in Sweden or Finland, which meant that Austrians did not necessarily end up better off economically after they moved to Brussels.

20. Interview, Finnish permanent representation to the EU, 2 May 1996.

21. See Lee Miles, "The European Union and the Nordic Countries: Impacts on the Integration Process," in Rhodes and Mazey, *The State of the European Union,* vol. 3, pp. 317–334.

22. See John Peterson, "The European Union: Pooled Sovereignty, Divided Accountability," *Political Studies* 45, 3 (1997), pp. 559–578.

23. Carl Bildt, "Importance of Nordic Influence in EU," *Financial Times, 22 November 1994*, p. 23.

24. See Miles, "The European Union and the Nordic Countries," p. 327.

25. This point is borne out clearly in European Commission, *Eurobarometer: Public Opinion in the European Union* 44 (Spring 1996), especially pp. 13–36.

26. Interview, Swedish permanent representation to the EU, 2 May 1996.

27. Interview, permanent representative to the EU (of a large member state), 26 October 1995.

28. Interview, Swedish permanent representation to the EU, 2 May 1996.

29. Quoted in *European Voice,* 13–19 June 1996, p. 15.

30. Wolfram Kaiser, "Austria in the European Union," *Journal of Common Market Studies* 33, 3 (September 1995): 422–423.

31. Interview, German permanent representation to the EU, 26 October 1995.

32. Quoted in *Le Monde,* 1 June 1996, p. 7.

33. Kaiser, "Austria in the EU," pp. 420–421.

34. See European Commission, *The Single Market in 1995: Report from the Commission to the Council and the European Parliament,* COM (96) 51 final, Brussels, 20 February 1996.

35. See European Information Service, *Monthly Report on Europe,* April 1996, p. II.2.

36. Interview, UK permanent representation to the EU, 7 December 1995.

37. See Peterson, "The European Union: Pooled Sovereignty, Divided Accountability."

38. Interview, former counselor in Swedish permanent representation to the EU, 5 June 1996.

39. Interview, Finnish permanent representation to the EU, 2 May 1996. See also David Arter, "The EU Referendum in Finland on 16 October 1994: A Vote for the West, not for Maastricht," *Journal of Common Market Studies* 33, 3 (September 1995): 361–387.

40. Quoted in *European Voice,* 19–25 October 1995, p. 19.

41. See European Commission, *Eurobarometer* 44.

42. The sectors treated here also were selected for Peterson and Bomberg, *Decision-Making in the EU.*

43. Interview, Swedish permanent representation to the EU, 2 May 1996.

44. European Information Service, *Monthly Report on Europe,* May 1996, p. III.10.

45. This characterization simplifies and aggregates the effects of enlargement. Sweden showed itself to be the most instinctively supportive of free trade, as illustrated by its opposition to removal of the term "free trade" from a negotiating mandate given to the Commission as the EU sought a trade pact with Mexico in 1996. In contrast, Austria joined France (and others) in blocking a Commission proposal to seek a free trade area with the United States in 1995.

46. Interview, Swedish permanent representation to the EU, 2 May 1996.

47. John Peterson, *High Technology and the Competition State: An Analysis of the Eureka Initiative* (London: Routledge, 1993), pp. 83–86; Eureka Secretariat, *Eureka Annual Progress Report 1995* (Brussels, 1996).

48. As a caveat, the first Finn to be appointed a director-general in the Commission in early 1996 was Jorma Routti at DG XII (research), formerly the president of a Finnish research agency.

49. See John Peterson, "EU Research Policy: The Policy of Expertise," in Rhodes and Mazey, *The State of the European Union,* vol. 3, pp. 394–395.

50. Alberta Sbragia, "Environmental Policy," in Helen Wallace and William Wallace (eds.), *Policy-Making in the European Union* (Oxford: Oxford University Press, 1996).

51. Kaiser, "Austria in the EU," p. 413.

52. Interview, UK permanent representative to the EU, 7 December 1995.

53. Christopher Preston, "Obstacles to EU Enlargement: The Classical Community Method and the Prospects for a Wider Europe," *Journal of Common Market Studies* 33, 3 (1995): 451–463.

54. European Council Presidency Conclusions, Turin, 29 March 1996 (Rome: Italian Foreign Ministry).

55. This view was strengthened after the leader of the British Labour Party, Tony Blair, made a strongly pro-EU speech before the Federation of German Industry in June 1996. At the time of Blair's speech, Labour enjoyed an approximate twenty-point opinion poll lead over the governing Conservative Party. See Robert Preston, "Blair Pledges Pro-Europe Election Fight," *Financial Times,* 19 June 1996; Peter Kellner, "Will the Tories Now Call an Autumn Election?" *Observer,* 23 June 1996, p. 17.

56. One implication of the EP's participation at the working-group level was that only the presence of the French socialist MEP (and former minister for European affairs), Elizabeth Guigou, prevented the meetings from being all male.

57. Rory Watson, "European Solidarity Wins the Day at Turin Summit," *European Voice,* 3–10 April 1996, p. 9.

58. Finnish official quoted in *European Voice,* 19–25 October 1995, p. 18.

59. Interview, Swedish permanent representation to the EU, 2 May 1996.

60. Finnish Permanent Representation, "Memorandum Finland and Sweden: The IGC and the Security and Defence Dimension—Towards an Enhanced EU Role in Crisis Management," Brussels, 25 April 1996.

61. Finnish Foreign Ministry, "Finland's Points of Departure and Objectives at the 1996 Intergovernmental Conference," report to the Parliament by the Council of State (Helsinki), 27 February 1996, pp. 37–41 (citation from p. 41).

62. Swedish Ministry of Foreign Affairs, "The EU Intergovernmental Conference 1996: Government Report 1995/96:30," submitted by the government to the Swedish parliament, Stockholm, 30 November 1995, unofficial translation, pp. 26–32 (citation from p. 27).

63. Austrian Permanent Representation, "Regierungskonferenz 1996, Österreichische Grundsatzpositionen," Brussels, March 1996.

64. Swedish Ministry of Foreign Affairs, "The EU Intergovernmental Conference 1996," p. 32.

65. Kaiser, "Austria in the EU," p. 420.

66. Quoted in Belmont European Policy Centre, "Challenge 96," 8 (May/June 1996), p. 12.

67. Interview, Finnish permanent representation to the EU, 2 May 1996.

68. The dilemma of small versus large states was exacerbated considerably by the commitment made to open accession negotiations with Cyprus, a "microstate" of 700,000 citizens, within six months after the conclusion of the IGC. The commitment was the price demanded by Greece to lift its veto on a trade agreement with Turkey in 1995. As Malta (with a population of only 360,000) had applied for membership at the same time as Cyprus (1990), it could hardly be denied EU membership if it was offered to Cyprus. Even after the election of a Euroskeptical Labor government in 1996, Malta did not officially withdraw its application.

69. Review by Norman J. Vig of Rhodes and Mazey, *The State of the European Union,* vol. 3 in *ECSA Review* 9, 2 (1996): 27–28.

70. Preston, "Obstacles to EU Enlargement," pp. 452–456.

71. See report on the Benelux summit of 7 February 1996 in European Information Service, *Monthly Report on Europe,* February 1996, pp. III. 5–6.

72. André Kirman and A. Mikka Widgrén, "European Economic Decision-making Policy: Progress or Paralysis?" *Economic Policy* 21 (October 1995): 423–460; Jan E. Lane, Reinert Maeland, and Sven Berg, "Voting Power Under the EU Constitution," in Sven S. Andersen and Kjell A. Eliassen (eds.), *The European Union: How Democratic Is It?* (London: Sage, 1996).

73. Miles et al., "Integration Theory and the Enlargement of the EU," p. 185.

74. Sjursen, "Enlarging the Union," p. 155.

75. Fritz W. Scharpf, "Negative and Positive Integration in the Political Economy of European Welfare States, in Marks et al., *Governance in the European Union,* p. 28.

76. Interview, Swedish permanent representation to the EU, 2 May 1996.

4

Strategies for the Eastern Enlargement of the EU: An Integration Theory Approach

Péter Balázs

The forthcoming Eastern enlargement of the European Union will most probably follow the traditional, federalist-based procedure in accordance with existing rules (Articles 237 and 228 of the Treaty). This approach requires the Central and East European Countries (CEECs)[1] accessing to the EU to commit themselves to the maximum in terms of integration rules and obligations, that is, to the *acquis communautaire,* probably with a rather long transitional period. In this respect the following basic question should be put and possibly answered before the end of the 1996 IGC of the EU: Is the traditional way (together with its criteria) appropriate for the EU in the special case of integrating "transition countries"? From the point of view of the future CEEC members of the EU, the same question could be reformulated as follows: Is the traditional way of joining the EU the right one for countries that come from a different economic and political system and are on the difficult path of political and economic transformation?

This chapter discusses these questions and tries to propose some theoretical and practical solutions. It examines the possible impact of integrating the CEECs into the existing EU structure established by the developed countries of Western Europe. From this aspect both positive and negative effects of integration on the transition countries can be considered. From the EU's point of view, the same question can be reversed; that is, the impact of the Central and East European transition on the integration process should be analyzed. More precisely, interest should be focused on the outcome of the CEECs' inclusion into the EU and its influence on the further evolution of the Union. Both formulations of the same question are legitimate and important.

However, the IGC may fundamentally change the actual provisions for admission of new member states. These modifications are not predictable. Their direction and extent will probably be interrelated with the internal transfiguration of the enlarged EU as well as its external relations. Further evolution of the EU, with special regard to the requirements and procedure for adding new members, is one variable in this analysis. Another variable is the complex and in most respects unprecedented phenomenon of transition taking place in the CEECs.

This chapter presupposes that integration of the CEECs will follow, mutatis mutandis, the example of the early years of West European integration. In fact, one can see a surprising discrepancy between the integration ambitions and integration abilities (or real possibilities) of the CEECs. They are willing to share far-reaching *federalist* EU objectives, namely, to subscribe to the commitments of the Treaty on European Union, but de facto integration is still below a level that could be considered as "transcending the nation-state." In theoretical terms, real integration on the Eastern periphery of Europe in the 1990s is following a simple *functionalist* rather than a more sophisticated and more committing *neofunctionalist,* let alone a federalist, way. In order to analyze these problems, one should first recall some basic theoretical explanations and strategies of the whole integration process. Among the various theories of understanding and strategies of guiding the integration process, I refer below to the two main poles that most influenced the early evolution of the EC: The construction of the EC, as the central element and model for the enlarging European integration process, was based on federalist and functionalist strategies.[2]

The main lesson of the following analysis is a warning against the full and unlimited applicability of classical Western integration theories and practices to the coming Eastern enlargement of the EU. The result of this attempt to give some theoretical background to the Eastern extension of the Western-based integration model is certainly not complete and mature enough to constitute a "theory of understanding" of the ongoing process and to predict coming developments. At this stage, it is only a contribution to a pragmatic strategy for enlargement. A deeper analysis of the motivations of states and interest groups on both sides, in the CEECs and in the EU, in connection with the political process of enlarging the integration would be a step for future research, which could lead us to modern integration theories related to political decisionmaking and international relations.

Since the beginning of fundamental political and economic changes in the late 1980s, Central and East European countries have considered integration to be one of the main tools in achieving transformation. Transformation itself should be understood as the process of transition from various forms of centralized (in some cases command) economies to market-based structures. Economic transition is accompanied by a parallel transition from monolithic political regimes toward multiparty democracy. In CEEC government programs, "modernization" is often used as a synonym for "transformation" and vice versa.[3] In a more systematic approach, modernization appears either as the objective of this transformation process or as its second phase, following one of stabilization.

In the transition countries of Central and Eastern Europe, integration is understood mainly as the process of joining the Euro-Atlantic organizations. According to CEEC vocabulary, getting closer to the developed center of Europe means above all full membership in the EU and NATO. Surprisingly, the Organization for Economic Cooperation and Development (OECD) is rarely mentioned in this respect. The European Economic Area is generally rejected by the CEECs as an unsatisfactory, halfway solution. This conception of integration does not usually involve uniting (i.e., integrating) these countries within their own neighborhoods either. Subregional integration among adjacent countries is considered a marginal issue, not closely connected to European integration.

None of the above key words—"transition" (or "transformation"), "integration," and "modernization"—has a clear definition. This is a major obstacle to the closer analysis of the interdependencies between the East European transformation process and the integration of European economic, political, and defense systems. The lack of clarity and of theoretical background is reflected by political improvisations and terminological confusion on both sides, in the CEECs and in the EU. Furthermore, if one tries to use the Western concept of integration[4] and apply it to the concrete situation of the CEECs and to their inclusion into Western-based international structures, some new problems arise.

Since the first enlargement of the EC, the methods of admission of new member states have been based on rules of "joining the club," on the acceptance of already existing commitments of the current members and their implementation after a clearly defined transitional period. This kind of leap onto a moving train presupposes similar political and economic systems in the old and the member states and, in particular, a high capacity of adaptation on the part of the newcomers. Against this background, the following important questions can be raised in connection with the Eastern enlargement. Is the transition process mature enough to be able to set the *maximum* integration requirements, that is, the *acquis* as a whole for all the coming Eastern members of the EU? And furthermore, is adaptation to the Western-based and untouchable *acquis communautaire* the best possible guideline for the retarded Westernization of the whole Eastern periphery?

European integration has been built on the establishment of a common legal order. The *perception of law* is in general deeply rooted in Western (Catholic-Protestant) society.[5] The Central–East European cultural heritage (e.g., of the Visegrád or Baltic countries) is identical to the Catholic-Protestant traditions of the West. However, beyond certain historical boundaries, different cultures—Orthodox and Islamic—dominate.[6] With the forthcoming Eastern enlargement, European integration steps far beyond its originally conceived borders and has to face qualitatively new cultural and conceptual challenges. The question is whether all Central and East European candidates for EU membership can adapt themselves to the existing model of integration, to its organizational, regulatory, and cultural characteristics. And from the other perspective, how far is the Western legal, political, and cultural model adaptable on the Eastern periphery?

The EU's characteristics are seen from the outside as given and unalterable. In fact the success of the West European integration process, its obvious prestige, and its influence have attached a high value to the existing model, making it appear the only and best variant of integration in Europe. The attraction of this Catholic-Protestant, legal-institutional structure is heightened by the wish of the Eastern periphery of Europe to Westernize, to modernize following the Western model. Does this methodology of integration and its final, albeit idealized objective accord with the basic political habits and wishes of the CEECs? Would the automatic extension of the Western integration model, based on a high degree of political solidarity, with shared moral and legal values and jointly developed systems, be at all feasible when a large number of CEECs are included in the process?

Specific Features of the Eastern
Enlargement of the European Union

Before proposing a set of answers to some of the above questions, one should highlight important differences between the characteristics of the integration process in Western Europe and its extension to the other half of the Continent.

In all previous enlargements, as it went from the Six to the Fifteen, the EC has either enlarged its own center or attached to this center its closest (Western) semiperiphery. The coming Eastern enlargement would be fundamentally different from all preceding enlargements in this respect, too. The basic problem of the applicability of traditional integration practices, methodology, and theories for the Eastern enlargement of the EU is rooted, even after 1989, in the existence of inherited division and systemic differences between the Eastern and Western partners. I take up the main features and consequences of this "integration gap" below.

Young Nation-States and Young Borders

The first and fundamental question is connected with the main purpose of integration itself. All theories and practices in Western Europe have as a basic objective of the countries (governments) participating in the integration process the transcendence of the nation-state, which is a limiting factor on the expansion of welfare and security. There may have been differences during the postwar history of European organizations about the extent, degree, and methods of integrating nation-states, but all participants shared the common objective of uniting—at least partly—their national structures, competences, and resources in order to reduce possible conflicts among nation-states. In the 1990s in Eastern Europe, one can see a strong antifederalist drive accompanied by a powerful tendency toward national reidentification. In fact three federal states—the Soviet Union, Yugoslavia, and Czechoslovakia—have disintegrated, giving birth to more than twenty new countries. Most of these new states are eager to define their national characters and to establish their national economies (customs systems, monetary systems, etc.). Some of these states never existed before or have been reestablished within artificial boundaries. National self-identification has taken various forms, from peaceful institution building to international conflicts to modify inherited or newly drawn state borders. Since the collapse of Soviet-type socialist systems, border disputes and national minority problems have created difficulties in bilateral relations, increased tensions between direct neighbors, and led to bloody conflicts; the cases of the former Yugoslavia and some members of the Commonwealth of Independent States (CIS) are well known.

Most state borders in Eastern Europe either are brand new or were drawn in 1920. Thus from a historical point of view, they are not ancient and certainly not deeply ingrained. In those Central and East European countries that have escaped the fate of the dissolving federalist states in the 1990s and have unchanged borders,[7] democratic and progressive forces have also encountered difficulties in justifying the historically young (ca. seventy-five years old) state frontiers to nationalist political forces, either in their own countries or in the region. In these circumstances, the symbolic abolition or even the transparency of state borders through integration is a rather sensitive question in Eastern Europe. In those cases where nationalist forces have gained a majority in parliament, new and exaggerated nationalism is in itself an obstacle to any deeper integration that would necessitate close cooperation with governments of neighboring countries.

The Meaning of "Integration" for the CEECs

When speaking about integration, politicians and public alike in the CEECs think first of aid and security granted by what they see as the rich and powerful West, followed by increased welfare and accelerated modernization with Western help. They would prefer to enjoy these benefits as members of a respected organization such as the EU. In their perception, integration is a rather happy event, a solemn admission into the club and not a troublesome technical process based on continuous political bargaining, on uniting competences and resources to find better solutions to common problems and progress toward a joint and remote political objective.

For these reasons, the CEECs do not foresee the same integration with their immediate, equally poor or even poorer neighbors. In fact, they will be rather surprised to find that the parallel integration of neighboring countries into the European center automatically means close links with each other, too. They hardly understand that the integration efforts of adjacent countries might go—in principle—as far as common participation in a federation. Opinion polls show that a sizable majority of East European citizens are in favor of joining the EU. No opinion polls have taken place so far on the question of a possible federation with neighbors (e.g., Slovakia with Poland, Romania with Hungary, etc.). Most probably the outcome of such a poll would be negative in whichever country the question were put to a referendum.

Security Policy Aspects

With Eastern enlargement the EU will for the first time in its history go beyond a sharp security policy border. In fact, the accession of former Warsaw Pact states to all three pillars of the EU, including the WEU, would bring about changes in the future balance of power in Europe. In the bipolar system, the neutral states of Europe constituted a no-mans'-land between NATO and the Warsaw Pact. They also had a special status from the point of view of economic integration. During the Cold War, the accession of neutral states to the EC was tacitly prohibited by the Soviet Union in accordance with the accepted interpretation of their—in every individual case still different—neutrality. (A good example of this was Finland, whose direct proximity to the Soviet Union did not even permit full accession to EFTA.) Joining the EU as full members became possible for neutral states only after the collapse of the Soviet Union.

The economic expansion of the Western system took the form of association agreements between the EC and a growing number of the CEECs, as well as free trade agreements concluded between EFTA and the same CEECs. Russia has so far not questioned the West's de jure occupation of the former buffer zone between NATO and the Warsaw Pact through the admission of neutral countries into the EU-WEU structure. Nor has Russia objected to the parallel extension of the West European preferential trading zone to former Council for Mutual Economic Assistance (CMEA) member states. At the same time, Moscow is keeping a jealous eye on the security status of its former allies and concentrating its attention and opposition on the enlargement of NATO. However, the road leading through the EU to WEU may equally determine the future security policy map of Europe and limit definitely the Russian sphere of influence in the eastern part of the Continent.

The Political Risk Factor

Eastern enlargement involves new political risks for the EU connected with the unprecedented political transition in the CEECs. These political risks have two different origins both linked to the political situation in the CEECs. *Internal* political risks derive from the immature status of the pluralistic political structures and democratic practices in the majority of the CEECs. In Eastern Europe most political parties from the prewar period or the late 1940s have not survived the four decades of hibernation under monolithic Soviet rule. New political formations are not yet mature. In addition, heavy government tasks absorb inexperienced political parties. In the CEECs, multiparty elections or even minor government crises may yet bring about unexpected political results in the coming decade. *External* political problems are rooted in the high risk from the above-mentioned disputed state boundaries and national minority problems. The UN, the Council of Europe, the Organization for Security and Cooperation in Europe (OSCE), and the European Stability Conference have made notable efforts to find or propose solutions to these questions. The European Stability Agreement inspired quarreling neighbors to conclude basic treaties with each other on neighborliness and friendly cooperation.[8]

The high-risk factor of unexpected internal and external political events in the CEECs has already created fears in Western countries that could slow down enlargement. The degree of this kind of political risk will depend on the timing and scope of the EU's Eastern enlargement. A large and early Eastern expansion of the EU would of course internalize the political risks much more than a more cautious, gradual enlargement process would.

Economic Gaps and Differences

The Eastern extension of European integration will have to face new and so far unknown systemic differences between the economies of the EU and the new member states. In some cases, depending again on the date and the extent of the coming Eastern enlargement(s), these differences are fundamental; in others they represent only a few and fading remnants of the previous divergent development. The beneficial effects of integration are expected to help the completion of the economic transition process and to bridge important differences in economic development levels. At the same time, in less-developed countries or at an early stage in the more-developed ones, the possible harmful effects of integration could endanger the achievements of transition and may lead to a growing peripheralization of certain CEECs.

Two different economic aspects of integration of the CEECs—systemic transformation and development-level gaps—are often mixed up or confused. The basic difference between them consists of their divergent time horizons. The legal and institutional tasks of economic transition—the establishment of the basis of a market economy—are medium-term objectives, whereas achieving a qualitative leap in the development level of a country is mainly a long-term goal. The ends of the two parallel processes have different time horizons, but their starts coincide. This means that their early progression is taking place in parallel. The cumulative effects of this twofold process increase the expected economic costs of the EU's Eastern enlargement, whoever pays the bill. Western hesitation about the share to be financed by the EU rests mainly on the uncertain and unpredictable nature of the real costs of transition.

Simultaneous Integration in Various Fields

Both the EU and the CEECs should pay special attention to the fact that from the very beginning of the political changes in Central and Eastern Europe economic, political, and military integration is progressing at the same time and in close connection. In the early evolution of West European integration, these three branches developed separately and took different forms. For this reason, there was less temptation to use them as substitutes for each other.[9] The unification of the three different pillars appeared only in the Maastricht Treaty, after more than thirty years of integration, and it remains a remote objective.

The sudden and unexpected changes in the CEECs have, at the same historical moment, raised the need to establish extendable (or new) structures that can satisfy the political, economic, and security requisites of an enlarging integration process in Europe. This parallelism can also lead to misunderstanding. The CEECs may consider any of the economic, political, or security integration processes as direct substitutes for each other (e.g., they might urge economic integration with a view to stabilizing security or insist on military integration in order to eliminate crime). In fact the three pillars of the EU mutually support and stabilize each other without being interchangeable. For this reason, their sequencing is an important element in the strategy outlined below.

Central and Peripheral Integration in Parallel

Another new and important phenomenon is that integration is developing not only between the European center and its Eastern periphery but among the countries at the periphery as well. This characteristic is rather specific if one compares it to the first two enlargements of the EC. Apart from the British and Irish and the Spanish and Portuguese, the new member states of the EC have established closer links among each other mainly inside the integration. The EFTA countries were an exception because in their case intensive cooperation developed among them before they joined the EU and in spite of geographical dislocation of certain EFTA members.

The specificity of the CEECs lies in their constituting a geographically compact bloc and also in their former membership in highly centralized structures, the Warsaw Pact and CMEA.[10] However, in spite of their contiguous location and seemingly intensive past relations, they were not closely integrated among themselves. In the Soviet system, integration developed mainly with a dominating regional center, the Soviet Union. After the collapse of that centralizing power, the whole structure has fallen apart, mutual trade has shrunk, and political tensions surfaced between neighbors. Three subregions along the old Yalta line offered new opportunities for integration: the Baltic Sea area, Central-Eastern Europe, and the Black Sea region. The first steps were taken by the Visegrád countries, which signed the Central European Free Trade Agreement (CEFTA).[11] The sophisticated methodology of their negotiations in 1991–1992 was reminiscent of the far too cautious approach of the EC to the new generation of Europe agreements in 1990–1991. This approach was not appropriate in the case of CEFTA given the limited trade coverage[12] and previous customs-free commerce of the CMEA system. The extension of CEFTA to new members also seems clumsy because of the uncertainty about the appropriate size and depth of subregional integration[13] and about its role in the overall process of European unification.

Breaking Up the Eastern Bloc

The organizations that have represented the Eastern bloc (i.e., the Warsaw Pact and CMEA) have been dissolved, but the West has still hardly differentiated its treatment of the former members of this artificial family. In fact, one can distinguish only two main differentiations so far: the so-called Associated Ten of the CEEC (Hungary, Poland, the Czech Republic, Slovakia, Romania, Bulgaria, Slovenia, Estonia, Latvia, and Letland) and the crisis areas. In any Eastern enlargement, the EU or NATO would take on board countries that have broken off from the Eastern bloc. For this reason, the admission of any of them into Western integration structures would have inevitable consequences for those not accepted. Most probably not all the CEECs can be admitted into the organizations of developed industrial states and certainly not all of them at the same time. Thus the East-West dividing line of the ex-bipolar system would be reestablished at other places and in other forms, creating new boundaries between "us" and "them," between "good" and "bad," between "eligible" and "noneligible" countries. This problem may create political difficulties, mainly because most CEECs tend to consider themselves "eligible," "good" countries in spite of obvious and important differences among them. Western organizations, first of all NATO and the EU, should sooner or later take firm positions on the eligibility and time tables for admission of new East European members. Explaining these decisions to the East European countries that will remain temporarily or permanently outside the scope of these organizations will be among the hardest political problems of the Eastern enlargement for most Western-based organizations.

A New Model of All-European Integration

The Model of Eccentric Circles

Eastern enlargement of the EU will have a strong impact on the whole integration process in Europe. To represent recent and future developments of European integration, I propose a dynamic model of eccentric circles (Figure 4.1), a denial of the well-known image of concentric circles suggested by Jacques Delors. After the political changes in Eastern and Central Europe, the concentric circles model has been overtaken in two respects. First, the model located all countries that did not attain the highest speed of integration outside the European Union. Second, it reflected an immobility, a stable integration pyramid of European states with the EU on the top. Unexpected political changes in Europe have brought dynamism into both aspects: The deepening and widening of the EU is thus better expressed by a new model of eccentric circles placed on a background that has its origins in the matrix of Lindberg and Scheingold.[14] I accept the political and economic dichotomy of integration strategies. At the same time, I propose to replace the important but still particular concept of transcending the nation-

Figure 4.1   The Eccentric Circles of European Integration on the Threshold of the Eastern Enlargement

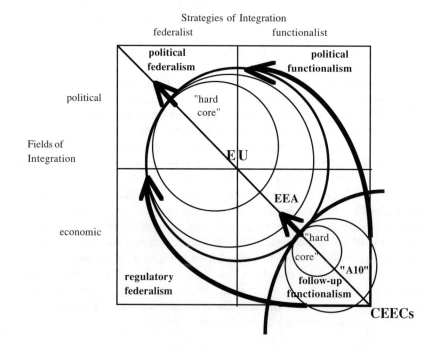

state by federalism and functionalism, that is, by the more polarized goals of those two main theories that have exerted the most influence on the evolution of European integration. The EU, as the center of European integration, goes in the middle of the matrix. It should be added immediately that this organization has never been and most probably never will be perfectly (or even approximately) balanced on the dividing line between economic and political integration or on the boundary between federalist and functionalist approaches. The mainstream of the evolution of integration points from functional integration of the participating states' economies toward their political federation. It should be stressed again that the idealistic goal of uniting all European states (or even an important number of them) in a federalist European "superstate" could not be attained in the foreseeable future.

In this model, deepening and enlarging are not in competition or in contradiction with each other, as they can be identified along the same main line indicating the evolution of integration. Deepening can be represented by the upper short arrow pointing toward political federalism. Enlarging is identical with the lower short arrow expressing the wish and efforts of the "hard core" of the CEECs to become members of the EU.

The Dynamics of the Eccentric Circles

The obvious existence of such eccentric circles demonstrates that in the 1990s the whole process of European integration was in strong movement. This movement was motivated by the need for a deep transformation that should correspond simultaneously to the requirements of a Western deepening of the EU, on the one hand, and to the necessity of an Eastern enlargement, a widening of the originally Western-based organization, on the other.

The eccentric circles are located along the line leading from economy-based functionalism toward political federation. From the point of view of integration positions and capacities, the West European states and the CEECs are both divided into three circles of different diameters. These circles are certainly not concentric, as their centers are moving at different speeds along the above-mentioned main direction of the supposed evolution of European integration. The first and smallest circle of the EU is its internal hard core, consisting of member states that are ready and able to move toward the federalist objectives faster than the rest of the Union.[15] This hard core has already taken an eccentric position, too. The second, wider circle consists of the rest of the member states. The third, largest circle is drawn by adding to the EU the (for the moment very narrow) sphere of the European Economic Area. Inside the rather wide circle of the CEECs, the first eccentric circle is the hard core formed by those countries that are leading the transformation process and would be the first to join the

EU as soon as Eastern enlargement begins.[16] The second, broader circle is composed of the rest of the ten associated countries ("A10").[17] The third, biggest circle includes all the remaining CEECs.

There are some striking differences between the hard core of the EU and that of the CEECs with respect to exclusivity and criteria. In the EU, member states striving to belong to the hard core do not see any exclusive status for themselves, that is, they do not reject the participation of others. Countries within the hard core satisfy clearly defined criteria, for example, those in the Treaty on European Union.[18] As far as the CEECs are concerned, they are competing with each other in their efforts to get closer to the center of European integration. This "beauty contest" is encouraged by the lack of sufficiently selective requirements defined for a hard core of the associated countries as preconditions of their future EU membership.

Each of the four fields of the background matrix of the eccentric circles represents one possible integration strategy. These four combinations of the fields and goals of integration help to classify those pathways along which European integration could progress in the coming decade, with special regard to its inevitable Eastern expansion.

Four Main Strategies for the Development of European Integration

Political Federalism

At the creation of the foundation of the European integration process, federalism, as a forward-looking political theory, was used to define and set long-term political objectives. Federalism had a strong impact on the further evolution of the institution-based structure of the EC. By the second half of the 1980s, it became increasingly evident that federalism had already reached the limits of its applicability in Western Europe. The ambivalent results[19] of referenda reflected a decrease in the popularity and attraction of the legal and institutional instruments of European unification. This "democratic deficit," some observers claim, testifies to the lack of transparency in the increasingly sophisticated decisionmaking procedure in the EU.[20] The political emphasis put on subsidiarity has also confirmed the slowing down—in some fields even the stopping—of the centripetal movement of national competences in integration. The federalist drive to shift competence to the integration organizations has, with the conception of the single market, probably reached the conclusion of its usefulness. The Maastricht Treaty has already stepped beyond the noninterference line of integration that national governments can admit as acceptable. Beyond this limit, the incursion of the supranational organization into national competences may decrease the political power of nation-based governments (e.g., by limiting their budgetary expenditure, modifying national trade and monetary policy, etc.).[21] Should integration no longer serve the interests of powerful business circles exerting pressure on governments, the deepening process may slow down or even stop. Insisting on federalist objectives has already exerted a selection effect on the development of the EU and provoked the separation of the hard core from the rest of the EU member states. In this light, political federalism is losing importance as the leading spiritual concept of European integration. Recent integration theories furnish new explanations for this phenomenon.[22]

In view of the inherited systemic differences, the integration of an important number of the CEECs within the EU cannot follow the classical federative, that is, political-institutional, path of integration unless their respective economies draw substantially nearer. Before any formal negotiation on the full accession of a wider circle of the CEECs, the economic gap between the East and West European countries involved—as demonstrated by price and wage differences, systemic divergence, the development-level gap, and so on—should be reduced. Otherwise the scope for conflicts of interest, in case of any attempt at their "internal" solution, would threaten the political foundations of the enlarged EU. Should the parties insist on a rapid implementation of the traditional way of enlargement, economic conflicts (e.g., in connection with reshaping the Common Agricultural Policy, redistribution of structural funds, definition of the conditions of the free movement of the workforce, etc.) would destroy the internal bargaining channels of the EU. The "internalization" of those kinds of conflict would certainly surpass the conflict-handling capacity of the Council based on (and limited by) the treaties, that is, joint objectives and methods. Heavy clashes of conflicting interests can better be dealt with in the external negotiation approach by the faceless Commission, in accordance with a negotiating mandate defined by the Council. In this case the Council, as the direct representative of the member states, does not directly handle the conflict itself but stays behind the scenes and coordinates the interests of the member states with each other as well as with the negotiating third party.

Regulatory Federalism

Functional integration of the Central and East European economies cannot follow the EC model either, as long as it is a precondition that real economic operators should appear in the CEECs; competition policy should be worked out and implemented, and comparable prices and wages should prevail on their markets. In practice, the establishment of realistic market conditions in the CEECs takes place in parallel with the implementation of preferential agreements,[23] whereas a minimum of competition policy regulations (e.g., on state aid, monopolies, protection of intellectual property rights, etc.) or the regulatory mechanisms of prices would constitute obvious preconditions to the conclusion of any free trade agreement. As for their legal convergence with the EU, the CEECs will most probably follow, mutatis mutandis, the model of the European Economic Area. The white book on legal harmonization issued by the 1995 June Cannes meeting of the European Council indicates the EU's wish to apply the relevant regulations deriving from the *acquis communautaire* outside the organization, in accordance with the provisions of the association agreements.[24] It should be noted that both agreements (European associations and the EEA) are, in spite of all their obvious differences, based on Article 238 of the Treaty of Rome. The extraterritorial application of the federalist-minded EU regulations indicates a possible fast-track integration, at least for the leading transition economies. This regulatory federalism gets around the slow mainstream of classical federative integration methods by introducing, without formal membership, the lion's share of the market regulations of the integration center.

Political Functionalism

Internal political stabilization in the CEECs, as a precondition of integration, presupposes a substantial improvement of their economic output. The key to political stability in the transition countries is economic welfare. But the association agreements concluded with the EU do not provide the CEECs with the necessary support to achieve these goals.[25] The full benefits of integration, including increased external financial help, cannot take effect either because of a mutual fear of the impact of the "four freedoms" (free movement of labor, capital, goods, and services). In the CEECs low prices of goods, energy, and transport as well as relatively low wages of workers, managers, and researchers have increased the interest of foreign investors. But the same factors are seen as a danger: the dumping of Eastern goods, services, and labor on Western markets. A rapid introduction of the "four freedoms" in the relationship between the EU (EEA) and the CEECs could promote an East-West equalization of prices and wages.[26] However, the inherited economic gap does not encourage the opening of Western markets to cheap goods, services, and labor from the East. Nor does the already proven superiority of the West in terms of competitiveness favor further market opening on the Eastern side. As long as the two partners are stuck in this vicious circle, this Catch-22 of integration, the prevailing economic differences constitute a serious obstacle to further closing up the gap, to reducing it with the help of integration.

However, economic integration (including solving the Catch-22 through more Western aid and assistance), is probably not the first step in integrating Eastern Europe into Western organizations. The heritage of the centralized economic and political systems requires a special approach. The functional integration of the CEECs should follow the three pillars of the

Treaty on European Union in a reversed order: Confidence building in justice and home affairs, as well as security measures, necessarily precede economic integration. The West European unification process, following the postwar consolidation, was based on an existing legal order, and it presupposed "normal" criminality in the member states. The sudden and fundamental political changes in the CEECs have challenged inexperienced authorities and limited financial resources. Police forces had been tailored to the needs of politically controlled and highly isolated (from the outside world) societies. Since the beginning of political transformation, the threat of imported crime and a flow of economic refugees from the East has haunted the West. For this reason, the EU has real and immediate interests in cooperating with the CEECs first in third-pillar issues, concerning justice and home affairs. Western motivation is also visible in the search for appropriate solutions to the security vacuum in the *Zwischenraum* (space) between the EU and the CIS. However, the solution to this depends mainly on the interests and reactions of Russia; it lies partly outside the scope of the EU's Eastern enlargement. Gradual military integration of would-be EU members into the structures of the WEU and NATO should perhaps precede economic integration. Individual admissions should fit into an overall and probably new European security system that includes Russia.

The mirror image of the three Maastricht pillars indicates a functionalist spillover effect of a political nature. A similar political functionalism played an important role in the early years of West European integration as well. The process of drawing the CEECs nearer could be facilitated by the levers of this political functionalism.

Follow-up Functionalism

In the subregional integration of the CEECs, the application of federalist strategies would not be appropriate in view of the strong antifederalist tendencies nourished by the emerging need for national self-identification. In theory, the acceleration of federalist integration could best solve the old-new problems of national minorities and accidentally drawn state borders in Central and Eastern Europe. However, the CEECs remain ambivalent toward and hesitant about the utility of subregional integration with each other. According to their political statements, these countries do not want to create any substitute for their direct and fast integration into the mainstream of European unification. It seems the CEECs have not yet understood the benefits of increased cooperation with their neighbors. Such integrative cooperation could enlarge the limited scope of individual national markets for both domestic and foreign investors. It could also testify to the ability of the CEECs to cooperate with each other as well as their maturity for higher degrees of integration. For most CEECs, however, the maximum real integration with the outside world probably still lies in the domain of functionalism. The rapid development of parallel preferential relations of individual CEECs with the EU has not reduced isolation among them. On the contrary, this structure has already resulted in dispreferential relationships between countries that once belonged to a former—special and close—preferential area.[27] The need to integrate the individual states of the eastern periphery of Europe with each other has been complicated by the disintegration of the three federative states (the USSR, Czechoslovakia, Yugoslavia), which has led to a multiplication of new nation-states and thus multiplied the number of possible bilateral relations among the CEECs.[28]

Subregional integration of the CEECs has begun by adapting the methodology of their new relations with the center of European integration. This follow-up functionalism should be complemented and transcended by their own initiatives. In practice, subregional integration among the CEECs still seems to be a retarded reaction to the centripetal movement of their drawing nearer toward the EU. For political reasons and out of theoretical considerations, subregional integration should go either in parallel with integrating the subregion with the center or even ahead of it.

Conclusions

European integration has been moving along the mainstream, starting with functional ties between partial economic activities and going toward objectives connected with federalist political unification. The two extremes are marked by efforts to accelerate integration toward political federalism by the EU's hard core, on the one hand, and by subregional follow-up functionalism on the part of a growing number of CEECs, on the other. This chapter has tried to explain why the implementation of these classical integration strategies is hindered in the new European context. In fact, the political federalism of the center and the follow-up functionalism of the Eastern periphery seem to be the slow tracks of European integration. At the same time, new and promising fast tracks of integration are emerging. Regulative federalism, the extraterritorial application of federalist-minded regulations of the EU, could promote the drawing together of the hard core of the CEECs with the single market. Political functionalism could help to create the confidence-building political basis for economic integration, just as it did at the beginning of West European unification.

The Eastern enlargement of the EU cannot take place as long as the EU defines itself as a homogeneous organization and regards the CEECs as a homogeneous bloc. Segmentation, both inside and outside the EU, is unavoidable. The time of federalist homogeneity in Europe is over. Multispeed integration is the structure appropriate to extension. The eccentric circles model indicates the need for differentiation. If differentiation can take an appropriate political form inside the EU, there is hope for differentiation among the Eastern candidates for EU membership, too. The hard cores are leading the process of differentiation among EU member states and the CEECs alike. However, their forward progress seems to be rather troubled by the lack of multispeed solutions at both ends of the integration trajectory. For this reason, neither the hard core of the EU nor the hard core of the CEECs could break out so far from the wider circle of countries (i.e., from the EU member states and from the associated countries, respectively) and step up onto the next, higher stage of integration in accordance with their political objectives and economic capacities.

From the viewpoint of the present analysis, a strategic dividing line inside the group of the associated CEECs could be traced on the basis of whether they are ready to transcend the nation-state. This selection criterion is clearly distinguishing the applicability of functionalist and neofunctionalist integration methods on the eastern periphery of Europe. As long as the turmoil of national reidentification prevails, most CEECs would probably prefer functionalist integration.

Notes

A first and more detailed version of this paper was published as CORE Working Paper 15/1995, Copenhagen Research Project on European Integration, Institute of Political Science, University of Copenhagen.

1. Terminological confusion prevails as well about the definition of the countries in question. With the collapse of the bipolar system, the previous simplified geographical categories (e.g., "Eastern countries" etc.) have lost their meaning. Definitions that allude to economic and political transition are acceptable (e.g., "partners in transition" of the OECD, etc.) but may cover a wider circle than the states directly connected with "European" organizations (e.g., Mongolia). Central and East European Countries are the transition countries belonging to "European" organizations (e.g., the Economic Commission for Europe of the UN and the OSCE). As the whole former Soviet Union, including the Central Asian republics, has been classified by international organizations in this category, the denomination is not geographically exact (in fact, it is erroneous). However, it is still the nearest definition to my approach, indicating the dominant European vocation of the countries in question. By "CEECs," I understand the former Soviet Union, the European members of the Warsaw Pact, and CMEA, the former Yugoslavia, and Albania.

2. This assessment is supported by the theoretical approach of Leon Lindberg and Stuart Scheingold, *Europe's Would-be Polity* (Englewood Cliffs, NJ: Prentice-Hall, 1970). Moravcsik stresses that "only the early variants of neofunctionalism predicted a steady development towards federalism"; (Andrew Moravcsik, "Preferences and Power in the European Community: A Liberal Intergovernmentalist Approach, in Simon Bulmer and Andrew Scott (eds.), *Economic and Political Integration in Europe: Internal Dynamics and Global Context* (Oxford: Blackwell, 1994), p. 32.

3. Communist ideology represented one of the most ambitious modernization programs of the century. However, this model failed, just like many other totalitarian attempts at rapid Westernization of the whole complex of economic, social, and

political life. These essays in modernization tried to introduce, with the help of a small political elite, imported Western schemes in peripheral countries.

4. In this context, it is not the scientific definition of "integration" that is important but its political perception. For the CEECs, to take a rather simplified approach, integration is the equivalent of full membership in the one-speed EU. According to the existing rules and practice of enlargement, any new member state is expected to accept the full package of integration rules and commitments and to implement them after a preagreed transitional period. One of the problems of EU enlargement is the multifunctional character of the organization. The EU has accumulated a wide range of competences, various functions difficult to handle at the same speed for a growing number of participants. Kelstrup points out that "sovereignty can be functionally specific." Of course one organization could hardly have several sets of legal obligations, but at least two different classes of membership, full and associate, exist in a series of international organizations. The 1996 Intergovernmental Conference of the EU could also find new and flexible solutions to this problem. Morten Kelstrup, "European Integration and Political Theory," in Morten Kelstrup (ed.), *European Integration and Denmark's Participation* (Copenhagen: Political Studies Press, 1992), p. 18.

5. An important though not fundamental duality inside the West European cultural heritage can be detected in the divergent natures of the Catholic and Protestant subcultures. This duality was also reflected in the different characteristics of the two main Western integration organizations: the Protestant Puritanism (i.e., efficiency through simplicity) of EFTA and the Catholic baroque ornamentation of the EU.

6. See Samuel P. Huntington, "The Clash of Civilizations," *Foreign Affairs* 72, 3 (1993).

7. Only five CEECs had unchanged borders in the 1990s: Poland, Hungary, Romania, Bulgaria, and Albania.

8. For instance, the Treaty on Good Neighborliness and Friendly Cooperation between the Republic of Hungary and the Slovak Republic was signed in Paris on 20 March 1995.

9. Economic and military organizations of Western countries, were created at different times and were not regarded as direct substitutes for each other. For example, the OEEC was established in 1947, NATO and the Council of Europe in 1949, the European Coal and Steel Community (ECSC) in 1952. However, the fiasco of the European Defense Community inspired the creation of the European Economic Community.

10. Exception is made for Albania and Yugoslavia.

11. The CEFTA was signed by Hungary, Poland, the Czech Republic, and Slovakia on 21 December 1992 and entered into force on 1 March 1993.

12. In the case of Hungary, by the time of negotiation of CEFTA, the market share of the EC was about 50 percent and that of the CEFTA partners about 5 percent.

13. Various, partly overlapping, subregional cooperation structures took shape after the political changes in Central and Eastern Europe: the Alps-Adria Cooperation, the Pentagonale became the Hexagonale, the Central European Initiative, and others.

14. Lindberg and Scheingold, *Europe's Would-be Polity,* p. 16.

15. I do not here want to enter into the debates about the extent of and criteria for this hard core.

16. Again, in this chapter I do not wish to name the countries belonging to the inner circle and to argue for a particular choice.

17. In accordance with the EU position taken on the Essen meeting of the European Council in December 1994, the ten associated CEECs are Poland, Hungary, the Czech Republic, Slovakia, Slovenia, Romania, Bulgaria, Estonia, Latvia, and Lithuania.

18. Listing member states in the first speed, that is, Germany, France and the Benelux, has turned out to be the political mistake in the proposal submitted by Wolfgang Schäuble to the Bundestag (CDU/CSU-Fraktion des Deutschen Bundestages, *Überlegungen zur Europäischen Politik,* September 1994.). Subsequent explanations—and excuses—gave a "nonlimiting" interpretation to the proposed hard core, making it conditional and not enumerative.

19. Since 1992, European referenda on integration matters, including the approval of the Treaty on European Union in some member states and the question of joining the European Economic Area or the EU in EFTA countries, have hardly brought convincing results. In five cases yes or no votes did not exceed 53 percent, in two cases 57 percent. The only exception was Austria, with 66.4 percent voting for EU membership.

20. The federalist model (or the federalization of the model) was not only inspired by member state endeavors to enhance integration but also, or mostly, by the integration institutions and their increasing number of employees in order to justify and substantiate their utility and usefulness. Rasmussen analyzed the role of the European Court in rendering the intergovernmental model of the EEC treaty a federalist institution. See Hjalte Rasmussen, *On Law and Policy in the European Court of Justice* (Dordrecht: Martinus Nijhoff Publishers, 1986).

21. See, for example, Marc Maresceau, "The Concept of 'Common Commercial Policy' and the Difficult Road to Maastricht, in Maresceau (ed.), *The European Union's Commercial Policy After 1992: The Legal Dimension* (Dordrecht: Martinus Nijhoff Publishers, 1993).

22. Moravcsik, "Preferences," pp. 39–52, analyzes national preference formation.

23. The first three preferential agreements concluded with CEECs were the association agreements signed between the EC and the Visegrád states (Poland, Hungary, and the then Czechoslovakia) on 16 December 1991. They were followed by free trade agreements on industrial goods between EFTA and the same countries. The trade provisions of the EC-Hungary and the EC-Poland association agreements entered into force ad interim on 1 March 1992 and in full on 1 February 1994.

24. For example, the Hungary-EC association agreement contains direct references to the provisions of the Treaty of Rome to be applied by Hungary, namely, Articles 85, 86, and 92, with vague provisions of implementation.

25. Market-access conditions have produced a reversed effective asymmetry resulting in growing trade deficits of the CEECs in their commerce with the EU. The PHARE program (Poland and Hungary Assistance for Economic Restructuring) has proved inadequate because of limited resources and extensive bureaucracy. The marginal inflow of aid and cautious foreign direct investment cannot compensate for the capital outflow in the form of debt service and trade deficit.

26. The equalizing mechanisms and effects of the "four freedoms" are presented in detail by Dudley Seers, "Theoretical Aspects of Unequal Development at Different Spatial Levels," Dudley Seers and Constantine Vaitsos (eds.), *Integration and Unequal Development: The Experience of the EEC* (London: Macmillan 1980).

27. For instance, the trade dispositions of the EC-Hungary and EC-Poland association agreements were implemented as of 1 March 1992. Customs duties on several products originating from the EC have gradually been reduced accordingly. While negotiations on CEFTA were still taking place, nonpreferential,

most-favored-nation (MFN) customs duties were applied in the bilateral Polish-Hungarian trade. This situation changed a year later: As of 1 March 1993, CEFTA entered into force. However, during the year of relative dispreference in their bilateral trade, various traditional products (e.g., Hungarian pharmaceuticals in Poland, Polish consumer goods in Hungary, etc.) were nearly eliminated from each other's markets. The situation is worse between the CEFTA members and other CEECs with association agreements with the EU that are not signatories of CEFTA (e.g., between Hungary and Romania).

28. This despite all the uncertainties of the post-Yugoslav peace process: There are as many as twenty-seven CEECs. The EU could conclude twenty-seven bilateral agreements with them. At the same time, these countries could maintain with each other 351 bilateral relations (e.g., conclude 351 bilateral trade agreements among each other) and could between them establish 702 diplomatic missions. Their relations with the outside world show a similar multiplication of the number of possible bilateral agreements, diplomatic missions, and seats in international organizations.

5

The Political and Institutional Consequences of Widening: Capacity and Control in an Enlarged Council

Bart Kerremans

Enlargement, Capacity, and Control

The European Union may be on the verge of a new enlargement. This will affect each of the EU institutions—their composition, their way of working, and their capacity to work effectively. In this chapter I deal only with such consequences on the Council of Ministers. The role of this institution has been the subject of much analysis and debate, but it is clear that it occupies a central position within EU decisionmaking and that its capacity to take decisions has a direct impact on the capacity of the EU as a whole to act and react. This capacity is the central—but not the sole—subject of this chapter. Instead, I analyze this capacity in relation to the position and the capabilities of each of the member states in an enlarged Council, that is, in relation to the problem of control. The issues of capacity and control are not specific to the EU Council, nor are they new problems for this institution. To a certain extent, every political system has to cope with them. As policy basically refers to the "authoritative allocation of values in a society,"[1] every polity has to deal with divergent opinions and interests on such values—some of which are represented or participate directly in the government—and has to be capable, despite the existence of such diversity, to take binding decisions for society as a whole. Therefore, every political system has to be able to filter a panoply of societal interests and opinions into a limited number of decisions, options, and choices, making the handling of the issues of capacity and control a precondition for decisionmaking.

The Problem of Capacity

Capacity refers to the probability that a political system, given the diversity of interests to which it is exposed, will be able to take decisions.[2] Key factors are the possibility of these interests to be translated into the governance system and the degree to which the governance system itself contains a mechanism that allows for the aggregation and transformation of divergent interests into collective decisions. The more diverse the interests are, the higher the burden of decisionmaking, as diversity increases the probability that political decisions will frustrate a greater number of interests in society or that such decisions reflect those interests less than expected or hoped for (e.g., in compromises).

Interests count only if they are translated into the governance system— if they become political interests. Such translation can be direct or indirect, depending on the access of the translators to the governance system, that is, on the relation between interests and decisionmakers. The structuring of the governance system will influence this access only partly. If the number of those who have direct access to the governance system is limited, part of the aggregation process will take place outside of this system, by the decisionmaker who has been convinced to defend a number of interests in the system. In such cases the decisionmaker will have made a selection and priority list of the interests to defend during the decisionmaking process itself, during interaction with the other decisionmakers. In the hypothetical situation where everybody has access to the governance system (e.g., Plato's polis), the burden of the aggregation is completely on the shoulders of the governance system itself, which makes decisionmaking much more difficult and therefore has a negative effect on the capacity of this system.

Even in cases where everybody has access, the governance system can increase its capacity by a particular set of rules concerning the way in which decisionmakers reach a decision. In case of unanimity, there will be low capacity since all participants have a tool to assure that their own interests will be warranted by the final decision. In cases of a simple majority, this is not the case anymore. The system increases its capacity since it can take decisions despite the opposition of some.

The Problem of Control

In the assessment of capacity, the perspective of the political system as a whole is used. In the assessment of control, the perspective is individualized. Control points at the extent to which each of the political actors[3] in a political system can determine the content of the decisions taken by that system. The relation to capacity is obvious: The more control each of the actors has, the less capacity the system will have. The opposite is not completely true, however. In cases where too much capacity reduces the control too much, the legitimacy of the system becomes problematic. This can affect the capacity of the system to take decisions and increase the costs of implementation. Otherwise stated, to secure its legitimacy and the implementation of its decisions, a political system needs to balance between capacity and control. This is true for local governments, national governments, and the political system of the European Union.

Capacity and Control in the European Union

Just like every other political system, the European Union has to cope with the problem of capacity and control. But there are reasons to argue that the problem is larger here than in most national political systems because of the mixture of intergovernmental and supranational mechanisms in its decisionmaking structures and processes. The EU consists of fifteen member states, each of which has a stake in seeing its interests translated into the joint decisions and all of which have an interest in the capability of the EU to take decisions and resolve problems. Both aspects are conditions sine qua non for EU membership. No state wants to belong to an international organization in which it has no say at all, especially not an organization as powerful and influential as the EU.

Yet what would be the attraction of an EU incapable of taking joint decisions? What would be the added value of an EU that wouldn't be able to materialize the benefits of cooperation by joint decisions? The EU would have remained an empty shell without any political and economic significance. Enlargement wouldn't have been an option either for the recent entries or for the Eastern and southern newcomers.

It is clear, therefore, that capacity and control are two options that most if not all member states would like the EU to have at the same time. They would like to have as much influence as possible on the decisions of the EU without endangering the capacity of this organization to act effectively, efficiently, and within reasonable time limits. The history of the EC/EU from an institutional angle is the story of a balancing between these two options.

Capacity and Control in Economic and Political Integration

The balance between capacity and control has been reflected in different ways, one of which concerns the relations among the major EU institutions, the other the way of working in the EU Council. In this chapter I pay attention only to the last.[4] The problem of balance has played its role mainly in the European Community (the first pillar of Maastricht) and much less in the Common Foreign and Security Policy (the second pillar) and in cooperation on justice and home affairs (the third pillar). This is because a large number of member states have perceived the process of European integration as an economic endeavor in the first place. Even member states that considered European integration a political project saw economic integration as an initial and important step to reach this objective. Whereas many member states had no difficulty overlooking the negative effect of their high level of control on the capacity of the European Union in political issues, no member state could afford this approach in the realm of economic integration. Balancing capacity and control therefore has been a constant consideration whenever it concerned decisionmaking in the Council on matters of the first pillar.

Balancing in the Council

So far I have mentioned three factors affecting the degree of capacity of political systems: the diversity of interests, the possibility of these interests to be translated into the governance system, and the degree to which the governance system itself contains a mechanism that allows for the aggregation and transformation of divergent interests into collective decisions. The last is crucial, since it can attenuate the effect of interest divergence on the system's capacity. The mechanism in a sense filters a large number of interests and priorities into a limited number of joint decisions. Probably the most successful aspect of the process of European integration is precisely this capacity to filter, as has been most obvious in the Council of the European Union.

Unanimity

From a formal perspective, the EU Council contains two filtering systems, one that gives priority to control and one that balances capacity and control. The first consists of the unanimity rule that gives every member state a veto. This allows for a maximum of control and hinders the decisionmaking capacity whenever the Council is exposed to divergent interests. The British obstruction policy in response to the beef export ban[5] is an extreme example of this. On their own, the British were able to block every decision on which unanimity was required. Whatever the reason for a blockage, unanimity makes the Council vulnerable and affects its capacity negatively. In case of unanimity, it seems there is no longer a filter.

In practice the situation doesn't have to be that dramatic. The practice of negotiation, issue linkage, and logrolling allows for decisionmaking. After all, the member states do have an interest in a European Union that can take decisions. But that doesn't reduce the vulnerability of the decisionmaking system to the intricacies and caprices of politics in each of the member states.

To say that a filter is completely absent is not quite accurate, however, even in cases of unanimity. The representatives of the member states in the Council (and the COREPER and the working groups) have to represent their member states as wholes. They are therefore obliged to aggregate numerous domestic interests into a national interest. The number of domestic interests that get direct access to the Council is thus limited.

Qualified Majority

Besides unanimity, the Council increasingly uses a decisionmaking system that reflects a particular balance between capacity and control: the qualified majority. Compared with unanimity, this system increases the capacity of the Council at the expense of a degree of control by the member states. Member states can be confronted with a legally binding decision of the Council despite their opposition. From a formal perspective, there is a possibility of minorization. In practice, consensus building is promoted. In order to avoid what it regards as a negative outcome, a member state has an interest in cooperation with the others unless it can form a coalition with other member states big enough—the blocking minority—to make it impossible for the rest to reach the qualified majority. From an individual point of view, therefore, the degree of control has been reduced. A member state needs other member states in order to determine the outcome of the decisionmaking process or prevent decisions that go against its own interests.

The qualified majority acts as a filter between the interests of the member states and the outcome of the decisionmaking process. No member state has the legal option to directly translate its own interests into the final decision; it needs the support of others. What makes it different from the unanimity rule is that a member state also needs the support of others to avoid decisions that run *counter* to its interests. The largest effect on the degree of control thus stems not from the qualified majority as such but from its corollary, the blocking minority.

That the qualified majority system increases the capacity of the Council decisionmaking and that this can be in the interest of every member state has been showed by the British attitude at the 1985 IGC, which resulted in the Single European Act. The Thatcher government favored the expansion of the scope of the qualified majority to decisions on the internal market since this program fitted quite well in her deregulation policies and "jeopardized British interests, as Thatcher assessed them, only in a few areas."[6] Moreover, the British government perceived it as a British interest that the EU Council would be able to take decisions on the internal market program despite the opposition of some member states against its liberal bias. Thatcher herself defended the qualified majority voting because "things which we wanted were being stopped by others using a single vote."[7] The British were willing to jeopardize their interests in a few areas in exchange for an increased capacity of the Council on a well-defined number of issues. Another country that could be called Euroskeptic,

Denmark, in the same way advocated the abolition of the right of veto in environmental protection and social rights in its memorandum of 1990.[8]

A similar example involves the French attitude toward the qualified majority. Whereas the French were at the root of the Luxembourg compromise of 1966, which basically made the legal possibility of qualified majority voting politically meaningless for sixteen years, they themselves were the first to ask for a vote again. This happened during the Belgian presidency of 1982, when the French requested a vote on agricultural prices so as to overcome British opposition because of the question of the *juste retour.*[9] The Belgian presidency called for the vote, and the British remained isolated. As Dinan put it, the vote itself seemed unimportant, "but its significance for the demise of unanimity" was great.[10] The real demise of the Luxembourg compromise took place only in 1986 with the reconfirmation of the qualified majority voting and the expansion of its scope by the Single European Act.

The French insistence on the vote is another illustration of the fact that member states sometimes have to give preference to capacity over control because blocking decisionmaking is against their interests. The scope of this interest may be limited, but it seems to have played an important role in a large array of issues. It equally indicates that governments concede control only if they perceive doing so as being in their national interest. As Lodge has indicated, "all [member states] are committed to maximizing their own potential" in Council decision making."[11]

The Widening Gap Between Capacity and Control

Enlargement is at the top of the European agenda and will have a major effect on capacity and control. Until now each member state could strike a balance between capacity and control; the distance between the two could be bridged. The qualified majority provided the EU Council a sufficient level of capacity without eroding the degree of control for each member state by too much. This was especially the case for the big member states (France, Germany, the UK, Italy, and Spain). Until 1995 two big member states could block the decisionmaking with the support of a small one. Since then two big member states need the cooperation of at least two small ones to halt the process. Before 1995 if a big member state couldn't enlist the help of another big one, it needed the support of three small member states; today it would need four.

The comparison between the situations before and after 1995 already provides some indication of the kinds of problems that will emerge in cases of further enlargements. The least one can say is that the distance between capacity and control increases with every new accession. With this growing distance, the trade-off between the two becomes politically more difficult to accept. New enlargements will turn this distance into a real gap, forcing member states to choose between preserving as much control as possible and endangering the decisionmaking capacity of the Union or maintaining that capacity and losing considerable control. In this section I provide evidence that the gap will widen; I then go on to illuminate the relationship between this gap and the dilemma between capacity and control.

The Formal Perspective

The Case of Unanimity.   From a formal perspective (in which bargaining practices in the Council are neglected), the relation between gap widening and enlargement is clear. In case of unanimity in the Council, the more member states you have, the more divergent views will have to be taken into account in order to avoid the use of vetoes. The larger the Union, therefore, the lower its capacity to take decisions in case of unanimity.

The perspective of control provides better results. Every member state contains a right of veto, enlargement or not. If one translates this into figures (between 0 and 1), control will be 1 (or the maximum) for each of the member states (see Table 5.1). The figure for capacity varies, however. Table 5.1 gives an overview of the results for an EC/EU with six, nine, twelve, fifteen, twenty-one, twenty-four, and twenty-seven member states.[12] It takes into account hypothetical enlargement rounds. The first would consist of the four Visegrád countries, Malta, and Cyprus. The second contains Bulgaria, Romania, and Slovenia. The third consists of the three Baltic states.

The Case of Qualified Majority.   The picture becomes more complicated with the qualified majority. Each member state's control is related to its share in the number of votes required to achieve the absolute majority.[13] If a member state adds its votes when a qualified majority has already been attained, its contribution doesn't result in more control since its additional votes were not necessary to take a decision. Table 5.1 presents the degree of control for each of the (current and prospective) member states. As a matter of fact, these figures reflect only the maximum degree of control. They hold only in situations where member states are able exactly to reach the qualified majority threshold (e.g., sixty-two votes in the current situation). Depending on the coalitions formed to reach the threshold, however, the real threshold can be a figure between sixty-two and sixty-seven.[14] In reality, therefore, the degree of control will fluctuate between a country's share in sixty-two and its share in sixty-seven votes.

The comparison of the control figures in an enlarging Council indicates that every member state loses with every enlargement: The larger the EU, the lower the degree of control for each of its member states. Take, for

Table 5.1   Control in the EU Council

Member State	Votes	EC 6 (12/17)	EC 9 (41/58)	EC 12 (54/76)	EC 15 (62/87)	EC 21 (79/112)	EC 24 (89/125)	EC 27 (94/133)
Belgium	5 (2)ᵃ	0.16	0.12	0.09	0.08	0.06	0.056	0.053
Netherlands	5 (2)	0.16	0.12	0.09	0.08	0.06	0.056	0.053
Luxembourg	2 (1)	0.08	0.04	0.03	0.03	0.025	0.022	0.021
Germany	10 (4)	0.33	0.24	0.18	0.16	0.12	0.11	0.10
France	10 (4)	0.33	0.24	0.18	0.16	0.12	0.11	0.10
Italy	10 (4)	0.33	0.24	0.18	0.16	0.12	0.11	0.10
United Kingdom	10 (4)		0.24	0.18	0.16	0.12	0.11	0.10
Ireland	3		0.07	0.05	0.04	0.037	0.033	0.031
Denmark	3		0.07	0.05	0.04	0.037	0.033	0.031
Greece	5			0.09	0.08	0.06	0.056	0.053
Spain	8			0.14	0.12	0.10	0.09	0.08
Portugal	5			0.09	0.08	0.06	0.056	0.053
Austria	4				0.06	0.05	0.044	0.042
Sweden	4				0.06	0.05	0.044	0.042
Finland	3				0.04	0.037	0.033	0.031
Poland	8					0.10	0.09	0.08
Czech Republic	5					0.06	0.056	0.053
Hungary	5					0.06	0.056	0.053
Slovakia	3					0.037	0.033	0.031
Malta	2					0.025	0.022	0.021
Cyprus	2					0.025	0.022	0.021
Slovenia	2						0.022	0.021
Bulgaria	5						0.056	0.053
Romania	6						0.07	0.06
Estonia	2							0.021
Latvia	3							0.031
Lithuania	3							0.031
Av. control		0.23	0.15	0.11	0.09	0.06	0.057	0.050

a. Figures in parentheses indicate the number of votes when the EC had only six members.

instance, Germany. In the best case (where a qualified majority is reached with the lowest possible number of countries), the degree of control for Germany diminished from 0.33 in the original EC to 0.24 after the first enlargement in 1973, to 0.18 in the EC of twelve member states, and to 0.16 in the current EU. This means that the current German degree is equal to the degree of control of Belgium between 1958 and 1972. New enlargements will further reduce this from 0.12 in an EU of twenty-one member states to 0.11 and 0.1 in a Union of twenty-two and twenty-seven member states, respectively. This is the case not only for Germany but for all the member states, as the average control indicates. This already evolved from 0.23 to 0.09 between 1958 and 1995 and will be further reduced to 0.06 and 0.05 with twenty-one and twenty-seven member states, respectively.

The meaning of these figures becomes clear if one looks at the difficulties in constructing qualified majorities from the perspective of each individual member state. Take again, for example, Germany. In the worst situation—with the highest possible number of member states to cross the qualified majority threshold[15]—Germany, in order to achieve this majority, had to find the support of four other member states in the original six-member EC. With the support of Luxembourg, Belgium, the Netherlands, and Italy, for instance, the Germans could achieve thirty-two votes, one vote above the required thirty $(1 + 2 + 2 + 4 + 4 = 13$ votes).

In the best situation—where the lowest possible number of member states cross the qualified majority threshold[16]—the support of two other large member states was sufficient $(4 + 4 + 4 = 12$ votes).

Today, in a European Union with fifteen member states, the situation is already radically different. In the worst case, Germany can reach the threshold only if it gains the support of at least twelve other member states.[17] In the best case, seven would be sufficient.[18]

The conclusion is clear. In terms of control, the enlargements of the European Union make it more difficult for each member state to influence the outcomes of Council decisionmaking. This is confirmed by the figures for an even larger EU. In an EU of twenty-one, for instance, Germany would need the support of seventeen others in the worst case and ten others in the best case. These figures are twenty and twelve in an EU of twenty-four, and twenty-three and thirteen in an EU of twenty-seven. For some new member states, this seems paradoxical. A country like Hungary that is very eager to join the Union will have a degree of control equal only to that of Luxembourg between 1958 and 1972.

One cannot expect, however, that the declining degree of control will benefit the capacity of the Union. On the contrary, enlargement is detrimental to capacity, as reflected in the number of member states required to achieve the qualified majority (QM) and in the related capacity figures (see Table 5.2).

The capacity figures clearly indicate that in the case of either unanimity or qualified majority, enlargement results in a loss of capacity. The qualified majority rule, a device that increases capacity, is not sufficient on its

Table 5.2 Capacity in the EU Council

Number of Member States Required to Reach the QM	EC 6 (12/17)	EC 9 (41/58)	EC 12 (54/76)	EC 15 (62/87)	EC 21 (79/112)	EC 24 (89/125)	EC 27 (94/133)
Lowest Possible Number	3	4	7	9	11	13	14
Highest Possible Number	5	7	11	13	18	21	24
Lowest Capacity QM	0.20	0.14	0.09	0.07	0.055	0.047	0.041
Highest Capacity QM	0.33	0.25	0.14	0.12	0.09	0.076	0.071
Capacity (Unanimity)	0.16	0.11	0.08	0.06	0.047	0.041	0.037

own to keep the capacity of the EU Council at its current level. In the case of unanimity, capacity declines from 0.16 (until 1972) to 0.06 (level in 1997) and 0.037 (with twenty-seven member states).[19] This is logical. The more member states, the more potential gridlock in the Council in cases of unanimity.

The qualified majority rule improves the situation a little bit (which was precisely its objective) but cannot cure the problem of the decline of capacity. In the current EU, the highest capacity is already equal to the capacity in case of unanimity in the former EC of nine. Its lowest capacity is already lower than its capacity in case of unanimity before 1995. In a Union of fifteen, therefore, and in the worst case, the problems with decisionmaking in the Council can be as big as those that occurred when the unanimity rule still applied in the Community of twelve. This becomes even more obvious if one looks at the number of member states required to reach the qualified majority.

In the Community of twelve, the support of eleven member states was required in cases where the larger member states were the most recalcitrant to support a Commission proposal. In the current EC, this figure is already thirteen. With the new enlargements, this figure will rise to eighteen (with twenty-one states), twenty-one (with twenty-four states), and twenty-four (with twenty-seven states). In the best case, the results are slightly better but still problematic. Whereas seven member states could reach the qualified majority (if all the big ones were supportive) before 1995, the figure is now eight states. It will increase further to eleven, thirteen, and fourteen member states in a Union of twenty-one, twenty-four, and twenty-seven member states, respectively.

Just as for control, then, enlargements will affect the capacity of the EU negatively, irrespective of the unanimity rule or the qualified majority rule. Despite the qualified majority, new enlargements will reduce the EU's capacity to a level lower than in the case of unanimity before 1995.

The Gap.   What may be more troubling is the widening gap between capacity and control that enlargement engenders. In 1958, in a Community of six member states, an acceptable level of capacity could be reconciled with a large degree of control for each of the member states. Even a country like Luxembourg had the chance to let its voice be heard. But even then some perceived the qualified majority as problematic (as during the empty-chair crisis of 1965).

The past enlargements have changed this picture. With every enlargement, it became much more difficult to reconcile a decent level of control with a decent level of capacity, as the British understood during the IGC of 1985.[20] The gap between capacity and control will widen further as the Union becomes ever larger. If the current decisionmaking rules remain unchanged, new enlargements will reduce both capacity and control. Both concepts are in a zero-sum situation. If the Union wants to preserve its current capacity level after new enlargements, an additional reduction in the member states' control will be required ("additional" meaning a loss of control beyond the loss they automatically suffer with an enlargement). Conversely, if the member states want to preserve their control, this will require an additional reduction in the EU's capacity, with all the risks of potential paralysis in Council decisionmaking.

The Perspective of Political Practice

Until now, my analysis has been based on Council decisionmaking in its formal dimension. I started from the assumption that in cases of qualified majority, decisions are taken by way of a vote. In most cases this is not true. The Council has developed a tradition of consensus-building. This has consequences mainly on the degree of control.

Consensus, Unanimity, and Control. As far as control is concerned, the consensus-building tradition of the Council gives the member states more control than would have been the case in decisionmaking by way of voting. But the possibility of voting exists, and every member state representative has to take that into account in the bargaining process. There is always a possibility of minorization by way of a vote. The degree of control may be higher, therefore, than in a pure voting situation; it is not as high as in the case of unanimity. Moreover, as the number of member states increases and it becomes more difficult to reach a consensus, there will be a higher probability that the Council will sooner resort to a real vote. One can thus assume that the degree of real control will become closer to its theoretical counterpart as the EU enlarges. In practice, then, the loss of control with every enlargement will go even faster than in theory.

Majorities, Minorities, and Control. Because of how the Council works, control is determined more by the blocking minority than by the qualified majority. This has consequences for the degree of control of each of the member states. In practice, Council decisionmaking takes place in the following way: The Commission submits a proposal that the presidency puts on the agenda of the COREPER. This body refers it to one of the working groups. If the group reaches a consensus, the COREPER refers the question to the Council, which ratifies the outcome. If it fails to reach a consensus, the COREPER deals with the proposal or refers it directly to the Council. Bargaining among the member states then takes place, on the assumption that there is still a blocking minority against a compromise proposal. This assumption is based on the statements of the member states' representatives during the deliberations, not on a vote. As long as the assumption of such a minority exists, the bargaining will continue. If the presidency thinks that no such minority exists anymore, it concludes the case with the assumption that a qualified majority exists. In such cases member states have the possibility to object or abstain. Abstentions make it difficult to achieve a qualified majority, however, since no votes are added to reach the threshold.

The consequence of this practice for control is clear. Control depends more on the assumption of the blocking minority than on the qualified majority. Control is largely determined, then, by the potential of each member state to build such a minority. Once again, however, control has been negatively affected by the past enlargements and will be in the future, as Table 5.3 indicates. But the effect is smaller than in the case of the qualified majority, especially for the larger member states.

Table 5.3   Control and the Blocking Minority

Number of Member States Required to Reach the Blocking Minority	EC 6 (12/17)	EC 9 (41/58)	EC 12 (54/76)	EC 15 (62/87)	EC 21 (79/112)	EC 24 (89/125)	EC 27 (94/133)
Votes Required for Blocking Minority	6	18	23	26	34	37	40
Lowest Possible Number	2	2	3	3	4	4	4
Highest Possible Number	4	5	6	8	11	11	14

If the big member states succeed in cooperating in order to veto proposals that are detrimental to their interests, they could limit the loss of control due to the enlargements. If they depend on the smaller member states to block decisionmaking, however, their loss of control will be bigger. As there is no reason to say that the interests of the big member states "naturally" converge on most EU issues, there is reason to believe that enlargements will seriously affect the capability of each member state individually to block Council decisionmaking. It is from this perspective that the British and Spanish reaction to the enlargement of 1995 can be understood.[21] Both countries wanted to keep the blocking minority at the former level (in terms of votes), namely, twenty-three votes. This would have preserved their degree of control after the accession of Finland, Sweden, and Austria, although it would have made it more difficult to reach the qualified majority: The increase from sixty-two to sixty-five votes would have required the support of an additional member state (compared with the situation at the time) in some cases (depending on the degree to which the larger member states supported a proposal). The other member states only partly conceded to this British-Spanish request. With the Ioannina compromise, an objection of twenty-three votes would entail the postponement of the issue (though it is not indicated for how long). The idea behind the compromise is that although it is legally possible to take a decision in case of the objection of twenty-three votes, in practice the presidency will continue to negotiate until the opposition of three more votes (which can mean one additional member state) has been overcome. In legal terms, this agreement has preserved the capacity of the EU. In political terms, however, it has eroded this capacity even more than has the enlargement with three member states. This very clearly indicates that for some member states the erosion of their control caused by the enlargements has reached its limits. Strangely enough, some of these states are the most fervent supporters of new enlargements. This will have to happen, however, at the expense of the Council's capacity and with the preservation of their current level of control.

Two remarks have to be added to this conclusion. First, as I have already indicated above, the increasing number of member states itself will make reaching a consensus much more difficult and can provide an incentive for the presidency to resort to a vote sooner. Second, more EU decisionmaking takes place according to procedures in which the role of the European Parliament is important. The feature of most of these procedures (e.g., the budgetary, the cooperation, and the codecision procedures) is that the Council has to work with deadlines. In these situations there is a higher probability that the Council presidency will have to resort to a formal vote in order to keep the procedure from ending (because the deadline has passed) without a formal decision. In such cases, control will be determined more by the qualified majority than by the blocking minority, which has negative effects on the degree of control and magnifies the negative impact of the enlargements.

Heterogeneity, Homogeneity, Capacity, and Control

The capacity of the EU and the degree of control of its member states is not determined simply by the share of each member state in the qualified majority or the blocking minority or the level of these majorities and minorities. It is equally determined by the degree of heterogeneity of the member states. If there are more member states but all share the same interests and policy priorities, the real effects of the enlargements would be small. An individual member state would have no difficulty finding support from others, whereas the Council would easily reach its majorities.

In the case of the European Union, however, it is clear that the enlargements will bring with them heterogeneity. The new member states will differ in many respects from the current ones and will intensify already existing conflicts. Two divides in the European Union will be especially affected by this: the north-south divide and the difference between big and small member states.

North Versus South and North Versus South Versus East

The enlargements to the east and to the south will bring into the EU a number of countries whose economic situations are generally worse than those of the poorest current member states (the only exceptions being Slovenia and Malta). To give an indication, the "richest" countries among the candidates, the Czech Republic and Hungary, achieve a gross national product (GNP) per capita less than one-third the GNP per capita of Greece. For countries like Romania, Bulgaria, and the Baltic states, the figure is less than one-sixth of the Greek GNP per capita. The effects of these figures on the EU budget have been analyzed elsewhere.[22] What is obvious from these analyses is that the new enlargements will intensify the existing conflicts within the EU Council on the revenues and the expenditures of the EU budget. Whereas the richer member states show an ever greater reluctance to pay more to the EU and require from it a higher level of efficacy, the southern member states are eager to increase the size of a budget from which they receive the most. In the past, this resulted in payoffs between the north and the south, as reflected in the linkage between the Internal Market Program and the doubling of the EU's regional policy budget from 1988 on and between the EMU and the Edinburgh Perspectives at the end of 1992.[23] The Edinburgh Perspectives increased the share of the regional policy budget by an additional one-third between 1995 and 1999 and increased the EU budget from 1.2 percent of the Union's GNP in 1995 to 1.27 percent in 1999. The difficulties in ratifying these perspectives not only for the UK but also for traditionally pro-EU member states like the Netherlands made clear that for the net contributing member states the size of the EU budget had reached its limits.[24] The 1995 enlargement of the European Union, which brought in Austria, Sweden, and Finland, further showed that these new member states—despite the hope of their southern counterparts—were not prepared to become large net contributors of the EU.[25]

And then there are the southern member states. In order to maintain their share in the expenditures of the EU, they plead for an "upward adaptation" of its size whenever the enlargements take place. If the size of the budget remains the same, they understand that they will receive less from it. Some of them would even become net contributors. Should the EU decide to provide only a small amount of money for the newcomers, an important argument for becoming an EU member would disappear for many of the current candidates. As Hasse has put it, the access to the finances of the EU's structural funds is one of the main reasons for the CEECs to become EU members.[26]

Whatever the outcome of this budgetary discussion, it is clear that the new enlargements will transform the current north-south division in the EU Council into a north-south-east one. As this will increase the potential for conflicts in the EU and as the Council decisionmaking system will be less able to ease such conflicts, this could become a serious problem for the EU Council's capacity.[27]

Big Versus Small

Most new member states of the European Union will be small states. This has caused some fear among the big member states that they will become a minority as far as votes are concerned although they provide the vast majority of the EU population. The issue showed up for the first time with the enlargement of 1995 and was one of the factors leading to the Ioannina agreement of March 1994.[28] Table 5.4 indicates that these concerns are only partly justified.

Table 5.4   Big and Small in the EU Council

	EC 6 (12/17)	EC 9 (41/58)	EC 12 (54/76)	EC 15 (62/87)	EC 21 (79/112)	EC 24 (89/125)	EC 27 (94/133)
Share of Population of Big Member States	87.3	87.2	84.2	79.2	76	75.4	69.2
Share Votes of Big Member States	71.4	68.9	63.1	55.1	50	49.6	46.6
Disadvantage of Population Versus Votes	15.9	18.3	21.1	24.1	26	25.8	22.6

As Table 5.4 shows, the big member states may form the majority of the EU population, but the enlargements will make them a minority in the Council. In the original EC of six[29] the dominance of the big states was reflected in their voting power. This diminished with every enlargement. It seems the next enlargement will be a turning point: The big states would lose their majority of votes in the Council if the EU enlarged from fifteen to twenty-one member states. This enlargement would also create the biggest difference between the share of the EU population and their share of the Council votes. This would reduce somewhat with the enlargements to twenty-four and twenty-seven member states (mainly because of the accession of Romania and the very small number of votes for the Baltic states and Slovenia).

The picture looks more dramatic than it is. With the qualified majority threshold at 71 percent of all the Council votes, a qualified majority composed of the small member states (i.e., the majority with the highest possible number of member states) would still reflect 55 percent of the EU population in a Union of twenty-one and even 59 percent in a Union of twenty-seven states. This means that it would remain impossible for the small member states to form a qualified majority without representing the

majority of the EU population. The fear of the big member states that the
Council would be able to take decisions against the will of the majority of
the EU population is without reason. Nonetheless, it seemed to be an
important subject at the 1996 IGC.

The difference between big and small remains relevant, however, as far
as capacity and control are concerned. As I have made clear above, the
maintenance of the current level of the qualified majority after new
enlargements will negatively affect both the capacity and control. Solutions
that aim at maintaining the EU's capacity (by lowering the 71 percent
threshold) become less feasible. Lowering the threshold would create the
possibility that a minority of the EU population would form a majority of
votes in the Council, which would throw off the balance between capacity
and control in an enlarged Council. The UK seems especially sensitive to
this question. As George has put it: "It remains important to the British
government not to allow the continued dilution of the ability of the larger
member states to block legislation, and to get the issue settled before the
next round of enlargement negotiations begins so as to avoid being put in
the position of having to threaten an enlargement that they wish to see in
order to defend a principle that they do not wish to see go by default."[30]
Likewise, in September 1995 the French president accepted the principle of
the extension of the scope of qualified majority voting on condition that the
voting weights would be revised "in a manner that would take into account
the demographic, economic and financial realities."[31]

For their part, however, the small member states, especially Denmark,
are equally anxious not to let Council decisionmaking be reformed so that
they would be marginalized in an EU dominated by the large states.[32] A
possible solution for these countries could be the reinforcement of the role
of the European Commission. That certainly fits into a typical small-state
strategy to counterbalance the power of the big member states with supranational devices.[33] But for countries like France and the UK, this seems to
be unacceptable.[34]

Perspectives for a Solution: The 1996 IGC

There is clearly a problem with the effects of the upcoming enlargements
on capacity and control in the European Union, and it threatens to paralyze
the Union with acrimonious discussions among the member states. At the
1996 IGC that is supposed to "improve Maastricht," the EU and the possible consequences of its enlargements are on the negotiating table. But far
from engendering a consensus on Council decisionmaking, the consensus
on the necessity of the enlargements hides a divergence of opinions on
decisionmaking. This is reflected in a quote from the report of the Reflection Group:

The Union must be able to take decisions but some members insist that it is not simply a matter of assisting the ability to decide. Its effectiveness will depend on such decisions having the backing of as many European citizens as possible. For this to be the case, the revision should keep the qualified majority threshold at an effective level and such decisions should not leave a significant proportion of the people of Europe in a minority. However, there is no specific option enjoying broad support in the Group when it comes to putting this into practice.[35]

As indicated above, the British position on the IGC indicates that reforms to Council decisionmaking have to benefit the degree of control of the large member states. There is no sign that a possible Labour government would take another position on that subject, although such a government would accept the extension of the qualified majority principle (in its current meaning) to issues such as social[36] (where the UK would accede to the Social Protocol), environmental, industrial, and regional policy. The Major government rejected this, emphasizing the central role of the member states in the European Union and hoping to preserve the possibilities of the Luxembourg compromise (a right of veto in order to protect a vital national interest).[37]

The position of the UK is a peculiar one compared to that of the other fourteen member states, who accept the principle of the extension of the qualified majority. Some of them want to limit this to particular policy areas; others (such as Belgium) defend a generalization of the qualified majority.[38] All member states seem to recognize that the introduction of the qualified majority in the Common Foreign and Security Policy is not feasible.[39]

A key issue concerning the Council and its decisionmaking is the balance between the big and small member states after the enlargements. In the different points of view on the IGC, one can distinguish three groups on this subject. The first group asks for a change in the voting weights (*répondération*), a second bluntly refuses this, and a third rejects the *répondération* but accepts a second criterion (besides the qualified majority) in Council decisionmaking. The first group consists of France, Spain, and the UK; the second Ireland, Greece, and Luxembourg; and the third Belgium, the Netherlands, Portugal, Sweden, and Denmark. Germany, although it does not reject the *répondération*, supports the introduction of a demographic criterion besides the qualified majority.

The position of France and the UK has already been outlined above. Both member states want a *répondération* in which demographic and eventually economic or financial criteria are taken into account. They are supported in this by Italy.[40] This would mean that their voting weight would increase at the expense of small member states like Greece, Portugal, and Ireland. These are not only small member states, but they also receive a large share from the EU budget (the financial criterion) and have poor economic performances (Ireland being the exception). Luxembourg would also lose part from its weight because it is the smallest member state in terms of population. It is clear, therefore, why countries like Luxembourg and Ireland reject such proposals outright. The principal argument used by Luxembourg is that a *repondération* is useless since the big-small divide has never played a role in any major issue. As Luxembourg foreign minister Jacques Poos put it, "to change the voting weights in the Council other than by extrapolating from the current weightings would be equivalent to changing the nature of the Union. A coalition of the small [states] against the big has never formed on an essential question."[41] The same argument has been put forward by the Irish government.[42] Greece supports only a "technical adaptation" after the enlargements, which basically means no *repondération* and the maintenance of the threshold on 71 percent of the votes.[43] The same opinion is defended by Finland, at least until the next enlargement; Finland wants to postpone any decision on adaptations until the accession negotiations.[44]

Spain takes a position quite similar to the one that it advocated during the discussions on the adaptation of Council decisionmaking with the EFTA enlargement.[45] Its central aim is to preserve Spain's capacity to form a blocking minority with the lowest possible number of other member states, preserving a kind of a veto for the southern member states. This would enable them to continue to force the richer member states to make side payments to the southern states in exchange for their support for market liberalization and monetary integration. The Spanish government therefore defends a formula by which two large member states and one small would be able to block decisionmaking in the Council. The formula might mean lowering the blocking minority to twenty-three votes, a *repondération* that has the same effect, or maintaining the current level of the blocking minority and introducing specific arrangements that enable a limited number of countries to block the decisionmaking in a specific number of issue areas.[46]

Belgium, the Netherlands, Portugal, Sweden, and Denmark recognize the problem of the balance between big and small and thus accept the application of a second criterion besides the qualified majority that would preserve the balance. This second criterion, which Germany defends as well, would consist of a majority of the population threshold. This means that decisions would be endorsed only if the achieved qualified majority reflected the majority of the population of the European Union.

Why are such solutions necessary in the current system? Table 5.5 shows that in no case can a qualified majority of 71 percent reflect a minority of the EU population. Admittedly, in the case of a qualified majority consisting of exclusively small member states (whenever possible), such a majority becomes smaller in terms of the population that it reflects, but it always remains a majority. The least representative (in terms of the

Table 5.5 Qualified Majority and Majority

	EC 6 (12/17)	EC 9 (41/58)	EC 12 (54/76)	EC 15 (62/87)	EC 21 (79/112)	EC 24 (89/125)	EC 27 (94/133)
Share of the Population of a Qualified Majority with the Lowest Possible Population	69.8	76.9	72.8	62.6	55	58.3	59
Share of the Population of a Qualified Majority with the Lowest Possible Number of States and the Lowest Possible Population	87.3	87.3	81.5	86.8	86.2	86.1	86.8
Loss of Representativeness	17.5	10.4	8.7	24.2	31.2	27.8	27.8

population) will be the qualified majority in a European Union of twenty-one member states, largely because of the accession of Malta and Cyprus. In that case, the lowest possible population represented in such a majority will be 55 percent of the EU population. The discrepancy would diminish with additional enlargements. In a Union of twenty-four and twenty-seven member states, the qualified majority of the votes will represent 58.3 and 59 percent of the EU population, respectively.

What Table 5.5 makes clear, however, is that the nonparticipation of the larger member states in the achievement of a qualified majority seriously affects the representativeness of the Council's decisions. The second row in the table provides the cases in which the lowest possible number of member states (and the lowest possible number of inhabitants) compose the qualified majority. In these cases all the big member states contribute to the majority since they have most of the votes individually. The third row of the table indicates the maximum loss of representativeness of a qualified majority compared with the most representative qualified majority, one consisting of all big member states. Once again, the EU of twenty-one member states will suffer the biggest loss because of the accession of Malta and Cyprus, two member states that will be largely overrepresented in the Council.

We can draw three conclusions from Table 5.5. First, discussions on a demographic threshold have no meaning in the current qualified majority system. Second, any change to the current qualified majority threshold in order to preserve the capacity of the Union can lead to a minority's being represented in a qualified majority. In political terms, this means that solutions for the preservation of the Council's capacity will be less acceptable to the big member states unless their small counterparts would accept a disturbance of the balance between big and small at their expense. There is no indication that this is the case. Third, it is in the interests of the degree of control of the big member states to discuss not the introduction of a criterion involving majority of the population but a demographic threshold that is higher than just 50 percent of that population. Still, such a solution would in a number of cases reduce the capacity of the Council even more than already will be the case with the upcoming enlargements.

Conclusion

As the European Union approaches what might be its next enlargements, the 1996 IGC provides the last opportunity for it to prepare its institutional framework. There are reasons for pessimism. As the enlargement will have a detrimental effect on both the capacity of and the control in the Council, the existing gap between the two will become a dilemma. At the 1996 IGC, the member states will have to choose between the preservation of either their control or the Council's capacity. This choice is made even more difficult as a consequence of the increasing divergence of interests among the member states. The intensification of the divisions between south and north and big and small after the enlargements and the member states' anticipation of this split will make a consensus on the required institutional adaptations all the more problematic. As the discussions on the EFTA enlargement have proved, this increases the probability of agreements like the one at Ioannina. Otherwise stated, the capacity of the Council and therefore of the European Union is in danger. By the first decade of the twenty-first century, there will probably be a larger Union. Whether this will mean expanded capacity remains an open question. Because this will necessitate a step forward in the institutional aspects of the integration process—although countries like Spain, France, and the UK object to this forward integration momentum—there is a greater likelihood that the dilemma of capacity versus control of the enlarged Council will be "resolved" at the expense of capacity. An ever more attractive EU is becoming the victim of its own success.

Notes

1. H. Keman, "Comparative Politics: A Distinctive Approach to Political Science?" in H. Keman (ed.), *Comparative Politics: New Directions in Theory and Method* (Amsterdam: VU Press, 1993), pp. 31–57.

2. Another word for "capacity" could be "governability." See R. Dahrendorf, "On the Governability of Democracies," in R. C. Macridis and B. E. Brown, *Comparative Politics: Notes and Readings* (Pacific Grove, CA: Brooks/Cole, 1990), p. 287. See also J. S. Migdal (ed.), *State Power and Social Forces: Domination and Transformation in the Third World* (Cambridge: Cambridge University Press, 1994); J. S. Migdal, *Strong Societies and Weak States: State-Society Relations and State Capabilities in the Third World* (Princeton: Princeton University Press, 1988); P. Hall, *Governing the Economy: The Politics of State Intervention in Britain and France* (Oxford: Polity Press, 1986); P. Katzenstein,

Small States in World Markets: Industrial Policy in Europe (London: Ithaca, 1985); J. E. Keman, *Over Politicologie: maatschappelijke conflicten en politieke consensus als paradox* (Amsterdam: VU Press, 1992).

3. The term "political actors" refers not only to the decisionmakers, that is, the direct participants in the governance system, but also to everyone who has the possibility to defend a political interest.

4. For an analysis of the effect of interactions between the Council and other institutions on the relative power of the member states and Council decisionmaking, see G. Garrett and G. Tsebelis, "An Institutional Critique of Intergovernmentalism," *International Organization* 50, 2 (1996) 269–300.

5. Which was in itself a reaction to mad cow disease.

6. The original approach of Thatcher to the qualified majority vote was not its formal inclusion in the Treaty. The British advocated "informal efforts to facilitate more majority voting." See A. Moravcsik, "Negotiating the Single European Act," in R. O. Keohane and S. Hoffmann (eds.), *The New European Community* (Boulder: Westview, 1991), pp. 49 and 61.

7. R. O. Keohane and S. Hoffmann, "Institutional Change in Europe in the 1980s," in R. O. Keohane and S. Hoffmann (eds.), *The New European Community* (Boulder: Westview, 1991), p. 17.

8. H. Banner, "Danish European Policy Since 1945: The Question of Sovereignty" and T. Lise Schou, "The Debate in Denmark 1986–91 on European Integration and Denmark's Participation," in M. Kelstrup (ed.), *European Integration and Denmark's Participation* (Copenhagen: Political Studies Press, 1992), pp. 321 and 344.

9. That is, the question of the imbalance between the British contributions to the EU budget and what they received from it.

10. D. Dinan, *Ever Closer Union? An Introduction to the European Community* (Boulder: Lynne Rienner, 1994), p. 121.

11. J. Lodge, "EC Policy Making: Institutional Considerations," in J. Lodge (ed.), *The European Community and the Challenge of the Future* (London: Pinter, 1989), p. 32.

12. Capacity is determined by the number of member states required for a decision in the worst possible case. In case of unanimity, this is just the opposite of the number of member states.

13. In the case of Denmark, for instance, the degree of control is 3/62 or 0.04. Denmark has only three votes, and sixty-two are required for a qualified majority. Table 5.1 gives an overview of the results of all the current and future member states.

14. Sixty-seven is the maximum number of coalition partners required to pass the threshold. This happens in the case where only the smaller member states support a proposal.

15. The highest possible number to cross the threshold is reached in the hypothetical situation where the large member states are the most recalcitrant in supporting a proposal. In such cases, majorities are composed by the small member states first.

16. This happens when the big member states support a proposal first.

17. $2 + 3 + 3 + 3 + 4 + 4 + 5 + 5 + 5 + 5 + 8 + 10 + 10 = 67$, whereas the threshold is sixty-two votes.

18. Germany + 10 + 10 + 10 + 8 + 5 + 5 + 5 = 63 votes.

19. The capacity figure ranges from 0 (no capacity) to 1 (maximum capacity).

20. S. George, "The Approach of the British Government to the 1996 IGC," *Journal of European Public Policy* 3, 1 (1996): p. 53.

21. C. Closa, "National Interest and Convergence of Preferences: A Changing Role for Spain in the EU?" in C. Rhodes and S. Mazey (eds.), *The State of the European Union*, vol. 3: *Building a European Polity?* (Boulder: Lynne Rienner, 1995), pp. 306–307.

22. R. Baldwin, *Towards an Integrated Europe* (London: Center for Economic Policy Research, 1994), and B. Kerremans, "Do Institutions Make a Difference? Non-Institutionalism, Neo-Institutionalism, and the Logic of Common Decision-Making in the European Union," *Governance* 2 (1996): 217–240.

23. G. Marks, "Structural Policy and Multilevel Governance in the EC," in A. W. Cafruny and G. G. Rosenthal (eds.), *The State of the European Union*, vol. 2: *The Maastricht Debates and Beyond* (Boulder: Lynne Rienner, 1993), pp. 391–410 ; M. Schakleton, "The Community Budget After Maastricht," in A. W. Cafruny and G. G. Rosenthal (eds.), *The State of the European Union*, vol. 2: *The Maastricht Debates and Beyond* (Boulder: Lynne Rienner, 1993), pp. 373–390; M. A. Pollack, "Regional Actors in an Intergovernmental Play: The Making and Implementation of EC Structural Policy," in C. Rhodes and S. Mazey (eds.), *The State of the European Union*, vol. 3: *Building a European Polity?* (Boulder: Lynne Rienner, 1995), pp. 361–390.

24. H. Wallace, "Fit für Europa? Reform und Erweiterung der Europäischen Union," *Integration* 19, 2 (1996): pp. 77–92.

25. B. Kerremans, "Enlarging the European Union to the East: Mission Impossible?" *European Studies Journal* 13, 1 (1996): pp. 1-31; H. Matthijs and B. Kerremans, *De publieke financiën en het begrotingsstelsel van de Europese Unie* (Antwerp: Intersentia, forthcoming); P. Luif, *On the Road to Brussels: The Political Dimension of Austria's, Finland's and Sweden's Accession to the European Union* (Vienna: Austrian Institute for International Affairs, 1996).

26. R. Hasse, "Réformes au sein de la Communauté européenne et transition de l'ordre économique et politique en Europe de l'est: influences réciproques," *Revue du Marché commun*, 1991, p. 553.

27. One cannot consider the applicant states as a homogeneous group (Wallace, "Fit für Duropa?" p. 82). This could but enhance the potential for conflicts in an enlarged Council.

28. F. Hayes-Renshaw and H. Wallace, *The Council of Ministers* (London: Macmillan, 1997), p. 55.

29. The figures for the EC of six and of nine are calculated with West Germany only. From the EC of twelve on, the unified Germany is taken into account. Furthermore, big member states are those that have more than five votes in the Council: Germany, Italy, France, the UK, and Spain. Among the future member states, only Poland and Romania have been ranked as big.

30. George, "The Approach of the British Government to the 1996 IGC," pp. 53–54.

31. *Agence Europe* 6559 (9 September 1995), p. 2.

32. George, "The Approach of the British Government to the 1996 IGC," p. 57.

33. For this reason, Banner was quite optimistic about Denmark's future position toward the EU's institutional integration. As he put it, "In the future we can expect Denmark to be not a reluctant European, but part of the inner circle of EC members, increasingly joining forces with the small states of the original EEC" (Banner, "Danish European Policy Since 1945," p. 323). He seems to be right. The Danish representative in the Reflection Group that prepared the agenda of the 1996 IGC equally defended the role of the Commission because "this is very important for the small member states" (my translation, *Agence Europe* 6612, p. 2).

34. The French minister of European affairs, Michel Barnier, declared to the European Delegation of the Assemblée Nationale that the role of the Commission has to be strictly restricted to execution (*Agence Europe* 6585, 16/17 October 1995, p. 4).

35. Reflection Group, *Reflection Group's Report* (Brussels, 1995), p. 34, point 103; See also Reflection Group, *Progress Report from the Chairman of the Reflection Group on the 1996 Intergovernmental Conference,* SN 509/1/95 REV 1 (Madrid, 1995), p. 12. Both reports are available on the Internet.

36. George, "The Approach of the British Government to the 1996 IGC," p. 60, and Task Force IGC, *The Future of the European Union: Report on Labour's Position in Preparation of the Intergovernmental Conference* (European Commission Task Force, 1995), p. 2. Published on the Internet.

37. *Agence Europe* 6689 (16 March 1996), p. 3.

38. *Agence Europe* 6739 (1 June 1996), p. 3.

39. Ibid.

40. Task Force IGC, *Position of the Italian Government on the Intergovernmental Conference for the Revision of the Treaties* (European Commission Task Force, 1996), p. 3. Published on the Internet.

41. *Agence Europe* 6728 (16 March 1996), p. 3.

42. *Agence Europe* 6705 (10 April 1996), p. 4, and Task Force IGC, *Ireland: Challenges and Opportunities Abroad: Irish White Paper on Foreign Policy* (European Commission Task Force, 1996). Published on the Internet.

43. Task Force IGC, *For a Democratic European Union with Political and Social Content: Greece's Contribution to the 1996 IGC* (European Commission Task Force, 1996), p. 4. Published on the Internet.

44. Task Force IGC, *Finland's Points of Departure and Objectives at the European Union's Intergovernmental Conference in 1996* (European Commission Task Force, 1996), p. 3. Published on the Internet.

45. Closa, "National Interest and Convergence of Preferences," and European Parliament, *Spain's Position with Respect to the 1996 IGC.* Published on the Internet.

46. Ibid., p. 5.

PART 2

─────

Common Foreign and Security Policy

─────

6

WEU After the
Second Maastricht

Joseph I. Coffey

As these words are being written, the European Union is holding an inter-governmental conference more informally known as the "Second Maastricht." The task of the IGC is to devise policies and procedures that will make the EU a more cohesive and more effective institution, with increased ability not only to formulate policy but to implement it. Although this applies to areas as diverse as the introduction of a common currency and the establishment of uniform standards for granting asylum to refugees, a major concern is how to implement the proposed Common Foreign and Security Policy, especially when that may require the use of the military instrument: in short, how to create the defense arm that the EU may need. This issue, unlike others, is driven as much by external events, such as the political situation in Russia, the European policy of the United States, and ethnic rivalries in Europe, as by internal ones. Hence, the EU may not have the leisure to postpone decisions on the Common Foreign and Security Policy and on movement toward the creation of a common defense policy until Maastricht III.

In this chapter, I try to explore this issue, which centers around the role to be assigned to the Western European Union, the EU's "chosen instrument" in defense policy, its capability to carry out that role, and its relations with the EU and other security organizations, notably NATO. In so doing, I must consider some of the major variables, ranging from competing visions of European security to the costs of defense, that will—or at least should—influence choices. It is necessary also to understand the position of the WEU today, the task with which I begin.

The WEU Today

The WEU, formally established in October 1954, bound seven European countries (Britain, France, the Federal Republic of Germany, Italy,

Belgium, the Netherlands, and Luxembourg) not only to cooperate in economic, social, and cultural fields but to engage in collective defense; in fact, Article V of the Brussels treaty bound signatories to afford any member subject to armed attack in Europe "all military and other aid and assistance in their power."[1] Over time, however, the social and economic functions of the WEU were transferred to the Council of Europe or the European Economic Community, which later became the EU, and the military responsibilities were assigned to NATO. Thus the WEU was for thirty years an organization without a mission. This changed in the 1980s, partly because of fears in Europe that the United States was decoupling from its position on that continent, partly because of the need to provide a security dimension to European integration, and partly, it must be admitted, because France saw in the WEU a way to play more of a role in matters affecting European security than it had been able to do since 1967, when it withdrew its troops from the integrated military command of NATO and ceased to participate in the deliberations of the Defense Planning Committee and the Military Committee.

Whatever its motivations, WEU began to assume a more active role, politically as well as militarily. In 1991 it was designated by the Treaty on European Union as an "integral part of the development of the Union" and given responsibility to "elaborate and implement decisions of the Council [of the European Union] which have defence implications."[2] Pursuant to this mandate, to its own sense of its missions and responsibilities (and, it would appear, to the desire not to be preempted by NATO), WEU in the last decade:

- Has increased its membership to include, in one category or another, all states belonging to the EU, the European members of NATO, and nine countries from Eastern Europe, a total of twenty-seven.[3] And while these states have different powers and responsibilities, all of them can engage in the discussion by WEU of its future role, the development of ideas about how to carry out that role, and the preparation of plans for contingency operations, should these be necessary.
- Has established not only a planning cell to prepare for contingency operations and to give military advice to the Western European Council (WEC) but a situation center to keep track of developments that might require action and a Political Military Group to add balance to the consideration of those actions to be taken. Since the WEU also has a Committee of Chiefs of Defense Staff, it is able to bring to bear on its proposed operations national military perspectives as well as those which originate within WEU itself.
- Has, at Petersberg, agreed that military units could be employed for

humanitarian and rescue tasks, peacekeeping tasks, and tasks of combat forces in crisis management, including peacemaking;[4] and has carried out explorations of particular crises that might require action. For example, the planning cell has studied circumstances under which the WEU might undertake peacekeeping missions in Africa, either alone or in association with the Organization for African Unity (OAU). And the planning cell has also prepared estimates of the kinds and levels of forces that might be required for various types of operations, including crisis management and peacemaking.

- More important, the WEU has taken steps that would enhance its ability to carry out those operations which are decided upon. It may, once it agrees to undertake military operations, call upon the Forces Answerable to the WEU (FAWEUs), which at the moment include the Eurocorps, the UK-Netherlands Amphibious Force, the Multilateral (Airborne) Division of the ARRC (Allied Rapid Reaction Corps), and, in the south of Europe, two new forces organized by France, Italy, Portugal, and Spain: Eurofor and Euromarfor. And it may in time of emergency look to NATO for authorization to employ these forces, many of which are also earmarked for use by NATO, and, under the CJTF (Combined Joint Task Force) concept, for the commanders and the staffs needed if they are to be employed effectively.[5]

- Has transferred to the WEU several former Eurogroup bodies that deal with logistics, communications, and long-term studies of operational requirements and has created a Western European Armaments Group (WEAG)[6]—reflecting the fact that the EU not only proposes to frame a common defense policy but might seek to establish a common defense, to whose attainment all these measures would contribute.

- Has adopted procedures to improve coordination between the WEU and the EU by harmonizing the terms of the presidents of the two bodies, synchronizing the dates and venues of their meetings, establishing close cooperation between the Council and the secretary-general of the WEU and the Council of Ministers of the EU and its Secretariat-General, and increasing its exchanges of information with other elements of the EU, including the Commission. It has also improved coordination between the WEU and NATO by establishing similar procedures for cooperation with the NATO secretary-general, synchronization of meetings, and transparency in decisionmaking, to include regular joint meetings of the WEU Council and the North Atlantic Council, cross-participation in the meetings of some committees, exchanges of documents, and so on.[7] Moreover, to facilitate this the Secretariat of the WEU was moved to Brussels, where it is in close proximity to the headquarters of both the European Union and NATO.

What Does It All Mean?

Had a time traveler from 1986 gone forward ten years, he or she would have been amazed at the progress of the WEU in defining its place in the "architecture of Europe," in identifying its missions, in enhancing its staff capabilities, and in improving its cooperation with the EU and NATO. Indeed, these are all significant developments, for which the members of the WEU must be given due credit. However, if one looks at these accomplishments not in absolute terms but in terms of their effect on the ability of the WEU to carry out its assigned tasks, the judgment may be different. These tasks, as defined in the WEU-related text adopted at Maastricht in December 1991, are:

- To "build up WEU in stages as the defence component of the European Union," with responsibility for elaborating and implementing "decisions and actions of the Union which have defence implications."
- "To develop WEU as a means to strengthen the European pillar of the Atlantic Alliance."
- To strengthen the operational role of WEU by "examining and defining appropriate missions, structures and means."[8]

Coordinating the Work of the WEU and the EU

The problems in implementing the first task range from relatively minor ones, such as the establishment of closer working relationships between the WEU and the EU, to the all-important one of who makes decisions with respect to actions the WEU should take. One of the issues for the IGC is how to achieve the long-sought synchronization of dates and venues of meetings and harmonization of working methods; for example, while the WEU is seemingly "trying to coordinate security and defence aspects in a single institutional framework," the Council of the European Union decides, on a case-by-case basis, whether "security questions discussed in the framework of the CFSP had implications in the defence area" and whether, therefore, the WEU should be called in.[9] Moreover, while recommendations made within the WEU have a clear progression from the working group to the Permanent Council to the Council of Ministers (see Figure 6.1), that is not the case in the European Union. There the Commission (which has a director-general for external political affairs), the presidency

Figure 6.1   The Structures of Decisionmaking

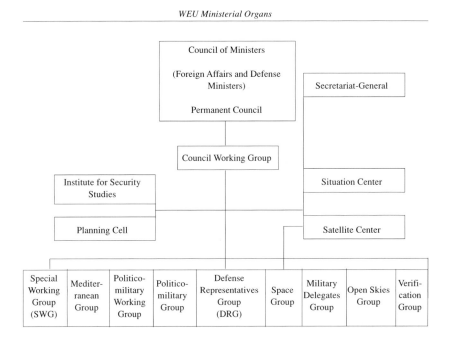

WEU Ministerial Organs

EU Council Secretariat-General

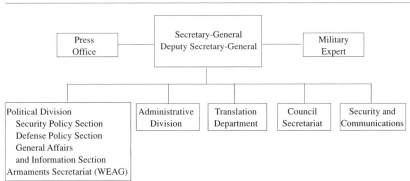

Source: Press Office, Western European Union, 23 January 1997.

of the Council of the European Union (which rotates every six months), and the Secretariat-General of the Council all are involved in drafting recommendations, which must ultimately be approved by the Council at the ministerial level, acting in accord with the principles laid down by the

European Council, which functions at the level of heads of state and government. At the moment, it is not altogether clear when and how the WEU can influence this decision process, though the CFSP working group of the Political Committee has proposed measures, such as coordinated sessions of respective bodies and joint utilization of experts, that could help—if they are ever implemented.

A more important problem is the division of responsibilities for handling crises between the European Union, which deals with the political, economic, and humanitarian aspects, and the Western European Union, which is supposed to deal with the military ones. As shown by experience in Bosnia, where the Implementation Force (IFOR) disclaimed responsibility for ensuring the safe passage of individuals throughout Bosnia guaranteed by the Dayton agreement or even for protecting the civilian police sent by the United Nations from attacks by armed mobs, such bifurcation of responsibility can hamper attainment of political objectives. What is needed, according to some of those involved, is for the Council of the European Union to establish procedures for facilitating the coordination of EU policies and programs with those of its military arm, the WEU, and for evaluating their effectiveness; these procedures should, moreover, be tested by crisis management exercises, in advance of their actual utilization.[10] Additionally, the WEU needs to improve its own decisionmaking processes, to establish clear channels of communication between the WEU Council and WEU forces in the field, and to ensure that there is a single chain of command leading from these forces to the proper authorities, whether in the field or in Brussels.[11]

Finally, at least for this part of the discussion, there is the question of who makes the decisions about the role to be played by the WEU. For one thing, the WEU and the EU not only have different memberships (with the former giving some voice to twelve states that do not belong to the latter) but different representatives from these states: The foreign ministers of the EU members sit on both the WEU Council and the Council of the European Union (more precisely, the General Council of the [Foreign] Ministers, since there are some twenty-odd functioning elements of the Council); in contrast the defense ministers and, in an advisory role, the chiefs of the defense staffs are found only in the WEU. Furthermore, while *all* members of the EU, including the four "neutrals" (Austria, Finland, Ireland, and Sweden) can vote in the EU, only the ten full members can vote in the WEU. Perhaps more important, the ultimate decisions in the EU, at least with regard to the role of the WEU, are taken by the European Council, consisting of heads of state and government, which has no counterpart in the WEU. Thus still on the table as the ICG begins its review of the Treaty on European Union are proposals ranging from the establishment of a WEU Defense and Security Council at the level of heads of state and government through variable procedures for voting on defense issues within the EU to the question whether that organization should incorporate the WEU in one form or another.

Defining the Relationship Between the WEU and the Atlantic Alliance

The second task assigned by the Maastricht Declaration is to "develop WEU as a means to strengthen the European pillar of the Atlantic Alliance," a task that requires some explanation. This directive was part of the compromise reached between "Europeanists," who saw the WEU primarily as an instrument of the EU and a means of extending European cooperation to a new field, that of defense policy, and "Atlanticists," who thought that NATO should remain the primary vehicle for consultation on and implementation of defense policies and that at most the WEU should act as a vehicle for the formulation of a "European" position. Moreover, the WEU is specifically charged with "acting in conformity with the positions taken in the Atlantic Alliance,"[12] a mandate that limits both its independence as a decisionmaking authority and its operational role.

There were essentially three ways in which the WEU could have carried out this task. One was to reshape both the political and the military structures of the Atlantic Alliance so that it became essentially bipolar. Under this scheme, the European members would formulate a common defense policy for discussion within the North Atlantic Council (NAC), organize and train the forces required to carry out their agreed missions so as to "balance" the North American contribution, and maintain among all NATO forces common procedures and as much interoperability as possible. This approach, however, was unacceptable to the United States, both because it would dilute its influence on NATO decisions and diminish its control over NATO operations and because it could result in the United States' being dragged into conflicts initiated by the European members of NATO, a danger that holds whenever those members conduct operations on their own. Moreover, the approach implied, if it did not specifically require, a redesign of European forces that would enable them to play a major role in "power projection," whether to Poland or to Kuwait, an outcome that might have delighted most Americans—but not many Europeans. As one analyst pointed out, any WEU military force will to some degree be "smoke and mirrors," since no EU member will want to build and pay for forces in addition to those already committed to NATO.[13] Thus, under present circumstances, the WEU has little to give the alliance that NATO does not already have.

A second possibility would have been to agree on a division of roles and responsibilities between WEU and NATO, which would, together with a corresponding earmarking of "separable but not separate forces," have enabled each organization to plan for, prepare for, and carry out different types of operations, in this way easing the political burden on NATO if not the military one. The WEU did, in the Petersberg Declaration of 1992, take a step in this direction by paying particular attention to "humanitarian and rescue tasks; peacekeeping tasks; and tasks of combat forces in crisis management, including peacemaking."[14] It might have been possible to make these tasks the main focus of the WEU, leaving to NATO responsibility for defense of the European continent against armed attack. This, however, was equally unacceptable in that it would have both relegated NATO to the role of a watchdog waiting for an intruder unlikely to come and hampered its efforts to broaden its role in European security and extend its relationship with nonmembers of NATO, as through the Partnership for Peace (PFP). Instead, NATO insisted on keeping its responsibility for "non–Article V operations," such as peacekeeping, a responsibility it has since reaffirmed.[15]

The final approach, the one taken, was to improve cooperation with NATO by, as noted earlier, endeavoring to synchronize the dates and venues of meetings, harmonizing working methods, and establishing closer cooperation between the two secretary-generals. Moreover, joint meetings of the two councils have been held regularly, documents developed by one organization have been exchanged with the other, joint meetings of experts have been held, and so on. (A further step, agreed upon in principle but not yet implemented, is for the WEU "to become actively involved in the Alliance's defence planning process" and for all European allies, whether members of WEU or not, to participate in WEU-led operations.[16]) For its part, NATO has pledged itself to support the development of the ESDI within the alliance, has agreed to facilitate the use by the WEU of NATO's collective assets and capabilities, and has undertaken to work out procedures for application of the CJTF concept to WEU operations. Although these latter procedures have not yet been approved, largely because of acrimonious debates over the degree of supervision and control to be exercised by NATO (for which read "the United States"), this approach could produce significant results.

Improving the WEU's Operational Capabilities

These results bear directly on satisfactory completion of the third task, that of strengthening the WEU's operational role by "examining and defining appropriate missions, structures and means." As noted earlier, building new structures within WEU was comparatively easy, but defining missions and developing means to carry them out is not. One reason for this is that while various elements of the EU, such as the CFSP working group of the Political Committee, are striving to formulate a CFSP, no document yet produced has received formal approval. Moreover, such drafts by the EU or the WEU as have seen the light of day are broad, covering everything from relations with Russia to the threat posed by organized crime, and focus more on desired outcomes than on policies designed to achieve these.[17] Nowhere in sight is a document that not only details the common interests of the members of the European Union but indicates which of these are vital (such as a defense against armed attack), which are essential (such as precluding the interruption of energy supplies transported by sea) and which (like violations of human rights) are more general in their nature and specifies the kinds of actions that should be taken if these interests are jeopardized.[18]

In one sense, this is as it should be, since security is a broader concept than defense, but it means that the WEU has been left largely on its own in defining defense policy and determining force requirements. (Granted, because all members of the EU participate in one way or another in the WEU, the latter organization has been able to proceed to develop its own version of the CFSP, but its decisions do not necessarily reflect the views of the Commission and other elements of the EU and lack the ultimate imprimatur of the European Council.) In carrying out this task, the WEU has, as is logical, begun by identifying the kind of threats to the interests of EU members that could require military action, threats such as that of an armed attack on a member state, a flare-up of ethnic rivalries in or out of Europe, and interruptions in the flow of oil. It has then gone on to note that some of these threats, such as that of a massive military confrontation, are a remote prospect, whereas others, such as ethnic conflicts, are all too likely. And it has fixed its attention on those kinds of operations where the WEU (and the EU) may be able to achieve effective results, namely, lower-level conflicts.[19] In other instances, such as that of armed attacks, it has either passed on to NATO responsibility or, as in the possible use of nuclear weapons against member states, relied on arms control measures, restrictions on the export of technology, and so on rather than opting for the introduction of ballistic missile defenses, as some have urged.

This decision to focus on lower-level conflicts, and particularly on crisis management and peacekeeping operations, reflects to some extent the level of political consensus; in fact, even the four "neutrals" have reportedly agreed that these are missions the EU could undertake.[20] Another factor, however, is that the WEU does not have the means to carry out large-scale military operations. The WEU planning cell is not really large enough to be effective, the organization has no overall military commander—and hence no subordinate ones either—and has therefore no functioning command structure, no communications net, no intelligence system. Furthermore, while most of the FAWEUs earmarked for the WEU have organic logistical support elements, the provision of food, fuel, ammunition, new equipment, and so on remains a national responsibility, and not even the UK and France have the capacity to provide these items in any quantity and at any reasonable distance. Thus while some planners would like to see the WEU provide an intervention force of 150,000 to 200,000 for Petersberg-type operations,[21] political leaders, in a rare display of realism, have concluded that WEU does not have "the assets to contemplate anything that involves a serious combat-related task" and hence should eschew large-scale operations.[22]

The WEU and the Second Maastricht

The ability of the WEU to carry out these three tasks will be affected in varying degree by the decisions reached—or not reached—at the Second Maastricht. Though it is impossible to forecast exactly what will happen in the ongoing meetings of the IGC, it is both possible and desirable to suggest some of the putative outcomes and to indicate the factors that will influence those.

As a prelude, it is necessary to note that the plates of the delegates to the IGC are heaped to overflowing with issues that are both important and complex. Among these are that of rationalizing the decisionmaking system to reduce its complexity and to enhance the commonality of procedures within the three pillars (economic and social matters, justice and internal affairs, and the CFSP); democratizing the system; and increasing its efficiency. In so doing, representatives of the member countries must also decide whether to move further toward political union (which would provide both an incentive to and a basis for the rationalization mentioned above) and if so what form the Union can take, given the differing views of the members. Moreover, it must do all this at a time when the EU is facing not only an institutional crisis but an economic one, that of high levels of unemployment and soaring costs of welfare, with severe social (and political) repercussions.

In this context, it would not be surprising if the development of a cohesive and meaningful CFSP (as distinct from the adoption of procedural reforms, as suggested by Ireland when it held the presidency of the Union in 1996) received somewhat shorter shrift than might be deemed desirable. Given the variety of interests and interest groups engaged, the division of bureaucracies into functional elements (such as foreign affairs, defense, economics, etc.) and the complexities of decisionmaking in *any* democratic country, this task would be a difficult one even for a national government. The IGC involves not one national government but fifteen, with varied geostrategic positions (Great Britain is "this blessed stone, set in the silver sea"), historical experiences, political persuasions, and national interests. In consequence, the task facing the EU is comparable to that which would have confronted the first Congress of the United States had it attempted to devise a CFSP agreeable not only to the thirteen former colonies but to the Spanish in Florida and the Louisiana Territory, the British in Canada, and the Indian tribes east of the Mississippi. In both cases, the prerequisite for a

CFSP that would give meaningful guidance on defense policy and force requirements would seem to be political union, which is only slightly more likely in Europe today than it was in North America 200 years ago.

The WEU's Operational Capabilities

In one sense, this is all to the good, since if it is to be "meaningful," any CFSP must be realistic, which in the defense field means taking account of the resources available to the countries that may be called upon to take action. Understandably, these resources have diminished with the end of the Cold War; the defense budgets of the European members of NATO have declined by more than 10 percent, the personnel in the armed forces have been reduced by more than 20 percent[23] (with more to come, as France shifts from a conscript to a volunteer army), and the procurement of equipment has dropped drastically. (To illustrate this latter point, in 1992 Britain, France, and Germany together produced only forty-eight combat aircraft, six armed helicopters, and fifteen tanks—barely enough to equip one company.[24]) The result has been not only cuts in the number of operational units (maneuver brigades, air squadrons, and naval vessels), amounting in the case of Germany to 30 percent and in that of the United Kingdom to over 40 percent, but also decreases in readiness for combat because of shortages in funds for training. Even more significant, there remain long-standing deficiencies in logistical support and in the air and sea lift required to move both troops and equipment over any distance. And to expect the countries of Europe to spend the money required to reverse these trends and to create forces capable of conducting significant military operations is both politically unreasonable and economically infeasible; even if the sums required are far less than the $107 billion per year additional for ten years estimated by the Royal United Services Institute,[25] the monies are unlikely to be forthcoming.

This means three things. For one, if the leaders of the EU accepted the argument that the Union, like any other political entity, must be able to defend itself and its member states, it would find this hard to do; even though the scale of any conceivable armed attack has fallen off drastically since the end of the Cold War, so, too, have the forces available to meet it. Thus one would expect that any preparations that the WEU makes to cope with external aggression on any scale are more likely to arise from its role as the European pillar of the Atlantic Alliance than from its responsibilities as the defense component of the European Union.

The second finding is that even the accomplishment of lesser tasks, such as those of committing the Eurocorps to intervention in another Bosnia or dispatching a task force of two divisions to deter aggression against one of the prospective EU members would place severe strains on the WEU.[26] Indeed, as the WEU Council of Ministers themselves stated,

the ability to conduct operations at the corps level will require "inter alia
. . . the use of the [Atlantic] Alliance's assets and capabilities, in particular
the successful implementation of the CJTF concept."[27] Only in smaller-
scale peacekeeping operations, at the brigade level or below, can the WEU
hope to operate on its own.

The third, if unpalatable, conclusion is that while the EU can carry out
political and economic measures aimed at implementing the CFSP, it is
utterly dependent on NATO for the conduct of most military operations.
This is true in part because the United States controls essential assets such
as air transport and satellite communications that it will make available
only through NATO. It is true also because that organization *does* have the
command structure, staff support, and communications net so desperately
needed by the WEU. Moreover, if the WEU is to train in peacetime for
operations in wartime (as all good military organizations should do), it can
do this only by "borrowing" NATO personnel and facilities. And although
NATO is willing to lend these items, the price that must be paid is, as noted
in the Berlin Communiqué of 3 June 1996, ultimate control by the Atlantic
Alliance. Thus plans for the "exercising of command elements and forces
for illustrative WEU-led operations" must be submitted *through* the
Military Committee and the NAC for review and approval.[28]

The WEU and NATO

This, coupled with other decisions taken at the ministerial meeting of the
North Atlantic Council in Berlin, suggests answers to a number of questions concerning relations between the WEU and NATO. As noted therein,
NATO may maintain "the ability to mount . . . non–Article V operations"[29]
(i.e., peacekeeping, crisis management, and contingency operations) with
the participation of all or some members of the alliance and of other
nations, such as those in the Partnership for Peace program; thus the idea of
a division of labor between NATO and the WEU is virtually ruled out.
Moreover, the North Atlantic allies are to be involved "across the command
and force structure" of NATO, which would further militate against a different role for these countries than for those in Europe.

Cooperation between NATO and the WEU, in the sense of exchanges
of information, consultations, joint meetings, and so on, is, however, to be
expanded, so that that way of strengthening the defense pillar will continue
to be practiced. What is less clear is whether a third approach, that of
reshaping the Atlantic Alliance into a bipolar organization, will be favored
or ruled out. On the one hand, the WEU *as an organization* is given direct
responsibility for defining illustrative WEU-led operations, for identifying
the forces (and headquarters elements) required for such operations, and for
preparing plans both for exercising headquarters and forces and for conducting operations, should the NAC approve implementation of these

plans. All of this suggests that members of the WEU (presumably including the associate members, some of whom also belong to NATO) are to speak with one voice in the NAC and other NATO bodies. In contrast, the ESDI (which the WEU embodies) is to be developed *within* the Atlantic Alliance, which must approve everything from the identification of forces to be made available to the WEU to plans for their training to their actual use—which NATO will continue to monitor. This clearly envisages a subordinate role for WEU.

Whether the latter will attain the status of an equal partner with the North Atlantic elements of NATO is problematical. For one thing, its mandate (to develop the capabilities required to carry out peacekeeping operations) is much more limited than that of NATO, which is also concerned with collective defense and "power projection." For another, the WEU is a supplicant for the use of NATO resources rather than a contributor, inasmuch as all the FAWEUs are also earmarked for use by NATO. For a third, there is no indication that any member of the Atlantic Alliance is pressing for a WEU that would have an equal voice with the North Americans in a revised NATO; in fact the French minister of defense has explicitly stated that his government opposes a "binary Alliance, with the European Union states on one side and the North American countries on the other."[30] Thus, the European pillar of the alliance will be both short and slender—if indeed it is to be a pillar at all, a concept the Foreign Office minister of the United Kingdom described as having been overtaken.[31]

The WEU and the EU

Although the decisions noted above may not answer fully the question of the future role of the WEU in the Atlantic Alliance, they do provide definitive indications of the limits on its relations with the EU. There is general agreement that these need to be strengthened if the EU is to achieve greater coherence in the fields of security and defense, improve its capabilities for crisis management, and arrange for effective and expeditious implementation of those issues with defense implications.[32] There is, however, little agreement as to how this should be done.

One option that has been discussed is that of reinforcing the partnership between the EU and an autonomous WEU. Essentially this would call for more of the same in terms of cooperative measures such as back-to-back meetings of senior officials and perhaps of the respective councils and their representatives, the establishment of joint task forces to conduct individual operations, the creation of coordinated and perhaps joint mechanisms for monitoring crises and planning responses to them, and so on.[33] Decisions would still be made separately within each body, perhaps on a consensus basis, perhaps on the basis of qualified majorities—with some suggesting that only full members of the WEU be able to vote in the EU on

CFSP issues with defense implications. And there are other proposals for creating a WEU summit that would meet back to back with the EU's heads of state and government, thereby reserving decisions on measures with defense implications to the highest political authorities.

Another option would be to move partway toward institutional convergence, through juridical or political commitments that would assign primary responsibility for some operations to one organization or the other. Thus the EU might be authorized to instruct the WEU to take action rather than request it to do so, and the WEU might bind itself to do this when so instructed. (Since its ten full members are also members of the EU, the WEU would in effect have accepted an assignment before receiving it.) Alternatively, the IGC might go a step further and establish legal commitments between the two bodies, spelling out the types of missions the WEU should undertake, the conditions under which EU decisions should be binding, and so on. In this case, the WEU would be subordinate to the EU operationally as well as politically.

Finally, there is the option of integrating the WEU into the EU as an end result of the process of developing an ESDI and of enabling the WEU to play an integral part in the development of the EU. Again, this could be done in a variety of ways, one of which would call for the EU's taking over the responsibility for collective defense given to the WEU by the Brussels treaty, which in any event can be denounced after 1998, and reorganizing itself to deal with both the defense and security aspects of the CFSP. Under one approach, the Council of (Foreign) Ministers of the EU could be expanded to include defense ministers, which would mean that working groups of Pillar II could have representatives from both foreign and defense ministries and perhaps from the military as well. Alternatively, a fourth pillar for defense, with its own secretary-general, its own council, and direct access to the European Council, could be set up—in which case the EU might have both a common European defense policy, to which all members would subscribe, and a protocol on collective defense that members could choose to sign if they wished. And under any one of these variants the EU itself, and not the WEU, would be the organization to establish relations with the Atlantic Alliance.

To take these in reverse order, the last is a very unlikely outcome, regardless of the form it takes. For one thing, it comes too close to the establishment of the EU as a supranational organization, which is the objective of some member states yet anathema to others. For another, it could tend either to force the "neutrals" into arrangements incompatible with their current positions (which are that they will endorse peacekeeping operations by the EU but nothing more) or to leave them outside some parts of the framework, in the latter case enabling them to enjoy the benefits of membership without incurring any obligations in the field of defense. (Indeed, given that decisions with a military defense dimension require unanimous consent, it would be possible for the neutrals to block *any* action going beyond their limited definition of "peacekeeping" unless, like Denmark, they agree not to participate in drafting such decisions and not to impede their implementation.) For a third, it would mean that associate partners of the WEU and those associate members (Iceland, Norway, and Turkey) that do not belong to the EU would be left dangling. For a fourth, while Germany and the Netherlands are supportive of integration in principle, the UK is strongly opposed, and France (which sees greater opportunities for exercising influence in a revised NATO) is ambivalent.[34] And most significant, the arrangements spelled out at the NATO meeting of 3 June 1996 (for which all ten of the full members of the WEU voted) treat the WEU as an independent actor, a status that would militate against its disappearance from the European scene.

The same problems might not arise in connection with rules that change the nature of the relationship between the EU and WEU, depending on what they are. If the EU is given the power to instruct the WEU to take action, leaving to that organization the decision on how to do so and who will do it, this is one thing—though it does mean that EU members who choose not to belong to the WEU would be able to vote for directives they would be under no obligation to support. If the EU is able to order the WEU to take specific actions, there is no need for the WEU as it now exists: These orders could be given directly to a chief of defense staff— though where he or she would get the troops needed to carry them out is another question. Even lesser changes, such as a revision of EU procedures that would give the European Parliament more of a voice in and the Commission more authority over security policy, would affect relations between the EU and WEU, whose role would be changed and whose status would be downgraded. Thus the outcome would depend on what procedural reforms are adopted by the EU, an issue with a history and a dynamism of its own.

This leaves, as the prime contender for adoption, the approach based on closer coordination between the EU and the WEC, which would then be in a position to serve as the bridge between the Union and NATO, which the British, for one, advocate.[35] Certainly more can be done here. It is, however, unlikely that even far-reaching measures, such as the establishment of the WEU summit or the setting up of joint WEU-EU task forces, can result in the development of joint policies, much less in coordinated action, unless the Common Foreign and Security Policy is marked by greater precision and specificity. And while this might be furthered by measures such as the appointment of a "single figure . . . answerable to the Council of Ministers" to represent the foreign policy of the Union to the outside world[36] (and presumably to suggest to the Council what that policy should be, though the British do not mention that), it depends largely on the willingness and the ability of the members of the EU to agree on *some-*

thing, however banal. But as Christoph Bertram reminds us, while institutions will take action only if their member governments are willing, they do make it easier for those governments to act,[37] so perhaps that will happen if this approach is taken.

Conclusions

The WEU has made significant progress since the late 1980s, particularly with respect to restructuring its internal organization and improving its procedures, but it is still far from what it could be. This is due in part to slow progress in implementing actions agreed upon earlier; for example, four years after the WEU Council called for closer working relations with the EU, the two organizations finally held their first meeting between working groups.[38] Furthermore, at the operational level analysts and officials today note the same list of deficiencies in available staff, command structure, communications, and so on that have been repeated year after year, with little change for the better and, until June 1996, little prospect for change. It is, therefore, understandable that the high-level group of experts concluded that "the inertia and impotence of the CSFP and WEU are the inward and outward reflection of a lack of capacity or will to act, particularly as regards the threat and/or use of force by the Union."[39]

The question before us is not, however, whether this harsh judgment is accurate but whether the WEU can, by virtue of decisions taken during the course of the IGC, move closer to achieving its three goals of becoming the defense component of the EU, strengthening its role as the European pillar of the Atlantic Alliance, and enhancing its capability to plan and conduct military operations. Put that way, the answer in all three areas must be no.

Why is this the case? As indicated earlier, it is improbable that the EU will seek to integrate the WEU into its framework, since this would require major adjustments in its structure and procedures, raise questions about both voting rights and responsibilities of the neutral members of the EU, and, to some, seem to edge too close to the creation of a supranational organization. Nor is it likely that the EU will seek a "convergence" with the WEU, which could require either major amendments to the Treaty of Maastricht or the adoption of new and binding agreements between the two organizations. Moreover, one cannot expect the IGC, for all the reasons given earlier, to adopt a CFSP that would both provide guidance to WEU and serve as a vehicle for the development and application of coordinated policies. The most one can look for is further measures to improve cooperation between the two organizations, perhaps accompanied by changes in the internal organization of the EU that would clarify and simplify responsibility for formulating and implementing security policy. With goodwill and hard work, these might even extend to joint decisionmaking and to the formation of a political-economic-military version of CJTFs, for employment in crises; absent that, we may have to wait another four years for a *second* meeting of the EU and WEU working groups.

Nor can we expect the IGC to do much toward strengthening the WEU as the European pillar of the Atlantic Alliance: Success here depends both on the definition of "strengthening" and on relations between NATO and the WEU. If "strengthening" means improving their ability to work together and if the Berlin Communiqué is any guide, then this is very likely to happen, though not on any scale requiring a restructuring of NATO. It will, however, happen by virtue of decisions taken by NATO, not by the IGC. But if "strengthening" means giving the WEU a more important role, which might enhance its status within NATO, this is unlikely to take place, as nothing suggests that the EU is going to authorize WEU to engage in power projection, much less grant it a mandate to develop capabilities for collective defense, in or out of the NATO framework. Thus the WEU may be further removed from becoming a pillar of the Atlantic Alliance than it was in 1991, when this objective was formalized by the WEU Council.

Finally, strengthening WEU's operational capabilities will, if it takes place at all, occur largely as a result of measures adopted by NATO, not by the IGC. The Berlin Communiqué promises help in the areas where WEU deficiencies have been pronounced: communications, intelligence, staff resources, and command structures; moreover, it offers to back up this assistance with both the training and the exercising of troops and commanders—measures that will go a long way toward filling certain gaps in the WEU's operational capabilities. The key word here is "certain," since these measures, however significant, will still leave the WEU without the transport facilities, the logistical support, and the other means of power projection that only the United States can provide. And though these may not be essential for the limited peacekeeping missions for which the WEU is now planning, they would be if the WEU takes on a larger role. Thus, somewhat ironically, the strengthening of the European pillar of the Alliance in terms of military capabilities will depend largely upon the largesse of the United States.

In short, the IGC in and of itself is unlikely to have any significant impact upon the fortunes of the WEU. In the future, as in the past, these will depend largely on the WEU's ability to make optimal use of its limited resources and to tailor its coat to fit the cloth. At the moment, the supply of cloth is limited by the decision of the EU that it does not require the defense capabilities that a "great power" should theoretically possess and is not prepared to use force to ensure the effective implementation of its foreign and security policy. Although an exception to this is made in the case of peacekeeping, it is not clear whether missions requiring sizable forces would be approved, though this may yet be put to the test in Bosnia. And while this approach may change if the United States once again seems to turn its back on Europe, if the situation on that continent takes a turn for the worse or if the European Union moves further and faster toward political integration than now seems likely, this is probably a matter for discussion in the "Third Maastricht," not the second.

Notes

The author wishes to acknowledge the comments and suggestions of Professor Michael Brenner and Gary L. Schaub Jr., Graduate School of Public and International Affairs, University of Pittsburgh; Professor Alberta Sbragia, director of the Center for European Studies, and Professor Phil Williams, director of the Ridgeway Center for International Security Studies, University of Pittsburgh; and Professor Richard Ullman, Woodrow Wilson School, Princeton University. As always, the author remains responsible for what is written here.

1. Reprinted, together with other relevant documents, in Arie Bloed and Ramses A. Wessel (ed.), *The Changing Functions of the Western European Union (WEU)* (Dordrecht: Martinus Nijhoff Publishers, 1994). This book also contains a brief history of the WEU (pp. xiii–xxx).

2. Article J.4(2) of the *Treaty on European Union* (Brussels: Office of Press and Information Services, 1993).

3. Full members of the WEU (Belgium, France, Germany, Greece, Italy, Luxembourg, the Netherlands, Portugal, Spain, and the United Kingdom) are committed to its development. They are bound by all the provisions of the Brussels treaty, including that on collective defense, are voting members of the Council of Ministers and the Permanent Council (which functions at the ambassadorial level), have representatives on all the working groups (including the newly established Political Military Group and Defense Planning Group), and have officers assigned to the planning cell, which works closely with another committee, the Chiefs of Defense Staff.

Observers, consisting of members of the EU who choose that status (Austria, Denmark, Finland, Ireland, and Sweden), are not bound by the provisions of the Brussels treaty. They may attend and, on request, be invited to speak at meetings of the WEU Council and the various working groups and may establish liaison with the planning cell. They may, with the permission of the WEU Council, designate forces for peacekeeping operations, as Austria, Finland, and Sweden did in sending a composite battalion to Mostar while they were observers.

Associate members include Iceland, Norway, and Turkey, who are members of NATO but not of the EU. They may participate fully in the meetings of the WEU Council (though they may not block a decision on which the full members agree); they attend meetings of working groups and subsidiary bodies; they may be associated with the planning cell through a permanent liaison arrangement; they may be able to participate in the implementation of decisions taken by member states and will take part on the same basis as full members in WEU military operations to which they commit forces.

Associate partners (the Czech Republic, Hungary, Poland, Slovakia, Bulgaria, Romania, Estonia, Latvia, and Lithuania) are all candidates for membership in the EU, with which six of them have treaties of association. These countries have voice but no vote in meetings of the WEU Council; may be invited to attend specific meetings of working groups, concerning whose activities they will be kept informed; may establish liaison arrangements with the planning cell; and may associate themselves with member states in decisions concerning humanitarian and rescue tasks, peacekeeping operations, and the use of combat forces in crisis management, including peacemaking. (WEU Council of Ministers, *Petersberg Declaration,* 9 June 1992, section III, part A, reprinted in Bloed and Wessel, *The Changing Functions of the WEU,* pp. 137–146; WEU Council of Ministers, *Kirchberg Declaration,* 9 May 1994, part II, in ibid., pp.191–202.)

    4. WEU Council of Ministers, *Petersberg Declaration,* section II, para. 4.

    5. Ministerial meeting of the North Atlantic Council, Berlin, 3 June 1996, *Final Communiqué* (hereafter, "Berlin Communiqué"), paras. 7 and 8.

    6. WEU Council of Ministers, *WEU Contribution to the Intergovernmental Conference of 1996,* Madrid, 14 November 1995, para. 38.

    7. Ibid., paras. 18–20, 25 and 29–32.

    8. "Declaration of the Member States of Western European Union Which Are Also Members of the European Union on the Role of WEU and its Relations with the European Union and with the Atlantic Alliance," Maastricht, 10 December 1991, paras. 2, 3, and 4.

    9. Assembly of the Western European Union, *Draft Order on a European Security Policy,* explanatory memorandum by Mr. Soell, rapporteur, n.d., p. 115.

    10. WEU Council of Ministers, *WEU Contribution,* para. 20.

    11. WEU Council of Ministers, *European Security: A Common Concept of the 27 WEU Countries,* Madrid, 14 November 1995, para. 175.

    12. Maastricht Declaration, para. 3.

    13. Jennone Walker, *Fact and Fiction About a European Security Identity and American Interests,* occasional paper (Washington, DC: Atlantic Council of the United States, n.d.), p. 10.

    14. WEU Council of Ministers, *Petersberg Declaration,* section II, para. 4.

    15. Berlin Communiqué, para. 7.

    16. Ministerial Meeting of the North Atlantic Council, NATO Headquarters, Brussels, 10 December 1996, *Final Communiqué,* para. 19.

    17. See, in this connection, WEU, *European Security,* chapter I, section I, C, on the new risks.

    18. Michel d'Oléon, in cooperation with Mathias Jopp, "The Way Ahead For European Defence Cooperation," in Laurence Martin and John Roper (eds.), *Toward a Common Defence Policy* (Paris: Institute for Security Studies of Western European Union, 1995), p. 103.

    19. WEU *European Security,* chapter I, section I, C; chapter II, para. 180.

    20. Republic of Ireland, Office of the President, *Proposed Changes to the Treaty of Maastricht,* conf. 2500/96, part A, section III, chapter 12, p. EN 94. It should, however, be noted that (1) some among the neutrals have suggested weakening the language of the Petersberg Declaration to replace the word "peacemaking" with the phrase "involving the use of military means," which could call for ambulances or water purification vehicles rather than tanks or guns; (2) there is strong opposition to introducing a universally binding mutual security guarantee, a point that will be taken up again later.

    21. *European Security Policy Towards 2000: Ways and Means to Establish Genuine Credibility,* first report, Brussels, 19 December 1994, p. 16.

    22. British foreign secretary Malcolm Rifkind, press conference following the Berlin meeting of the NAC, quoted in *Survey of Current Affairs* 26, 6 (June 1995): 226.

    23. "International Comparisons of Defence Expenditure and Military Manpower in 1985, 1993 and 1994," *The Military Balance, 1995/96* (London: International Institute for Strategic Studies, 1995), p. 264.

24. *UN Register of Conventional Arms,* quoted in Trevor Taylor, "West European Security and Defence Cooperation, Maastricht and Beyond," *International Affairs* 70, 1 (January 1994): 12.

25. Cited in *Economist,* 25 February 1995, p. 20.

26. Gert de Nooy makes this suggestion in "Capabilities," in Martin and Roper, *Toward a Common Defence Policy,* p. 39.

27. WEU Council of Ministers, *WEU Contribution,* para. 40.

28. Berlin Communiqué, para. 7. The italics are mine.

29. Ibid.

30. Charles Millon (minister of defense of France), "France and the Renewal of the Atlantic Alliance," *NATO Review* (May 1996): 16.

31. David Davis, speech to the Transatlantic Forum, Washington, 23 June 1996, excerpted in *Survey of Current Affairs* 26, 7 (July 1996): 272.

32. WEU Council of Ministers, *WEU Contribution,* para. 100.

33. Ibid., para. 56. The discussion that follows is drawn largely from paras. 56–92 of this document, though it does not go into all the details presented there.

34. For these and other national positions, see North Atlantic Assembly, *Structure and Functions; European Security and Defence Identity (ESDI) and Combined Joint Task Forces (CJTF),* draft general report, May 1995, Rafael Estrella, general rapporteur, pp. 2–10.

35. Davis, *speech.*

36. Foreign and Commonwealth Office, *The British Approach to the European Union Intergovernmental Conference 1996,* n.d., para. 41.

37. Christoph Bertram, *Europe in the Balance: Securing the Peace Won in the Cold War* (Washington, DC: Brookings Institution, 1995), p. 13.

38. WEU Council of Ministers, *Birmingham Declaration,* 7 May 1996, para. 16.

39. *European Security Policy Towards 2000,* p. 4.

7

Problems and Possibilities: The Development of the CFSP from Maastricht to the 1996 IGC

Stephanie B. Anderson

The Maastricht Treaty on European Union sought to revitalize European influence on international events by replacing European Political Cooperation with a Common Foreign and Security Policy (CFSP) that would encourage the dozen, and later fifteen, member states to speak with one voice on the world stage. EPC had been in existence since 1971 but worked mainly as a forum for discussion of foreign affairs outside the Community context. The CFSP components intensified political cooperation by implementing, under certain circumstances, a qualified majority voting system.[1] However, major loopholes in the CFSP and a lack of political will among the member states[2] have undermined EU efforts to speak with a single voice on international events.

During the Maastricht negotiations, disagreement between two factions, the "integrationists" led by France and Germany and the "Atlanticists" led by the United Kingdom, resulted in weak foreign and security policy components. The flaws became especially obvious during the crisis in what was Yugoslavia. Even after the installation of the CFSP in November 1993, the EU made little impact on the war in Bosnia. The lack of political will among EU member states was so striking during the Bosnian crisis that many European government leaders realized the weakness of the European Union as an international actor and turned to the United States for leadership in the Balkans. Even external political affairs commissioner Hans van den Broek had to admit: "This policy is in its infancy and so far has registered only partial success."[3]

The integrationist countries want to strengthen the CFSP and have put it high on the agenda for the 1996 IGC. New proposals to streamline the decisionmaking process and for Combined Joint Task Forces to strengthen the EU's military arm may well enhance the CFSP's credibility. The question is whether the reforms can rectify the structural problems found in the CFSP and whether these changes can help the EU face the challenges of enlargement, a common defense, and bringing the members states together to speak with a unitary voice.

The Development of the CFSP

Although the roots of the CFSP can be found in EC cooperation, EPC, and the resuscitation of the WEU, much of the motivation among the member states to intensify cooperation in foreign and security policy came from the EC's dismal performance in the Gulf War. The Gulf War was particularly significant in evaluating the performance of Europe's foreign policy cooperation for several reasons: (1) It was the first major crisis to take place in the post–Cold War world; (2) it occurred just before the start of the 1991 IGC; and (3) it brought to the forefront Europe's problems in influencing the course of international events. To rectify EPC's shortcomings, the member states put forth a number of reforms. The new Treaty on European Union was supposed to "render [the EU's] institutions more efficient—to ensure the unity and coherence of the union's economic, monetary and political action, *define and implement a common foreign and security policy.*"[4]

In one of the clearest cases possible of international misconduct, the Community was unable to present a united front during the Gulf War. Although the Community quickly denounced the Iraqi invasion, the three most powerful countries, Great Britain, France, and Germany pursued independent policies. The UK immediately identified itself with the United States and even went so far as to put its military units under U.S. command. France sent forces but kept command while trying in vain, as Christopher Hill put it, "to get its erstwhile Iraqi partners off the hook on which they had impaled themselves."[5] Constitutional restrictions stopped Germany from sending troops; although they helped fund the mission, they were criticized for not doing more: "How can there be a common European policy when the British and French take ground losses in Kuwait and the Germans keep themselves deliberately aloof?"[6]

After the Gulf War, the member states and the Community institutions tried to analyze why the Community had such little influence internationally. Blaming the absence of an EC military dimension for the uncoordinated effort in the Gulf, Belgium's foreign minister complained that Europe was "an economic giant, political dwarf and military worm."[7] Jacques Delors, president of the European Community, immediately after the Gulf War appealed to the member states for EC reform if the Community were to play a larger role in world affairs:

> It is true that the very first day—2 August 1990—the Community took the firm line expected of it. It confirmed the commitment of its member states

to enforce sanctions, the first line of dissuasion against aggressors. However, once it became obvious that the situation would have to be resolved by armed combat, the Community had neither the institutional machinery nor the military force which would have allowed it to act as a community. Are the Twelve prepared to learn from this experience?[8]

Having "learned" of their collective shortcomings in the political field, member states such as Belgium, Luxembourg, the Netherlands, Italy, Spain, Germany, and to a lesser extent France sought to reform European Political Cooperation. These integrationist countries supported the adoption of qualified majority voting to the proposed Common Foreign and Security Policy to streamline decisionmaking and to enable the Community to react to international events with greater speed. The Dutch endorsed "the idea of majority voting in the Council and [we]re prepared to study possibilities for the extension of majority voting to the 'new competences' and 'external relations.'"[9]

The integrationists also supported the inclusion of defense within the European Community (with the important exception of the Netherlands).[10] From the Gulf War, the French learned that its forces "possessed virtually no independent intelligence or airlift capacity and were compelled to rely on U.S. support."[11] Therefore, in French eyes, Europe needed an EC or WEU rapid deployment force with logistical support independent from that of NATO and the United States. Similarly, the Italians supported the incorporation of the Western European Union directly into the Community: "The proposal to transfer to the Union the competencies presently being exercised by WEU would in this respect only be a logical consequence of the decision to realize a qualitative improvement in the process of European integration."[12]

Atlanticists, such as Great Britain, Portugal, and Denmark (and the Netherlands on the issue of defense), opposed using qualified majority votes in foreign and security policy and the inclusion of defense in the Community. They believed these measures would compromise the sovereignty of the member states and undermine the Atlantic Alliance. In 1990 Douglas Hurd, the British foreign minister, proposed strengthening the WEU but warned of the "certain danger" in duplicating NATO's functions.[13]

As a result of the disagreements between the integrationists and the Atlanticists, the CFSP provisions were based on lowest-common-denominator agreements and were weak. For example, the member states were evenly split over whether to take CFSP decisions by qualified majority vote. Of the big three members, France and Germany supported QMV, although France supported it to a lesser degree than Germany; the UK opposed it. As a result, the provisions say the minimum: The Council can decide at any time to vote on whatever matters by a qualified majority; however, to put matters up to a majority vote, a consensus is required, thereby giving each country a veto. Furthermore, if any subject is too sensitive, any state can require that decisions be made by consensus.[14]

On the inclusion of defense, France and Germany supported it; the UK opposed. Overall, seven countries (Belgium, France, Germany, Greece, Italy, Luxembourg, and Spain) were for the inclusion; five were against. Vague language was the solution providing the minimum for both sides. The French and the Germans got a statement calling the WEU an "integral part of the development of the Union,"[15] implying that the WEU was to act as the EU's defense arm. The British were able to incorporate another statement seemingly delaying the inclusion of defense indefinitely: "The common foreign and security policy shall include all questions related to the security of the Union, including the eventual framing of a common defense policy, which *might* in time lead to a common defense."[16] In this way, both sides were satisfied by doing the bare minimum.

EPC Versus CFSP: Same Bottle, Different Label?

According to one official, "The CFSP is not just changing the label on the bottle," but since the installation of the CFSP in November 1993, European involvement on the world stage has not changed greatly. The first five tasks undertaken by the CFSP—"support for the Middle East peace process, the Balladur stability pact, efforts to end war in former Yugoslavia, help in monitoring elections in Russia and South Africa—were picked for convenience and topicality."[17] As mentioned earlier, the Yugoslav crisis highlighted the shortcomings of the European Community in influencing international events.

When the Yugoslav crisis first broke out in June 1991 during the height of the CFSP negotiations, the Europeans seized the opportunity to show off the EC's new international stature. Jacques Poos, Luxembourg's foreign minister representing the Council presidency, declared: "It is the hour of Europe, not the hour of the Americans."[18] However, the inability of the member states to act in unison in Yugoslavia or even to come to a common position on recognition of the Yugoslav republics stymied European foreign policy and seemed to make a mockery of the commitments under discussion in Maastricht.

The inadequacy of the CFSP components became apparent when their installation made no difference in EC policy toward the Bosnian crisis. *El Pais* reported: "The EU Common Foreign and Security Policy has been in existence on paper for 100 days. In that time, the only action taken has been the sending of observers to the Russian elections, with the situation in Bosnia being seen as a glaring example of EU inaction."[19]

After the mortar attack in Sarajevo, Bosnia-Herzegovina, the European press strongly criticized the EU. The right-wing *Le Quotidien de Paris* headlined its account of the EU meeting "Bosnia: Not Even an Ultimatum!" The left-wing *Libération* agreed, stating the twelve EU states were "incapable of imposing an ultimatum on the Serbs."[20]

Individually, France and Britain have contributed respectively 6,800 and 3,400 troops to the United Nations peacekeeping mission in the Balkans.[21] That two of the most prominent EC member states could not lead the Community to a common position on the Balkans indicates significant problems of structure and political will.

Financing the CFSP

Another debilitating problem for the CFSP was the question of how it should be financed. Although the states agreed upon the need for a Common Foreign and Security Policy, there was no consensus on how to pay for it. As a result, while the Western European Union was to "be developed as the defense component of the European Union,"[22] it did not have enough money for "paper clips."[23] Alfred Cahen, former secretary-general of the WEU, frustrated with the lack of funds, said, "If the Europeans want this, they'll have to pay."[24]

At a time of reduced threat, justifying huge defense expenditures is difficult for any government. The end of the Cold War promised peace dividends to be spent on welfare, not warfare. Thus the CFSP and the fledgling defense identity through the WEU have suffered for lack of funds. No money was allotted to the CFSP in the 1994 EU budget. Planned moves to send observers to Russia and South Africa to monitor elections in December 1993 and April 1994 had no funding allocated. As a temporary compromise, the Commission chose to transfer money from the external actions section of the 1994 budget as necessary.[25]

Discussions have been under way since 1994 regarding whether CFSP funds should come from the individual states or the EU common fund. The dilemma is not easily solved for two reasons: The EU does not know how much money it will need for CFSP, and the EU is not yet sure where the money should come from. According to one EU diplomat, the problem is serious: "The point is that the costs will grow as the list of our actions grows and we lack a framework for funding. . . . We need to find a solution to this quickly."[26]

In general, the member states prefer not to foot the bill for the CFSP. As one EU diplomat put it, "The member states want to keep a firm grip on foreign policy but, if possible, they would rather not pay for it."[27] At the same time, the member states are reluctant to let the common budget fund the CFSP for several reasons: It is already overtaxed, it would give the Commission a larger role in the execution of the CFSP, and it would give the European Parliament a say in the CFSP although the Maastricht Treaty makes no mention of the EP in this field. Since the European Parliament has the final word on the Union's budget, allowing the common budget to fund the operational expenditures would give the Parliament undue influence over the CFSP.

Ultimately, there were three different proposals:

- Paying for CFSP actions with the Union budget and having the Council Secretariat administer it. Britain and France argue that operations should be administered by the Council because it is the member states acting together who make the decision.
- Paying for CFSP actions with the Union and having the Commission administer it. This is what is the majority favor on the grounds that the Commission already has the expertise and staff.
- Paying for CFSP through national contributions, laying down a set percentage for each country. Britain is said to be most in favor of this system. The issue of who would administer is the same as in the first two options.[28]

Agreement on this topic proved so difficult that after five months of discussion, the Council chose to drop the issue. According to one diplomat, "We may talk about it but it's just not ripe for a decision, so we will probably need to continue work at a lower level."[29] As late as October 1994, even the European Parliament could not decide what stand to take on the issue.[30] As of June 1996, the member states had generally agreed that the Community budget should in principle fund operational expenditures but that under certain conditions the Council would have the final word.[31]

Changes in Attitudes Toward the CFSP

In anticipation of the second IGC, Jacques Santer, the new European Commission president, highlighted the need to reform the CFSP:

> The instability of the continent of Europe is glaringly obvious: military and social conflicts, conflicts of identity and culture, environmental problems, the growth of organized crime networks—all these are compelling reasons why we should move further forwards towards defining a common security and defense model—a model which works and has credibility.[32]

The opportunity for making real progress in the 1996–1997 IGC exists. Changes in attitude among the some of the key players (specifically, the United States, Great Britain, and France) mean that consensus should be easier to achieve. Furthermore, the additions of different military arrangements shared between NATO and the Europeans have belayed concerns over how a European defense identity and the Atlantic Alliance would function together.

President Bill Clinton of the United States has been more supportive of a European defense identity than his predecessor, George Bush. Under Bush's presidency, the ambassador to the EC, James Dobbins, sent a démarche to the different EC member states warning them not to undermine NATO. To quote Ambassador Dobbins, "Europe was proceeding precipitously without adequate consideration of the relationship between the WEU, the EC and NATO and of their interrelated functions."[33] In contrast, Clinton has welcomed European defense cooperation. Robert Hunter, his ambassador to NATO, explained:

> The cold-war argument that the alliance needed centralised military direction, and that a robust WEU could interfere, no longer applies. We support the WEU as a means of preventing the renationalisation of defense. The WEU will help to focus minds on security, and thus aid the EU's attempts at common foreign and security policies; and it will, like NATO, provide a home for the Germans. Furthermore, the more the European allies help themselves, the more Congress is likely to pay for transatlantic defense.[34]

This change in U.S. attitude helps to reassure the Atlanticists that the United States will not perceive European efforts to strengthen their defense identity as attempts to undermine NATO.

The British have also changed their attitudes toward the United States, the French, and European defense cooperation. First, the change in the U.S. attitude has made the British less suspicious of a European defense identity. At the same time, the Yugoslav crisis led to disagreements with the Americans over policy in the Balkans and closer military and political cooperation with the French. Although the United States took an active role in making policy toward Yugoslavia, it refused to send troops. In the words of one British diplomat, "I feel like saying to the Americans, Why don't you put your troops where your bloody mouth is?"[35] The U.S. withdrawal of ships participating in the arms embargo in the Adriatic further antagonized the UK.[36] From Yugoslavia, the British learned that they could not depend on the Americans to involve themselves in conflicts in Europe; the Europeans needed their own independent military capacity. In the words of Lord Owen,

> I don't think we can go on relying on America . . . having quite the same commitment to European defense. I think the lesson of that is that the Western European Union (WEU), an inter-governmental defence organisation, European-based, will have to be strengthened. I think Britain is going to play a much wider and deeper role in the WEU, and in European defense within NATO in a broad sense, than they've ever done before.[37]

In contrast, French and British cooperation bloomed under the Yugoslav crisis. As the two major countries that sent ground troops to former Yugoslavia, France and Britain worked closely together. The two member states have come to a new understanding on defense. The British have come to believe that there are times when the Europeans will need an independent defense force, and the French have taken a less antagonistic view of NATO. In January 1993 the French agreed to put the Eurocorps under NATO command if Article 5 of the Washington treaty were invoked,[38] and it reintegrated its military into NATO at the end of 1995. In November 1994 the UK and France unveiled a new joint airborne command with a permanent headquarters and multinational staff that may be more significant than the Eurocorps. The joint air command will create units for use by the Western European Union.[39] The French and the British seem to agree on almost all issues regarding a European defense identity but one. Jean-Marie Guehenno, France's ambassador in the WEU, explained: "We say that these steps are to promote the political goal of European Union; but the British will not say that."[40]

In addition, since 1991 many of the proposed structures and military arrangements that would operate under the WEU have been spelled out, alleviating concerns as to how the WEU would operate, especially with regard to NATO. The Petersberg Declaration of 19 June 1992 defined the mandate of the WEU, stating that it would be used in humanitarian and rescue tasks, peacekeeping tasks, and crisis management, including peacemaking. In the Kirchberg Declaration of May 1994, the WEU reached an agreement as to which multinational arrangements would be FAWEUs to perform the aforementioned Petersberg tasks.

The Eurocorps is one of the most important tools the WEU has at its disposal. The French, along with the Germans, in October 1991 proposed upgrading the joint Franco-German brigade to that of a Eurocorps that could become the nucleus of a European army. Originally the 4,200-man Franco-German brigade, established in 1988, was simply a symbolic expression of Franco-German cooperation. Today any EC country can participate in the Eurocorps. At first the Eurocorps was not supposed to be answerable to any security organization, including NATO and the WEU. Later, in January 1993, the French placed the Eurocorps at the disposal of the Atlantic Alliance and the WEU if needed in a crisis. The Eurocorps, with its 50,000 German, French, Spanish, Luxembourg, and Belgian troops headquartered in Strasbourg, France, was made operational in December 1995.

Another major advance in defining the relationship between NATO and an independent European defense force was the creation of the Combined Joint Task Forces, agreed upon in January 1994. Both the Gulf War and the Yugoslav crisis demonstrated that the Europeans were lost without NATO (read "U.S.") military command, control, and communications (C^3) infrastructure and without access to NATO intelligence support.[41] The CJTF would make NATO's infrastructure separable for use by the European allies so that ad hoc units and equipment could be made available when the North American (again, read "U.S.") contingent would either be unwilling or unable to take part.

Other forces that would be at the WEU's disposal if need be are the UK-Netherlands Amphibious Force and the recently established Eurofor and Euromarfor. In 1995 France, Spain, Italy, and Portugal established a joint land force known as Eurofor, an infantry and light artillery force based in Florence, and a naval force called Euromarfor led by a French aircraft carrier. At UK insistence, a provision was added that these new forces will also be at the disposal of NATO if need be.[42]

These changes in attitude of the Americans, British, and French have facilitated NATO-EU cooperation and helped in closing the gap on security and defense policy between the member states within the European Union.

IGC 1996—Reforming the CFSP

Although there was a partial rapprochement between the Atlanticists and the integrationists between 1991 and 1996, especially between the French and British, there still exist differences of opinion on the same two questions: qualified majority voting and the inclusion of defense, that is, the exact relationship between the WEU and the EU. In addition, in the 1996 IGC the three new neutral member states, Sweden, Austria, and Finland, are also participating. When they joined in January 1995, they agreed to accept all the *acquis communautaire*. Nevertheless, none of these countries belong to the WEU, and they have proved difficult to pin down on the issue of defense.

Italy's Silvio Fagiolo, chairman of a group of EU foreign ministers' representatives who have met weekly to negotiate changes to the EU's treaties in the 1996 IGC, has said that "the vast majority of countries recognise the need to [find ways] that will allow us to avoid the limitations of unanimity."[43] Only two countries oppose qualified majority voting— Greece and Britain. Greece refuses to give up its veto because of problems in its relations with Turkey.[44] Britain likewise sees no need for the member states to make decisions by qualified majority vote. In the words of Douglas Hurd, "The key to successful and coherent foreign policy cooperation is persuading your partners of the force of your arguments, not resorting to the procedural means of a vote to overrule their point of view."[45]

Commissioner Hans van den Broek, the former Dutch foreign minister, argues that it is the absence of qualified majority voting that paralyzes the Union:

Unfortunately, the CFSP's basic device, the "common action," has proved to be fundamentally flawed. It requires unanimous agreement by the fifteen and so is subject, at best, to the rule of the lowest common denominator and, at worst, to the national veto. . . . Unanimity is a recipe for paralysis and the continued predominance of national interests. The situation is hard enough with fifteen member states but imagine what it would be with twenty-five or thirty. The challenge is to find a formula which will facilitate decision-making and moreover ensure a genuinely Union approach. This can only be achieved, in my view, by basing decision-making in principle on qualified majority votes.[46]

As of June 1996, possible solutions under consideration ranged from the use of a reinforced majority formula to facilitate the usage of QMV to the explicit recognition in the Treaty of a member state's prerogative to oppose majority voting when an essential interest is at stake. The member states have also discussed allowing "national interest" to be invoked only at the level of the European Council. Another possibility is changing procedure for deciding when decisions are taken by QMV: If a member state calls for a decision normally decided by majority vote to be decided by unanimity, then the request may be rejected by qualified majority vote.[47]

The member states have also promised to reform the WEU during the 1996 IGC. Van den Broek has said:

I agree with the suggestion that the IGC should take an evolutionary approach in the defense area, and that it should spell out the subsequent steps to be taken. In a first phase, the so called "Petersberg tasks" could be incorporated in the EU Treaty, making them tasks for the CFSP. These tasks include humanitarian and rescue missions, crisis management, peace keeping and, indeed, peace enforcement. The EU would then establish the policy framework while the WEU would acquire an enhanced operational capability to implement those policies. The development of a European armaments policy would also be included in the first phase. This would lead in time to a second phase in which the EU and the WEU would be merged. Membership in this merged Union would logically prepare the way for membership in NATO, because of overlapping mutual defense obligations.[48]

Although it is in its embryonic stage, the Europeans have great expectations for their new offspring. The WEU has already investigated becoming Europe's antiballistic missile system coordinator, creating a Standing Baltic Sea Force to monitor the Baltic, and perhaps even controlling a European nuclear policy.[49]

On defense, van den Broek believes that "if Europe is to become a real political union, and an equal partner of the United States, it needs a convincing security and defense identity."[50] Britain supports multinational cooperation but is against the formation of a European army, navy, or air force.[51] A possible solution that might be acceptable to all, including the new neutrals, is the formation of a fourth pillar for defense, added to the temple structure of the Union. Encased in its own pillar, defense would not be under the jurisdiction of Community procedures and institutions (one pillar) and would be separate from the EU's foreign and security policy procedures (another pillar). In this way, those countries that wanted to preserve their neutrality (Ireland, Sweden, Austria, and Finland) could still participate in the CFSP without having to participate in defense cooperation.[52]

Challenges for the CFSP

"Officially, nothing important happened in Dublin as regards the Intergovernmental Conference on the review of the Maastricht Treaty."[53] As of December 1996, the draft treaty negotiated during the 1996 IGC is only the basis for further discussions. French foreign minister Hervé de Charette called work done in the IGC mediocre.[54] If the CFSP is to be successful, the EU needs to face many challenges including disputes over structure, enlargement, defense.

Structural Challenges

As the Gulf and Yugoslav crises demonstrated, the European Union needs a strong decisionmaking mechanism to yoke the member states in place and to present the world with a single voice when confronting international events. It also needs more resources to back up militarily, if need be, whatever diplomatic initiatives the Union undertakes. The CFSP structure formulated in 1991 does not adequately address these problems. Five years later, in September 1996, a common position on the U.S. raids on Iraq was stymied because of France's opposition. In a case where it was "one against fourteen," Santer took the opportunity to point out how the CFSP structure needed reform if the EU were to avoid a recurrence of this type of situation.[55]

As during the Maastricht negotiations, disputes involving the UK, France, and Germany have stalled proceedings. Major disagreements over structure in the 1996 IGC included institutional reform and the adoption of a "flexibility clause" that would allow those member states inclined to participate in certain projects to do so without prejudice to those who refused. In terms of institutional reform, Germany wants to integrate the CFSP more closely into the supranational framework of the Union, giving the Commission a more prominent role in its operations. Both France and the UK are determined to keep foreign and security policy strictly intergovernmental.[56] John Major opposed the "flexibility clause" on the grounds that the wrong type of flexibility "could blow the Union apart."[57] As in other issues, a Labor victory and Tony Blair as prime minister could alter some final decisions from Amsterdam.

A stronger structure may not be the answer. Ferdinando Riccardi, editor of *Agence Europe,* argued that "until the Fifteen share the same views on concrete issues and external relations, there will be no common foreign policy and the establishment of rigid institutional rules will not only prove useless but might even be counterproductive."[58] In any case, without consensus on institutional reform, French president Jacques Chirac warned that the EU would not be able to accept new members from Eastern and Central Europe.[59]

Enlargement

A further challenge to the CFSP is enlargement. Many of the Central and Eastern European countries have announced their intention to apply for membership, and through the European agreements the EU has already strengthened relations with many of these countries. The closest relations are with the Visegrád countries, the Czech Republic, Poland, and Hungary. Considering the difficulty of finding consensus among fifteen member states, any institutional reform must face the question of whether the CFSP would be able to function with even more members. Even after institutional questions are resolved, the issue remains which countries should be allowed in and at what time. In addition, before these countries can join, their status with NATO must be resolved vis-à-vis the United States and Russia.

Defense

France and Germany have great expectations for a European defense policy that may well include a nuclear component. They have also assured U.S. officials that any joint nuclear policy would take place within the NATO framework.[60] If so, relations among NATO, the EU, and the WEU must be made very clear, as must be the status of the neutrals. Although in July 1996 the neutrals (Ireland, Sweden, Finland, and Austria) said that they would support the inclusion of peacekeeping, armed humanitarian actions, and crisis management in a revision of the Maastricht Treaty, there is strong domestic resistance to Austria's joining NATO, and no reason to believe the other countries would join.[61]

Living Up to the Spirit of the CFSP

Perhaps the greatest challenge the CFSP faces is how to reconcile fifteen different national interests and positions into a common Union policy.

During the 1991 IGC, when consensus was elusive, the solution was vague language and lowest common denominator agreements; more detailed plans would emerge from the next conference. Again, in the 1996 IGC, certain issues, especially structural reform, the budget, and the inclusion of defense, have proven contentious. However, the member states' leaders will have to come to an agreement so as not to go home empty-handed and to save face for the Union. If no progress can be made on these issues, the leaders may well choose additional minimalist solutions and vague language to smooth over the cracks until a real decision can be made sometime in the future.

Notes

1. Based on general guidelines established by the European Council, the Council of Ministers defines and implements the Common Foreign and Security Policy. Consensus remains the norm, but if the Council unanimously designates an issue area subject to joint action, then the implementation of joint actions can be determined by QMV. As it stands, if a country that had been in the minority were forced into adopting a policy through qualified majority voting, the country could take any measure to fulfill the objective, or even no action, if it so chose, as long as it did not act to undermine the agreed upon objective. Thus the CFSP would afford the member states both the unity on the world stage they had been seeking and considerable leeway in making foreign and security policy.

2. France, Germany, Italy, Belgium, the Netherlands, Luxembourg, Great Britain, Ireland, Denmark, Greece, Spain, and Portugal were the twelve member states at the time of the Maastricht treaty negotiations. In 1995, Finland, Austria, and Sweden joined. The coming into force of the Maastricht Treaty changed the European Community to the European Union, but only the EC retains legal personality. I use "EC" and "EU" interchangeably.

3. Stephen Nisbet, "Commission Looks for Better Days on CFSP," *Reuters,* 17 June 1994.

4. Kohl-Mitterrand Letter to the Irish Presidency, 19 April 1990, emphasis in the original, *Agence Europe,* 20 April 1990.

5. Christopher Hill, "EPC's Performance in Crises," in Reinhardt Rummerl (ed.), *Toward Political Union: Planning a Common Foreign and Security Policy in the European Union* (Boulder: Westview, 1992), 144.

6. François Heisbourg, quoted in Scott Anderson, "Western Europe and the Gulf War," in Rummel, *Toward Political Union,* 158. Extreme criticism over their refusal to send troops sparked a constitutional debate in Germany over whether to change existing policy.

7. Ibid., 147.

8. Delors, "European Integration and Security," *Survival* 102 (March–April 1991); emphasis added.

9. Text of the Letter Addressed to Mr. Giulio Andreotti by Ruud Lubbers, in F. Laursen and S. Vanhoonacker (eds.), *The Intergovernmental Conference on Political Union: Institutional Reforms, New Policies, and International Identity of the European Community* (Maastricht: European Institute of Public Administration, 1992), 315.

10. The Netherlands have always been a strong integrationist country and sup-

ported moves to strengthen the European Community. However, the Dutch have also always been ardent supporters of NATO and did not want the EC to compete with NATO by taking on traditional security affairs.

11. *Agence Europe,* 30 January 1991.

12. "Italian Proposal on Common Foreign and Security Policy, 18 September 1990," in Laursen and Vanhoonacker, *The Intergovernmental Conference,* 292.

13. *Agence Europe,* 16 October 1991.

14. Maastricht Treaty, Articles J.3 and J.4. Even if the states do decide matters by a QMV, Article J.3 provides escape clauses including special provisions for when a "change of circumstances arises which has a substantial effect on a question subject to joint action" or if "major difficulties in implementing a joint action" arise. In addition, if "imperative need[s]" occur, article J.3(6) allows individual member states to follow independent courses of action. Also, QMV does not apply to matters with "defence implications."

15. Maastricht Treaty, Article J.4(2).

16. Maastricht Treaty, Article J.4(1). Emphasis is my own.

17. Nisbet, "Commission Looks for Better Days."

18. *Financial Times,* 1 July 1991.

19. From *El Pais,* 7 February 1994, p. 2, as reported by *Reuters,* 7 February 1994.

20. *Reuters,* 8 February 1994.

21. *United Press International* (UPI), 9 March 1994, and *Reuters,* 10 March 1994.

22. Treaty on Political Union, Annex V, "Declaration of the Member States of Western European Union Which Are Also Members of the European Union on the Role of WEU and Its Relations with the European Union and with the Atlantic Alliance," para. 2. All the members of the European Community are members of the WEU with the exception of Denmark, Sweden, Austria, Finland, and Ireland, which have observer status.

23. Interview with WEU official, Brussels, 8 April 1993.

24. Alfred Cahen, former secretary-general of the WEU, Paris, 28 April 1993.

25. "Commission Proposes Budget Compromise for CFSP Funding," *Reuters,* 19 January 1994.

26. Nicholas Doughty, "EU Faces Dilemma over how to Pay for CFSP," *Reuters,* 12 January 1994.

27. Ibid.

28. "Council May Not Discuss CFSP Funding," *Reuters,* 11 May 1994.

29. Ibid.

30. "The Common Foreign and Security Policy" (A4-28/94-Willockx), European Parliament Session News Press Release, document date 25 October 1994.

31. *Agence Europe,* 18 June 1996.

32. Jacques Santer, "The European Union's Security and Defense Policy: How to Avoid Missing the 1996 Rendez-vous," *NATO Review* 43 (November 1995): 4.

33. Interview, Ambassador James Dobbins, U.S. Mission to the European Communities, Brussels, 25 March 1993.

34. *Economist,* 25 February 1995.

35. Ibid.

36. Ibid.

37. *Independent,* 14 November 1994.

38. Also known as the North Atlantic Treaty. Article 5 outlines the procedures for collective defense in the case of an armed attack.

39. *Independent,* 1 November 1994.

40. When those words were relayed to a British diplomat, he exclaimed: "We can't say it because of the *Daily Mail*." The *Daily Mail* is an influential, Conservative-leaning British newspaper. *Economist,* 25 February 1995.

41. Assembly of the WEU, WEU Planning Cell, WEU Document 1421, Paris, May 1994, in Patricia Chilton, "Common, Collective or Combined Defense as the Path to European Security Integration," paper presented at the European Community Studies Association Conference, 11–14 May 1995, Charleston, South Carolina, 19.

42. *Financial Times,* 2 June 1995.

43. Jeremy Gaunt, "EU Anxiously Seeks Stronger Foreign Policy Voice," *Reuters,* 8 May 1996.

44. Ibid.

45. Douglas Hurd, "Developing the Common Foreign and Security Policy," *International Affairs* 70 (1994): 422.

46. European Commission Press Release, Speech/95/215, document date 19 October 1995, Hans van den Broek, "The Common Foreign and Security Policy: The Challenges of the Future," Europees Instituut voor Bestuurskunde, Maastricht, 19 October 1995.

47. *Agence Europe,* 19 June 1996.

48. Van den Broek, "The Common Foreign and Security Policy."

49. Craig Covault, "WEU Seeks European Missile Defense Plan," *Aviation Week and Space Technology,* 18 January 1993, p. 25; "WEU Urges New Baltic Sea Force," *Reuters,* 5 December 1995; William J. Kole, "Western Europe—Defense (Common Nuclear Force?)," *Associated Press,* October 1995.

50. Van den Broek, "The Common Foreign and Security Policy."

51. *Independent,* 1 November 1994.

52. Ibid., 21 November 1994.

53. Ferdinando Riccardi, *Agence Europe,* 17 December 1996.

54. Charette said the "Irish paper accurately reflected the 'mediocrity' of the work of the IGC." *Irish Times,* 14 December 1996.

55. *Agence Europe,* 10 September 1996.

56. *Irish Times,* 18 September 1996.

57. Ibid., 14 December 1996.

58. *Agence Europe,* 25 July 1996.

59. Ibid.

60. *New York Times,* 25 January 1997.

61. *Financial Times,* 23 July 1996. According to a poll, 60 percent of Austrians would vote against NATO membership in a referendum. *Financial Times,* 6 August 1996.

8

What's Wrong with the CFSP? The Politics of Institutional Reform

Michael E. Smith

In November 1993, after a difficult ratification process, the Maastricht Treaty on European Union finally entered into force. Among its most notable innovations was the replacement of European Political Cooperation with a Common Foreign and Security Policy. This new mechanism was heralded as an improvement over EPC, which for years was little more than a secretive "gentlemen's club" in the view of those who took part in it. The CFSP was made part of the European Union's single institutional framework, its administrative structure in Brussels was strengthened and linked to that of the European Community, and its decisionmaking procedures permitted qualified majority voting under certain conditions. EC-level actors such as the Commission and the European Parliament saw their roles in the CFSP formalized and legitimized, while defense matters were finally included in the CFSP after years as a taboo subject under EPC.

Yet the CFSP has been a serious disappointment, if not a dismal failure, in the view of its practitioners, informed observers, and even EU citizens.[1] CFSP actions have been more modest than anticipated,[2] and many of these had to be haphazardly improvised, as most of the details on the CFSP were ambiguous or unspecified by the TEU. Majority voting for the CFSP has not been successfully attempted, and delays have plagued the implementation or funding of joint actions. The Commission has been attacked by some when it exercises its right of initiative in the CFSP and criticized by others for not asserting itself more. States seem to decide at whim the extent to which the European Parliament should be involved in the CFSP, and they have paralyzed the system in some cases (Greece over Macedonia and Turkey) or circumvented it in others (France in Rwanda and the Middle East). In the former Yugoslavia, the supreme test of the new CFSP according to some critics, the EU toiled for years only to see the fruits of its groundwork harvested by the United States with the Dayton accords. Similarly, in the Middle East, the United States and Norway claimed credit for peacemaking in the region despite two decades of patient work by the EC under the Euro-Arab Dialogue.

Why has the transition from EPC to the CFSP been so difficult? A number of reasons for the CFSP's difficulties could be mentioned: a severe shortage of political will, a more complex post–Cold War international environment, the fact that expectations for the CFSP (and for the TEU as well) were raised too high by officials eager to ratify Maastricht, the normal "breaking-in" period required of new procedures, and a preoccupation with other internal and external issues.[3] These problems are complicated by the different cultures, histories, and foreign policy traditions of fifteen member states. However, there is an astonishingly high degree of consensus among EU elites that much of the problem is due to the institutional design of the system itself. Indeed, compared to another TEU goal, Economic and Monetary Union, the CFSP can hardly be considered a robust mechanism: It lacks a clearly defined objective, measurement criteria to achieve it, a timetable for institutional change, sanctions for defectors, and a central bureaucracy with a firm mandate for its operations.

Thus, this chapter shows the extent to which institutional characteristics weaken the CFSP as a mechanism for making the EU a more potent global actor, and it examines the potential for institutional reform at the 1996–1997 IGC of the EU. Rather than focus on a particular policy outcome, I analyze the CFSP as a policy process involving procedures developed under EPC and, increasingly, EC actors. In general, the Title V provisions on the CFSP emulated the EPC tradition: incremental change based on habits and informal norms. However, the TEU effectively rekindled the decades-old debate between intergovernmental and supranational visions of political cooperation. This controversy is a result of the new potential for more involvement of EC actors in the CFSP, the greater binding nature of the CFSP as compared to EPC, and the deliberate inclusion of difficult issues (namely, security and defense) in the CFSP.[4]

More specifically, the Commission and the EP cannot be kept at arm's length as they were under EPC, while the stature of the Committee of Permanent Representatives was also raised after the TEU was ratified. However, the Treaty did not specify in great detail what roles these institutions should play in the CFSP because such cooperation was still a difficult subject for several member states. Hence the division of labor among and within EC institutions became highly contentious issues after the CFSP was implemented. Since the wording of Title V was imprecise on a number of issues, states increasingly feared that any new procedures would set precedents for the CFSP that could limit their options later or would empower EC actors to a greater degree than they desired. The result has been much confusion when actors attempt to utilize the CFSP system, whose decision-making rules still set it apart from the EC's supranational procedures that have developed over several decades. Moreover, with its weak or unspecified CFSP provisions, the TEU inadvertently encouraged EC actors to change their administrative structures and working habits in ways that now complicate the EU's external political relations.

Since the CFSP is based upon a dual structure—that of EPC and the EC's own institutions—the analysis here requires a sensitivity to both inter-governmental and supranational-institutional theoretical perspectives. Like EPC before it, the CFSP clearly is far from supranational because of the limited involvement of the Commission and the EP, the formal exclusion of the European Court of Justice, and the ability of member states to block qualified majority voting in Council (Article J.3[2]). Governments still dominate the process of setting broad guidelines for the CFSP (and the EU) at the European Council level. But neither is the CFSP as intergovernmental as its EPC legacy might lead one to believe: EC actors do play important roles in the policy process, governments alone do not control all options, and a more complex and binding set of norms than those outlined in the TEU affects state behavior under the CFSP. Particularly where CFSP joint actions involve EC competencies (such as the imposition of economic sanctions), governments must exhibit a respect for EC actors and procedures. Also, the innovative transgovernmental network developed earlier under EPC, which links foreign ministries and the Commission, is still in place, allowing the involvement of foreign policy bureaucrats in national capitals and in Brussels, sometimes to the irritation of governments.[5]

While it would be naive to argue that a mere change in rules could have enabled the EU easily to resolve situations as complex as Bosnia, it is also true that decisionmaking mechanisms can improve or discourage the prospects for common action. They have a conditioning effect on policy outcomes and state interests, even when they are as loosely articulated as in the CFSP system. Here institutional structures are important for fielding proposals, choosing options, supplying resources for the CFSP (particularly those of the EC), and implementing CFSP actions or representing the CFSP abroad. Further, CFSP insiders consistently stress the value of habitual processes of socialization, building trust, and the adoption of pragmatic working habits in a decentralized system with no real compliance mechanisms. Indeed, they now complain that the informal, clublike EPC atmosphere has been changed in two ways. First, several developments brought a number of new officials into the CFSP who are still being socialized to the system: the 1995 enlargement, the confused mergers of EC and EPC working groups, and the increased involvement of (and changes within) COREPER and the Commission with regard to the CFSP. Second and perhaps more important, the CFSP policy process is far more formal, legal, and bureaucratized than EPC ever was, and officials fear being locked into rigid rule systems.[6]

As I discuss in this chapter, the change of policymaking style from EPC to the CFSP, the CFSP's weak institutional structure (compared to other EC policy areas), and the heightened sensitivity of states to legal precedents make CFSP decisionmaking a far more demanding and combative process than that of EPC. With these difficulties, the 1996–1997 IGC reform debate is dominated by a perception that the EU's external relations (if not the TEU itself) as presently designed cannot work as desired—with enhanced coherence, effectiveness, and visibility[7]—in an EU of twenty or more states. Recent failures and the prospect of enlargement have lent a sense of urgency to the old question of CFSP institutional reforms, but it seems the most ambitious changes—effective compliance mechanisms, involvement of the ECJ, and true majoritarian decisionmaking procedures—are unlikely at present. Thus the CFSP, like other controversial EU policy areas, will most likely proceed under the banner of "flexibility" so that a continually shifting group of member states (but not a permanent "hard core") can proceed with joint actions if and when they desire.

The Modesty of Maastricht:
Interinstitutional Dilemmas and the Fear of Precedent

It is not necessary to rehearse all the CFSP's provisions here; most observers agree there are only four notable differences between it and EPC. First, the CFSP represents a stronger commitment to common policies. Article J.2 requires member states to "ensure that their national positions conform to the common positions of the CFSP." Second, decisionmaking rules permit CFSP joint actions to be initiated and/or implemented by qualified majority voting in Council (Article J.3). Third, security issues are fully included in the CFSP, including the "framing" of a common defense policy, "which might in time lead to a common defense." The Western European Union is directed to "elaborate and implement" any decisions that have defense implications (Article J.4). Fourth, the CFSP is part of the single institutional structure of the EU; the Council of Ministers and the Commission must ensure "consistency" between the EC and the CFSP (Articles C and J.8). Hence the TEU replaces the "High Contracting Parties" language of EPC with terminology that conforms to existing EC usage. Although EC and CFSP procedures still vary, there is no more practical distinction between EC policy and the CFSP (the Single European Act, of course, had maintained such a distinction); the General Affairs Council of EU foreign ministers deals with all issues regardless of the pillar from which they originate.[8]

   As noted, most of these provisions were codifications of existing practices. There had been no practical distinction between the EC and EPC for years in the view of most officials involved with EPC; Maastricht finally recognized this. The "new" instruments of common positions and joint actions were generally based on tools under the EPC regime; the TEU essentially created a new and far more complicated procedure—with multiple veto points—for taking joint actions. This involves broad guidelines from the European Council, unanimous decisions by the Council of Ministers on both *specific actions* and the *definition of later decisions* (implementation, timing, funding, etc.) that can be taken by QMV, and final QMV decisions (if any) to complete the joint action. Actions with defense implications are, of course, excluded from this procedure. The change to QMV seems innovative, but again EPC admonished states not to impede the formation of a consensus.[9] Similarly, the use of EC sanctions as a CFSP action now specifically requires a unanimous decision in Council before the EC can act according to its usual procedures (QMV). This already was typical practice (though the decision was taken in EPC, not in Council) but had not been stated so clearly in treaty form. Now it should no longer be necessary, as it often was under EPC, to invoke, say, Article 113 (the Common Commercial Policy) to provide superficial legal justification for the use of EC instruments for political ends.[10]

Other CFSP provisions regarding Commission and EP involvement also reflected EPC traditions. Although the Commission now has a formal "right of initiative" (shared with member states), it had quietly suggested policies under EPC. Significantly, Article J.5 says the CFSP is still directed by the Council presidency; the presidency state (or the troika of the presidency state and the previous and next states to hold the presidency), not the Commission, also represents the CFSP abroad. Equally, the EP gained no significant powers; it must be "consulted" on CFSP decisions, but the Council largely determines the extent to which the EP can be involved on a practical basis. The EP can also make recommendations, ask questions, and hold an annual debate on the performance of the CFSP, weak powers it already enjoyed under EPC. Finally and perhaps most significant, the ECJ is specifically excluded from the CFSP (and justice and home affairs).[11] In both the second and third pillars, then, states made sure European Court decisions would be unlikely to make political cooperation a supranational or Community affair.

However, when the EU attempted to implement these "innovations," controversies quickly arose over the division of labor in the CFSP process. Officials soon realized the difficulty of merging two distinct political and legal cultures: the EC and EPC/CFSP. The first task was to set the agenda for potential CFSP actions. Since the TEU negotiations could not produce agreement on "essential European interests" to be served by the CFSP,[12] a general clause was preferred that allowed the European Council to define the scope of the CFSP as needed (Articles D, J.3, and J.8). In a decision taken soon after Maastricht, the Lisbon European Council (26–27 June 1992) defined a number of specific geographical and functional areas open to joint action in the CFSP.[13] When the CFSP entered into effect in November 1993, these areas became the object of the first CFSP joint actions.[14] Yet as critics and CFSP officials have argued,[15] these broad guidelines, set down only a few times a year at most, provide little substance for policy. Also, the European Council is usually concerned with EC, not CFSP, issues, and its attention does not often focus on the implementation or quality of CFSP actions. Instead, as under EPC, policy details and follow-up are left largely to foreign ministers and the CFSP transgovernmental network involving foreign ministry officials, COREPER, and the Commission. These actors clearly dominate "normal" policymaking in the CFSP; European Council instructions would disappear without their input.

Hence, the Commission and the Council of Ministers, not the European Council, ensure the consistency of the EU's external relations in terms of economic, development, and security policies under Articles C and J.8(3).[16] Although consistency in foreign affairs has improved compared to EPC, there has hardly been a coherent strategy. As under EPC, a haphazard mix of instruments has been applied: Some are regulatory in nature (such as control of dual-use goods, the demining initiatives, action against blinding laser weapons), while others involve diplomatic conferences (such as the Stability Pact or the Nonproliferation Treaty renewal conference), minor temporary operations (monitoring elections, supporting peace plans), or substantial commitments of EC resources (aid to Africa, Bosnia, and Palestine; administering Mostar).

EC actors have not taken the mandate for consistency lightly, however; a striking development is that Council and Commission officials have been paying far greater attention to the legality of CFSP actions, particularly those which involve EC resources or competencies (such as dealing with international organizations). Officials are drafting CFSP texts with the understanding that legal precedents are being set, even if EC treaty articles are not invoked. This is a significant change from EPC, which makes the CFSP a far more bureaucratic and thus contentious process, since it can affect future choices. The first "dualist" EC/CFSP legal act, a decision to control the EU's exports of dual-use goods, required much debate among officials,[17] but this encouraged the establishment of "model common positions" to avoid repetitive legal arguments in the CFSP.[18]

Since Maastricht, then, EU states have become very sensitive to the implications of this change in political cooperation, and ideological debates continually erupt over the wording of texts, which are viewed as more legally binding than those produced under EPC. States fear that any new decisions will set precedents for the CFSP that may bind them later or that will involve the Commission or EP to a greater degree than they desire. For example, the Commission's CFSP agenda setting has been criticized by EU states, particularly its involvement in any security-related areas, such as the demining efforts or the Korean Energy Development Organization (KEDO). More so perhaps than under EPC, the Commission serves as a point of access by outsiders for CFSP-related actions; both KEDO and the

New Transatlantic Agenda agreed between the EU and the United States depended in part on Americans' lobbying the Commission.[19] These successes mean outside pressure on the Commission for CFSP action will only continue. The conniving and procedural debates that most CFSP decisions have provoked reflect a textbook case of what might be called "path-dependency phobia," or fear of the way current decisions in a complex environment can limit future options.[20] That the Commission and Council legal services are deliberately attempting to legalize all CFSP texts with EC language does not ease states' fear of the "contamination" of the CFSP by EC actors and procedures.

Fear of precedent also affects the choice of CFSP voting rules. It is not surprising that QMV for the CFSP has been strongly resisted; Article J.3(2) allows states unilaterally to veto the definition of which decisions could be taken by QMV, and they often exercise this option. Controversies over decisionmaking and the involvement of EC actors have similarly caused funding headaches for most CFSP actions, particularly the EU's administration of Mostar. Officials attempted to sort out CFSP funding at a Council meeting on 13 June 1994, where they agreed that CFSP "administrative" expenditure would be charged to the EC budget. CFSP "operational" financing would typically come from member states, but a unanimous vote enables them to use EC money instead. If so, France and Britain wanted such funds to be under the "Council" line, but a majority of states (and the EP) held out for a CFSP operational line in the Commission budget (line III-B-8), which now includes funds for CFSP actions previously decided and a small reserve fund.[21] As the CFSP is "noncompulsory" expenditure in the EC budget, the EP has the right (under Article 203) to approve all CFSP disbursements. These disagreements and the notorious unreliability of individual member state contributions to fund the CFSP (as in Mostar) resulted in CFSP funds' being "illegally" taken from existing EC budgets (for example, development, agriculture, or cooperation) for several months on an ad hoc basis to avoid having to create a permanent CFSP line in the budget that the EP can control. These budgets involve hundreds of millions of ECUs, some of which were creatively diverted to pay for CFSP actions, while the CFSP itself had an operational reserve fund of only ECU 32 million in 1995–1996.

Besides procedural difficulties, the entire tri-pillar structure of the TEU has been attacked, since it is difficult to achieve consistency with separate decisionmaking systems. The CFSP may already be "contaminating" the first pillar; when there is a conflict between the decisionmaking rules of the EC and those of the CFSP, those of the second pillar dominate.[22] It seems similarly little attention has been given to the links between the CFSP and EMU. After EMU, financial sanctions will fall under the authority of the European Central Bank if the EU's finance ministers have their way. But this is not definite, and there is likely to be a controversy when the first such case arises.[23] There is also the potential discrepancy between an "EMU hard core" and a "CFSP hard core," which may not consist of the same states. Similarly, coordination between the CFSP and justice and home affairs (JHA) has not been seriously attempted, although some JHA areas (such as asylum policy and cooperation on terrorism) are functionally linked to the CFSP (and "political union" comprises both) and can be manipulated to support it.[24] Ironically, in recent years EU polls have revealed an increasing amount of support for the notion that cooperation in foreign policy and crime *above all other policy areas* should be handled at the EU level, and governments will need to confront these demands.[25] Other changes in the EU, such as recent developments in European Union citizenship provisions and the establishment of the first common EU missions in Nigeria and Tanzania,[26] may hasten the pressures for intensified CFSP/JHA cooperation (and stronger rules), if not for political union itself. With such limited coordination between pillars, it is clear the European Union still appears to be a union in name only.

Intrainstitutional Changes: Bureaucratic Politics and the CFSP

Since the TEU's CFSP decisionmaking rules were so convoluted, they inadvertently stimulated the creation of several new working habits and procedures to improve the implementation of the CFSP. The past several years have seen much policy experimentation as EC actors attempted to determine—and widen—the extent of their authority in the second pillar. A new element of EC-style bureaucratic politics has been introduced in the CFSP: Under EPC, bureaucratic politics in individual national capitals led to the dominance of political cooperation by foreign ministries; under the CFSP, bureaucratic politics have changed the Commission and COREPER, who now have their own internal CFSP dynamics and compete to a certain extent with political directors in the EU capitals. A duplication of authority now exists between the informal transgovernmental network created under EPC (and retained by the CFSP) and the institutions in Brussels that are involved in the CFSP.

For example, in what became an ill-fated attempt to create a quasi foreign ministry for itself, the outgoing Delors Commission split its Directorate-General I for external economic relations into two parts. All EU external political relations were to be handled by the new DG IA under a single commissioner; desk officers for this directorate were to be taken from other DGs and commissioners' cabinets.[27] Since this created a backlash inside and outside the Commission, a second reorganization under Commission president Jacques Santer redistributed portfolios among several external relations commissioners along functional and geographic lines so that each commissioner now handles both economic and political relations for his or her geographic area. The distribution of portfolios has worked as well as it can in a system that involves up to seven commissioners for external relations and is still susceptible to turf battles and confusion.[28]

To improve coordination and avoid such battles, Santer has further instituted regular *"relex* group" (for *relations extérieures*) meetings of the six commissioners (plus himself) who have external relations portfolios, meetings of Commission planning staff, and meetings of cabinet officials involved in the CFSP as well.[29] This has been especially helpful in promoting cooperation between, say, DG I for external economic relations and DG VIII for development, both of which are related to the CFSP (and which did not always share information with each other under EPC). Since the Commission lacks many tangible resources for influencing the CFSP, it has been more creative in the way it makes its administration of external funding (such as the huge PHARE and Technical Assistance to the Commonwealth of Independent States [TACIS] programs) and its negotiation of association agreements subject to political criteria, even though some member states strongly oppose this power.[30] Finally, the Commission is permitted a voice in all security and defense matters as well and was involved in the Nonproliferation Treaty renewal conference, the EU's initiative on demining war-torn areas, and KEDO.

Since the CFSP is now formally handled by the Council of (Foreign) Ministers, a number of changes were made in COREPER as well. COREPER is often overlooked by analysts of EU policymaking who focus instead on governments or the Commission/EP/ECJ, but it has become a far more influential actor in the CFSP process compared to the EPC regime. CFSP-related changes in COREPER were considered at Maastricht; however, negotiators disagreed on what practical arrangements should be formalized in the TEU, so they wisely left these "details" to be decided during the Treaty's implementation stage.[31] They anticipated that the division of labor between COREPER and the political directors in national capitals (who meet as the Political Committee, or "PoCo") ultimately would have to be addressed. PoCo had dominated the EPC system, but it would now have to share some authority with COREPER, since EC/CFSP matters were increasingly linked and always meant to be consistent. Over the past few years, three important changes here took place.

First, COREPER prepares all Council meetings now, and technically it has the ability to ensure consistency between the CFSP (prepared by PoCo) and the EC (prepared by COREPER), but it is unclear what would happen if COREPER and PoCo disagreed, since neither body has primacy over the other. To clarify this function, a second change involved attaching a new "CFSP counselor" to each permanent representation after a July 1994 agreement. After a year of experimentation, COREPER recommended that CFSP counselors meet as a group on a regular basis (two times a week or more) to contend with the demands of political directors who do not always understand the legal and technical links between the CFSP and the EC. More important is that the CFSP counselors (who consider themselves the CFSP workhorse) now handle *all matters relating to the imposition of sanctions as a CFSP instrument,* currently the strongest tool the CFSP has. Third, relevant EPC working groups were merged with their EC counterparts into single units in order to improve the coordination between EC and CFSP affairs.[32]

Thus, if knowledge of a political system's rules is a source of power, then COREPER and the CFSP counselors in particular are now in a more advantaged position thanks to these changes, as they are the primary, day-to-day junction between the EC's complex political system and the foreign policy traditions and preferences of individual member states. This is especially true concerning financing the CFSP from the EC budget or using EC economic tools for CFSP ends, domains where COREPER's expertise about what can and cannot be done (and how quickly and efficiently) is crucial. The CFSP counselors have also improved the quick response ability of the CFSP, such as during the November 1995 executions of playwright Ken Saro-Wiwa and eight other Nigerian political activists. Since the African working group meets infrequently, the CFSP counselors and the Commission quickly stepped in to consider proposals on how the CFSP should react.

Finally, the TEU also mandated a small change in the EPC secretariat that might have implications after the IGC. The CFSP secretariat was permanently placed in the Secretariat-General of the Council of Ministers and directed to serve it as well, not just the presidency. The political functions of the CFSP and the existing external economic functions of the EC unit were established as two departments under a new director-general. These are largely staffed by experts from foreign ministries at the discretion of the presidency. The new CFSP secretariat is larger than the previous EPC unit, but it is still small, with a staff of about sixty. It has no hope of competing with the Commission in resources or expertise. It has also been kept on a very short leash; states have "gagged" it, in the words of one official, when it attempts to advance policies.[33] However, as I discuss below, it is possible that this unit (or officials from it) will constitute a new CFSP analysis and/or planning unit. Until this happens, ad hoc CFSP policy planning will likely be dominated by the Commission's planners and those of member states.

The Politics of CFSP Reform at the Intergovernmental Conference

With these problems of implementation and lingering institutional questions, CFSP reform became a major priority of the 1996–1997 IGC.

Although, as usual, expectations about the CFSP still vary among states and the lack of political will is correctly blamed for many of the CFSP's problems, most actors were convinced that some institutional changes would help improve the CFSP process. It is hard to deny that statements made by officials during the TEU ratification process and the early stages of Yugoslavia raised expectations so much that the CFSP, based as it was on the informal EPC process, could not possibly meet the demands forced on it. And still there have been some successes, such as the Stability Pact with Eastern Europe.

However, many believed the CFSP represented an old solution to internal and external problems bound up in the vague notion of "political integration." With enlargement looming, the IGC appeared to be the last manageable opportunity the EU had to give itself an effective tool for projecting political power. A diagnosis debate over the CFSP's problems began in the run-up to the IGC, although many of the issues and options were ones that have been considered for years. Official proposals for CFSP reforms began to circulate in Brussels and among member states, most of which would not have required major treaty changes. A "Reflection Group" under the chairmanship of Carlos Westendorp, Spanish secretary of state for European affairs, prepared the IGC agenda between June and December 1995. The group's treatment of CFSP reform as a high priority on the IGC agenda was strongly endorsed by the Madrid European Council (15–16 December 1995). Among other goals, the Council committed itself to equipping the EU for external action and common security.[34] While the Spanish presidency had much to be proud of, the Italian presidency suffered a shaky start because of domestic economic and political instability and Britain's policy of "noncooperation," a response to the EU's ban on British beef. This policy did not end until the Florence summit on 21–22 June 1996, holding up both IGC discussions and regular business in the EU. Italy was also criticized for its timidity about using the CFSP (or encouraging the EU in general) to help resolve the military confrontation between Greece and Turkey over the Aegean island of Imia/Karadak in early 1996.

However, at the formal opening of the IGC in Turin on 29 March 1996, EU foreign ministers specifically directed their representatives to the IGC to:

1. Define principles for the CFSP and the areas it covers;
2. Define the action needed to defend the EU's interests in areas reflecting these principles;
3. Create procedures and structures for taking decisions; and
4. Agree upon suitable budget provisions for joint actions.[35]

Although the IGC was dominated by talk of EMU, by the start of the Irish presidency in July 1996 several meetings had been held on the CFSP, and Ireland had further agreed (under pressure from the French) to hold a special IGC summit in mid-October to give more momentum to the reform process. Ireland also managed to produce a draft revision of the Maastricht Treaty, which was welcomed at the Dublin European Council (13–14 December 1996). With the IGC agenda set, what follow are seven general areas of CFSP reform around which consensus had emerged (to varying degrees), based on the positions of EU member states and EC-level actors.

CFSP Policy Analysis and/or Planning Unit

Article J.8 of the TEU stipulates that the PoCo (Political Committee) is charged with "monitoring" the international situation and providing opinions to the Council at the request of the Council or on its own initiative. Many are not satisfied with this arrangement, given the size, power, political ambitions, and problems of the EU. They also blame it in part for failing to anticipate problems such as Yugoslavia and Rwanda and for failing to encourage a common analysis of (and solution to) such problems. Hence some type of analysis, planning, early warning, or crisis prevention unit—a CFSP think tank—is likely to be created, as virtually all member states, the Commission, and the EP support this idea. It was the strongest area of consensus in the Reflection Group, and it was also the *only* area of consensus during the first IGC meeting on CFSP reform, held on 6–7 May 1996.[36] The Irish draft revision of the TEU reflected this consensus for such a unit.

There was some contention over the extent to which the CFSP analysis unit should be able to *plan* or *initiate* common foreign policies.[37] This is the most important issue, since the CFSP needs a source of policy ideas that is seen as independent of all member states (as in the role the Commission plays in the first pillar). There was also controversy over whether a new official should be created to direct this unit (see below). A new unit within the Council Secretariat-General, supported by experts from capitals and the Commission, was the most likely possibility. The extent to which such a unit will actually be permitted to do the work asked of it and will significantly improve the CFSP is still open to question. States realize that an effort must be made to tie together all relevant planners and permit them to monitor developments, field proposals, draft texts, and prepare common analyses of major external problems facing the EU. The proposed link with the new Policy Coordination Group in NATO and the strengthening of links with planners in the WEU will be especially important. However, if this reform is not complemented by others outlined below, it will be a cosmetic change only. Planners in national foreign ministries, for example, do not always see their concerns addressed by higher officials, so CFSP insiders are not putting much confidence in the planning unit alone.

Reforming CFSP Decisionmaking Rules

Article J.3 of the TEU provides for QMV on certain CFSP matters that have been decided unanimously by the Council, a two-stage (or more) process. Such matters were unspecified by the Treaty. QMV on CFSP actions has not been successfully attempted, although states have "refrained from insisting on a consensus" on several CFSP decisions.[38] There was wide agreement that the CFSP needs to be able to take decisions quickly without being held hostage by obstructive member states, a realization strongly encouraged by the British policy of noncooperation. Officials were considering a decision process whose rules would vary according to the type of task or tool being considered, such as the so-called Petersberg tasks (after a June 1992 WEU meeting where they were discussed): conflict resolution, crisis management, rescue and humanitarian operations, peacemaking, and peacekeeping. According to the Irish draft TEU revision, common positions could be taken by QMV, but joint actions or decisions with defense or military implications would require unanimity. States could abstain from these actions or decisions by formally declaring so, but they would still be required to show "mutual solidarity" with the EU. The new principle of decisionmaking "flexibility" in the Irish draft TEU revision (also known as a coalition of the willing, consensus minus one, reinforced/enhanced cooperation, active/positive/constructive abstention, or differentiated integration) would permit the willing and able EU states to implement Petersberg tasks while avoiding the appearance of a permanent CFSP hard core. Stricter changes, such as the loss of voting rights and the imposition of sanctions against states who opt out of (or defect against) CFSP decisions, were not being seriously considered.

While there may be problems applying QMV to the CFSP (such as measuring compliance or defining CFSP tasks in advance), there was some room for compromise for the EU to strike a balance between consensus and efficiency in the CFSP. Some states (Belgium, Greece, Germany, and France) supported making priorities areas for CFSP action part of the TEU and linking such priorities to QMV decisionmaking. Also, the Benelux states tentatively accepted that the "big five" could have more voting weight in Council, but only if they surrendered some authority to the CFSP (these states were also unwilling to give up their own commissioners). On 27 February 1996, France and Germany reached agreement on "Guidelines for the CFSP" in Freiburg: stability in neighboring regions east and south of the EU, stronger transatlantic links, and closer relations with Russia and Ukraine. They further agreed on distinguishing between CFSP "decisions in principle" (requiring unanimity) and "implementation decisions" (QMV or constructive abstention). Like most EU members, they believe abstainers from military action should still provide political, and possibly financial, support for a common action, perhaps through a "political solidarity

clause" written into the TEU. Such a clause is included in Article J.1(4) of
the Irish draft revision of the TEU, which also eliminates Article J.3(2) so
that states cannot unilaterally veto the definition of CFSP decisions that
could be taken by QMV. Belgium, the strongest supporter of a communita-
rized CFSP, also suggested that QMV should be required for all Commission proposals on the CFSP. In an unexpected move, Denmark, too, supported QMV, but on the condition that the present pillar structure of the EU
be maintained.

However, Greece still urged consensus in areas where members have a
"vital interest," and France wanted it in "sensitive areas" (foreign, defense,
and internal security policy), requirements that could easily neutralize the
practical impact of any decisionmaking reforms. Ireland, Finland, Sweden,
and Britain were even more opposed to QMV for the CFSP.[39] At least all
but Italy and Sweden were willing to allow exceptions to the implementation of joint actions; most agreed that they must find an institutional way to
square the circle: A majority must not be prevented from acting by a minority (or by one), while a minority (particularly neutrals) should not have
tough decisions imposed on it. Flexibility appeared to be the only way to
achieve this.

Strengthening the External Representation of the EU

There was general agreement that the EU presidency, despite is useful features, demands more and more of the state that holds it. In addition, there is
the usual discrepancy between the status of large EU states and that of
small states when they hold the presidency. The troika framework is also
"ridiculously burdensome" in the words of one Commission official, an
attitude shared by many others.[40] The presidency/troika is also intimidating
to nonmembers; in external matters, often two or three officials from a nonmember state have to sit across the table from a dozen or more EU representatives, which inhibits frank discussion. Trust between a horde of rotating negotiators for the EU and any external interlocutors has to be
constantly rebuilt.

At the IGC, officials were attempting to clarify two major presidency
functions: managing the EU's normal business and representing the EU
abroad. Representation is highly relevant to the CFSP, and France has
strongly supported the creation of a High Permanent Representative to give
a "voice and face" to the CFSP. Michel Barnier, French minister for
European affairs, suggested a "president of the Union" or "secretary-general of the CFSP" appointed (and revocable) by the European Council for two
to five years to represent the EU's foreign/defense policy. This person
would be a "politician acting as an official" for the EU. The idea found little support, although the Germans tentatively approved it during the
Franco-German summit at Freiburg and it was still alive after the first few

meetings of the IGC.[41] Kohl's Christian Democratic Party, however, later rejected the idea in a policy paper released in September.[42] Typically, there was much speculation (but little agreement) about who would first hold this office: A commissioner, the Council secretary-general, the head of the Council's external relations secretariat, the director-general of DG IA, and former French president Valéry Giscard d'Estaing have been mentioned.[43] Britain, however, preferred that any new official would be lower in rank than desired by France, and the small states feared that the new official would always be someone from the larger EU states.

Naturally, the EP and the Commission strongly opposed the idea of a new high official for the CFSP. Instead, and like most other states, they preferred a presidency-Commission "tandem," where two officials, one delegated by each actor, share responsibility for representing the CFSP.[44] The Italian presidency also suggested including a new paragraph 3a in Article J.5 so that the Council could assign "executive authority" to the presidency, the troika, or the Commission on a case-by-case basis. This is a likely compromise, and it already worked well for the Stability Pact and the Transatlantic Agenda. This remains a difficult area for reform; if agreement is not reached, temporary representatives for the EU/CFSP probably will continue in specific areas,[45] possibly along with the tandem. Supporters of federalism still want representation to be handled by the Commission president or vice president, since the Commission could easily take advantage of its vast overseas network of delegations, which is more extensive than that of some member states. And any EU representative must also be provided with more authority, resources, and flexibility to be successful, as both Hans Koschnick and Carl Bildt learned the hard way in the Balkans.

A related issue concerning external representation involves creating a legal personality for the EU. Since the EU has no legal personality (unlike the EC, the European Coal and Steel Community, and the European Atomic Energy Community [Euratom]), it cannot conclude agreements or join international organizations using the CFSP mechanism alone. Instead, weak "memorandums of understanding" or convoluted "mixed agreements" that refer to EC competencies have to be drafted. These are difficult to negotiate, and there are unresolved questions about their enforcement. For example, the EU could not become a board member of KEDO despite its financial contribution of ECU 5 million to that body, and legal advisers are continually reminding CFSP officials that they lack the authority to make a particular agreement.[46] The Italian presidency advanced some suggestions to handle this problem, such as giving the EU full legal personality or giving the EU the ability to conclude agreements in certain sectors. The Irish draft revision of the TEU endowed the EU with full legal personality vis-à-vis its member states (where the Commission represents the EU) and external states and organizations (where the presidency, assisted by the Commission if appropriate, represents the EU). This provision would not apply to agreements involving the use of military means. However, most states were either indifferent or only moderately concerned about this issue; Britain and to a lesser extent Denmark were strongly opposed to such a change (Denmark would also be constitutionally required to submit the IGC agreement to a referendum).

Defense and the CFSP-WEU Relationship

Clarifying the roles of the WEU, the CFSP, and NATO is one of the most contentious issues facing the EU, and the developments in this area are beyond the scope of this chapter.[47] I offer only a few comments here. First, it is clear the CFSP has had very little to do with security or defense. So far only four minor security-related issues have been directly addressed by the CFSP: the mine-clearing directive, the Nonproliferation Treaty renewal, the control of exports of dual-use goods, and the goal to prohibit blinding laser weapons. Only one Article J.4(2) WEU/CFSP action has been taken: the Council decision of 27 June 1996 to have the WEU prepare contingency plans to support the emergency evacuation of EU citizens from a third country if necessary (WEU support of the EU's administration of Mostar was not an official request by the EU made under Article J.4[2]). This was as much a symbolic decision for the IGC process (to show critics of reform that all CFSP instruments had been used at least once) as it was a practical CFSP action.[48] In addition to this extremely modest record of joint EU/WEU action, the WEU is rarely if ever present at General Affairs Council CFSP meetings, and links between the Commission and the WEU are poorly developed. Commission relations with NATO are much better than those with the WEU.

Second, there was finally a majority in favor *in principle* of merging the EU with the WEU but much disagreement over the details. It is obvious that the only compromise will be a gradual, minimalist approach, as on EMU, even though France and Germany are solidly behind the merger.[49] This would involve a timetable for increasing the lower-level links between the EU and WEU and enhancing the "operability" of the WEU, as it is still deficient in reconnaissance, intelligence, and transport. The WEU is unlikely to be the "army of the EU" soon; instead, this role will be played by the Eurocorps for now (although some, such as Denmark and Austria, are still opposed to such a role). This small land force (50,000 troops), which became operational on 30 November 1995, is independent of but linked to the WEU, and the two forces began joint exercises in December 1995. More important, major decisions by the WEU and NATO during ministerial meetings in mid-1996, following the French rapprochement with NATO, finally confirmed that the WEU and/or Combined Joint Task Forces with NATO could carry out military operations without U.S. involvement but with the logistical support of NATO.[50] These developments, though still in their early stages, threaten to eclipse the nascent European Security and Defense Identity of the CFSP since the European Union seem neither ready nor able to act more independently of NATO.

Third, it is now possible that a clear, formal distinction will be made between security and defense in the IGC treaty revisions. This distinction, which the Commission supports as well, has already been made during domestic ratification debates over the Single European Act (in Ireland and Denmark) and over the TEU (in Germany and Austria) to include these states in security-related collective actions. With this idea, security matters would involve the Petersberg tasks, EC/WEU resources in most cases, and would permit the involvement of all EU states and the Commission (even with military matters). Defense would be strictly limited to territorial defense of the EU/NATO members, which would be handled by NATO states in coordination with the EU. An annex to whatever agreement is produced at the IGC would permit EU states who are not full members of NATO (Austria, Finland, Ireland, and Sweden) to opt in to the NATO/WEU defense structure if and when they choose. After Ireland assumed the EU presidency in July 1996, these four states tentatively agreed to support the inclusion of Petersberg tasks in the TEU (and they appear in the Irish draft revision), an encouraging development to be sure, but one that is still as vague on its details as the CJTF concept. These changes would be linked to new QMV rules noted above, so that security tasks could be taken on by a coalition of the willing, while defense would remain an intergovernmental decision of alliance members. Britain, however, was still opposed to writing these changes into the TEU.

Defense Equipment Cooperation

The EU is similarly confounded by the number of ad hoc arms production agreements involving small coalitions of its members. There is wide agreement that some sort of coordination—and potentially a formal European Armaments Agency or West European Armaments Organization—should be established among these groups and industries. Article 223 of Maastricht, which permits state protection of domestic arms industries, may be revised or revoked, as it effectively discourages mergers or acquisitions of defense manufacturers. Its most important purpose perhaps is as a bargaining chip to obtain a reciprocal pledge from the United States to give up its "Buy American" defense procurement policy, but neither side seems willing or able directly to confront this issue. At present the sensitivity of the issue (not to mention fears of Commission involvement in approving such acquisitions or mergers) means Article 223 will likely be retained in the near future. France and Britain are still the most vocal opponents of revoking Article 223, while the other states are indifferent or only slightly in favor of it.[51]

Predictably, this controversial topic did not see much consensus either in the Reflection Group or during the early IGC talks, but there was recognition that if Europe wants to increase its share of the shrinking global arms market it must change its research and procurement practices, given the very large economies of scale required by these industries. Opposition to direct Commission involvement or the revocation of Article 223 does not preclude other cooperative measures, of course; Britain was approved to join the proposed Franco-German arms agency (set up in 1995) on 4 June 1996, and France and Germany (at their Dijon summit, 6 June 1996) formally agreed to give a new push to defense cooperation and to "review" their twenty-seven bilateral arms programs, which would extend to joint procurement. Similarly, the Commission is already poised to take steps toward improving the competitiveness of the EU's approximately ECU 50 billion defense industry, having outlined a number of proposals in a January 1996 communication. According to this communication, between 1984 and 1992 domestic demand in EU defense industries fell by 30 percent, exports were cut in half, and the industry shed 37 percent of its workforce. As Martin Bangemann, EU industry commissioner, bluntly put it, "If the EU wants a CFSP, then it has to choose between a domestic arms industry or buying military hardware from America."[52] The Commission wants to apply single market rules to the defense industry and foster joint armaments research and production, but since France and Britain still fear potential Commission influence in military affairs through the backdoor channel of industrial policy, major change in the near future is unlikely.

Improving the Financing of the CFSP

EU members have also become very sensitive to the need to make the financing of CFSP actions more reliable and consistent. All except Britain support or at least are not strongly opposed to permanent funding of the CFSP from the EC budget, instead of placing earmarked CFSP funds under the Commission's budget line. This would involve the Commission and the EP to a much greater degree than the British desire. A possible option is the creation of a CFSP emergency fund in the EC budget that could be used at the Council's discretion. A CFSP line in the Council's budget is another option, but the Commission and EP would be strongly opposed to this. CFSP/WEU actions requiring "military means" would be exempt from the EC budget in principle, but there was no further definition of this idea. Any changes will require tricky language, as the EP must still approve nonobligatory funds and has threatened to use its budgetary control of the CFSP to make states respect its views. Under the current system, delays of up to six weeks occur when the EP must approve the use of CFSP funds in the Commission's budget. The EP has been pressing for an interinstitutional agreement on this issue since December 1993 and may see one following the IGC. Resolving the functional link between the WEU and the CFSP will mean little if member states continually show reluctance or an inability to provide material resources for foreign and security policy.[53]

Enhancing the Role of EC Institutions in the CFSP

Finally, states were split on whether to fully "communitarize" the CFSP, or to adopt mere procedural changes for it. Only the Benelux, Germany, Italy, Austria, and surprisingly, Greece emerged early in favor of CFSP communitarization. The ECJ will be left out of the CFSP again for the foreseeable future, since most states were either indifferent or only moderately supportive of its involvement (except Britain and Denmark, who were opposed). For their part, both the Commission and the EP naturally want more EU control of the CFSP. The EP has called for, among other things, a stronger EU defense policy that includes security guarantees, more use of QMV combined with the ability of states to "opt out" of joint actions, supervision of the CFSP by the EP and national parliaments, an interinstitutional agreement on financing the CFSP, the inclusion of an EP delegation at international conferences, the deletion or revision of Article 223, and some structural changes: a CFSP analysis/assessment unit, an EU diplomatic service and "civilian peace corps," and EU intelligence-gathering equipment (including satellites).[54]

However, most member states, particularly Britain, Ireland, Finland, and France, opposed the expansion of the EP's limited CFSP powers. The Commission was somewhat more pragmatic about what it wanted to achieve: an analysis unit, better decisionmaking procedures, an EU legal personality, directing the CFSP with a presidency-Commission tandem, judicial review of the CFSP, reducing or limiting the number of commissioners, and more secure funding for the CFSP with an interinstitutional agreement. It has also suggested that the PoCo be permanently moved to Brussels (to the Council) and that a Council of Defense Ministers be established.[55] All states except Britain wanted the Commission to make greater use of its right to make CFSP proposals. Finally, the Council of Ministers was opposed only to a role for the ECJ in the CFSP and to the revision of Article 223; it was generally supportive of or indifferent to everything else.[56]

In sum, if twenty years of EPC is any guide, we should not expect dramatic changes to the CFSP at the 1996–1997 IGC unless a major crisis stimulates the EU to act. Even after the IGC began, it appeared to be in a state of suspended animation because of two factors: very little change of opinion on the part of most actors and the combination of British opposition and its policy of noncooperation with the EU/IGC. The period through December 1996 was marked by timid prenegotiation discussions and reactions to papers put forward by the Italian and Irish presidencies. The major

CFSP bargains were made at Maastricht, and the agenda should not move far beyond what was outlined above. More important perhaps were that Germany and France were reaching agreement on changes they wanted to make, NATO and the EU/WEU had worked out arrangements to put more teeth in the EU's defense policy, and the neutrals did not seem to be actively blocking such a move. But the negotiations should continue well into 1997, and a few officials were privately hoping that a change in Britain's government after the May 1997 elections would break the deadlock against major institutional reform. Also, the Irish presidency's draft treaty revision, completed in time for the Dublin European Council of 13–14 December 1996, did not reflect any major departure from the compromises discussed above (although it does include slightly enhanced definitions of "common positions" and "joint actions").

Conclusion

The EU is increasingly desperate to become a potent international political actor, if only to be able to confront the challenges generated by instability in neighboring regions. After twenty years of informal political cooperation, the CFSP is the EU's primary tool for this task, but many officials are profoundly dissatisfied with the way it has worked. Although Yugoslavia has unfortunately—and perhaps unfairly—become the outstanding symbol of the ineffectiveness or irrelevance of the CFSP, it made EU states realize that adherence to a common position could at best impair its bargaining positions during crises and at worst paralyze the EU into following an action no state would have wanted. The Dayton accords also showed that the EU will play only a supporting role in crisis situations where military force is an option. And even when agreement on a proper action is reached, the lack of a permanent CFSP financial infrastructure delays and erodes the impact of a joint action. Causes of these problems are varied and complex; however, even if the CFSP isn't "broken," EU states are actively looking to an institutional fix for it. This might make them worse off; national solutions are sometimes the only alternative when the EU can't or won't act (or takes too long to act). As weak as EPC was, its participating officials still recall with nostalgia its pragmatism, secrecy, and flexibility.

Despite the obstacles, Europe's obstinate efforts to overcome differences, find common interests, and cooperate politically have much value— even if primarily symbolic—in world politics. This chapter focused on the expression of these efforts in terms of CFSP procedures and policies. The CFSP's institutional structure is not its only problem, of course; rules are not a substitute for political will. But EU states definitely think that institutions affect cooperation, and they are serious about reform. More important, they are looking to EC solutions for the CFSP. These include using QMV, delegating to the Commission for negotiations and implementation, establishing a legal personality for the EU, securing EC funding for the CFSP, strengthening the CFSP apparatus in Brussels, and using or adapting EC competencies (trade, development aid, a single-market–influenced defense industrial policy, etc.) to support the CFSP. At present only Britain and to a lesser extent Denmark are preventing some of these options from being utilized. Thus the prospects for CFSP reform are better than one might expect, given the sensitivity of foreign policy cooperation among independent states. Even without major decisionmaking reform, all states agree that a CFSP "hard core" (such as with ad hoc contact groups or coalitions of the willing), at least on military questions, is temporarily inevitable, and they are all somewhat predisposed to more EC influence in the CFSP.

As a policy process, then, the CFSP still cannot be considered in supranational terms, but it is more sensitive to the EC's actors and rules, more consistent, and more binding than intergovernmentalist theories suggest. To be sure, member governments still exert most influence in the CFSP, the CFSP "executive" in the form of the presidency or the Commission is still very weak, the EP and ECJ have very limited roles, and domestic politics in the form of public opinion or lobbying rarely intrudes on CFSP deliberations in any consistent or significant way. Since member states have not been able to make the symbolic advance to a more central direction in foreign political relations, at present they control the policy process. But only a small minority of states is holding up the transfer of more authority to EC institutions, and even these states agree that the system is unworkable if they demand consensus at every stage in the process.

The prospect of enlargement, a "political necessity and a historic opportunity," according to the December 1995 Madrid European Council, profoundly enhances this fear, as states realize that insistence on unanimity will paralyze a system with twenty or thirty members. EPC was created in part to help the EC cope with its first enlargement, and the next one poses monumental problems. The CFSP is only one of them, but it must be considered a fundamental part of the EU's enlargement strategy in light of the worst-case scenario of the Balkans. Given the current negotiating positions and NATO's creation of CJTF as an insurance policy, a Europe of intersecting hard cores—EMU, social policy, Schengen, and so on—seems inescapable at present, but this should not necessarily dilute the EU if core membership criteria and their associated obligations are very clear. EU members are sensitive to hostage holding by consensual rules and to free riding on the CFSP; those who consistently choose to free ride on the difficult decisions or actions of others may have to pay for such conduct, especially in the areas of security and defense. Critics of the CFSP should recall that it took two decades of work to use QMV for the internal market and to encourage states to bring EPC closer to existing EC structures; the same could happen with other hard-core policy areas.

At least the 1995 enlargement of Austria, Finland, and Sweden showed that new member states, even neutral ones, can accept and contribute to the goal of EU foreign and security policy cooperation (although of course no demanding security-related actions have been taken under the CFSP). NATO is looking east, and both the Commission and Germany should be able to play leading roles in confronting the problems faced by enlargement. Although "variable geometry" may be the only practical solution to defense cooperation in the near future, more difficult questions, such as the extent to which the new members' security problems will become the EU's security problems, will not be addressed at the IGC. These must await the enlargement negotiations, at present scheduled to take place six months after the end of the IGC. Thus while Yugoslavia and Dayton may have helped focus the EU's attention on the CFSP's shortcomings, the real tests—the CFSP after enlargement, its relationship to the WEU and NATO, and the question of supplying it with material resources in terms of military equipment—are yet to come.

Notes

This chapter is part of a wider project on the institutionalization of European Political Cooperation and its transition to the Common Foreign and Security Policy. The methodology involved elite interviews with officials from the U.S. mission to the European Union and with EPC/CFSP policymakers at the Commission, the Committee of Permanent Representatives (including COREPER II, or the permanent ambassadors to the EU), the European Parliament, the Council Secretariat-General, and several EU member state foreign ministries. An earlier version of this chapter was presented at the Tenth International Conference of Europeanists, Chicago, 14–16 March 1996. I am grateful to the Council for European Studies and the 1995–1996 U.S. Fulbright European Union program for their financial support of the research on which this chapter is based. For their advice and assistance I would also like to thank Russell Dalton, Viscount Etienne Davignon, Roy Ginsberg, Patrick Morgan, Simon Nuttall, John Peterson, Wayne Sandholtz, Philippe de Schoutheete, Penny Turnbull, and the officials who agreed to be interviewed for this research.

1. For general official consensus on the shortcomings of the CFSP, see Reflection Group, *Reflection Group's Report for the 1996 IGC* (Brussels: European Community, 1995), pp. 39–49; and Council of Ministers, *Report of the Council on the Functioning of the Treaty on European Union* (Luxembourg: Office for Official Publications of the European Communities, 1995), part 5. For informed outside analysis, see Roy H. Ginsberg, "Principles and Practices of the European Union's Common Foreign and Security Policy: Retrospective on the First Eighteen Months," paper prepared for the fourth international conference of the European Community Studies Association, Charleston, South Carolina, 11–14 May 1995; Roy H. Ginsberg, "The European Union's Common Foreign and Security Policy: An

Outsider's Retrospective on the First Year," *ECSA Newsletter* 7 (Fall 1994): 13–16; and Elfriede Regelsberger and Wolfgang Wessels, "The CFSP Institutions and Procedures: A Third Way for the Secon Pillar," *European Foreign Affairs Review* 1 (July 1996): 29–54. European citizens' groups complained about the failings of the CFSP (among other things) at public hearings organized by the European Parliament in preparation for the IGC. *European Report* 2111, 28 February 1996.

2. Between 1 November 1993 and 1 July 1996, the CFSP produced twenty-six common positions, thirty joint actions, and nearly 200 declarations. However, nearly half of the positions and actions were related to the former Yugoslavia and Mostar (eleven positions, thirteen actions). Most of these are listed in Commission of the European Communities, *Commission Report on the Functioning of the Treaty on European Union* (Luxembourg: Office for Official Publications of the European Communities, 1995).

3. Some of these reasons are suggested in the *Reflection Group's Report,* para. 148.

4. For a more detailed comparison of EPC and CFSP institutional structures, see Michael E. Smith, *The "Europeanization" of European Political Cooperation: Trust, Transgovernmental Relations, and the Power of Informal Norms* (Berkeley, Calif.: Center for German and European Studies, 1996).

5. EPC has usually been analyzed as an intergovernmental process. See Susanne J. Bodenheimer, "The Political Union Debate in Europe: A Case Study in Intergovernmental Diplomacy," *International Organization* 21 (Winter 1967): 24–54; William Wallace, "Political Cooperation: Integration Through Inter-governmentalism," in Helen Wallace and William Wallace (eds.), *Policy-making in the European Community* (Sussex: John Wiley and Sons, 1983); and Alfred E. Pijpers, "European Political Cooperation and the Realist Paradigm," in Martin Holland (ed.), *The Future of European Political Cooperation: Essays on Theory and Practice* (London: Macmillan, 1991).

6. Interviews with COREPER, Commission, and Council Secretariat-General officials, Brussels, 1995–1996.

7. According to the Conference of the Representatives of the Governments of the Member States (IGC), *The European Union Today and Tomorrow: A General Outline for a Draft Revision of the Treaties,* completed during the Irish presidency, 5 December 1996 (hereafter, "Irish draft TEU revision").

8. For more details, see Geoffrey Edwards and Simon Nuttall, "Common Foreign and Security Policy," in Andrew Duff, John Pinder, and Roy Price (eds.), *Maastricht and Beyond: Building the European Union* (London: Routledge, 1994); M. R. Eaton, "Common Foreign and Security Policy," in David O'Keeffe and Patrick M. Twomey (eds.), *Legal Issues of the Maastricht Treaty* (London: Wiley Chancery Law, 1994); and Simon J. Nuttall, "The Foreign and Security Policy Provisions of the Maastricht Treaty: Their Potential for the Future," in Joerg Monar, Werner Ungerer, and Wolfgang Wessels (eds.), *The Maastricht Treaty on European Union* (Brussels: European Interuniversity Press, 1993).

9. Article 30.3(c), Single European Act.

10. This was accomplished by replacing Article 228 of EEC treaty with a new Article 228 in the TEU and adding Article 228(a), which specifically applies to CFSP actions that call for the use of EC sanctions.

11. Article L, TEU, specifies that the ECJ enjoys no powers in the second pillar (it is also excluded from the third pillar, JHA). However, thanks to Article M, the ECJ could technically have jurisdiction over a CFSP (or JHA) decision that runs counter to procedures of the first pillar (EC).

12. The closest they came, perhaps, was during the October 1990 foreign

ministers meeting in Asolo, Italy (the so-called Asolo list), but they could not agree on which items should be included in the final treaty.

13. These areas included Central and Eastern Europe, the Maghreb and the Middle East, and several security issues (Conference on Security and Cooperation in Europe [CSCE], disarmament and arms control in Europe, nuclear nonproliferation, and controlling the transfer of arms technology to third countries). See Council of Foreign Ministers, "Report to the European Council in Lisbon on the Likely Development of the Common Foreign and Security Policy (CFSP) with a View to Identifying Areas Open to Joint Action vis-à-vis Particular Countries or Groups of Countries," *European Union Bulletin,* June 1992.

14. These included the Stability Pact in Central and Eastern Europe, support for the Middle East and Yugoslavia peace processes, and support for transitions to democracy in South Africa and Russia.

15. Joerg Monar, "The Foreign Affairs System of the Maastricht Treaty: A Combined Assessment of the CFSP and EC External Relations Elements," in Joerg Monar, Werner Ungerer, and Wolfgang Wessels (eds.), *The Maastricht Treaty on European Union* (Brussels: European Interuniversity Press, 1993), p. 140. Also, interviews with Commission and COREPER officials, Brussels, 1995–1996.

16. For more on the "consistency" issue, see Nanette Neuwahl, "Foreign and Security Policy and the Implementation of the Requirement of 'Consistency' Under the Treaty on European Union," in David O'Keeffe and Patrick M. Twomey (eds.), *Legal Issues of the Maastricht Treaty* (London: Wiley Chancery Law, 1994).

17. Council decision 94/942/CFSP; OJ L 367 (31 December 1994).

18. See the "Mode d'emploi concernant les positions communes définies sur la base de l'Article J.2 du Traité sur l'Union Européene," internal Council document 5194/95 of 6 March 1995. Casting combined EC/CFSP agreements as "administrative" in nature has helped to reduce disagreements over the ability of the CFSP legally to use EC tools. Interviews with COREPER officials and officials of the Commission and Council Secretariat legal services, Brussels, 1995–1996.

19. Interviews with Commission officials and U.S. diplomatic officials involved in the KEDO and New Transatlantic Agenda negotiations, Brussels, 1995–1996.

20. On path dependency, see Stephen D. Krasner, "Approaches to the State: Alternative Conceptions and Historical Dynamics," *Comparative Politics* 16 (January 1984): 223–246; and Paul Pierson, "When Effect Becomes Cause: Policy Feedback and Political Change," *World Politics* 45 (July 1993): 595–628.

21. *European Report* 1958, 15 June 1994; *Agence Europe,* 15 June 1994; interviews with Commission and COREPER officials, Brussels, 1995–1996.

22. For example, QMV could have been used to disburse funds to Mostar, and while states chose to "avoid insisting on unanimity" here, several time-consuming joint actions to disburse funds were still required. Sanctions against Haiti led to confusion over whether EC rules or CFSP rules would dominate; those of the CFSP did. Interviews with COREPER officials, Brussels, 1996. Also see Commission of the European Communities, *Commission Report on the Functioning of the Treaty on European Union,* p. 57.

23. Personal communication with Simon Nuttall, 3 April 1996.

24. For example, note that the common visa policy, which can be manipulated as a policy tool in both the CFSP and JHA areas, is actually an EC competency under Article 100c of the TEU. For more on the links between the CFSP and JHA, see Malcolm Anderson, Monica den Boer, and Gary Miller, "European Citizenship and Cooperation in Justice and Home Affairs," in Andrew Duff, John Pinder, and Roy Price (eds.), *Maastricht and Beyond: Building the European Union* (London: Routledge, 1994).

25. Eurobarometer surveys since June 1993 consistently reveal that out of up to twenty-two policy areas in which citizens Europe-wide preferred EU decision-making to national solutions, three of the top four areas in each survey were components of political union (i.e., CFSP or JHA areas). In the *Standard Eurobarometer of Autumn 1995* (survey 43), the three areas of political union where citizens preferred EU decisionmaking were Third World cooperation (78 percent), the fight against drugs (77 percent), and foreign policy (70 percent).

26. For example, a Council decision of 19 December 1995 (OJ L 314/73/1995) on common protection of EU citizens provides that citizens of any EU state have the right to assistance from the embassies or consulates of any other EU state in a third country if their own consulate is inaccessible. The Council of Foreign Ministers meeting in Luxembourg (6 October 1995) approved a CFSP common position (not published in the official journal) favoring the consolidation of the EU's missions and representations. But Britain will not participate, although it shares embassies with other EU states. *European Report* 2074, 11 October 1995.

27. Interviews with Commission officials, Brussels, 1995–1996. Also see Simon J. Nuttall, "The European Commission's Internal Arrangements for Foreign Affairs and External Relations," *CFSP Forum* 2 (1995): 3; and David Allen and Michael Smith, "External Policy Developments," *Journal of Common Market Studies* 32 (August 1994): 68.

28. Besides President Santer, the commissioners who currently share external relations portfolios are Hans van den Broek (CFSP shared with Santer; oversees DG IA for external political relations); Leon Brittan (DG I for external economic relations with the developed world); Manuel Marin (DG IB for external economic relations with the developing world); João de Deus Pinheiro (DG VIII for development); Emma Bonino (European Community Humanitarian Aid Office, an arm of the Commission); and Yves-Thibault de Silguy (DG II for economic and financial affairs).

29. Interviews with Commission officials and Commissioners' cabinet members, Brussels, 1995–1996.

30. The Interim Partnership and Cooperation Agreement with Russia was perhaps the most noted example. Its implementation was temporarily delayed by Commissioner van den Broek during the Chechen rebellion. Interviews with Commission officials, Brussels, 1995–1996.

31. "Declaration on Practical Arrangements in the Field of the Common Foreign and Security Policy," annex to the Treaty on European Union (declaration no. 28).

32. "Création du groupe de conseillers PESC," internal COREPER document, 26 July 1994; based on a Political Committee decision of 2 July 1994, "Recommendations of the Political Committee to the General Affairs Council," internal Council document, 18 July 1994. Interviews with COREPER officials, Brussels, 1995–1996.

33. Interviews with Commission, Council Secretariat-General, and COREPER officials, Brussels, 1995–1996.

34. *European Report* 2094, 20 December 1995.

35. The Italian presidency conclusions of the Turin European Council, which opened the IGC on 29 March 1996, are reproduced in *European Report* 2121, 3 April 1996.

36. Interviews with Reflection Group members and IGC negotiators, Brussels, 1996. Also see *European Report* 2130, 8 May 1996, and *Agence Europe,* 8 May 1996 and 15 May 1996.

37. The Reflection Group, for example, was opposed to the idea of allowing the proposed unit to initiate CFSP positions or actions. See their report, para.

152–153. The Irish draft TEU revision suggested the planning unit could prepare "policy options papers" on its own initiative or at the request of the Council or the presidency.

38. According to interviews with Commission and COREPER officials, member states did not insist on unanimity on the antipersonnel mine clearing directive, financial sanctions against Bosnia-Herzegovina, some disbursement decisions for Mostar, and a decision on the prohibition against making payments under contracts caught by the embargo against Haiti.

39. *Agence Europe,* 8 March 1996, 15 March 1996, 22/23 April 1996.

40. Interviews with Commission and COREPER officials, Brussels, 1995–1996. The Irish draft TEU revision suggests that the troika framework could be amended to include only two member states: the presidency and the next member state to hold it.

41. *Agence Europe,* 10 February 1996, 15 May 1996, 8 June 1996.

42. The Christian Democrat Union (CDU) paper on the IGC said that the enhanced visibility provided by a new CFSP high official would not offset the risk of "later complications" regarding institutional matters and the breakdown of tasks. The CDU also called for participation by Commission personnel in the proposed CFSP planning unit, an idea opposed by France. *Agence Europe,* 18 September 1996.

43. Interviews with Commission and COREPER officials, Brussels, 1995–1996. The Irish draft TEU revision, via a new article, J.8(b), provides for the secretary-general of the Council to assist with external representation. Also see Lionel Barber, "Dr. K's Riddle Still Awaits an Answer," *Financial Times,* 22 April 1996.

44. See Commission of the European Communities, *Commission Opinion on Reinforcing Political Union and Preparing for Enlargement,* COM(96)90 (Luxembourg: Office for Official Publications of the European Communities, 1996). Also, talk among large states of creating a special "team presidency" for security and defense matters provoked much criticism from small states, and Belgium publicly stated it was strongly opposed to this idea. *Agence Europe,* 12 June 1996.

45. *Agence Europe,* 8 June 1996. The habit of creating ad hoc special representatives for EU (or for the state holding the presidency) is slowly taking hold. These include, among others, Lords Carrington and Owen, then Carl Bildt, for Bosnia; Hans Koschnick (later Ricardo Perez Casado, then Martin Garrod) for Mostar; Aldo Ajello, for the Great Lakes region of central Africa (Rwanda, Burundi, and Tanzania); and Federico Roberto, then Kester Heaslip, for Cyprus.

46. Interviews with officials of the Commission and Council Secretariat legal services, and with COREPER officials, Brussels, 1996.

47. For more on the WEU issue, see Lawrence Martin and John Roper (eds.), *Towards a Common Defence Policy* (Paris: Institute for Security Studies of the WEU, 1995), and Chapter 6 in this volume.

48. This CFSP decision was not published in the official journal, and Denmark opted out of this decision. But the Danes also said they would not impede the development of closer cooperation among member states in this area. *Agence Europe,* 29 June 1996; *European Report* 2045, 3 July 1996; interview with COREPER official, Brussels, 1996.

49. For example, according to the Irish draft revision of the TEU, the wording of Article J.4 would change to "the *progressive* framing of a common defence policy *in the perspective of* a common defence. . . . The Union *will avail itself of* the WEU to elaborate and implement decisions and actions of the Union which have defence implications" (emphasis added to reflect textual changes).

50. *European Report* 2083, 11 November 1995; 2085, 18 November 1995; 2131, 11 May 1996; no. 2137, 5 June 1996. Also see the Birmingham Declaration of the WEU ministerial meeting (7 May 1996); and the final communiqué of the North Atlantic Council ministerial meeting in Berlin (NATO doc. M-NAC 1-96-63), 3 June 1996.

51. For more on this issue, see Pierre de Vestel, *Defence Markets and Industries in Europe Time for Political Decisions?* (Paris: Institute for Security Studies of the WEU, 1995), and Saferworld, *The Future of the European Defence Industry* (Brussels: Club de Bruxelles, 1994).

52. The Commission's ideas for enhancing the competitiveness of EU defense industries are outlined in the *Commission Communication on the Challenges Facing the European Defence Industry* (Brussels: Commission's Spokesman's Service, 1996). The quote is from *European Report* no. 2094, 20 December 1995. Interviews with members of the reflection group and IGC negotiators, Brussels, 1996. Also see *European Report* 2102, 27 January 1996, and *Agence Europe,* 26 January 1996.

53. CFSP funds still represent only about 0.15 percent of the total Community budget. In addition, this money has been overwhelmingly devoted to the former Yugoslavia; of ECU 110 million (ECU) for the CFSP in 1995, fully ECU 60 million went to Mostar; of about ECU 60 million for the CFSP in 1996, about half went to Mostar. See the EP's *Report on the Financing of the CFSP* (Willockx Report), EP documents 209/630, 18 October 1994.

54. The EP's views are put forth in the *Report of the Committee on Foreign Affairs and Security on Shaping the European Community's Common Foreign Policy* (Aldea Report), EO documents 201/471, 23 October 1992; the *Report on Progress Made in Implementing the Common Foreign and Security Policy (November 1993–December 1994)* (Matutes Report), EP documents 211/241, 24 April 1995; and the No. 5 *Briefing on the CFSP (Third update) of the EP Task Force on the IGC,* EP documents 165/569, 19 October 1995.

55. The Commission's official views are found in the *Commission Report on the Functioning of the Treaty on European Union; and the Commission Opinion on Reinforcing Political Union and Preparing for Enlargement.* Also see the (unofficial) report of the Commission's "High-Level Group of Experts on the CFSP" entitled *The Foreign and Security Policy of Europe for the Year 2000* (Durieux Report) (Brussels: Commission's Spokesman's Service, 1995); interviews with Commission officials, Brussels, 1995–1996; and *Agence Europe,* 29 December 1995.

56. See Council of Ministers, *Report of the Council on the Functioning of the Treaty on European Union,* part 5.

9

France, the CFSP, and NATO

Ronald Tiersky

Maastricht Economics and Chirac's Reform

Only a few years ago, NATO was belittled as an institution that had lost its raison d'être with the Cold War's end. So much a creature of the Cold War, it was unable to find or to create a new and useful purpose. Thus it seemed destined to wither rather than be transformed, faced with a European defense pillar that would soon manage European security problems without the United States.

Bosnia—the big European powers' desolate failure to stop war and "ethnic cleansing"—changed all that. Bosnia demonstrated clearly that Europeans are not yet ready to act on their own in a situation requiring major military action. As even the neo-Gaullist French president Jacques Chirac said on 1 February 1996 in his speech to a joint session of the U.S. Congress, NATO is necessary to European security and "doesn't work without U.S. leadership." Absent the United States in NATO there might today be a Greater Serbia and a Greater Croatia, with a rent Bosnian Muslim people and a rump Muslim governmental "entity" between the two, neither nation nor state.

In 1996–1997 it was European Union plans for an independent Common Foreign and Security Policy and a European Security and Defense Identity that were weakened, set back in schedule and substance. The CFSP and ESDI are still likely to materialize; it could be said that a CFSP already exists to some extent and an ESDI is real in the form of several projects more or less in process. But this will happen at a slower pace and with less self-affirmation than the EU's strongest protagonists had hoped.

NATO, which is already militarily transformed rather than withered and which is expanding rather than dying, now looks to be fundamental to European security for years to come, perhaps for the entire next period in European international relations. A common EU foreign policy may become a more effective European diplomatic voice, but the Europeans are of necessity putting their security eggs in NATO's basket. At the July 1996 Berlin summit, it was agreed that the ESDI will be built *inside* NATO and not as a freestanding, independent WEU European military force. When Chirac succeeded the socialist François Mitterrand in May 1995, the issue of whether the new president would step back from the outgoing president's Europeanism was vital. There have been both changes and continuities, for while any country's national interests tend to be constant or at least long term, they can be pursued in different ways. But the degree of Chirac's Europeanism has been remarkable.

The developing post–Cold War era requires big adaptations in Europe, and Chirac has had the merit of starting to make the big innovations necessary in French defense and security policies, even if he doesn't have the self-confidence or geopolitical sense of Mitterrand (at least Mitterrand during his first term). But what is particularly instructive in a larger sense is that the differences between Mitterrand and Chirac are not what stereotyped understandings of Gaullism and left-wing policy would have supposed.[1]

It is a mistake to define "Gaullism" eternally as de Gaulle's policies of the 1960s. Circumstances change and thus policies, even if basic values remain the same. As Stanley Hoffmann said, Gaullism is more an attitude than a policy. Like the national interest, the "*gaullien*" mindset is neither right nor left but both: national.

First of all, Chirac has confounded the stereotyped expectation that a neo-Gaullist would back away from European integration. Having campaigned in 1995 with the national-oriented promise that reducing unemployment would be his "priority of priorities," he has instead maintained Mitterrand's "European" choice of the "strong franc" achieved through high interest rates to support the currency's exchange rate. The result has been a worsening rather than amelioration of unemployment plus continued economic austerity, but the Single European Currency project remains on track, with Germany and France at the core of it.

The justification for this Bundesbank policy, as with Mitterrand, is the "European" priority, meeting the Maastricht convergence requirements to qualify France for membership in the Single European Currency. Ruled out is new government deficit spending to create jobs, almost certain to increase inflation, budget deficit, and national debt alike: The hardest convergence target is to reduce government deficit spending from 5 percent of GDP in 1995 to the 3 percent required when the first Euro membership list is decided in early 1998.

"La Pensée Unique" and Its Discontents

Chirac's choice of Europe against a national priority of raising employment is what "anti-Maastricht" critics had begun, already before Mitterrand's departure, to call "*la pensée unique*." Loosely translated, this Maastricht orthodoxy, this "single way of thinking," asserts that there is only one sensible strategy and policy for French development today, namely, "Europe." The Euro is in this view a necessity.

Critics say that the *pensée unique* is an excessively conservative, Bundesbank-defined vision of Europe. It is a low-growth recipe in which fear of slipping further behind an economically dominant Germany works budgets and exchange rates to meet arbitrary convergence criteria. The European priority thus fails to justify France's punishing national unemployment rate—in late 1996 pushing 13 percent, about 3.5 million people—and the unnecessarily low economic growth rate that limits job creation and squashes the rising living standards to which the French have become accustomed.

French unemployment, it is true, has been on a persistent upward curve for twenty years under three different presidents, whether with solid or weak parliamentary majorities or the two "cohabitation" governments.[2] Le Pen's National Front (FN) has profited, and so has the French Communist Party (PCF), which has stabilized its long political decline, both playing the old role of protest party, or *tribun,* speaking for the disadvantaged.

The Chirac-Juppé government's promise, which appears weak at best, is that only a year or two more of austerity is necessary, that tax cuts have begun, and that once the Euro is launched an expansion-oriented policy will be possible again.

Chirac's Military Reform and Turn Toward NATO

In contrast with his embrace of Mitterrand's economic, monetary, and social policy, Chirac already in his first year launched a great reform of Mitterrand's legacy of defense, military, and security policies.

A new round of nuclear testing in the French Polynesian islands of Mururoa and Fantgoufre was announced, breaking with Mitterrand's moral high-ground moratorium on nuclear testing begun in 1992. Chirac was accused of reneging on France's commitment to a new total nuclear test ban treaty, when in fact the new round of tests would achieve the capacity for laboratory simulation testing in the future, precisely so the French commitment to a total test ban treaty could be honored, as it was when France and over 100 other nations, including the United States, signed the new accord on the first day possible, 24 September 1996.

A second Chirac innovation was his reversal of France's NATO policy and a new French attitude toward the U.S. military responsibility in post–Cold War Europe. This welcoming of the U.S. military presence and abandonment of the idea of an independent European second pillar based on the WEU and the EU's CFSP resulted from the lessons of the Bosnian debacle.

In Washington in early February 1996, President Chirac called upon the United States not to go home but to remain permanently engaged in European security affairs; he even welcomed U.S. leadership of NATO as necessary. Chirac said that the Europeans' failure to stop the wars in Bosnia demonstrated that a European-only CFSP and defense structure doesn't exist and won't exist for some time. NATO is thus the only realistic European security system, and its expansion to the east is the most certain way to stabilize the region between Germany and Russia. NATO isn't credible without U.S. leadership, and the U.S. presence in Europe is the sine qua non of guaranteeing peace and development in Central and Eastern Europe, the former Soviet bloc countries.

This reevaluation prompted Chirac to announce his intention to return France to some of NATO's central military command institutions.[3] A full French return to a suitably reformed and updated NATO integrated command, meaning one acceptable to the French, seemed a fait accompli, until in August 1996 the French put forward a proposal for a rotating European Armed Forces South (AFSOUTH) command at Naples, which the Americans rejected. This dispute continued, though it seemed likely to be settled by the NATO Council meeting scheduled for late spring 1997.

What happened to Gaullism? Either Chirac was betraying the heritage or adapting the *gaullien* attitude to the 1990s, to a post-Yalta, post–Cold War world in which France was even less capable of going it alone than before. Vis-à-vis NATO and in relation to the Maastricht agreement to create a Common Foreign and Security Policy, Mitterrand seems in a sense the last *gaullien* French president. Or else Gaullism-as-pragmatism is even more flexible than almost anyone thought possible.

In 1996, in a Europe finally beyond Yalta, with the Soviet Union relegated to the dustbin of history and U.S. isolationist tendencies rather than U.S. imperialism the greater danger to European independence, peace, and prosperity, what sense would it make to play the 1960s Gaullist game? Between a tottering Russia susceptible to populist nationalism and a United States looking inward, how could France create post–Cold War political leverage and diplomatic freedom to action? With France's main alliance the permanent partnership with unified Germany, with France's European power dependent on its ties to Germany, could the old French flirtation with a Russian *alliance de revers* be revived, could it still move the United States?[4] Probably not.

Chirac's strategic policy, Gaullist or not, must bring France into a post–Cold War international system on the basis of France's real strengths, stripped of outdated notions of grandeur, glory, and status. Mitterrand might have done likewise, but fatally ill and "cohabiting" politically with the conservative Balladur government for his last few years in office, he hadn't the strength to carry off Chirac's two first-year successes in European security problems: (1) prodding the Clinton administration to lead military action in Bosnia, leading to the Dayton agreement and NATO's reinvigoration; and (2) launching a military reform to turn French capabilities toward post–Cold War conditions.

The CFSP Paradox and Chirac's Military Reform

The French military reform and turn back toward NATO in 1996—assuming the dispute over the AFSOUTH command doesn't reverse it—are part of a multinational, ongoing transformation of European security structures, East and West, which resulted from the collapse of the Soviet Union and the Soviet bloc states.

In France Chirac has launched a thorough transformation of the French military, whose size and capabilities, including nuclear weapons, are being radically shrunk along with the size of the military budget. Consequently French policy toward its EU partners and the CFSP negotiations in the 1996–1997 IGC are also taking a new shape.

Military reduction was not an easy decision politically for Chirac, since downsizing means adding unemployment to unemployment in an economy where successive thresholds of "unacceptable" unemployment (2 million, 2.5 million, 3 million) have been transgressed. Additionally, because French military installations are unusually significant to rural towns, a large number of local and regional economies will be damaged by military base closings. The Maastricht convergence crunch, although not the single cause of austerity, has driven Chirac's defense and military downsizing further than it would have gone in flush times.

The 23 February 1996 Chirac plan for downsizing and modernizing the French military will create a British-style army, meaning a rapid reaction force capable of quickly melding with the other forces, in particular with a German quick reaction conventional force also in the works. This reconfiguring of French military forces, plus a French offer to discuss "all" matters, even nuclear, with NATO partners, showed that Chirac wanted rapidly to implement France's return to NATO's integrated command.

Chirac's military reform concerns not only numbers but the basic structure and configuration of the armed forces, including nuclear weapons. First was a long-debated abandonment of conscription. This should have been more controversial than it was, given historical social and ideological resonances on both the political right and left ("the sacred republican bond of the army and the nation" or the "people's army"). Yet opinion polls showed about 70 percent of respondents favorable to the end of conscription. A "professional," all-volunteer French army will emerge over several years, replacing the Jacobin-Republican conscription army. Furthermore, French strategic thinking is being reoriented from defense, in its Cold War meaning, toward general security problems, including terrorism. The much-maligned Eurocorps, theoretically operational since fall 1995 as a classic conventional armed force, is being sent to Bosnia as part of the "after IFOR" peacekeeping operation.

The uniformed military will shrink from 500,000 to 350,000, or more exactly, excluding the paramilitary gendarmerie, from 400,000 (about 50 percent ten-month conscripts) to 250,000. This means a cut in forces of about one-third and a budget cut of about one-fifth.[5] This smaller military is to be molded around four elite units with the capacity of rapid deployment abroad, to face the kinds of ad hoc crisis situations planners foresee as the likeliest job of French soldiers in the post–Cold War world. Chirac's military reform will also abandon the Gaullist goal of self-sufficiency in all weapon types. This means a restructuring of the defense and arms industry (mergers and streamlining), whose exports as a consequence will drop temporarily, adding to employment and balance-of-trade difficulties. Overall, the Chirac plan is not a mere shrinkage of numbers and budgets but part of an allied cooperative restructuring among the major EU military capabilities, in which post–Cold War national force levels, capabilities, and strategies are being "harmonized," made more complementary—in a word, more Europeanized.

The less shiny causes of downsizing are two: France, like other European powers, just cannot afford a full-range military operation as in the past; and in the Gulf War in 1991, the French learned humiliating lessons about their military insufficiencies. France had trouble mustering barely 15,000 troops for Desert Shield and Desert Storm, whereas British forces were double that size despite a smaller army overall. The French were also less effective in fighting terms: unable to participate in night bombing raids for lack of night radar, for example, and forced to rely completely on U.S. transport.

By 2001, a French full battle force of 50,000–60,000 men is to be deployable, quickly and at distance. No more will the usual French military operation consist of a few hundred soldiers jerry-dispatched to put down a coup d'état or to replace a president somewhere in former French Africa. Germany, as noted above, is also developing a nonconscript "crisis reaction force," about 55,000 strong, to be in place by 1999. With the British and other smaller, similar EU forces, a rapid reaction, post–Cold War European military force of perhaps 250,000 is envisageable in the medium term.

Even the sacrosanct nuclear *force de frappe* is not being spared. The eighteen land-based Albion Plateau (Provence) missiles, symbolic embodiment of the *force de frappe,* were simply closed up in summer 1996, meaning that with surprisingly little fanfare one leg of the nuclear triad, albeit the least valuable and most vulnerable, was amputated. Air-launched missiles and, most important, the nuclear submarines remain. But one fewer nuclear submarine will be built, leaving a fleet of four as opposed to the five scheduled under Mitterrand. Last, Chirac decided, as a gesture to

German sensibilities, to dismantle France's short-range Hades missiles, whereas Mitterrand had had them stored but not destroyed.

Rethinking the future of French nuclear weapons is significant for CFSP, ESDI, and general European security alliance calculations. The French deterrent will remain under French decisionmaking authority, but a European-level *dissuasion concertée,* a "concerted deterrence," may emerge from the CFSP/WEU discussions. A "consultative nuclear deterrent" with Britain could emerge, as well as some consultation on nuclear (and other "ABC" issues—atomic, biological, and chemical weapons) with the EU's nonnuclear powers, especially Germany.[6]

In sum, Chirac's defense and military reform is not a camouflaged scheme to allow military preparedness, patriotism, and self-esteem to slip softly into the night. It is a broad-gauged, genuine modernization years in coming, which might be seen, especially by longtime critics of the gap between French means and Gaullist rhetoric, as admirable in its marriage of Europeanism, Atlanticism, and realism.

As for NATO, having France back in its central command institutions would be a new "unity in diversity," giving the lie to predictions that the end of the Cold War would, by robbing it of its raison d'être, prove fatal to NATO. A reformed NATO is to be Europe's principal security, not the CFSP/WEU/ESDI.[7] Instead of "NATO or nothing," NATO would be reformed, be made relevant to new sorts of missions, reintegrate the French and Spanish in the command structure, and make an expansion to the east combined with reassurances to Russia.

France, the EU, and NATO Enlargement

Questions of NATO enlargement—what new members and what pace and order—have been a first priority since Soviet collapse made Eastern expansion thinkable. Expansion will affect each NATO country differently, according to factors such as geography, size and military power of the member state, and national ambition. NATO's enlargement also raises issues of the relation between European integration and European security, of the intersection between EU and NATO development. European security and European integration are, in fact, increasingly linked and overlapping problems. In certain ways they have even become the same problem, since almost all Central and Eastern European countries would like to be members of both the EU and NATO. Admission in one organization will create added legitimacy for admission to the other.

It is interesting to notice that any new EU member country receives ipso facto a security guarantee, since any threat to an EU member's territory (e.g., some future Russian threat to a Baltic state) will of necessity be seen as a threat to all EU members' security, thus invoking a response that leads back to NATO. So membership is not only a privilege given to candidate countries but a new burden on the two integrated communities, NATO, and the EU. At a minimum, there is much Community financing involved. At a maximum—in the case of NATO's Article 5 guarantees should a member state come under military attack—there is a promise to defend the borders of new and more distant countries that, additionally, are closer to Russia than the old NATO border.

For France, NATO enlargement does not hold the significance it does for Germany, whose new eastern border, the eastern border of the former East Germany, remains NATO's nearest approach to Russia. For France, however, enlargement of NATO would have substantial consequences beyond those of security, in particular for European integration. The French policy on European Union enlargement is acceptance in principle but reticence in practice. As far as the East and Central European applicants to the EU are concerned (the Visegrád countries first of all, i.e., Poland, Hungary, and the Czech Republic), France is seen as a kind of friendly adversary or rather an adversarial friend.

Former president Mitterrand believed that French interests required a "variable-speed" Europe of concentric circles rather than simple expansion for all comers: It would be composed of the present EU as the core, a quasi federation, with a larger "European confederation" around it, which conceivably, in its loosest tie, one day could even encompass Russia.[8] Expansion for some or most East and Central European countries would stop at treaties of association rather than full membership. The resulting confederation would therein avoiding shifting the EU's center of gravity too far eastward and too much under Germany's sway. Nor would it swamp the "little Europe" European Union, already enlarged from twelve to fifteen countries.

In a "little" EU, France has, at least in theory, more leverage over Germany and the other partners. The decisionmaking process is less unpredictable and more controllable, meaning that France in principle can have more influence. In a smaller European Union, furthermore, France "embodies" and represents a weightier agricultural, southern, and Mediterranean group of countries against the German industrial north. The Union has a balance that a new Eastern enlargement would significantly alter.

Of course a larger decisionmaking Council could mean less direct influence for all countries, Germany included. But Germany, for moral and security reasons, believes the EU must be enlarged to the east, and naturally it is geographically, economically, and financially the country most responsible. In fact EU enlargement eastward is Germany's major foreign policy task in the coming period.

NATO enlargement has, in a sense, already occurred or at least begun with the incorporation of the former East Germany. East Germany's collapse into union with West Germany under Article 23 of the Federal

Republic's Basic Law obliged the Western powers to deal with the Soviet Union, not only on the principle of NATO membership of the eastern German Länder but on practical issues such as stationing NATO troops and nuclear weapons. If the USSR were allowed to put conditions on the latter, an unacceptable precedent would be established of a Soviet *droit de regard* over NATO business.

In 1996 NATO Council documents and formal communiqués repeated, to the attention of a Russia in which Boris Yeltsin was presiding over shaky economic modernization and an ominous struggle for political power, that enlargement had been decided. Enlargement had become a question only of when, not if. The important NAC communiqué issued in Berlin on 3 June 1996 made a solemn declaration on this matter, and a formal NATO study, commissioned in 1995, laid out the purposes, principles, and modalities of enlargement, including the vital matter of what guarantees candidate countries not chosen for the first stage can expect from NATO.[9]

The unexpectedly successful Partnership for Peace programs made up a good part of these encouragements and recommendations. Candidate member governments saw in PFP activities just how far their own militaries had to go to meet NATO standards, how costly raising quality would be, and—of prime importance—what civil control of the military really means in principle and practice.

A permanent U.S. leadership role in European security was, as already noted, solicited by Jacques Chirac. His success in convincing a reluctant Clinton administration to lead in several days of bombing attacks on the Bosnian Serb military positions brought an unexpectedly rapid halt to the killing. On his state visit in early February, Chirac said to a joint session of Congress,

> Today, as yesterday, the world needs the United States. . . . [Your] political commitment to Europe and military presence on European soil remain an essential factor in the stability and security of the Continent. . . . France is ready to take part fully in this process of renovation [of NATO], as witnessed by the announcement a few weeks ago of its rapprochement with the military structures of the organization.[10]

By the time of the 3 June NATO communiqué, Chirac had further announced agreement that the European ESDI second pillar of NATO would (as the Germans and British had wanted, against earlier French opposition) be built *within* NATO rather than stand alone. This meant that the Western European Union, the future military arm of the CFSP, would operate only under mandates and implementation instructions from the NATO Council. Because the United States has a veto power in the NAC, U.S. acceptance of a strong ESDI was won.

In the future there may be certain "Europeans-only" NATO missions, without U.S. troop participation, in which the WEU would use NATO's separable but not separate, U.S.-provided, technologically advanced and heavy equipment (strategic lift, logistics, satellite intelligence, and command-and-control equipment). Of course there is a possibility of future European-U.S. disagreements, but this was so in the old NATO. The Europeans know their interest is not to push NATO-CFSP disagreements beyond a certain point. Among the Europeans, French comportment will draw much attention, and Europeans will be very aware of isolationist tendencies in the U.S. Congress. The Europeans will go far, especially after the 1994 scare when Republicans won control of both houses of Congress, to avoid making the United States' NATO role into a major issue in U.S. domestic politics.

In summary, contrary to what had been predicted by alarmists in 1989–1991, the Europeans in post-Yalta Europe have to worry more about pushing the United States out of Europe than about U.S. "hegemony" in European affairs. The current French-U.S. conflict over the AFSOUTH command will most likely be seen in this regard as a passing storm rather than a turning point.

The CJTF and NATO's Future

NATO's attractiveness, as opposed to a self-standing European pillar built on an independent WEU, is increased by the unusual instance of a new idea—the Combined Joint Task Force—proving itself in practice before the name was conceived. The multinational IFOR in Bosnia, which included units from NATO countries and from several non-NATO countries as far away as Pakistan, was not originally conceived as a CJTF, but it became the first example in fact. IFOR, despite all its problems, was a relative success. Criticized for not having arrested indicated war criminals Radovan Karadzic and General Ratko Mladic, nevertheless its primary initial objective of separating the armies, cantoning weapons, and policing the cease-fire frontiers has gone well.

This CJTF approach in NATO interventions could plausibly work widely in future European security crises. Moreover, it is not dependent on U.S. involvement. In 1992–1993 few Europeans took seriously the new Clinton administration's proposals to withdraw the United States to the margins of post–Cold War European security. Today, Europeans fear to the contrary that the minimum contingent of U.S. soldiers on the ground in Europe is the last European hold on a reliable U.S. security commitment in Europe.

Chirac's shift back toward NATO, like the end of conscription, has caused no trembling by party coalitions or concern in domestic public opinion. French popular resentment of NATO's U.S. hegemony seems to have diminished, along with all sorts of other ideological-political cleavages in an increasingly banalized French political culture.[11] The end of the Cold War coincided in France roughly since the late 1970s with the end of left-right ideological hatred reaching back sinuously, in its roots, to the French Revolution.

Conclusion

It might be said that French policy is moving closer to NATO command institutions only after it has ceased to matter and that a French policy less worried about U.S. hegemony is natural after the end of the Cold War. Gaullist France, making its point about independence, paid for its absence from the command structure in several concrete ways: reduced military quality and interoperability and self-exclusion from military consultation and action. Today France will gain more from rejoining the integrated command than will NATO, which had long ago adjusted to France's absence. France needs the post–Cold War NATO integrated command more than the command needs France. But both will profit.

In arguing the United States back into active leadership in European security, Chirac seems to have intuited that France's future European security distinctiveness can be a power of energy and provocation, mainly of Washington. This contrasts with a venerable British strategy of influencing rather than confronting the United States. It is also a French response, adequate or not, to the shock of hearing the Bush administration speak openly of Germany as the United States' new "partner in leadership" in Europe.

Notes

1. See Ronald Tiersky, "France, Germany, and Post–Cold War Europe," in Desmond Dinan (ed.), *Encyclopedia of the European Union* (Bolder: Lynne Rienner, 1998). Some of the material in this article comes from that earlier analysis.

2. After a brief decline after Chirac came to power, the 12 percent rate of the 1990s, of which young people and the long-term unemployed are the largest parts, resumed. Yet the French average growth rate of 2.5 percent in 1987–1995 outclassed several countries whose governments devalued and kept interest rates low, for example, the UK (1.7 percent in the same period) and Italy (1.9 percent).

A good new analysis of the *pensée unique* controversy and recent French economic and social results is Jean-Marcel Jeanneney, *Ecoute la France Qui Gronde* (Paris: Arléa, 1996). See also the first important book on this subject, Jean-Paul Fitoussi, *Le Débat Interdit: Monnaie, Europe, Pauvreté* (Paris: Arléa, 1995).

3. The French defense minister would attend NATO meetings, including those where nuclear policy was discussed, and France would rejoin the permanent Military Committee, which is where the national military chiefs of staff meet. France would also become active in international military staff training programs,

beginning with the NATO Defense College and the Oberammergau College, as well as the NATO situation center, all of which are under jurisdiction of the Military Committee.

4. On the classic realpolitik French *alliance de revers* policy, see Pierre Hassner, "The View from Paris," in Lincoln Gordon (ed.), *Eroding Empire: Western Relations with Eastern Europe* (Washington, DC: Brookings Institution, 1987), pp. 190–192.

5. See Ronald Tiersky, "French Military Reforms and Strategy," *Strategic Forum* #94 (November 1996), pp. 1–4.

6. In 1992–1995 President Mitterrand first suggested a possible Franco-British European nuclear doctrine as part of an independent European defense pillar and CFSP.

7. Spain, also outside the integrated command in similar but not identical circumstances, was set to rejoin the full integrated command in mid-1997. The alliance's newest member (1982), Spain never was inside the integrated military command. Russian policymakers sometimes have suggested, without success, a "Spanish solution" for Poland and other East and Central European NATO candidates.

8. See Ronald Tiersky, *France in the New Europe: Changing Yet Steadfast* (New York: Wadsworth/ Harcourt Brace, 1994), chapters 9–10.

9. "Final Communique," M-NAC-1 (96)63, of the ministerial meeting of the North Atlantic Council in Berlin, 3 June 1996, and "Study on NATO Enlargement," 27 June 1996.

10. Quoted in *New York Times,* 1 February 1996.

11. See Tiersky, *France in the New Europe.*

PART 3

AN EU SOCIETY?

10

Environmental Policy: Deepen or Widen?

John McCormick

While debates rage about the merits of expanding the powers of the European Union and the implications of subsidiarity, relatively few doubts remain about the value of EU activity in the field of environmental protection. A joint EU response has advantages over separate national responses in part because many environmental problems are transboundary in nature and in part because differences in environmental standards create trade distortions, posing a threat to the completion of the single market. There is also wide public support for an EU response; a 1995 Eurobarometer poll found that 82 percent of Europeans consider environmental protection an "immediate and urgent problem" and 69 percent believe that decisions on the environment should be taken at the EU level rather than at the national level.[1] In short, the logic of making environmental policy at the level of the EU rather than the member states acting independently is widely understood.

However, recent developments suggest that a watershed has been reached in the evolution of EU environmental policy and that a fundamental reappraisal of methods, goals, and priorities is under way. Not only have the member states been involved in an intensive discussion through the IGC about the future of European integration, but the Santer Commission has made clear its preference for stimulating more and legislating less, hence it is becoming increasingly common for the Commission to amend existing environmental legislation rather than to develop new legislation. The balance of policymaking power has also shifted since the accession of three environmentally progressive countries (Austria, Finland, and Sweden) and promises to shift again as EU membership expands to Eastern European states with weaker records of environmental protection.

This chapter assesses the record to date on the development of EU law and policy on the environment, outlines a number of problems that need addressing, and identifies a number of emerging trends that may lead to fundamental changes in the way the EU approaches environmental management. It analyzes the implications of the last round of expansion and the potential consequences of Eastern expansion and argues that the time may be ripe for an emphasis on consolidation rather than expansion.

The Evolution of the Environmental Dimension

There was little in the Treaty of Rome that could be interpreted as giving the EEC competence in the field of environmental policy. Just as the environment was not a policy concern of most national European governments during the 1950s and 1960s, so it was low on the agenda of European integration. The few environmental initiatives taken consisted either of legislation promoted by Euratom and aimed at reducing the dangers of radiation, action based on Article 2 of the Treaty (which mentioned in a very general way an interest in the quality of life, the "harmonious" development of economic activities, and "balanced" expansion), or action based on Article 100 (which provided for harmonization of the laws of the member states "as directly affect the establishment or functioning of the common market"). The catchall Article 235—which allowed the Council of Ministers to take action to achieve the goals of the Community where the Treaty had not explicitly provided powers—was also occasionally used as justification.

Community interest in environmental policy heightened following the 1972 UN Conference on the Human Environment, held in Stockholm. This drew the attention of national governments for the first time to the problems of the global environment, prompting the establishment of national environmental ministries and a rapid growth in the development of environmental regulation.[2] It also became much more clear within the Community that the strengthening of national legislation in member states such as West Germany and the Netherlands was causing trade distortions that compromised the construction of the common market.[3] A meeting of the heads of government of the member states in Paris in October 1972 resulted in agreement on the need to accelerate Community action. A small Environment and Consumer Protection Service with fifteen staff members was set up in 1972 and attached to DG III (then responsible for industrial policy), and in 1973 a Standing Committee on the Environment was created in the European Parliament. The same year saw the publication of the first in what would become a series of Environmental Action Programs (EAPs), setting out a general policy direction for the Community.

There was still no clear legal basis for Community action, however, and while more environmental laws were developed and adopted, most were still based on Articles 100 and/or 235. The validity of using Article 100 was upheld by the Court of Justice in a 1980 ruling in which it argued that "provisions which are made necessary by considerations relating to the environment and health may be a burden upon undertakings to which they apply, and if there is no harmonization of national provisions on the matter, competition may be appreciably distorted."[4] Whichever article was used, decisionmaking in the Council of Ministers demanded unanimity, which meant that one member state could block legislation and that because legislation often had to be watered down to the level of the lowest common denominator, the final content of the legislation often imposed only minimal requirements on member states.

Three significant changes came in the 1980s. In 1981 a reorganization of the Commission in the light of Greek accession resulted in the transfer of environmental responsibilities from DG III to a reformulated DG XI, which has since been responsible for environment, nuclear safety, and civil protection. In 1982 the third Environmental Action Program emphasized the importance of taking preventive action to protect the environment and established the principle that environmental concerns should be integrated into all Community policies, thereby giving DG XI considerable influence and pushing the environment further up the policy agenda. Finally and most significant, the 1987 Single European Act gave the Community legal competence in environmental matters by adding Title VII (Environment) to the Treaty of Rome. This confirmed the underlying goals and principles of Community environmental policy and introduced qualified majority voting for environmental measures designed to harmonize national laws in the interests of completing the single market. It was now impossible for any one member state to block proposals, and reluctant member states were encouraged to work harder toward reaching agreement. Since decisions taken by QMV are subject to the cooperation procedure, another consequence was to give more influence to the European Parliament.[5]

The Community also became more active in financing environmental programs, beginning in 1984 with Community Operations Concerning the Environment (COE), which was followed in 1987 by Action by the Community Relating to the Environment (ACE). The reform of the structural funds in 1987 provided the opportunity to extend Community funding to include capital investments for projects that would improve the quality of the environment. This is now undertaken most actively through L'Instrument Financier pour l'Environnement (LIFE). Meanwhile, the Community also became more involved in international negotiations on the environment, playing a key role in reconciling the different positions of the member states and helping promote agreement, for example, on the 1985 Ozone Layer Convention and the 1992 Climate Change Convention.

Concerns about the quality of the data upon which Community policy was based led to the creation in 1985 of the CORINE (Coordinating Information on the Environment) program, whose work was institutionalized in 1990 with agreement to create the European Environmental Agency, which finally began work in 1994. The agency is not a policymaking or implementing body but generates and provides data to the Commission, helps identify new ideas for legislative and policy initiatives, and coordinates the work of the European Information and Observation Network (EIONET). One of the EEA's first tangible projects was the preparation and publication in 1995 of a lengthy survey of Europe's environment (the Dobris Assessment), which provided the most comprehensive picture to date of the state of a regional environment anywhere in the world.[6] Unfortunately, the picture it painted was of progress in some areas but of continuing or worsening problems in many others.

In 1991 Maastricht further refined EU powers by making "sustainable and non-inflationary growth respecting the environment" a fundamental goal of the EU (Article 2), reiterating the importance of the "precautionary principle" (the notion that the EU should take action if there was a suspicion that an activity might cause environmental harm rather than waiting until the scientific evidence was clear), and giving legal force to the application of subsidiarity to all EU policy sectors. Voting by qualified majority has become standard procedure for most environmental measures, and the codecision procedure has given Parliament more powers to amend draft legislation.[7]

By the end of 1995, the EU had adopted 540 regulations, directives, and decisions relating to environmental issues.[8] In terms of their content, most were directed at controlling chemicals and pesticides (27 percent), air pollution (13 percent), and freshwater and marine pollution (11 percent) and protecting nature and wildlife (8 percent). In terms of legislative tools, directives have been the most popular, accounting for 54 percent of environmental laws, with regulations accounting for 25 percent and decisions the remainder. As Table 10.1 indicates, the output of environmental legislation as measured by adoptions grew steadily to a peak in 1994, when sixty-six new pieces of environmental law were adopted. Given the emphasis of the Santer Commission on consolidation rather than the development of new legislation, it may be some time before similar levels of output are reached again. In addition to these legislative tools, the EU has also adopted a variety of nonbinding opinions, recommendations, conclusions, declarations, and resolutions on the environment and since the early 1990s has relied increasingly on the development of green and white papers, attempting to generate policy discussions rather than new laws.

Current Problems

Progress to date on the development of EU environmental policy and legislation has been impressive, and there is little doubt that EU initiatives have helped encourage member states to improve environmental quality. The EU's water and air is cleaner, there is more public awareness of the threats

Table 10.1   The Adoption of EU Environmental Laws

	New Laws Adopted[a]	Amendments[b]	Total Laws Adopted
1958–1972	5	4	9
1973	3	2	5
1974	2	1	3
1975	9	1	10
1976	8	1	9
1977	8	2	10
1978	7	1	8
1979	8	6	14
1980	10	4	14
1981	6	7	13
1982	12	7	19
1983	8	10	18
1984	13	8	21
1985	10	17	27
1986	14	10	24
1987	6	24	30
1988	12	19	31
1989	17	18	35
1990	14	13	27
1991	18	22	40
1992	15	14	29
1993	25	25	50
1994	30	36	66
1995	5	23	28
Total	265	275	540

a. Regulations, directives, decisions.
b. Amendments, elaborations, derogations, supplements, etc.

posed by chemicals to food and water, fish stocks are better managed, the EU is quieter (nearly forty pieces of legislation on noise have been agreed on), and differences in environmental standards pose less of a handicap than before to trade among the member states. In the case of poorer states such as Greece, Spain, and Portugal with little in the way of preexisting environmental policies, almost all their activities in this area have been driven by the obligations of EU membership. However, a number of problems remain, and the changes that may come out of the IGC and out of the accession of new members such as Poland and Hungary emphasize the need for the EU—most notably the Commission—to take stock.

First, the Dobris Assessment made it clear that despite progress to date much remained to be done:

- Although ambient levels of sulfur dioxide (SO_2), lead, and particulates have declined, many European cities still exceed World Health Organization (WHO) guidelines on air quality, thanks mainly to heavy concentrations of road vehicles. The volume of road traffic in Western Europe is expected almost to double between 1990 and 2010, leading the Dobris Assessment to conclude that the benefits of technological improvements could be canceled out by growth in the number of vehicles on European roads.[9]

- Between 1970 and 1990, energy consumption in the EU grew by 1.3 percent annually; intensive agriculture continues to exert pressure on natural habitats, intensifying the threat of extinction for 45 percent of Europe's reptiles and 42 percent of its mammals, introducing increasing amounts of nitrogen and phosphorus into surface waters, and emitting acidifying ammonia into the atmosphere.
- While the production and consumption of ozone-depleting chlorofluorocarbons (CFCs) and halons has fallen almost to zero, levels of chlorine have increased by nearly 600 percent, and the ozone layer over Europe thinned by 6–7 percent between 1979 and 1994.
- Across much of Britain, Germany, and the Benelux states, deposition of acidifying SO_2 and nitrogen oxides exceeds critical loads (the level at which damage to ecosystems begins to occur).
- Per capita municipal waste production more than tripled between 1980 and 1992, although the proportion going into landfills fell as the use of incinerators grew.
- Freshwater is overexploited and polluted by sewage, pesticides, and industrial waste, and pollution continues to be a problem in many coastal zones and marine water.[10]

Second, as the membership and powers of the EU have grown, so its decisionmaking processes have become more convoluted and the time taken to develop new environmental laws and policies has lengthened. DG XI officials often complain that while it once took two to three years to develop a new piece of legislation, the process may now take as long as six to seven years for more complex proposals. This is a blessing in the sense that it allows more interested parties to be involved in the policy development process and so promotes democratic decisionmaking and greater reflection on the potential implications of policy. But it is a curse in that it makes it difficult to respond quickly to worsening problems. Part of the trouble lies in limited resources: Although DG XI had a staff of nearly 490 and an annual budget of ECU 137 million ($168 million) in 1996,[11] it is still only a middle-ranking DG in terms of its size and powers and is both understaffed and underbudgeted given the scope of its responsibilities. Its most serious shortcoming lies in its inability effectively to oversee the implementation of EU law, a flaw that fundamentally devalues the output of new laws and policies.

The problem is also partly structural. EU decisionmaking procedures have become increasingly complex as the focus of policymaking has shifted away from the formal processes outlined in the treaties to informal processes. These have evolved in part to simplify decisionmaking but also in part to ensure as much agreement as possible among interested parties before a legislative proposal leaves the Commission for consideration by the Council and Parliament. This is a noble objective, but it has come at the cost of encouraging frequent and often lengthy interactions involving DG XI, the cabinets of interested commissioners, officials from other interested DGs, COREPER, representatives of the member states in Council working groups, Parliament and its committees, the Economic and Social Committee, national bureaucrats, representatives of non-EU governments where necessary, representatives of industry, and nongovernmental organizations (NGOs).

Another structural problem relates to the challenge of policy integration. Maastricht declared that "environmental protection requirements must be integrated into the definition and implementation of other Community policies" (Article 130r[2]), a requirement that applies to no other EU policy area but whose implications are ambiguous. Jans points out that the definition of "environmental protection requirements" is unclear, that questions have been raised whether the principle implies that environmental policy has a measure of priority over all other EU policy areas, and that nothing is said in Maastricht about how conflicts between environmental protection and the goals of other policy areas should be resolved. It also raises the interesting legal question of whether or not the legitimacy of an action of the Council or the Commission in the fields of transport or agriculture, for example, could be challenged on the basis that it infringed or did not fully take into account the environmental implications.[12] Despite the ambiguities, DG XI made policy integration a priority of its management plan for 1996, helping prompt an internal reorganization called MOVE (Management, Organization, Vision, Environment), aimed in part at improving coordination within DG XI and at helping DG XI keep up with developments in other units of the Commission.

Third, problems are caused by the imbalance of interests involved in the development of EU law. Like most units of the Commission, DG XI has become adept at identifying and working with outside parties with an interest in the form and content of environmental legislation. However, those interests are unequally represented. Writing about EU administration in general, Middlemas notes the role of "peak organizations or federations" and "corporate players" and the importance of interdependence and "bargaining through networks in a densely structured game" concluding that the EU system provides little protection for weaker interests and "privileges the more efficient ones."[13] This is abundantly true of environmental policy, where industry has considerably more influence than do environmental NGOs.

The development of legislative proposals invariably involves DG XI officials in discussions not only with the member states and other interested DGs but with specific manufacturers (for example, negotiations on vehicle emissions have seen the active involvement of Europe's major auto manufacturers, such as Renault, Fiat, and BMW) as well as Brussels-based industrial lobbies and federations such as the European Chemical Industry Council, Eurelectric (representing public and private electricity generators), and the European Crop Protection Association (representing pesticide manufacturers). Groups such as these have developed an influential symbiotic relationship with the Commission and are actively involved in the development of new laws and policies from the earliest stages. Not only do they represent distinct communities with specific interests, but they are well organized and funded, have a vested interest in the negotiations given that they are centrally involved in the implementation of subsequent legislation, employ technical experts or consultants who can provide the Commission with badly needed information and respond authoritatively and persuasively to the often detailed technical content of DG XI proposals, and are adept at quantifying the costs and benefits of such proposals.

By contrast, two other sets of interests are relatively poorly represented in the DG XI policymaking process: the European Parliament and environmental NGOs. MEPs and their support staff are overworked and have relatively little in the specialist technical knowledge and background often required of participants in the development of environmental legislation. Moreover, Parliament is not required to defend its position until it is presented with a finished proposal from the Commission. The result is that Parliament is rarely involved in the critical early stages of the development of new legislation in the Commission, and MEPs are rarely able to offer constructive input into the development of proposals until much later in their evolution. By the time they see proposals, they have already been the subject of intensive discussion involving the Commission, industry, the member states, and the Council of Ministers. MEPs by then have relatively little to add, and the Commission has little incentive to do more than pay lip service to the opinions of Parliament. In short, the role of Parliament in initiating or influencing the development of proposals is marginal.[14]

NGOs, too, are failing to live up to their potential. Richardson suggests that DG XI has been helped in its deliberations (on water policy, at least) by "a politicised, mobilised, and effective constituency of environmental groups,"[15] but this is a debatable proposition. Not only is the constituency of environmental NGOs at the European level harder to define and its collective views more difficult to outline and represent, but there is a common perception both inside and outside DG XI that the NGOs have few of the strategic advantages enjoyed by industry. By their nature, NGOs tend to have to focus on a broad variety of issues, so their staff are rarely experts and rarely in the position authoritatively to oppose the arguments of industry. NGOs are also poorer, have fewer staff, and are not well placed to employ expert consultants. They are routinely invited to attend Commission advisory committee meetings but seldom have the time, thereby absenting themselves from the early stages in the development of law and policy. The consequences are illustrated by the lobbying associated with the 1994 packaging and packaging waste directive (94/62): A study found that of the 279 lobbying entities that contacted DG XI as the directive moved towards adoption in 1990–1993, just over 70 percent represented trade and industrial interests, while less than 4 percent represented environmental interests.[16]

The source of NGO weaknesses is both structural and organizational. The Brussels offices of groups such as the World Wildlife Fund and the European Federation for Transport and Environment are professional and effective to the extent that they can be, but their resources are thinly stretched and there is surprisingly little coordination among them. Although the seven major NGOs have worked together informally in recent years and have influenced policy development in various ways,[17] it is difficult not to conclude that more could be done, even with limited resources, to improve NGO input into the development of EU law and policy. Nowhere is this more true than with the European Environmental Bureau (EEB), an umbrella body that claims to represent more than 160 national organizations with 11 million individual members. Theoretically, it is in a good position to take a leading role in improving the quality of NGO influence, but it has suffered from poor administration, and its influence on the Commission and Parliament has been modest at best.

The result of these tendencies is that EU environmental law and policy reflects more fully and accurately the priorities and positions of corporate Europe than it does of environmental NGOs and European consumers. The imbalance may become even more marked as the Commission develops more voluntary agreements with industry, an approach that was given priority status by the Commission's work program for 1996. If the EU is to be more responsive to the needs of Europeans as a whole, then the Commission needs to work more closely with environmental NGOs, but those NGOs also need to improve their performance in a way that encourages the Commission to solicit their input and opinions on a more regular basis.

Finally, there is the problem of the "implementation deficit." The Commission has been productive in quantitative terms in the development of new law and policy on the environment, but questions have long been raised about its record in implementation. Only since the early 1990s have the Commission and the Council begun to pay more attention to improved implementation, which is listed in the fifth EAP as one of five priorities for the Commission. The annual Commission reports on the implementation of EU law now routinely show a mixed performance on environmental legislation and in 1995 revealed that suspected breaches were more common in the environmental field than in any other field except completion of the internal market.[18] Not only is there considerable variance in the transposition of EU law into national law (ranging in 1994 from 76 percent in Italy and 82 percent in Britain and Portugal to 98 percent in the Netherlands and 100 percent in Denmark), but even where laws have been transposed, there are doubts about the efficacy of practical application. The Commission has traditionally relied heavily on complaints as a method of detecting noncompliance, but the numbers of complaints may say more about the culture of a member state than they do about real levels of application.[19]

The reasons for poor implementation are many and varied. Haigh notes the complications arising out of the sheer number of pieces of EU legislation in force, the difficulties of assessment arising out of the many different goals of environmental law (from limiting emissions to setting environmental quality standards and restricting the production of selected substances), and the often very different time frames involved in implementation. He also cites the many different national, regional, and local authorities that may take part in implementation (and variations in their levels of staffing and training), the large number of different projects subject to laws such as the 1985 directive on environmental impact assessment, and ambiguities in reporting requirements.[20]

Demmke notes the difficulties arising from differences in administrative structures among EU member states. The transposition of EU law into national law, for example, calls for cooperation and coordination among four local government units in Belgium, seventeen in Germany, eleven in Austria, autonomous units in Spain, regions in Italy, *départements* in France, and so on.[21] Other problems include the costs (which some member states are better able to meet than others), the variable quality of information provided by the member states to the Commission, the vagueness of the wording in many environmental directives (e.g., the "best available technology" for emissions control or the "safe disposal" of waste), the broad-ranging nature of many directives, the lack of public involvement in monitoring application, and—most fundamental—the Commission's lack of powers of enforcement.

Attempts have been made to improve the record since 1992 with the creation of IMPEL (the EU Network for the Implementation and Enforcement of Environmental Law). This brings national environmental enforcement authorities together informally at biannual meetings chaired jointly by DG XI and the member state holding the presidency of the EU. It aims to improve implementation by encouraging the exchange of information and experience and improving communication between the Commission and the member states. Although IMPEL has its uses, the creation of a new committee and process to discuss the shortcomings of existing committees and processes is not the answer. The need for time to reflect lends weight to the current tendency in the Commission to draw up fewer new laws and to concentrate instead on improving the efficacy of the existing body of laws. Problems in implementation are due only in part to misunderstandings, ambiguities, and misapplication; a more essential problem is caused by the barriers preventing the Commission from adopting one of the most basic powers of a bureaucracy, the power of enforcement. Until the Commission has the power to oblige national governments to transpose EU law into national law, to closely monitor the application of EU law, and to compel relevant national and local authorities to apply the law and report on its application, problems with implementation will remain. However, to give the Commission those kinds of powers would radically alter the balance of power between the EU and the member states.

Emerging Trends

The IGC will undoubtedly lead to changes in the structure of EU decision-making and the relationship among the EU institutions, but changes have already begun to emerge that involve fundamentally new approaches to making policy and achieving policy goals.

The Changing Balance of Member States

The expansion of EU membership until 1995 meant relatively few problems of adjustment, even though richer and poorer states have brought very different priorities and assumptions to the environmental policy debate. The tensions that existed between lead states and laggard states are well established in the literature;[22] some states have been in favor of tighter regulation (notably the Netherlands and Germany), while others have not (notably Britain). Tensions might have worsened with the absorption of East Germany, but it imposed more costs on the former West Germany than on the rest of the EU. By contrast, the 1995 enlargement brought three environmentally progressive states into the Union (Austria, Sweden, and Finland), shifting the balance toward a more aggressive pursuit of rigorous environmental standards. The expansion of membership to countries such as Poland, Hungary, and the Czech Republic will likely broaden the gulf between the leaders and the laggards, increasing the political tensions in making policy.

Austria, Finland, and Sweden made clear from the outset their expectations for more stringent environmental controls. The environment was high on their lists of concerns during negotiations on accession, and the three states were allowed a four-year transitional period following accession, during which they were to be allowed to maintain stricter standards than those prevailing within the rest of the EU (the so-called horizontal solution). Their expectation was that at the end of this period (January 1999), there would be common standards across all fifteen member states and that the twelve older members would have met the standards of the three new-comers rather than the three having to lower their standards to the level of the older members.[23] This transitional period encouraged the Commission to take a more ambitious approach to environmental issues, the pressure for which was heightened by rumors in early 1996 that representatives from Austria, Denmark, Finland, Germany, the Netherlands, and Sweden had met to discuss the possibility of creating an "Eco-Schengen" grouping aimed at coordinating pressure for more rapid progress on implementing environmental legislation.[24]

A cautionary note is injected, however, by the challenges of integrating new Eastern European members. It is already clear that they have much to do to meet the environmental policy conditions required for entry; among the problems that have emerged are the superficial quality of the dialogue so far between the EU and the Eastern Europeans, the lack of basic infor-mation and statistics, the absence of national strategies, poor monitoring and enforcement of national law, and the priority given to economic growth over environmental protection.[25] The process of adjustment has already been anticipated to some extent in cooperative programs aimed at helping Eastern European states make their economic transition. For example, the PHARE program was created in 1989 to provide assistance to Poland and Hungary but has since expanded to almost all the states of Central and Eastern Europe. Its environmental element, initially reactive in the sense that it focused on providing equipment, studying specific problems, and helping establish standards and regulations, has shifted to a focus on sup-porting activities linked to national environmental policy implementation. In its first five years of operation (1990–1995) it made available about ECU 430 million to environmental and nuclear safety projects. However, not only has the administration of PHARE been criticized, but it will take considerably larger sums of money to pay for the adjustments needed to bring Eastern European states closer to the environmental standards preva-lent in the EU.

Economic Incentives and Effect-based Solutions

EU policy and legislation on the environment has so far concentrated main-ly on a "command and control" approach based on legislating changes in the sources of environmental problems, for instance, limiting emissions from road vehicles and combustion plants, setting limit values for dis-charges of dangerous substances into water, placing limits on noise levels from machinery, and so on. A combination of worsening economic prob-lems such as unemployment, the need for the EU to become more competi-tive on the global market, and doubts about the efficacy of source-based approaches has encouraged a move toward cost-effectiveness and more flexible solutions tailored to different environmental conditions.

The shift toward economic incentives is exemplified by the emphasis in the fifth EAP and the Commission work program for 1996 on voluntary agreements, economic instruments such as eco-taxes, and the overall goal of sustainable economic development. The record so far on putting these goals into practice has been mixed. A directive on environmental impact assessment of public- and private-sector projects was adopted in 1985 and amended in mid-1996, but a proposal for an EU-wide CO_2/energy tax has proved controversial, meeting with the opposition of Britain and several southern member states and delays within the Council and Parliament. Work was also under way in mid-1996 on an initiative aimed at drawing up voluntary agreements between industry and local authorities.

The tendency toward effect-based solutions to environmental problems is exemplified by the EU program on acidification, which has so far aimed mainly at setting limits on motor vehicle emissions, airborne concentrations of suspended particulates and lead, and the sulfur content of fuel and at encouraging a sliding scale of percentage reductions in emissions of SO_2 and NO_x. At the core of the program is the 1988 large combustion plant directive, which aims to cut SO_2 emissions overall by 58 percent by 2003 and NO_x emissions by 30 percent by 1998 (although SO_2 targets run as high as 70 percent for Belgium, France, Germany, and the Netherlands, whereas emission *increases* are allowed for Greece, Ireland, and Portugal). While such approaches have been useful and SO_2 emissions had fallen by 47 percent for the twelve members of the EU between 1980 and 1993,[26] the inclination among European scientists since the late 1980s has been toward policy based on differences in the sensitivity of different environments to acidifying pollutants. The "critical load" approach attempts to quantify pollutant thresholds at which harmful effects occur in different ecosystems[27] and thereby to set emission limits based more on protecting sensitive ecosystems than on across-the-board percentage reductions. In mid-1996 DG XI was in the early stages of developing a strategic approach to acidification, with the objective of reaching the target outlined in the fifth EAP of not exceeding critical loads anywhere in the EU. This effect-based approach is becoming an increasingly common element of the EU approach to environmental protection.

Consolidation Rather Than Expansion

It has become clear in recent years that the Commission in general—and DG XI in particular—has moved away from launching new initiatives and more toward consolidation of its existing activities. This is in part due to the legal force given by Maastricht to subsidiarity, which has encouraged the Commission to screen legislative proposals for their conformity with the principle of subsidiarity, leading to the tabling of fewer new proposals and the withdrawal of some.[28] Table 10.1 shows clearly that while amendments, elaborations, and derogations have been a part of the DG XI legislative calendar since the beginning, the relative volume of new legislation and amendments has changed significantly. Although 70–90 percent of the environmental laws adopted by the Council of Ministers in the late 1970s consisted of entirely new regulations, directives, or decisions, the proportion was down to 45–55 percent by the early 1990s. Of the twenty-eight pieces of legislation adopted in 1995, all but five were amendments of existing laws.

The trend was confirmed by the Commission's work program for 1996. These programs have not always proved reliable predictors of actual achievements (the waters are muddied by the difficulty of foreseeing how the Council will receive every new legislative proposal), but the 1996 program was notable for its emphasis on discussion rather than legislation. The theme of the program was "stimulating more and legislating less,"[29] and although only nineteen entirely new pieces of legislation were proposed, the Commission promised nearly fifty action plans and thirty-five measures aimed at stimulating public debate. In the environmental field, only two legislative initiatives were proposed (on organic compound emissions caused by the use of solvents and on action to be taken on end-of-life road vehicles). Meanwhile, the Commission suggested fostering public discussion on reaching voluntary agreements with industry, the use of green levies and charges, the need to improve implementation, and future directions on noise, waste, and recycling.[30]

The IGC and the Future

The environment was added to the agenda of the IGC barely two weeks before the conference opened, largely at the instigation of the more environmentally progressive Scandinavian member states.[31] At the opening meeting in March 1996, the Italian presidency noted the importance of making environmental protection more effective and coherent at the level of the Union, with a view to promoting sustainable development. Denmark, Finland, and Sweden made clear their support for this view and for the need to ensure greater integration of environmental policy with other policy areas, notably agriculture, transport, industry, and European networks. Calls were made for discussion on the need to improve enforcement and implementation, clarification of the implications of subsidiarity in relation to environmental law, greater public access to EU documents and to Council discussions on legislation, the extension of majority voting to all environmental decisions, and renewed attempts to have the right to a healthy environment included in Treaty provisions.[32]

There is little question that much has already been achieved as a result of EU initiatives on the environment but equally little question that new approaches are needed to address the many problems that remain. The existence of these problems along with weaknesses in the "command and control" approach offered by regulation and legislation and shortcomings in the enforcement of EU law has encouraged the Commission to shift increasingly toward solutions based on economic incentives, voluntary agreements with industry (which in a sense confirm the already close association that exists between the Commission and industry), and more flexible solutions tailored to fit the different needs of different environments and member states. These will surely provide the Commission with more effective tools with which to approach Western Europe's environmental problems, allowing the EU to build on an already impressive record in this critical policy area.

Notes

Much of the material on which this chapter was based was collected during my secondment to DG XI in summer 1996, and many of the arguments I raise here—and the conclusions drawn—are based on interviews conducted both inside and outside the Commission with officials and lobbyists who often preferred that their views and comments remain anonymous.

For their help in making the secondment both possible and fruitful, I would like to thank Jonathan Davidson, Tom Garvey, and Pat Murphy. I would also like to thank the staff of the DG XI library for their help in searching for documents and other information and to the many individuals I interviewed for their often candid and insightful comments. Finally, my sincere thanks to the Office of Faculty Development and the Office of International Programs at Indiana University for their welcome and valuable funding support.

1. European Commission, *Europeans and the Environment* (Brussels: DG XI Documentation Centre, 1995).

2. John McCormick, *The Global Environmental Movement,* 2d edition (London: Wiley, 1996), chapter 5.

3. Robert Garner, *Environmental Politics* (London: Prentice-Hall, 1996), pp. 120–121.

4. Case 92/79, 18 March 1980, *Commission v. Italy* [1980] ECR 1115, [1981] 1 CMLR 331.

5. Nigel Haigh, *Manual of Environmental Policy: The EC and Britain* (Harlow: Longman, 1992), p. 2.3.

6. David Stanners and Philippe Bourdeau (eds.), *Europe's Environment: The Dobris Assessment* (Luxembourg: Office for Official Publications of the European Communities, 1995).

7. Haigh, *Manual of Environmental Policy,* p. 2.3 note 5.

8. John McCormick, *The Greening of Europe: Environmental Policy and the European Union* (London: Wiley, forthcoming).

9. Stanners and Bourdeau, *Europe's Environment,* chapter 4, note 6.

10. For more information, see ibid. and European Environment Agency, *Environment in the European Union 1995* (Luxembourg: Office for Official Publications of the European Communities, 1995), chapter 4.

11. Directorate General XI (Environment, Nuclear Safety, and Civil Protection), *Management Plan 1996* (Brussels: DG XI, 1996).

12. Jan Jans, "Objectives and Principles of EC Environmental Law," in Gerd Winter (ed.), *European Environmental Law: A Comparative Perspective* (Aldershot: Dartmouth, 1996).

13. Keith Middlemas, *Orchestrating Europe: The Informal Politics of European Union, 1973–1995* (London: Fontana, 1995), pp. xv–xvi.

14. Shirley Williams, "Sovereignty and Accountability in the European Community," in Robert O. Keohane and Stanley Hoffmann (eds.), *The New European* (Boulder: Westview, 1991), p. 160.

15. Jeremy Richardson, "EU Water Policy: Uncertain Agendas, Shifting Networks and Complex Coalitions," *Environmental Politics* 3, 4 (Winter 1994): 139–167.

16. M. H. Porter, "Cross-national Policy Networks and the EU's Packaging and Packaging Waste Directive." Paper presented to an EU-sponsored conference in Sonderberg, Denmark, April 1995. Quoted by Alan Butt Philip, "David Versus Goliath? The Challenge for Environmentalists in the Making and Implementing of EU Environmental Policy," paper presented at the European Community Studies Association conference, 11–14 May 1995, Charleston, South Carolina.

17. See, for example, the publications *Greening the Treaty* and *Greening the Treaty II,* published in 1990 and 1995, respectively, by a consortium of environmental NGOs based in Brussels.

18. *Official Journal of the European Communities,* OJ C 254, vol. 38, 29 September 1995.

19. *ENDS Report* 249 (October 1995): 37–38.

20. Nigel Haigh, "Effective Environment Protection—Challenges for the Implementation of EC Law," paper presented to a joint public hearing on implementation and enforcement of EC environmental law, European Parliament, Brussels, 30 May 1996.

21. Christoph Demmke, European Institute of Public Administration, comments made to the joint public hearing on implementation and enforcement of EC environmental law, European Parliament, Brussels, 30 May 1996.

22. See, for example, Sbragia, Alberta, "Environmental Policy," in Helen Wallace and William Wallace (eds.), *Policy-Making in the European Union,* 3d edition (Oxford: Oxford University Press, 1996).

23. "New Members Want Tougher Standards," in *Environmental Liability Report* (ELR) 029 (January 1996): 4–5.

24. "Six States Form 'Eco-Schengen,'" *ELR* 032 (April 1996): 8.

25. "Long Way to Go Before Accession," ELR 029 (January 1996): 7–8.

26. UN Economic Commission for Europe, *Strategies and Policies for Air Pollution Abatement,* ECE/EB.AIR/44, table 1 (New York: United Nations, 1995).

27. K. R. Bull, "An Introduction to Critical Loads," *Environmental Pollution* 77, 2/3 (1992): 173–176.

28. Haigh, *Manual of Environmental Policy,* p. 2.3, note 5.

29. *ENDS Report* 250 (November 1995): 35–36.

30. European Commission, "Commission's Programme for 1996," supplement to *Bulletin of the European Union,* COM (95) 512 final.

31. *ENDS Report* 255 (April 1996): 40–42.

32. Ibid.

11

EU Social Policy After Maastricht: The Works Council Directive and the British Opt-Out

Robert Geyer & Beverly Springer

EU social policy entered a new era with the adoption of the Maastricht Treaty. The development of that policy had been hampered by British opposition in the Council and the requirement that the Council adopt most social policy directives by unanimous vote. Proponents of social policy were unable to overcome these obstacles and rally support in an environment where social policy was never a high priority. The Treaty created qualified majority voting in the Council for most areas of social policy, strengthened the powers of the Parliament (always a strong supporter of social policy), and with the inclusion of the Social Protocol introduced a method to bypass the British veto. The adoption of the European Works Councils directive in 1994 represented the first victory in a twenty-year struggle by proponents of social policy to get a proposal for worker participation through the Council. The victory was made possible by the Social Protocol, whereby Britain lost its ability to block the proposal, as it had all previous ones dealing with worker participation.

   Although the history of the post-Maastricht era is short, enough evidence exists to discern possible trends in social policy and, most important, to draw some preliminary conclusions regarding the impact of the European Works Council directive. The purpose of this chapter is to examine these trends and to look at the impact of the European Works Council directive, particularly as it affects the United Kingdom, the member state not formally covered by the directive. That many corporations have voluntarily extended participation to their employees in the United Kingdom raises questions about the viability of the British "opt out." The final section of the chapter includes speculations regarding the significance of the research for integration and the ability of member states to pursue an à la carte Europe.

Social Policy in the Post-Maastricht Era

Social policy fills an uneasy place in the panorama of EC policies. It serves a number of objectives: providing for the free movement of labor, fulfilling concepts of social justice, harmonizing different national policies, and perhaps building support for European integration among the citizens of the member states. The legitimacy of social policy has always been contested. It has fervent supporters and tenacious opponents. National labor unions compose the core of the supporters of social policy; the European Trade Union Confederation (ETUC) is their voice in Brussels. The opposition is spearheaded by the Union of Industries of the European Community (UNICE), the counterpart of the ETUC and the voice of business interests in Brussels. The ETUC finds allies in DG V, the divisions of the Commission where social proposals are drafted, and in Parliament, where the Social Democratic Party group and the Democratic Christian Party group dominate and are generally sympathetic to social concerns. UNICE is supported by the prevailing economic paradigm and the sensitivity of political leaders in the Council to warnings that social policy makes European firms less competitive than U.S. or Japanese firms in the contest for global markets.

Two major documents are landmarks in the decade preceding the Maastricht Treaty, and both continue to influence the present era. The Social Dimension, the social policy counterpart of the white paper on the internal market, lays out proposals to protect employees from possible negatives arising from the creation of the single market. The Community Charter (Social Charter) of the Fundamental Social Rights of Workers is the workers' bill of rights; it ties together social policy and human rights as they relate to the workplace. The EU has a role, which it shares with the member states, in protecting those rights.

The Treaty on European Union provides the legal basis for the current era of social policy. The framers of the document were forced to go to extraordinary lengths in order to reach agreement on the provisions for social policy, which is dealt with both in the body of the treaty and in the Social Protocol. The text of the treaty leaves relatively unchanged the provisions for social policy found in the Single European Act. The Social Protocol, however, makes major changes: It allows the members of the EU, with the exception of the United Kingdom, to adopt policies related to the objectives of the Social Charter despite British opposition. Such policies require only a qualified majority vote in the Council, except for policies dealing with social security, protection of workers when their employment contract is terminated, codetermination or related topics, conditions of employment for third-country nationals, and financial contributions for promotion of employment (except the Social Fund).[1] The latter measures require a unanimous vote in the Council by all members of the Council with the exception of the United Kingdom. A policy adopted under the Social Protocol is in force in all member states except the United Kingdom, but British firms operating in other member states must comply with the policy for their operations in the other member states. Social policy may also be made by the social partners (primarily the ETUC and UNICE), who may negotiate an agreement that in some cases may be adopted by a Council decision following a proposal from the Commission.

Ten months after the Maastricht Treaty went into effect in November 1993, the Council adopted the EWC directive, signaling for many a new and more hopeful era for social policy. The promise of the new era is tempered by the prevailing economic climate and the commitment to create a single currency in 1999. Economic objectives are top priority. Any proposal will be examined to ensure that it does not harm the competitiveness of European firms or add to the deficit of national governments.

In general, social policy in the post-Maastricht era, with two notable exceptions, has been characterized more by continuity than by new developments. The actors continue to work on proposals that have been around for years and even decades. Little has happened on the legislative front. Following the acceptance of the EWC directive (one of the notable exceptions), the Council did not adopt another social directive (one on health and safety) until December 1995. In the span of this chapter, we cannot trace the entire history of social policy in the new era, but we can consider three facets of social policy that illustrate the characteristics of this post-Maastricht era: employment policy, equality policy, and social dialogue. The first is a major concern of the EU today, the second is a traditional policy, and the third is a potentially important development that may provide a new channel for making social policy. All three policies are priorities for Sweden, Finland, and Austria, the newest members of the EU.

Employment rather than social policy per se has taken the center stage since 1991. Despite the promise of the single market, Europe has not been able to generate enough jobs for its population. The job market expanded between 1985 and 1990, but then the situation took a dramatic turn for the worse between 1991 and 1994, when the number of employed decreased by 4 percent, the worst decline in the postwar period.[2] A number of highly publicized documents trace the EC efforts to improve the situation. The 1993 "White Paper on Growth, Competitiveness, and Employment" emphasized job creation through major infrastructure building programs.[3] It also laid down the premise on which all subsequent discussions on employment have been developed, linking competitiveness and job creation. According to the premise, high European labor costs are a major reason for the loss of competitiveness. "European Social Policy," a white paper issued the following year, remarked that "competitiveness is crucial for wealth and job creation and . . . labour market policies . . . need to be reoriented."[4] The employment problem dominated the agenda whenever social policy was discussed in meetings of the European Council. The Essen Council cited five specific requirements that must be met if Europe is to create jobs. The third point poses the most difficult challenge: "Reducing non-wage labour costs extensively enough to ensure that there is a noticeable effect on decisions concerning the taking on of employees."[5] The point was reiterated in the 1995–1997 Medium-Term Social Action Program.

The crux of the problem facing the EU is how to resolve the inherent contradiction between job creation through increased competitiveness and the preservation of traditional employee protections. EU leaders argue that they can square the circle by trimming protections and setting European standards so that member states have a level playing field for social costs. Workers keep their basic protections, but employers gain flexibility and lower labor costs. The plan, called the European social model, is promoted as a preferred alternative to the harsher U.S. model, in which jobs are created but protections sacrificed.

The EU employment policy has had high visibility but little focus. Observers have the sense that those responsible for it are still searching for solutions and are hampered by a lack of support in the member states where employment policy has traditionally resided. The policy has had modest successes in setting up a number of vocational education schemes, the creation of a European employment agency, and the completion of previous programs. Padraig Flynn, the European social affairs commissioner, admitted that the European social model is not working as it was intended.[6] In January 1996, as Italy assumed the presidency of the Council, the Italian minister of labor reiterated the refrain that labor costs must be reduced in order to create jobs.[7] In early 1996 Jacques Santer, the president of the Commission, abruptly launched a new initiative, calling on the social partners (primarily UNICE and the ETUC) to work with him to reach a "European Confidence Pact" to ease the unemployment problem. His model was the German social pact in which the government, labor, and employers negotiated a package of concessions in order to encourage job creation. The social partners (and many in the EU as well) were surprised by the initiative. They initially supported it, but then the leader of UNICE expressed serious reservations. Undeterred, Santer called a major tripartite conference for June 1996. This new initiative on employment illustrates what appears to be an increasingly strong trend in the EU: Interest groups are co-opted into the policy arena and called on to assume responsibility for formulating and implementing social policy.

While the employment issue holds center stage in the EU, the equality program has had an interesting if less visible history in the post-Maastricht era. The program, based on Article 119 of the Treaty of Rome, has extensive support in the Commission, Parliament, and organizations active in Brussels. It has been a useful supplement to national programs that protect the rights of working women. Its supporters, although disappointed by their failure to insert special provisions in the Maastricht Treaty, hoped to use the Social Protocol to advance proposals blocked by the British. They have had one major success and one significant disappointment, and one objective is still under discussion. Three recent or ongoing issues that give insights into the status of the equality program today are the parental leave policy, the burden-of-proof directive, and the fate of the latest framework program.

The parental leave policy is the second notable success in the social arena in the post-Maastricht era (the adoption of the EWC directive being the other). The Commission first proposed a directive on parental leave in 1983, but the proposal failed to gain the requisite unanimous vote in the Council. Belgium revived it in 1993 during its presidency of the Council. In 1994, instead of pursuing a traditional legislative strategy, Commissioner Flynn asked the social partners to reach an agreement under the provisions of Article 4.2 of the Social Protocol of the Maastricht Treaty[8]—the first use of that article. In December 1995 the social partners reached an agreement that the Commission adopted, adding to it a clause that banned racial discrimination in the application of the law. The agreement, passed by the Social Affairs Council on 29 March 1996, is binding on all the member states (except the "opted-out" UK). It provides parents with a minimum of three months' leave before a child's eighth birthday, but member states may provide longer leave. Employees are entitled to the leave no matter what type of employment contract they have or what size firm employs them. They also have a guaranteed right to return to work following their leave.

The adoption of the directive is a major victory for supporters of equality policy but is perhaps more significant for the process of its adoption than for the substance of the directive. The Maastricht Treaty of course provided the possibility, but the interesting point is that this directive was shaped in a dialogue by the social partners, bypassing the usual process of policymaking. The social partners found the necessary consensus that had eluded participants inside the EU. As in the case of the employment policy, the social partners were called upon to play a new and significant role.

The case of the proposed burden-of-proof directive shows another use of the social partners. The proposal, which would make employers responsible for supplying proof in cases of sex discrimination, had been before the EU for a number of years without action by the Council. The Commission revived it in the new era but faced the opposition of both UNICE and Britain. In contrast to the parental leave policy, the burden-of-proof proposal moved into new territory. Parental leave has wide public support, and all but three member states already had such policies; no such groundwork exists for the burden of proof. The EU would not be setting a minimum standard but imposing one that would require changes in most member

states. Employers had an effective argument when they said that the proposal would burden them with new costs and responsibilities. Because the
Commission could not find grounds for a consensus, Commissioner Flynn
asked the social partners to join in the negotiations under the provisions of
the Agreement on Social Policy and the Social Protocol. Under Article 3 of
the agreement, the Commission consulted the social partners in July 1995,
then drafted a new proposal that moderated the burden of proof so that
responsibility would be shared by both the employer and the employee concerned. In February 1996 Flynn gave notice to start a new round of consultations with the social partners, but agreement is unlikely in the present situation.

The third topic relevant for equality policy in the post-Maastricht era is
the fate of the fourth Equal Opportunities Action Program, which ran into
serious opposition when it came before the Council. The objection of the
United Kingdom was predictable, but German opposition raised serious
concerns. The program was adopted only after the proposed budget was cut
by 50 percent to provide ECU 30 million over the life of the program
(1996–2001). The previous budget was ECU 32.9 million. Since the EU
now consists of fifteen members rather than twelve, Belgium, supported by
eight other members, argued that the new amount would not even be adequate to meet the commitments made at the Beijing UN conference.[9]
Germany had objected to the program and questioned the right of the
Commission to introduce such action programs because they infringe on
the sphere of national governments. Following the budget cut, Germany
accepted the program, but the limited funding and the opposition of
Germany do not bode well for equality policies.

The social dialogue provides a very different type of policy from the
employment policy or equality policy. The policy was formalized in the
Single European Act (Article 22, which amends Article 118 of the Treaty of
Rome). The article charges the Commission to develop a dialogue between
management and labor that could lead to relations based on agreement
between the two groups. The possibilities of the dialogue were expanded by
the Maastricht Treaty as noted above to include actual policymaking for the
EU.[10] The process has moved slowly and erratically. The social partners
have held dialogue on common concerns such as education and the introduction of new technologies as well as on parental leave.[11] Currently, a
number of bodies exist for the purposes of social dialogue; the Commission
regularly consults twenty-eight organizations. Structures exist for social
dialogue for different economic sectors. The Standing Committee for
Employment provides an umbrella structure for joint discussions with the
Council. In October 1995 the social partners held a dialogue in Seville to
precede the European Council during the Spanish presidency. The event
gave a new prominence to social dialogue and placed the joint interests of
business and labor squarely before political leaders when they assembled in

Madrid. The meeting may become a regular feature of the events leading to European summits. Commissioner Flynn announced a new initiative for social dialogue in January 1996 in order to devise better means to link the different levels of discussion and to ensure that it leads to tangible outcomes.[12]

This short overview of social policy in the 1990s provides a perspective for understanding the context in which the EWC directive was formed and is being implemented. Several points should be reiterated: Most of the work is a continuation of work long in progress; new initiatives are difficult to find in this cautious era. Consolidation, not innovation, is the order of the day. The possibilities of the Maastricht Treaty have not emboldened the drafters of social policy—they have not written a social dimension for the Economic and Monetary Union the way Jacques Delors did for the 1992 initiative. And yet the Maastricht Treaty has helped to break up old logjams and to allow the adoption of proposals long pending. The Commission has been able to dust off old proposals in order to send them along new policy channels created by the Treaty, though it still cannot force through the Council proposals (such as the burden of proof) where a political consensus is lacking. Perhaps the most important point is the increasing significance of the social partners. The parental leave directive is a new form of law-making for the EU. If the social partners succeed on the burden-of-proof directive, they may find the Commission turning to them with other controversial proposals. UNICE and the ETUC have moved a long way from their hostile relations in the 1980s, both organizations having changed and institutionalized a modus vivendi. This development needs to be studied and considered carefully.

The EWC directive differs from the policies discussed above in that many regard it as the harbinger of a new era in which the EU will gradually define a European industrial relations system. Others oppose the principle of such a system, and still others argue against its feasibility. If the directive, which has its roots in the German industrial relations system, can be successfully implemented in other systems, the argument against a common system will be weakened. The United Kingdom represents the toughest test because its industrial relations system is widely perceived as distinctly different from systems on the Continent. The issue of a common social policy or a social policy à la carte is one the drafters of the Maastricht II Treaty must address. They will no doubt be influenced by the findings regarding the EWC directive.

A Brief History of the EU's Works Councils Directive

As is evident in its founding treaties, the EU has always had within it a corporatist vision of labor-management cooperation.[13] The EU has been attempting to promote European industrial democracy for more than twenty years. The adoption of the EWC directive is the first victory in that effort.

The earliest attempts at creating EU industrial democracy were linked to the efforts to forge an EU company law.[14] Because the Germans feared that a regulation for a European company would give German firms a means to escape their national codetermination legislation by opting for the European law, they demanded that the regulation include an acceptable form of worker participation. The regulation failed in the face of British opposition. This pattern of German insistence on worker participation and British opposition to such participation persisted from the 1970s to the 1990s.

Throughout the 1970s and 1980s, the Commission searched for an acceptable form of worker participation. The form had to be flexible enough to accommodate the different industrial relations systems in countries such as France and Italy and to meet the demands of employers but at a level high enough to protect the German system and to meet the demands of those who advocated industrial democracy.[15] All attempts at reform consistently met with British opposition. The British industrial relations system had no tradition of worker participation along the lines known on the Continent.[16]

The 1980 Vredeling Directive (named after then EC social affairs commissioner Henk Vredeling, a Dutch socialist) was one of the most famous and controversial proposals in the history of worker participation.[17] Opposition to this proposal from European and international employer groups[18] and the British government was fierce. The proposal was revised in 1983 in order to meet the objections,[19] but the Conservative British government continued to oppose the measure and vetoed it in the 1983 Council. The proposal was again revised in 1986 and 1989.[20] Both attempts were blocked, and the proposal was seen as indefinitely shelved.[21]

The SEA and the white paper did little to revive industrial democracy within the EC. It was not until Delors presented the Social Dimension in 1988 that issues of industrial democracy returned to the EC agenda.[22] He called for the adoption of the European Company Statute, the Vredeling proposal, and a Community Charter of Fundamental Social Rights. The Social Charter was subsequently adopted as a declaration by eleven members of the Council. Articles 17 and 18 of the Charter encouraged the creation of information and consultation between the two sides of industry. Meanwhile, a new and more flexible version of the European Company Statute was issued,[23] but both the British government and UNICE were strongly opposed to it. This proposal appeared to have been permanently shelved by the Council,[24] but it reappeared again in 1995. The Council on the Internal Market considered it in May 1996. According to the Maastricht Treaty, the proposal required only a qualified majority vote for adoption.

Although the vote was possible, both Germany and the United Kingdom rejected it (for opposite reasons), so the Council decided not to call a vote. A qualified majority may be legally adequate, but it is not politically adequate when two of the largest members are opposed.

The Maastricht Treaty had a complicated effect on the development of European industrial democracy policy. On the one hand, the Treaty strengthened the consultative powers of the European Parliament (generally a strong supporter of European industrial democracy), created qualified majority voting in the Council for some areas of social policy, encouraged labor-capital "consultation,"[25] and gave the Council the "opt-out" clause with which it could bypass the British veto. On the other hand, tensions raised during the prolonged ratification struggle brought EU social policy development to a near standstill. This stasis was accentuated by a number of developments. First, in order not to antagonize British (especially Conservative) voters, EC social policy was put on hold until after the British general election of April 1992.[26] Following the victory of the Conservatives in that election, Britain took its turn as president of the Council from July to December 1992. The newly reelected Conservative government wanted to stifle any EU social policy development[27] and could do this with relative ease since most attention was directed toward overcoming the Danish rejection of the Maastricht Treaty in June 1992.

At the beginning of 1993, the Danes took over the presidency of the Council and were determined to bring social policy back to the forefront.[28] Following the events at the Hoover factory in France,[29] the ETUC increasingly lobbied for some kind of legislation on European works councils. In response, the Danes revived the modified Vredeling proposal that had been put aside in 1989. In June 1993 the British threatened to veto the proposal, and it was shelved again.[30]

With the final ratification of the Maastricht Treaty in November 1993, however, EU commissioner of social affairs Flynn decided to push the proposal forward in early 1994 through the use of the Social Protocol in the Maastricht Treaty. This was the first use of the protocol to get around the British veto. According to the protocol, several steps must be taken in order to surmount the British veto. First, the social partners must be consulted. If an agreement between the partners has been reached, then the Commission must approve it. If no agreement is reached, then the Commission must rework the proposal and return it to the social partners for a second consultation. If no agreement is reached at this point, the Commission has the right to put the proposal before the Council for a vote by the eleven.

In January 1994 Flynn put the proposal before the two social partners. Primarily because of employer resistance, no agreement was reached between the social partners. The Commission then revised the proposal in February, eliminating the requirement of a specific form of works councils, extending the time for implementing the councils from one to two years, and strengthening the employers' right to protect "vital" information.[31] This weakened proposal was returned to the social partners in mid-February for the second consultation. However, once again, no agreement was reached.[32] On April 13 Flynn announced that the consultations were over and that a legislative solution was the only way that works councils could be implemented. The ETUC strongly supported Flynn's action; the UNICE strongly condemned it.[33] At the 23 June 1994 meeting of the Social Council, the EWC directive was passed by a vote of ten to zero (Portugal abstained). It was then reviewed and passed by the European Parliament and became a directive following its second reading in the Council on 22 September 1994.[34] After more than twenty years of legislative struggle, the EU finally has a substantial law for the promotion of European industrial democracy.

As of late 1996, the directive applied to sixteen countries (the fifteen EU countries minus the UK, plus the two EEA countries, Iceland and Norway) and demands that "community-scale" firms (with over 1,000 workers with at least 150 in two or more of the involved European countries) must form a European Union works council or a "procedure for informing and consulting employees" in these firms.[35] The directive implies that firms should attempt to set up their own forms of works councils that are most suitable for their particular needs, though the councils must have between three and thirty members, representatives from all of the European countries in which the firm operates, and be informed about the firm's general structure, economic situation, and future developments in employment, investment, and overall development strategy.[36]

The directive provides for a two-year grace period for the member states to implement the directive, thus coming into force on 22 September 1996. Many European firms moved quickly to establish works councils before the deadline for various reasons, uppermost of which was the desire to avoid national- or European-level state intrusion into the particular formation of the European works councils structure. Article 13 of the directive states that the directive shall not apply where "there is already an agreement, covering the entire workforce, providing for the transnational information and consultation of employees." According to officials at UNICE and the ETUC, in May 1996 120 voluntary agreements were in place and they expected and got over 200 negotiated by September as employers rushed to take advantage of the voluntary period.[37]

Finally, given the success of the works councils directive, the focus now is on implementation rather than on expanding EU legislation in this area. The one major exception to this was the Commission's proposal in November 1995 to revive key pieces of legislation (the fifth directive and Vredeling proposals) that related to the councils.[38] As yet, little has come of this strategy.

The European Works Councils Directive and the UK

When the EWC directive was passed using the Social Protocol in September 1994, John Major and the British Conservative government saw it as just the sort of Eurocratic meddling in national affairs that they had been warning about all along. The British social policy opt-out, negotiated at Maastricht, was designed exactly to keep Britain out of these supposedly costly, bureaucratic, nondemocratic, anti–free market entanglements. As the language of the protocol states: "acts thus adopted by the Council and any financial consequences of measures taken in application of [the last indent of Article 118, 3] shall not be applicable to the United Kingdom." In essence, by opting out the UK demanded the right not to be affected by the policy in any way and clearly expressed its opposition to the policy in general. However, as we shall see, the EWC directive has had a substantial direct and indirect impact on the development of British politics and industrial relations.

Obviously, the main political parties took the directive very seriously. For the Conservatives, it is another example of a federalist, bureaucratic, socialist, and centralizing EU directive that would make the functioning of British firms more expensive, lower competitiveness, curb growth and employment, and ruin Britain's chances for becoming the Hong Kong of Europe. The Conservatives had been deeply divided over Britain's relationship to Europe, but this was one EU directive that could unite most of the party into an anti-EU position and was a clear justification for Major's social policy opt-out. Although Euroskeptics see this as a reason for staying out of the EU and Eurosupporters as a rationale for playing a more active role in it, both sides within the Conservative Party could agree that the directive should be opposed and would help to put some "clear blue water" between their policies and those of Labour.

The Liberal Democrats, reflecting their long-term support for the EU and belief that individual rights, including employee rights, should be protected by law, support EU social policy and the EWC directive. They believe the works councils will help protect the "weak and vulnerable" and encourage an industrial and commercial culture based on trust and cooperation. Their vision of a humane and competitive British industrial society resembles the model of Continental social capitalism.[39]

In many ways the position of the Labour Party with regard to the EWC directive is similar to that of the Liberals. They hope works councils will help create a more socially acceptable capitalism that accords with new prime minister Tony Blair's notion of a "stakeholder society."[40] The EWC directive is popular with party members, many of whom have been suspicious of the EU. Despite its substantial transformation, or "modernization," the Labour Party remains deeply divided over integration into the EU.[41] However, the trade unions in general support it, and it can be used as a device for pressuring the Tories and showing that Labour is a mainstream social democratic party of Europe.

The peak associations of British industrial relations view the works councils in various ways. The Confederation of British Industries (CBI) has publicly opposed the directive and defended the UK's social policy opt-out; privately, however, leaders have taken a much more pragmatic line.[42] One affiliate of the CBI, the Engineering Employers Federation, openly supports works councils.[43]

The Trades Union Congress (TUC) has been deeply divided over the EU but has become more pro-EU since the late 1980s.[44] It opposes the British social policy opt-out and strongly backs the EWC directive. Many leaders of the TUC believe that the EU social policy offers the TUC the means to bypass the Conservative British government and obtain basic labor and employment rights via Brussels. Industrial democracy via the EWC directive is much more attractive to TUC members in the current climate than it was when discussions began in the 1970s and British unions were still powerful inside the workplace.

TUC affiliates differ in their reaction to the EWC directive depending on a number of factors. UNISON, which for the most part represents public-sector workers, had shown little interest in the directive. As large pieces of the public sector have been privatized, however, concern has grown. The majority of these privatized operations were taken over by European multinationals, which are covered by the directive for their Continental operations, and they have given British workers the right to take part in the new councils.[45]

The big, private-sector unions, such as General, Municipal, and Boilermakers' Union; Amalgamated Engineering and Electrical Union; Transport and General Workers Union (TGWU); and Union of Shop, Distributive, and Allied Workers (USDAW), view the directive as extremely important. As an AEEU document states: "The European Works Council Directive is a major step forward for the involvement of employees in the decisions which affect their working lives. . . . For UK employees and trade unionists the goal must be to circumvent the Government's opt-out at every opportunity. . . . If successful, we will make the opt-out an irrelevance and pave the way for its inevitable reversal."[46] The officials we interviewed within these unions emphasized that the impact of the EWC directive will depend on the culture and position of particular firms. They do not expect works councils to become effective in firms such as Marks and Spencer and many U.S. firms that have a history of opposition to unions and worker organizations. But they do believe that other, more "confident" firms view works councils positively and are already establishing them. Union officials also believe that some firms are setting up works councils in anticipation of the new Labour government's move to end the opt-out. A USDAW document noted: "The Labour Party is committed to signing the European

Union Social Chapter so the return of a Labour government at the next general election would make absolutely certain that USDAW members will be participating in EWCs."[47] A key forthcoming battle for the TGWU and other major unions will be the negotiations over works councils at General Motors.

Officials in all of the union organizations with whom we spoke (eight major organizations have been affected) agreed that the works councils would not have developed without the EU directive. They had a positive orientation toward the EU but were realistic in their expectations regarding the EWC directive. They emphasized that the battle over works councils was just beginning and at a minimum the councils "will encourage the sharing of best practice, to make sure that we get the same terms as the best available in Europe."[48]

Conclusions

The Maastricht Treaty has created a new dynamic in EU social policy. The Treaty has made it possible to revive old proposals long blocked and channel them along new and more successful routes. Still, it is evident that social policy remains secondary in the hierarchy of EU policy. EMU, international competitiveness, the market, and unemployment are the top priorities and do not provide parameters in which bold or large-scale proposals for social policy could be developed.

This assessment of social policy in the post-Maastricht era does not lead to high expectations for the outcomes of the current IGC. Predictably, labor seeks a complete end to unanimous voting on social policy proposals in the Council. Employment remains the number-one concern of labor unions, however, so they are hampered by the need to defend any proposals they make against charges that their suggestions will harm the competitiveness of European firms in the global market. Given the existing economic paradigm, the initiative rests with employers who oppose any expansion of social policy. As Eurochambres, the European Association of the Chambers of Commerce (Brussels), which represents 13 million businesses, has argued in a memorandum for the IGC: "There are no further areas where the introduction of Union legislation impacting on the employment relationship would be useful. . . . Any further interventions are likely to be highly damaging, particularly for SMEs [small and medium-sized enterprises]."[49]

It is clear as well that the institutional changes of the Maastricht Treaty, particularly the Social Protocol, were essential to the EWC directive's final success. The protocol gave the EU a legislative strategy for surmounting the British veto. However, one must also recognize the general weakness of the proposal in relation to its earlier versions. The limiting of the number of firms affected, ability of the workers to demand information, types of works councils to be created, and powers of the councils in the final version are clear indications of the degree of labor compromise that was necessary for the directive's passage. In essence, the success of the EWC directive represents a combination of institutional change and political compromise that demonstrates the relatively weak position of labor and social policy within the EU.

Ironically, it appears that the EWC directive has had a substantial impact on the UK. Despite the UK's social policy opt-out, the UK has not really been able to opt out on the level of either political or industrial relations. As noted earlier, both the Labour and Liberal Parties were determined to end the opt-out. Unions intend to pressure firms to include Britain in the formation of the councils. As some employees from the UK gain experience in European works councils, the unions will have a strong case that others should not be denied the opportunity. Many firms see the councils as a logical extension of a European-wide strategy. In policy terms, the opt-out has been a failure. However, it is politically popular within the Conservative Party and is one of the few elements of John Major's EU policy that the majority of the party can support.

These conclusions lead in a number of intriguing theoretical directions. First, the limited developments of EU social policy since 1991 and the success of the EWC directive provide contradictory evidence for arguments regarding a "structural bias" in the EU that prevents it from furthering social policy. Various authors have argued that because of the pluralistic nature of the EU, its institutional and ideological orientation to free markets, the relatively disorganized and fragmented structure of the European labor movement, and other factors, the Union is structurally biased against the development of a strong and substantial social policy.[50] On the one hand, this bias would appear to be upheld by the limited development of social policy in the post-Maastricht period. A number of major institutional innovations were put into effect by the Treaty, but only a few legislative results actually occurred. On the other hand, the EWC directive, despite its obvious weaknesses, did pass, marking a substantial precedent and victory for European labor. The social partners' successful negotiations on the parental leave agreement also raise the possibility that a new channel for social policy may emerge through the social dialogue and that the social partners may reach agreements that elude the political actors in the Council and the Commission. It is a development worth watching. The post-Maastricht period thus gives no clear indication of a social policy bias.

Second, the impact of the directive on the UK seems greatly to challenge the ability of any member state to pursue opt-out or à la carte strategies. The spillover from the directive has clearly affected British politics and industrial relations. However, one of the main reasons it had so much impact on Britain was that it was strongly opposed only by the Conservative Party. It was not unpopular with the British public, and the other two main parties supported it, undermining the Conservative government's position against it. On a different issue (EMU, perhaps), where opposition parties are less supportive, public opinion more oppositional, and other member states more divided, an opt-out could actually work and be politically popular as well.

Third and finally, the question of opt-outs and their effectiveness should be a core concern for theorists of European integration. On one side, Europeanists should be expected to cheer the failure of the British opt-out as an indication of the overall level of integration and the inability of any one state to step outside of that process. On the other side, our conclusion that the failure of the opt-out was largely due to British political elites' divided opinion on the policy indicates that national factors still play a key role in the success or failure of a given opt-out. It would be useful to explore the role of opt-outs in allowing reluctant partners a degree of flexibility within an integrating framework and to study how different nations use the opt-outs to obtain distinct national and European goals. Another important reason for the failure of the opt-out has direct implications for the issue of a common European industrial relations system. Many employers in multinational corporations have decided that the opt-out is not useful; they do not deem it a sound industrial relations practice to deny to one part of their workforce a benefit that is mandated by the EU for the rest of their workforce. It will be interesting to see if the drafters of the Maastricht II Treaty take these implications into account.

Notes

1. Articles 2.2 and 2.3 of the Social Agreement of the Treaty on European Union.

2. Commission of the European Communities (CEC), *Employment in Europe* (Brussels: CEC, 1995), p. 8.

3. CEC, "White Paper on Growth, Competitiveness, and Employment," *Bulletin of the European Communities,* supplement 63/93, 1993.

4. CEC, *European Social Policy: White Paper,* COM (94) 333.

5. CEC, *The European Councils: Conclusions of the Presidency 1992–1994* (Brussels: CEC, 1995), p. 141.

6. ETUC, *European Trade Union Information Bulletin,* 2/1995, p. 2.

7. *Agence Europe,* 19 January 1996.

8. ETUC, *European Trade Union Information Bulletin,* 4/1995.

9. Centre for Research on European Women, "CREW Reports," Brussels, 11/12, 1995, p. 3.

10. The provisions for the social dialogue are found in Article 188b of the Treaty and Article 3 of the Agreement on Social Policy.

11. CEC, *European Social Dialogue: Joint Opinions,* documentary series, undated.

12. Padraig Flynn, "The Social Dialogue at European Level," *Frontier-Free Europe,* January 1996.

13. See Martin Rhodes, "The Future of the 'Social Dimension': Labour Market Regulation in Post-1992 Europe," *Journal of Common Market Studies* 30, 1 (March 1992); Paul Teague and John Grahl, "European Community Labour Market Policy: Present Scope and Future Direction," *Journal of European Integration* 13, (Fall 1989); Wolfgang Streeck and Philippe Schmitter, "From National Corporatism to Transnational Pluralism: Organized Interests in the Single Market," *Politics and Society* 19, 2 (June 1991); Beverly Springer, *The European Union and Its Citizens* (Westport, CT: Greenwood Press, 1994), pp. 61–63.

14. Michael Shanks, *European Social Policy, Today and Tomorrow* (New York: Pergamon Press, 1977), p. 48; Beverly Springer, *The Social Dimension of 1992* (Westport, CT: Greenwood Press, 1992), pp. 83–97.

15. W. Daubler, "The European Participation Directive—A Realistic Utopia?" in Paul Kapteyn (ed.), *The Social Policy of the European Communities* (Leiden: Sijthoff, 1977).

16. Chris Brewster and Paul Teague, *European Community Social Policy: Its Impact on the UK* (London: Institute of Personnel Management, 1989, pp. 74–75.

17. For more details on this directive, see R. Blanpain et al., *The Vredeling Proposal: Information and Consultation of Employees in Multinational Enterprises* (Boston: Kluwer, 1983); Lammy Betten (ed.), *The Future of European Social Policy* (Boston: Kluwer, 1989).

18. U.S. employers were also active in opposing the proposal. See "Europe's Unions Are No Match for America's Multinationals," *Economist,* 16 October 1982, p. 77.

19. Brewster and Teague, *European Community Social Policy,* p. 76.

20. EC Commission Documents, COM (90) 581 final (OJ C 39, 15 February 1991).

21. CEC, *Completing the Internal Market: Community Social Policy* (Brussels: EC, 1992).

22. CEC, *The Social Dimension of the Internal Market: Interim Report of the Intergovernmental Working Party,* special edition of Social Europe (Luxembourg, 1988).

23. EC Commission Document, COM (89) 268/1 and 2 (OJ C 263, 16 October 1989).

24. CEC, *Completing the Internal Market.*

25. *Treaty on Political Union,* Annex IV, Articles 118, 118a, 118b, and 118c.

26. "EC Ministers Put EC Social Policy on Hold Until After UK Poll," *Financial Times,* 15 March 1992.

27. In an unusually open display of dissent, Vasso Papandreou (the retiring EC commissioner for social affairs) complained, "We are at the end of 1992, and on the eve of the Single Market, our hopes have come to nothing. . . . The British presidency has been effective as to its aim which was to take as few [social policy] decisions as possible" (*Agence Europe,* 5 December 1992).

28. "Working Program for the Danish Presidency," *Agence: Europe, Documents,* 22 January 1993.

29. In March 1993 a French Hoover factory chose to close down its operations and transfer its activities to a low-wage and less-regulated area in Scotland. To European trade unions, this seemed like a perfect example of the kind of "social dumping" that a free market EU was capable of producing.

30. "Major to Use Veto on Euro-works Councils," *Financial Times,* 5–6 June 1993.

31. *Agence Europe,* 7–8 February 1994.

32. For more details, see Michael Gold and Mark Hall, "Statutory European Works Councils: The Final Countdown?" *Industrial Relations Journal* 25, 3 (1994).

33. *Agence Europe,* 15 April 1994.

34. *Official Journal* L 254/64, 30 September 1994. The title of the final directive is Council Directive 94/45/EC of 22 September 1994.

35. Council Directive 94/45/EC, Article 1.

36. For an excellent review of the directive see Mark Hall et al., *European Works Councils: Planning for the Directive* (London: Eclipse Group, 1995). Also see R. Blanpain and P. Windey, *European Works Councils: Information and Consultation of Employees in Multinational Enterprises in Europe* (Louvain: Peeters, 1994). See as well the *European Industrial Relations Review* (1994).

37. Many in Brussels expect that a number of the voluntary agreements will not stand up in court.

38. Caroline Southey, "Brussels Dusts off Blocked Laws," *Financial Times,* 16 November 1995, and Robert Taylor, "Proposal to Extend Works Councils in Europe," *Financial Times,* 28 November 1995.

39. Liberal Democratic Party, *Making Europe Work for Us—The Liberal Democratic Vision for Europe* (1994).

40. Will Hutton, *The State We're In* (London: Vintage, 1995).

41. Stephen George, *Britain and European Integration Since 1945* (London: Basil Blackwell, 1991); Robert Geyer, *The Uncertain Union: British and Norwegian Social Democrats in an Integrating Europe* (Hampshire: Avebury, 1997); Eric Shaw, *The Labour Party Since 1979: Crisis and Transformation* (London, Routledge, 1994); Martin Smith and Joanna Spear (eds.), *The Changing Labour Party* (London, Routledge, 1992).

42. Confederation of British Industries, *European Works Council Directive—Options for the Future* (1996).

43. Robert Taylor, "Engineering Employers' Group Backs EU Works Councils," *Financial Times,* 22 November 1995.

44. Andrew Taylor, *The Trade Unions and the Labour Party* (London, Croom Helm, 1987); Paul Teague, "The British TUC and the European Community," *Millennium* 18, 1 (1989); Paul Teague and John Grahl, *Industrial Relations and European Integration* (London: Lawrence and Wishart, 1992).

45. This information was obtained through an interview with a research director at UNISON.

46. AEEU, *European Works Councils,* March 1996, p. 19.

47. USDAW, *European Briefing* no. 2, August 1995, p. 25.

48. "Starting from Scratch—Creating a Works Council," *MSF at Work,* April 1996, p. 12.

49. *Agence Europe,* 6 January 1996.

50. Peter Cocks, "Towards a Marxist Theory of European Integration," *International Organization* 34, 1 (1980); Rhodes, "The Future of the 'Social Dimension'"; George Ross, "After Maastricht: Hard Choices for Europe," *World Policy Journal* 19, 3 (Summer 1992); Streeck and Schmitter, "From National Corporatism to Transnational Pluralism."

12

The EU and Women: Virtual Equality

R. Amy Elman

Within the European Union,[1] sexual (in)equality has been conceived within the parameters of economic considerations because the unification of Europe is foremost an economically inspired plan. Indeed the founding constitution of the European Community, the 1957 Treaty of Rome, stipulates in Article 119 that member states should apply the principle of sexual equality through "equal pay for equal work." Despite this pronouncement and others similar to it, sexual inequality persists both within and outside of European wage-labor markets. The economic situation of women in Europe is grim; poverty remains persistent and pervasive.[2] This suggests that economic palliatives, albeit necessary, are insufficient in ending women's subordination, economic and otherwise.

Whether women's equality lies beyond the grasp of European policy is impossible to answer definitively. This chapter explores the ways in which the rhetorical repudiations of sexual inequality can both enhance and impede concrete acts on behalf of women. To this end, it commences with a historical overview of the EU's equal opportunity law and concludes with a critical analysis of the remedies currently afforded, including the promise of democratization, which was explored at the 1996 Intergovernmental Conference. My argument is that while Eurocrats and others have legitimized some women's concerns, they have undermined the possibility for a more radical agenda, one that would transcend the liberal understanding of equality as sameness and dominance as (quantitative) difference. In consequence, women are conferred "virtual equality," equitable rhetoric that when pragmatically applied often proves disappointing.

Article 119 and Case Studies of Challenge

Considerations of "women's policy" necessarily begin with a discussion of the Treaty of Rome and its incorporation of Article 119, the only article to make explicit mention of women.[3] It does so by reference to "the principle that men and women should receive equal pay for equal work." Through the ideological prism of contemporary feminism, the article has since been understood as an essential vehicle for the promotion of women's rights.

Historical investigations into the article's adoption reveal that sexual equality was hardly its intent. Women were conspicuously absent from the deliberations. The Commission had no women members, and the Social Committee that was later formed to advise the Commission on the article and related issues had only two women; the other ninety-nine members were men. The request to palliate sex discrimination resulted not from a constituency demand from women themselves but in large part from France. France's post–World War II adoption of an equal pay policy prompted its promotion of a European-wide policy in the treaty negotiations of 1955–1957 that would protect it from other member states. France feared those states could undercut its labor costs by employing women at lower rates than men. France's request for equal pay legislation was neither extreme nor innovative. According to Michel Gaudet, who was present at the negotiations, "The other governments would not have accepted equal pay just because France wanted it. It was already a legitimate issue and in the public domain."[4]

Prior to the adoption of the Treaty of Rome, the International Labor Organization (ILO) ratified Article 100, a 1951 convention that promoted the principle of pay equity and legislative intervention against wage differentials between men and women. The very wording of Article 119 corresponds closely to Article 100.[5] Article 100 proved theoretically consistent with ILO's wish to emphasize the value of jobs as opposed to differentiating between the employees who performed them. In practice, however, unions were reluctant to insist on the implementation of this convention. They argued that pay equity is best achieved through collective bargaining and is wholly dependent on the power of labor to best represent the interests of wage earners. Sex-based differentials were thus excused through the careless contention that women workers have the power effectively to partake in a collective bargaining process, the outcome of which would be as beneficial to them as it is for their male counterparts.

A decade later autonomous feminist movements noted and then challenged the discrepancy between women's lives and the promises of equality that various constitutions, conventions, and treaties claimed to offer. In 1966, when women at a Belgian munitions factory struck, demanding improved working conditions and equal pay, their banners exclaimed, "Give us Article 119."[6] Article 119 was thus evicted from relative obscurity. The Belgian government revised its labor law, allowing equal pay cases to be referred to the European Court of Justice, Europe's highest court and, arguably, its "least accountable institution."[7]

In 1971 two Belgian lawyers, Eliane Vogel-Polsky and Marie-Thérèse

Cuvelliez, brought a case before the ECJ on behalf of flight attendant Gabrielle Defrenne and unsuccessfully invoked Article 119 against Sabena Airlines. *Defrenne I* was the first case concerning gender (in)equality to come before the Court. The airline's employment policy required sex-based differentials with regard to wages and pension plans. The case focused specifically on the exclusion of (female) flight attendants from the more generous pension schemes extended to the (male) flight crew. The Court responded that although occupational pension schemes might be covered by Article 119, the Sabena scheme was primarily statutory and thus fell outside of the Court's remit.[8] In consequence, although the Court implied that some schemes would be considered as pay, gendered differentials were legally maintained despite the redress that Article 119 appeared to offer. That Belgian women were the first formally to insist on European remedies against sex discrimination is not surprising, as it was within Belgium that women had greater access to (Brussels) and knowledge about Community institutions.[9]

A persistent Vogel-Polsky pressed the Court to reconsider *Defrenne,* which it did in 1976. In *Defrenne II,* pensions were not directly at issue. Instead, compensation was sought for sex-based wage differentials. In 1976 the Court ruled that although Article 119 failed to cover statutory pension schemes, it did directly effect member states as regards pay. Discriminatory pension and retirement schemes persisted, but Belgium could no longer claim that European law lacked standing because it had failed to incorporate it into national law.

Choosing to credit the judges with an enlightened position, few EU commentators have accounted for the Court's apparent conversion. A prominent analyst, by contrast, quotes a former ECJ judge who concedes that the Court is composed of "impressionable people" and argues that the ECJ "was responding to political activism among women."[10] Catherine Hoskyns believes that feminists influenced Europe's policymakers, yet Hoskyns neglects consideration of the Court's own agenda. These factors are not mutually exclusive.

In 1976 the Court asserted its expertise over a burgeoning policy area, one gaining greater significance as women throughout Europe mobilized for equal rights. Through a more interventionist posture, the Court enhanced its prestige. Although its second *Defrenne* ruling made equal pay directly binding on member states, the ECJ took no action against sex-based social security schemes or retirement ages. These matters, it insisted, rested with member states. By exercising such restraint, the Court carefully solidified its power as final arbiter of European law.

This second ruling on Article 119 is pivotal, as it appears to have provided concessions to all involved. For itself, the Court established its competence concerning equality legislation. Member states retain(ed) considerable independence to ignore and/or enact legislation that transcends the parameters of "equality" so narrowly conceived. Last, the Court provided women some redress; "member governments and private organizations alike realized they could no longer simply ignore Article 119."[11] Still, throughout the Community problems of enforcement persisted. Action was necessary to ensure compliance to the Court's changing will.

Equality Directives

The Court's emerging concern for women's workforce participation paralleled other Community developments. At the 1972 Paris summit, preparations for an enlarged Community included a Social Action Program that was to contain a section on women. The European Commission was to develop a program that would "achieve equality between men and women as regards access to employment and vocational training and advancement, and as regards working conditions including pay." To promote these goals, the Council of Ministers adopted three equality directives.[12]

The Council of Ministers adopted the first equality directive, the equal pay directive, in 1975.[13] It introduced the principle of equal pay for "work of an equal value." Until then the ECJ had construed Article 119 to mean merely equal pay for the *same* work. High levels of occupational segregation by sex obstructed the application of this sameness interpretation. The principle of "equal value" enlarged the possibilities for redress.

The second directive, adopted the following year, concerned equal treatment.[14] Both Article 119 and the equal pay directive cover women once they are in the wage-labor market; the equal treatment directive encourages women's entrance into the market by discouraging discrimination that precedes their participation. The directive thus focused on ending discrimination in vocational training, hiring, and promotion practices. As well, it called for improved working conditions.

The last equality directive of the 1970s, involving social security, forbids discrimination with regard to benefits.[15] This 1978 social security directive subverts the notion that women could or would wish to rely on the institution of marriage for fiscal security. It was hoped that a more equitable set of benefits would provide an added incentive for women to join the wage-labor market. In addition, it offered the chance to homogenize Europe's diverse array of social security schemes.

Only two equality directives have been adopted since, both in the 1980s. One extends the application of the principle of equal treatment to occupational social security schemes.[16] The other extends the principle of equal treatment to self-employed women (including pregnant women), whose occupational status and ensuing pay and benefits were unclear.[17] In 1992 the Council of Ministers adopted another, more specific directive concerning pregnancy.[18] Few, however, regard it as an "equality directive," as it was promoted primarily as a health and safety measure.[19] The pregnancy directive establishes minimum requirements for maternity leave throughout the Community and prohibits the dismissal of pregnant employees.

By promoting equality through directives as opposed to regulations, the European Community denied itself the interventionist powers necessary to pursue sexual equality rigorously. Directives are based on the voluntary compliance of the member states, which are expected to promote sexual equality; limited recourse is offered when the expectation is disappointed. By contrast, regulations are binding in law and are automatically incorporated into the national legal systems. Like the European Court of Justice, both the Commission and Council of Ministers appear to have exercised restraint. They passed on a more forceful approach, seeking instead to enhance their authority. In this manner, the "application of the Equality Directives has further clarified and consolidated the effective parameters of Community law."[20] The meaning of these directives for women remains less clear.

The equality directives have met with mixed reviews. Since their adoption, a plethora of equality claims have cluttered courts and tribunals throughout the European Union. Given the sheer volume of cases, an exhaustive and precise analysis is impossible to provide. Most analyses of their impact have thus concentrated on one or two member states. However, even single case studies fail to generate consensus.

Focusing most on Germany and somewhat less on Ireland, Hoskyns suggests that the equality directives often helped tip the legal balance in women's favor.[21] Myra Marx Ferree, writing exclusively on Germany, is less enthusiastic. She argues that without meaningful penalties the directives held "no immediate practical effect."[22] Writing from Ireland, Ailbhe Smyth remarks that claims for employment equality had been forcefully articulated by Irish feminists and by the state's mainstream First Commission on the Status of Women prior to the adoption of the directives. Moreover, she notes their implementation has required constant vigilance from the women's movement and trade union women.[23] According to Ferree and Smyth, women often successfully negotiated policies against discrimination despite such directives. According to Hoskyns and others, such legislation precipitated an increased awareness of sexual discrimination and enhanced the willingness of member states to confront the problem.[24] Despite such disagreements, most scholars agree that the equality directives offer relief in particular cases of overt sex discrimination while *indirect* discrimination persists.[25] This predicament prompted Sonia Mazey to conclude that "the major limitation of the Directives . . . is that they provide women with no more than formal equality with men."[26]

Analyzing directives through case law, though important, may exaggerate the reach of directives by referring only to those actually engaged in opposing or embracing them. In consequence, scholars frequently ignore several important issues.[27] First, employees often remain ignorant of the possible relief directives provide. Second, research in Great Britain revealed that even those trained in labor law possess an inadequate understanding of equal pay and equal treatment cases.[28] Third, those with a legitimate claim and legal awareness often lack the resources necessary to obtain counsel. Few states provide thorough assistance for claimants, who are likely to have less power and fewer resources than their employers. Last, despite efforts to protect claimants from vengeful employers, women employees are particularly reluctant to initiate grievances for fear of retribution. High unemployment and economic recession exacerbate this fear. These obstacles led a former legal adviser to Britain's Equal Opportunities Commission to conclude that "the political will to provide effective means for enforcing the principles contained in Directives is absent: lip-service is paid but no real support is given."[29]

Most forms of discrimination go unchallenged; few cases are likely to reach the attention of authorities, much less a court. Cognizant of the legal impediments, the European Commission is preparing a directive that shifts some of the burden of proof in sex discrimination cases away from those alleging violations. After plaintiffs provide precise and consistent factual evidence, defendants would be expected to prove that no infringement of sexual equality occurred.

Typically, the equality agencies within the member states have had the most experience in direct dealings with women suffering from discrimination. These agencies produced guidelines and general information to help alleviate ignorance, decrease the fear of claimants, provide counsel, and improve working conditions for women within their countries.[30] Similar responsibilities have been entrusted to organizations at the Community level.

Equality Agencies

In 1976 the Commission appointed a small Women's Bureau to monitor and implement the equal treatment directive and the European Social Fund. The fund was originally established by the Treaty of Rome to "improve employment opportunities for workers." It was "to be the principle vehicle through which unemployment was confronted."[31] Although the fund provided relief to those generally disadvantaged, the original guidelines contained a specific line for local employment programs for women.[32]

Situated within the division of employment, industrial relations, and social affairs (DG V), the Women's Bureau was charged to resolve problems pertaining to women's work. Yet this charge was constrained by several factors. Key among them was that the equal pay directive remained within the domain of another department, the wage policies division. If it were to be effective, the parameters of its responsibilities would have to expand. The bureau thus kept abreast of numerous developments, many of which fell outside its formal jurisdiction. In this manner it would slowly establish authority beyond its original confines.

Within four years after its inception, the bureau helped generate a European-wide network among the newly established equality units from within the Community. This network convened in 1980 at a conference in Manchester, England. Those in attendance desired more effective connections with one another and the Commission. Their final objective was to augment the existing equality directives. To this end, they stayed within the acceptable bounds of "equality" discourse: "Future EC policy should be based on the individualisation of benefits, positive action to desegregate the labour market, the provision of a wide variety of child-care facilities, and the development of 'appropriate' leave arrangements."[33]

The following year, in 1981, the European Commission extended an invitation to the various equality agencies throughout Europe to work more closely with it to improve the formulation and implementation of European equality legislation. By the end of the year, this ad hoc group became the Advisory Committee on Equal Opportunities for Men and Women. This name is not insignificant. Under the guise of promoting sexual equality, the Commission obscured the existence of women's subordination; it simply placed women and men together in search for equal opportunities as if one sex held no power over the other.

Action Programs

Women members of the European Parliament were concerned that with few women in senior positions within Community institutions and insufficient mechanisms of enforcement, equality law would remain a rhetorical claim, not an authentic aspiration. They began meeting as an informal group in 1980 and in 1984 evolved into a permanent committee, the European Parliament Committee on Women's Rights. Together with the Women's Bureau and the Advisory Committee on Equal Opportunities, the committee lobbied the Council of Ministers to take further action.

Convinced of the need for greater vigilance, the Council of Ministers adopted four action programs. Like all social policy, these programs represent the use of "political power to supersede, supplement or modify operations of the economic system in order to achieve results which the economic system would not achieve on its own."[34] All four of these programs sought to increase women's presence in the wage-labor market and strengthen the force of existing equality legislation. As Claire Duchen explains, "Much work carried out on behalf of women in the EC is in the context of the Action Programme."[35]

The objective of the first of these action programs (1982–1985) was to consolidate women's employment rights through positive action. This meant the funding of nontraditional educational and job-training programs intended to desegregate the labor market. The program also proposed two of the above-mentioned directives that were later adopted in the 1980s: one concerning occupational pensions and the other self-employment.

The second action program (1986–1990) appears to have responded to the concerns raised in Manchester. It emphasized the promotion of parental leave programs and support for childcare facilities to help parents "combine roles" of work and family. To this end, it developed the above-mentioned pregnancy directive and broached the issue of men's avoidance of parental responsibilities. The EC later responded with a 1992 Council recommendation on childcare.[36] This policy statement, the first equality measure to target male behavior, "encouraged" men to increase their participation in the care of children. Still, children remain women's responsibility— in discourse and practice. In its statement for the Beijing World Conference on Women in 1995, the Commission maintained that the "lack of adequate childcare facilities remains the major obstacle to women's full and equal participation on the labour market."[37] While the availability of childcare is important, it is no cure-all for women's disparate labor participation. Detached from broad-based efforts to counter sex discrimination, childcare programs perpetuate the sexual division of labor they were designed to eliminate—childcare workers are primarily women. In consequence, responsibility for childcare merely shifts from one group of women to another.[38]

The third action program (1991–1995) focused on improving the status of women through efforts to boost their presence in communications and decisionmaking. Prior to this period, women were conspicuously excluded from the first decades of Europe's construction and had only limited access to its most powerful institutions. For example, the European Commission had no women commissioners during the first thirty years of its operation. By 1997, five of twenty commissioners were women. Women similarly increased their percentage in Parliament, from 19 percent in 1989 to over 25 percent in 1994. This impressive increase is not, however, always enthusiastically received. Those who regard themselves as central to the struggle for women's liberation find that they are sometimes pilloried as impediments to sexual equality by some who insist that their principal function may be the legitimation of sexist establishments. Stated simply, bolstering women's political presence may afford the EU (and, more specifically, the Commission) a legitimacy it earlier lacked in its asserted embrace of (gender) equality. This suggests that while women's enhanced presence within the establishment is not insignificant, assessing gender (in)equality is not merely a matter of determining women's numerical presence within standard political institutions as opposed to the substance of the policies they promote.

The emphasis on increasing women's political presence coincided with more general efforts taken at Maastricht to democratize the Community. These efforts included augmenting EP power and establishing a concept of "European citizenship," the purpose of which is "to deepen European citizens' sense of belonging to the European Union."[39] Despite such reforms, enthusiasm for unification waned as Europe entered into its worst postwar recession in 1992. Indeed several national referenda revealed the fragile credibility accorded to the project of unification.[40]

During this period, efforts were also maintained to increase women's presence in the labor market, particularly in male-dominated sectors. In accordance with this goal, the Commission suggested that "an employer with a choice between equally qualified candidates should give preference to women."[41]

Although a fourth program is currently under development (1996–2000) to "mainstream" (i.e., integrate) sexual equality into all activities and program areas, aspects of the third action program are under reproach. A 1995 ECJ ruling (*Kalanke*) insists that member states may not impose affirmative action programs that afford women absolute priority for job appointments or promotions. The implications of this ruling will take time to become clear. It is not, for example, certain if the ruling will extend to voluntary programs in the private sector. The Court's decision provides little guidance for distinguishing between permissible and impermissible plans to achieve sexual equality. In fact, one interpretation of the decision appears to contradict the spirit of the Treaty on European Union.[42] A frustrated Commission is thus considering ways to best interpret the judgment. It has, for example, suggested that the Court condemned only rigid applications of affirmative action. Nonetheless, confusion persists and, with it, calls for clarification.

Given the dynamic and dispersed nature of public policy generally and "women's policy" in particular, a conclusive assessment of these action programs is difficult. Nonetheless, one should credit them with the development of several notable legal initiatives. The programs also facilitated the growth of a women's policy network and the initiation of job-training and educational programs for women. Whether these and similar efforts (including the emergence of the latest action program) will endure the challenges to affirmative action posed by the *Kalanke* ruling remains at issue. The reach of that ruling may eventually extend beyond the labor market, illuminating the need for more thorough considerations of what equality is and how best to achieve it.

"Equality" Assessed

The most significant effect of the aforementioned "women's policies" has not necessarily been in the specific redress and opportunities they provide but rather the ideological foundation they helped to foster. Through the construction and implementation of these policies and programs, the EU claims the authority to both articulate and arbitrate "equality" as it defines it.

The expectation that the incorporation of women within capitalist labor markets, replete with intrinsic economic and social disparities, facilitates sexual equality is riddled with irony. Yet, almost without contention, European initiatives declare that strides for equality must foremost be taken at places of work. This has obvious implications. Logically, acceptance of this plan implies that women should focus on obtaining sexual equality through increasing their presence in the wage-labor market. Few consider that the effect of this focus might compromise efforts in other areas.

In claiming to combat inequities associated with work, the EU has been able to evade action against sexual inequality elsewhere.[43] To be more specific, because the agenda of the European Union is primarily economic, issues involving sexual abuse and violence against women have often been deemed extraneous or inconsequential. This assumption belies the complexities of sexual politics, overlooking the extent to which issues such as abortion, reproductive technologies, woman battery, rape, and prostitution are at once deeply political and economic. Those demonstrating the greatest interest in these issues are often found within Europe's least powerful institutions, such as the Parliament.[44]

The general reluctance to regard the sexual subordination of women as political in nature, economic in consequence, and worthy of Union action has led to a partial embrace of equality by the architects of Europe. For example, Jalna Hanmer asserts that the EU's failure to incorporate action on violence against women in its social policies conspicuously undermines its promotion of equal opportunities.[45] Yet even the inclusion of (legal) assurances to combat such problems can prove deceptive.[46] The example of abortion is instructive. Although the European Court of Justice ruled that abortion is a service to which all European citizens are entitled and unification involves a harmonization of laws that would seem to support this, the politics of integration permitted Ireland the autonomy to deny women this right of European citizenship.[47] And while the EU recognizes sexual harassment as sex discrimination when it transpires in the wage-labor market, it does not regard the problem as injurious when it happens elsewhere or is inherent to an industry, as in the production of pornography. This suggests that the EU takes action against sexual discrimination only when it fundamentally hampers production and diminishes profits.[48]

That the EU should be interested in promoting "women's interests" at all is politically significant. Although access to the labor market may prove beneficial to women, the Union's access to women's relatively inexpensive and well-disciplined labor advances the interests of capital across member states and, more specifically, the men living within them. For them, "women's equality" has meant "a more efficient use of human capital, more incomes to tax, more skilled labor to fill their labor shortage," and greater support for their political systems.[49] Economic liberalism serves as the primary incentive for social initiatives.[50]

When the Commission chose to examine the formulation and implementation of equality law, it conferred the task to a newly established ad hoc body, the Advisory Committee on Equal Opportunities for Men and Women. As suggested earlier, by the time of the committee's founding in 1981, a significant change in public discourse had begun to occur. Within a decade after the emergence of strong women's movements in Europe, one began noticing the queer withdrawal of the word "women" from discussions pertaining to sexual equality. The very existence of women was called into question by postmodernists and others who suggested that the term was imprecise and essentialist.[51] Concern for women was equated with political solipsism and soon replaced by a "larger" regard for all people. Women's liberation was swiftly subsumed by a call for "gender equality."

Gender neutrality set the context for the continued bureaucratization and recent mainstreaming of those issues that are currently identified as "gender" or "equality" issues. In 1994 the Women's Bureau was renamed the Equal Opportunities Unit. In a rhetorical coup, women's experiences of subordination were obliterated; women became "equals." The subsequent suggestion that affirmative efforts to promote women are superfluous gained considerable support by 1995 when the ECJ ruled on *Kalanke*. The tide may be turning against women's few achievements. The institutions of Europe remain powerful by appearing permeable to the pressures of public opinion.

Even those Eurocrats supportive of affirmative action frequently espouse principles and assumptions used to undermine it. On the eve of International Women's Day 1996, the commissioner for employment and social affairs declared that focusing on women is "no longer valid," that instead a "partnership between women and men" is imperative if sexual equality is to be achieved.[52] But "partnership" cannot precede substantive steps to equality; the notion of "partnership" assumes that sexual equality has already been achieved. Men's relative power over women is thus cloaked by a veneer of reciprocity and goodwill.

Efforts to improve the transparency and democratic accountability of the European Union were considered, often behind closed doors, at the 1996 IGC. Having restricted access to these discussions, the Commission insists "ordinary people must *feel* actively involved" (my emphasis).[53] Writing for *Women of Europe*, Michel de Meulenaere exposes the absurdity of this "grandiose paradox." With barely 15 percent of all Europeans even knowledgeable about the IGC, he notes that the incessant chatter of "giving people a voice" is disingenuous.[54] For Meulenaere, the Commission's claims of a democratized Europe fail to mask its insincerity. Nonetheless, such deceit seems pardoned by rhetorical claims of democratizing Europe. Equality is affirmed in the abstract. In a similar vein, the Reflection Group, composed exclusively of men, submitted a draft agenda that suggested that "the Treaty should clearly proclaim such European values as equality between men and women, non-discrimination on grounds of race, religion, sexual orientation, age or disability."[55] This implies that clearly proclaiming equality a European value will result in its fruition. As yet, no sign has emerged from these meetings that the Union is prepared to depart from this embrace of "virtual equality," which provides the thrill of justice without any obligation to secure it.

Women in Europe were only peripherally involved in the determination of what equality is and how best to achieve it. Until recently, women were conspicuously absent from Europe's deliberative bodies. Even those within the former Women's Bureau, whose responsibilities in part entailed the authoritative enunciation of women's interests, were often unable effectively to intervene on behalf of women. Consequently, women are at a particular disadvantage with regard to the politics of integration. Despite their recent advances, they generally lack the financial and other resources with which to organize effectively. This fact is often obscured by the emphasis extended to women's achievements (e.g., the increased presence of women in the EP), raising doubts concerning the need for continued vigilance. Realizing equality necessitates a greater willingness to assess candidly the conditions that continue to conspire against women.

Notes

1. It was only after the Treaty on European Union (the Maastricht Treaty) had come into force, in 1993, that the European Community became more commonly known as the European Union. The former is often invoked with reference to the central activities of the European Community prior to this treaty. I often use the terms interchangeably, though am inclined to use the term "Community" when referring to matters prior to 1993.

2. M. Daly, "Europe's Poor Women? Gender in Research on Poverty," *European Sociological Review* 8 (1992): 1–12.

3. For a detailed history concerning the adoption of Article 119, see C. Hoskyns, *Integrating Gender: Women, Law and Politics in the European Union* (London: Verso, 1996), chapter 3. For a legal appraisal, see E. Ellis, *European Community Sex Equality Law* (Oxford: Clarendon Press, 1991), chapter 2.

4. Hoskyns, *Integrating Gender*, p. 54.

5. Ellis, *European Community Sex Equality Law*, p. 41.

6. C. Hoskyns, "The European Union and the Women Within: An Overview of Women's Rights Policy," in R. A. Elman (ed.), *Sexual Politics and the European Union: The New Feminist Challenge* (Oxford: Berghahn Books, 1996), p. 16.

7. G. Caldeira and J. Gibson, "The Legitimacy of the Court of Justice in the European Union: Models of Institutional Support," *American Political Science Review* 89 (1995): 359.

8. In general, statutory schemes are state-administered retirement pensions for all workers, whereas occupational pension schemes arise from the particular relationships employees have with specific employers.

9. Hoskyns, *Integrating Gender,* p. 129.

10. Ibid., p. 91.

11. S. Mazey, "European Community Action on Behalf of Women: The Limits of Legislation," *Journal of Common Market Studies* 27 (1988): 68.

12. For a detailed legal exploration of these directives, see Ellis, *European Community Sex Equality Law.*

13. Council Directive 75/117/EEC, OJ L 14, 19 February 1975, p. 19.

14. Council Directive 76/207/EEC OJ L 39, 14 February 1976, p. 40.

15. Council Directive 79/7/EEC, OJ L 6, 10 January 1979, p. 24.

16. Council Directive 86/378/EEC, OJ L 225, 12 August 1986, p. 40.

17. Council Directive 86/613/EEC, OJ L 359, 19 December 1986, p. 56.

18. Council Directive 92/85/EEC, OJ L 348, 28 November 1992, p. 1.

19. I. Ostner and J. Lewis, "Gender and the Evolution of European Social Policies," in S. Leibfried and P. Pierson (eds.), *European Social Policy: Between Fragmentation and Integration* (Washington, DC: Brookings Institution, 1995), pp. 159–193. The authors note that "pregnancy and maternity were treated not under the rubric of gender equality but as matters concerning working conditions, under the label of 'sickness,'" p. 166.

20. Mazey, "European Community Action on Behalf of Women," p. 70.

21. Hoskyns, *Integrating Gender,* p. 122.

22. M. Ferree, "Making Equality: The Women's Affairs Offices in the Federal Republic of Germany," in D. M. Stetson and A. G. Mazur (eds.), *Comparative State Feminism* (London: Sage, 1995), p. 99.

23. A. Smyth, "The Contemporary Women's Movement in the Republic of Ireland 1970–1990," in A. Smyth (ed.), *Irish Women's Studies Reader* (Dublin: Attic Press, 1993), pp. 245–269.

24. See, for example, E. Collins, "European Union Sexual Harassment Policy" in Elman, *Sexual Politics and the European Union,* pp. 23–33; A. G. Mazur, "The Interplay: The Formation of Sexual Harassment Legislation in France and EU Policy Initiatives," in Elman, *Sexual Politics and the European Union,* pp. 35–49.

25. Indirect sex discrimination refers to those factors other than sex that militate against women. These include but are not limited to job requirements, working conditions, grading structures, and job evaluation schemes. For further explanation, see A. Byre, "Applying Community Standards on Equality," in M. Buckley and M. Anderson (eds.), *Women, Equality and Europe* (London: Macmillan, 1988), pp. 29–30.

26. Mazey, "European Community Action on Behalf of Women," p. 77.

27. Jennifer Corcoran proves a notable exception. See J. Corcoran, "Enforcement Procedures for Individual Complaints: Equal Pay and Equal Treatment," in Buckley and Anderson, *Women, Equality and Europe,* pp. 56–70.

28. Ibid., p. 64.

29. Ibid., p. 68.

30. Most of these agencies were established in the 1960s and 1970s. For an examination of these organizations throughout much of Europe (and North America), see Stetson and Mazur, *Comparative State Feminism.*

31. E. Moxon-Browne, "Social Europe," in J. Lodge (ed.), *The European Community and the Challenge of the Future* (New York: St. Martin's Press, 1993), p. 153.

32. The Commission has begun to investigate the impact of such funds and

explore the possibilities for their enhancement. In March 1996 a conference convened with this purpose.

33. Hoskyns, *Integrating Gender,* p. 125.

34. T. H. Marshall, *Social Policy* (London: Hutchinson, 1975), p. 15.

35. C. Duchen, "Understanding the European Community," *Women's Studies International Forum* 15 (1992): 18.

36. Council Recommendation 92/241/EEC, OJ L 123, 8 May 1993, p. 16.

37. Commission of the European Communities (CEC), *The European Community Facing the Challenges of the 4th World Conference on Women* (Luxembourg: Office for Official Publications of the European Communities, 1995).

38. A similar situation exists for other responsibilities associated with women. For example, more and more relatively privileged women throughout Europe are employing poor women as domestics. Thus the burden of such work has merely shifted from one group of women to another, while men are able to evade responsibility. In consequence, the gendered inequities associated with such labor are maintained.

39. CEC, *Intergovernmental Conference 1996: Commission Report for the Reflection Group* (Luxembourg: Office for Official Publications of the European Communities, 1995), p. 21.

40. In 1992, Danish voters rebuffed the Treaty on European Union, only later accepting the modified Edinburgh treaty. In November 1994, Swedish voters supported a consultative referendum by a mere 52 percent. Two weeks later, Norwegians opposed EU entrance by the same percentage. Sweden's accession was particularly welcomed by those who regard it as enlightened and thus an effective promoter of women's rights throughout Europe. The country enjoys this reputation despite evidence to the contrary. See, for example, R. A. Elman, *Sexual Subordination and State Intervention: Comparing Sweden and the United States* (Oxford: Berghahn Books, 1996). Sweden's wage-labor market is among Europe's most gender segregated.

41. CEC, *Equal Opportunities for Women in the Community* (Luxembourg: Office for Official Publications of the European Communities, 1993), p. 6.

42. Under the Social Protocol, the Treaty insists that the Union "shall not prevent any Member State from maintaining or adopting measures providing for specific advantages in order to make it easier for women to pursue a vocational activity or prevent or compensate for disadvantages in their professional careers."

43. Elman, *Sexual Politics and the European Union.*

44. S. Baer, "Pornography and Sexual Harassment in the EU," in Elman, *Sexual Politics and the European Union,* pp. 51–65; D. Leidholdt, "Sexual Trafficking of Women in Europe: A Human Rights Crisis for the European Union," in Elman, *Sexual Politics and the European Union,* pp. 83–96.

45. J. Hanmer, "The Common Market of Violence," in Elman, *Sexual Politics and the European Union,* pp. 131–145.

46. C. Delphy, "The European Union and the Future of Feminism," in Elman, *Sexual Politics and the European Union,* pp. 147–158.

47. This was accomplished by Ireland's insertion of a protocol in the Treaty on European Union. In her astute discussion of Irish abortion rights and the EU, Ailbhe Smyth reveals the impossible situation faced by the women of Ireland. See A. Smyth, "'And Nobody Was Any the Wiser': Irish Abortion Rights and the European Union," in Elman, *Sexual Politics and the European Union,* pp. 109–130.

48. Baer, "Pornography and Sexual Harassment."

49. L. Leghorn and K. Parker, *Woman's Worth* (London: Routledge & Kegan Paul, 1981), pp. 78–79.

50. G. Majone, "The European Community Between Social Policy and Social Regulation," *Journal of Common Market Studies* 31 (1993): 153–170.

51. See J. Kristeva, "La Femme, ce n'est jamais" (A woman can never be defined), an interview by "psychoanalysis and politics" in *Tel quel* (Autumn 1974), translated and quoted in E. Marks and I. de Courtivron (eds.), *New French Feminisms: An Anthology* (New York: Schocken Books, 1981), pp. 137–138. For a critique of the politics of postmodernism, see S. Brodribb, *Nothing Mat(t)ers: A Feminist Critique of Postmodernism* (North Melbourne: Spinifex Press, 1992). More recently, Christine Delphy persuasively objects to those insisting that post-modernism and "French feminism" are inseparable. C. Delphy, "The Invention of French Feminism: An Essential Move," *Yale French Studies 87* (1995): 190–221.

52. "Speech by Mr. Padraig Flynn, Conference on the Structural Funds and Equality of Opportunity Between Women and Men," Brussels, 7 March 1996, 4.

53. CEC, *Intergovernmental Conference 1996: Commission Opinion—Reinforcing Political Union and Preparing for Enlargement* (Luxembourg: Office for Official Publications of the European Communities, 1996), p. 9.

54. M. de Meulenaere, "Citizenship: Will a Conference Suffice?" *Women of Europe Newsletter* 60 (1996): 2.

55. Reflection Group, "Reflection Group's Report," SN 520/95 (Reflex), (Luxembourg: Office for Official Publications of the European Communities, 1995), p. 4.

PART 4

MONETARY UNION

13

Enhancing Europe's International Monetary Power: The Drive Toward a Single Currency

Peter H. Loedel

As the members of the European Union reevaluate the desire to proceed with Economic and Monetary Union, a sense among Europeans that long traditions of economic power and national sovereignty are coming under threat has unleashed vigorous debate. The success of European integration in general and the intergovernmental conference designed to further propel European integration in particular hinges in large part on the attainment of EMU. For many leading Europeans, the completion of EMU will crown a nearly fifty-year process of European political integration. Broad consensus exists that after the fall of communism Europe needs deeper political integration to hold it together. A narrower consensus also exists, albeit among leading European politicians such as Chancellor Helmut Kohl of Germany, that suggests that a Continent linked through one currency and a common central bank is the safest way to ensure Europe will not again go to war with itself. This line of reasoning also predicts that failure to find common themes will end in a hopelessly fractured Europe and economic decline. Success in the historic monetary experiment over European monetary integration could create a competitive, powerful bloc, with France and Germany as its anchors. As German finance minister Theo Waigel has suggested, "Europe's only chance to stand its ground against other continents is if it joins forces."[1] Despite all the technical minutia surrounding EMU negotiations, there is indeed something larger, politically and historically, surrounding the process of European monetary integration.

This chapter explores these themes and the broader political and historical context of EMU by examining the interrelationships among member states of the European Union, the European Monetary System (EMS), and the United States.[2] As European heads of state, finance ministers, and central bankers reassess the movement toward EMU brought on by the ongoing IGC, they should be aware that failure to complete EMU would weaken

Europe's voice in international monetary affairs—and international affairs more generally. I argue that unless Europe can successfully complete EMU, Germany will retain a dominant role in European monetary governance. This dominant role—and the problems associated with this role—will also be transmitted to EMS-U.S. monetary relations. Within monetary policy, the EU will thus remain a hollow actor without significant international impact. Internationally, Germany's monetary voice, not Europe's, will continue to be enlarged. While this may not be a concern to some in Germany (in fact it may please many), continuation of the German approach to monetary leadership in Europe will result in continued tension and turmoil within the EU, especially in terms of the debate over the deepening and widening of the EU.

First, I develop a conceptualization to understanding monetary affairs in Europe that incorporates the basic triangular interaction of the dollar, the EMS, and the Deutschmark (DM).[3] Beginning with the Werner Report in the early 1970s, Europeans have called for a coordinated European exchange rate policy vis-à-vis the dollar. In fact the decision to proceed with the EMS and EMU was in large part a policy response to dollar volatility. In other words, European monetary integration is driven greatly but not exclusively by external constraints and pressures of the U.S. dollar–dominated international monetary system. However, the goal of a coordinated European exchange rate dollar policy or united European "voice" on global monetary affairs has never come to fruition. Instead, European efforts at exchange rate management have focused on individual European responses to the basic interaction of the dollar and the DM. Via the DM, the EMS often acts as a transmission mechanism of international monetary volatility and dollar "shocks" to Europe. At the center of my analysis, Germany has become the pivot point between international and European monetary governance. While some analysts might argue that Germany has provided an effective stabilizer to such shocks, Germany's central role in the operation and management of the EMS has created notable problems of asymmetry and unequal adjustment. The second section of this chapter further develops these themes with a brief historical account of the EMS.

The third section of this chapter surveys the issues and challenges facing European monetary integration today. I examine the current debates over some of the difficult political points to be negotiated, including rewriting some of the Maastricht principles on monetary convergence, reevaluating the timetable for EMU, and, at a maximum, rethinking the entire EMU project. I pay special attention to the nature of the international monetary context and what role it will play in determining the outcomes of the IGC.

I conclude by examining the question of the compatibility between widening and deepening in the monetary context, a crucial point centered on the ongoing IGC. I suggest that EMU is a worthy goal and that EMU can provide not only Germany but the whole of Europe a greater influence in questions of global monetary governance. In sum, within the realm of monetary affairs and with EMU, the EU could increasingly shape international monetary affairs in the form of a coordinated European exchange rate management strategy. Deepening EMU must remain a priority for the EU. Moreover, the failure to clarify particular components of the Maastricht Treaty pertaining to external exchange rate management will result in further monetary divisions within Europe. Finally, deepening should not be set off from enlargement to new members. Nonetheless, enlargement will prove problematic as long as the established patterns of EMS operation continue.

Argument and Framework:
The Triangulation of Europe's Monetary Policy

Competing explanations of European monetary integration have zeroed in on the importance of political imperatives, on economic and financial issues, on the impact of European institutions, on the logic of "economic spillover," and on strategies of high-inflation countries to "import" price credibility from Germany. These explanations are important and embrace powerful understandings as to the causes of European monetary integration. Their focus, however, is on the internal forces functioning among European nations and within Europe proper.

This chapter argues that explanations of European monetary integration should also highlight and analyze external forces—primarily U.S.-driven instability in the international monetary system. As Henning has succinctly noted, "When, over the decades, the members of the Community were divided over or uncertain about exchange rate stabilization, global monetary and exchange rate instability helped to nudge the reticent among them along the path toward monetary integration."[4] Community members have consistently pursued regional monetary stability and monetary integration in the face of U.S. exchange rate policies that many scholars consider indifferent and noncooperative.[5] The notion that Europe stands to gain from a larger international monetary voice was clearly noted by the European Commission during the bargaining leading up to Maastricht. For example, the Commission noted that a "Community that was united and well organised in its economic and monetary affairs would be better able to secure a world policy mix more favourable to the interests of the global economy."[6] In addition, the Commission's report entitled *One Market, One Money* suggested that global power gains from monetary integration. Specifically, "the United States can exploit this asymmetry by making its policy choices in a non-coordinated fashion without suffering much from a similar behavior of European nations. The effect of EMU would be to aggregate 12 economies into a single major block whose degree of interdependence with the US, Japan, that the rest of world would be meaningful."[7] In sum, a strong political purpose of European monetary integration has always been to develop a stronger European voice in global monetary affairs.

Although the European Commission and French officials, among others, have recognized the importance of greater European say in global monetary affairs, it has been Germany that has devised the European monetary strategy toward the United States. This strategy, however, has done more to shield Germany than Europe and to solidify the DM as the anchor currency of the EMS. In fact other EMS member states, not Germany, have borne a disproportionate share of the adjustment to external, U.S. monetary disturbances. In other words, the DM plays a crucial role as the transmission agent of dollar volatility into the exchange rate mechanism (ERM) of the EMS. The primary cause of the asymmetrical functioning of the EMS and the unequal distribution of adjustment to dollar instability has been Germany's rigid insistence that the "anchor currency country [Germany] must be geared primarily to achieving price stability" such that stability throughout the system can be safeguarded.[8] This mismatch between political purpose (developing a European counterpole to U.S. monetary power) and economic function (the DM as anchor of the EMS) has been at the center of the problems confronting European monetary integration.[9]

In order to provide a more solid analytical footing for examining Europe's and Germany's monetary affairs, we thus need to develop a framework that illustrates the complex interaction of Europe and Germany within the U.S.-led and G7-governed international monetary system. I argue that this interaction can best be conceptualized and analyzed within a framework identifying a triangular or tripartite relationship, a relationship that Hugo Kaufmann has termed the most interesting interaction of the international monetary system.[10] The use of the tripartite framework for this purpose is not new.[11] The triple dimension of German monetary policy and its interaction between internal and external preferences and interests is implicit, if not explicit, in most works addressing this issue area. In contrast to previous accounts, however, which tend to lack much formal conceptualization, the present study is systematic in its application to the analysis of European monetary integration and exchange rate management.

Kaufmann cites as the most important problem area in international monetary relations the "triangular interaction between the Deutsche Mark, the United States dollar, and the functioning of the European Monetary System."[12] A symbiotic interaction of these three points on the policy axis of German monetary policy (Figure 13.1) indicates the potentially complex policy arena within which Europe's monetary affairs operates.

As Figure 13.1 suggests, at the center of the analysis and this triangulation is Germany and the role of the DM. The basic monetary objectives of German monetary authorities must be balanced, however, with the

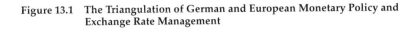

Figure 13.1   The Triangulation of German and European Monetary Policy and Exchange Rate Management

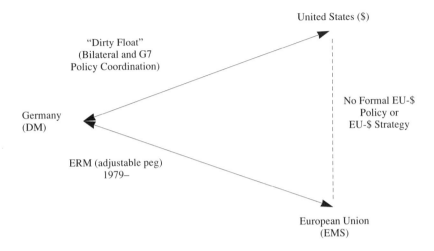

monetary concerns of Germany's particular European policies—especially continuing integration of the EU and the operation of the EMS—and Germany's key role within the larger global monetary arena, especially bargaining with the United States, G7 summitry, and G7 attempts to govern the international monetary system through "policy coordination."[13]

This triangular relationship, then, leads one to ask some particularly useful yet rather basic questions: What role does the DM play between the dollar and the EMS, and what are the consequences of Germany's central role in this relationship to questions of monetary integration in Europe and the international monetary order? The answers to these questions provide the insights into how tensions within Germany, within the European Union, and in the international monetary order are interrelated and how the triangulation of interests influences and complicates monetary policy and exchange rate management within both Germany and Europe.

At the core of this triangulation lies the Deutschmark, the pivotal element between the dollar and other EMS currencies. If, for example, the United States and the dollar were to exert strong pressure on Germany's monetary authorities to tighten their domestic monetary policy, such a policy decision would be quickly transmitted throughout the EMS as other EMS members adjusted their policy to keep their currency pegged to the anchor of the ERM—the DM. Because of this role, Germany must consider how its own domestic monetary policy and its dollar-DM policy may impact its European partners. As another example, when the U.S. Federal Reserve focuses on the relationship between the dollar and the DM in its exchange rate and/or interest rate policy, European central bankers have to decide for themselves whether and how they intend to react to this policy. They cannot simply rely on the Bundesbank to pursue a policy course that is congruent with "European" interests. This disparity in response can provide fertile soil for disagreement between the Bundesbank and the Federal Reserve, on the one hand, and the Bundesbank and EMS partner central banks, on the other.

A second important aspect to this tripartite arrangement is that there is no "EMS-dollar policy," either from the U.S. or German perspective.[14] When there is such reference, it usually pertains to the desirability of a DM-dollar policy. A joint European dollar float would be possible, however, only as long as the EMS partners accept, in the absence of a single EMS currency, one member currency that would function as the key currency and decides "European" exchange rate policy. While Germany plays the key currency role, differing domestic monetary objectives and exchange rate goals between Germany and other EMS members often lead Germany to conduct its own intra-EMS exchange rate policy in order to defend its currency against dollar volatility. Finally, differing preferences on appreciation and depreciation among European states and an unequal distribution of currency diversification (as short-term capital often moves first into Germany and not into other countries of the EU[15]) complicate matters further.

In short, the triangulation of European monetary policy places immense demands, pressures, and responsibilities upon Germany and Germany's European partners. As a result, the EMS, as the monetary arm of the EU, does not retain an identity of its own with separate and distinct interests vis-à-vis the United States or the dollar. I argue somewhat pessimistically that the EMS has not represented the monetary interests of "Europe" but mainly Germany's interests. The relationship of the EMS to other major international actors, in particular the United States, is not comparable, for example, to that of the trading relationship involving the United States, the WTO, and the EU. Moreover, the United States has not recognized the EMS as a separate and distinct entity in terms of global monetary governance. Previously established patterns of monetary interaction in the form of the dollar-DM relationship complicate EU and EMS operations. In sum, problems and tensions with the EMS translate into larger problems within the EU and its overriding movement toward union. The Europeans must shore up this weak foundation of monetary integration or else face continued division.

Decisive Junctures in the Path
Toward European Monetary Integration

A brief history of monetary integration from 1979 through the mid-1990s can illustrate the decisive junctures under which European monetary integration was driven by external factors and how Germany emerged to become the dominant actor of the EMS. From the beginning, in 1979, the EMS was designed to create an extensive European region of monetary stability through which constraints and pressures brought about by dollar policies and exchange rates could be more widely shared. After the buffeting brought about by the locomotive policies of U.S. president Jimmy Carter, it was German chancellor Helmut Schmidt, along with French president Valéry Giscard d'Estaing, who recognized the importance of a counterweight to U.S. global monetary influence by creating a "zone of monetary stability" and to avert appreciation of the DM against other EC currencies. As a dollar shield, the EMS was the regional complement to efforts at creating a new global monetary order that would seek to mend the passive dollar policy of the United States. The EMS was not designed to be a deliberate attempt to weaken U.S. power. Rather, it represented an attempt to denationalize global reserve holdings, a function that special drawing rights (SDRs) had only inadequately performed, and an effort to distribute global monetary influence commensurate with economic power. Most important, the EMS was designed in principle to be symmetrical in operation such that adjustment would be spread equally among members.

The first four years of the EMS, however, did not prove very successful either in shielding European currencies from global shocks and instability or enshrining the principle of symmetry. Member states pursued differing macroeconomic policies in response to unilateral U.S. monetary policy and indifference toward G7 exchange rate management. Nevertheless, with French and German political persistence and frequent use of realignments within the EMS, the EMS survived more or less intact. But this four-year period left its imprint on the function of the EMS: Germany emerged as the dominant political and monetary actor (the DM was not and still has not been devalued within the EMS); France and other member states would face devaluation and more painful macroeconomic adjustment.

March 1983 would prove decisive, marking the second phase of the EMS, which ended with the so-called Gleneagles summit of September 1986. The decision by the French government to remain within the ERM of the EMS would prove both a blessing for further monetary integration as well as a curse for its overall long-term stability. With France choosing to devalue the franc and implement restrictive policies to control inflation, as opposed to continuing Keynesian expansion programs implemented by Mitterrand in 1981, Germany and the German monetary norm of fiscal rectitude, low inflation, and Bundesbank rigor would come to politically and monetarily anchor the EMS. France, indeed most EMS members, willingly began to internalize what would become the stringent Maastricht criteria. Germany would become the primary counterpole in Europe to the dollar and U.S. global monetary leadership. Although never the formal policy of France or other EMS members, it would de facto be with Germany that the United States would negotiate the decade's leading global monetary agreements on behalf of the EMS. The triangulation of Germany's and Europe's monetary policies was complete.

More important for my argument here, the international monetary environment of the 1980s encouraged the French decision to stay within the ERM.[16] The appreciation of the dollar against the franc and other European currencies placed inflationary pressures on Europe, especially France, where it was already high. For France, leaving the relative safety and credibility of the ERM for the instability of global markets driven by U.S. exchange rate policy and Reagan dollar neglect proved an unfavorable option. Moreover, in a reflection of the shifting balance of power and tides, when the United States stepped up pressure on Germany and the Bundesbank to undertake fiscal and monetary stimulus, the Europeans—most notably the French—sided with the Germans. In 1977–1978, under similar conditions, the French had sided with the United States. A more cohesive European voice on global monetary affairs was slowly emerging, cemented in the Gleneagles summit of 1986, which codified a unified European response to U.S. pressure. With Germany at the head, the Europeans would resist continued U.S. calls to further European monetary stimulus and would direct their respective central banks to pursue joint efforts to buttress the value of the dollar against the DM. As the Luxembourg finance minister Jacques Poos stated, Europe wanted "to speak with one voice toward the U.S."[17] The primary problem for some Europeans was that the language spoken was most often German.

During the third phase of European monetary integration (1987–1991), Germany did bend to some of the concerns and pressures of its European partners. In 1987 the Europeans decided to solidify new arrangements within the EMS to make coordination and cooperation stronger. The Basel-Nyborg agreement on intramarginal interventions, although hotly contested by the Bundesbank, strengthened the functioning of the ERM and solidified and promoted European monetary cooperation during a period in 1987 when transatlantic macroeconomic relations between the Plaza and Louvre accords were tempestuous. In many respects, the move by Germany to accept some of the potential constraints brought about by Basel-Nyborg proved fortuitous and strategic. When U.S. treasury secretary James Baker's criticism of German monetary and fiscal policy following the Louvre accord unleashed global market jitters (resulting in the infamous 1987 Black Monday market crash), Baker flew to Frankfurt (and not Brussels, London, or Paris) to meet with Bundesbank and German Finance Ministry officials. As Germany emerged ever more powerful in global monetary affairs, the United States would encounter maturing German monetary influence. Germany's growing monetary influence did not, however, translate into an enlarged "European" influence on global monetary affairs. Instead, European officials would hope that Germany would speak for Europe's interests.

This hope was not a strong enough guarantee for some Europeans who wanted a more concrete arrangement. This arrangement would be Maastricht. The period from 1989 to 1991 leading up to Maastricht proved relatively stable in terms of DM-EMS-U.S. relations and supportive of the negotiations of the details of Maastricht. The lack of any major "external" monetary shock would prove important for success at Maastricht. Nonetheless, the international monetary environment was clearly a significant factor in solidifying the compromise of Maastricht and EMU. The Europeans realized that the respite from external U.S. pressure was momentary—especially given the ongoing deficit problem in the United States and Bush's pledge of no new taxes to remove the deficit. In terms of dollar policy, this would mean that downward pressure would continue to be placed on the value of the dollar in the markets as well as political pressure to talk down the dollar to combat the trade deficit. While Japan certainly was the primary target, Germany's continued surpluses remained an inviting target. With the Berlin Wall crumbling, the Soviets dismantling the iron curtain and control over Eastern Europe, and the Cold War ending, U.S. attention was temporarily diverted to the Gulf War and solidifying a "new world order." Monetary issues were not paramount for the United States—good for the short term but dangerous for the long-term stability of the international monetary system.

The outcome at Maastricht in December 1991 is well known, and I do not need to restate it in any great detail.[18] The Europeans agreed to create a single currency, with an independent European central bank, and developed a timetable (1997 at the earliest, 1999 at the latest) and mechanisms (convergence criteria[19]) to deliver member countries to union. The details of Maastricht generally reflected German concerns and desires, although the Europeans, especially the French, sought and received the German pledge to relinquish the DM and the Bundesbank's control over European monetary policy. This is an important point that is underemphasized in accounts and understanding of European monetary integration. True, the Europeans would now formally follow the German macroeconomic model,[20] but the Germans would also at some date give up their singular influence over European-wide monetary policy. If the strict timetables and programs were to hold firm, the benefits to Europe in terms of its global economic and monetary power would be immense. Moreover, the symmetry so sought after in the original design of the EMS would finally be attained. Europe would finally retain the possibility of speaking with one voice on global monetary matters.

The problem, of course, would be the period from 1991 to that date in 1997 or 1999 (the fourth phase) when EMU would theoretically arrive: Germany would keep its preeminent anchor position within the EMS. Pressure would also still come from external sources. The other EMS member states would continue to shoulder the adjustment to German and U.S.

policy. In other words, the triangulation of Europe's and Germany's monetary policies remained. Although the euphoria over Maastricht may have masked these powerful continuities, it would not take long for everyone to realize that everything was still much the same as before Maastricht.

The complications within the EMS brought about by the yearlong EMS crisis of 1992–1993 again clearly illustrated the ongoing complexity of the DM-EMS-dollar triangulation. Despite the pledge of all governments, including Germany, to move to a single currency and monetary policy in Europe, Germany remained dominant within the operation of the ERM. With inflationary pressures brought on by German unification pushing German interest rates to historic highs in the fall of 1992 and into the summer of 1993, the choice and trade-off between exchange rate stability and monetary autonomy proved too exacting for some EMS members. Some countries (Britain) left, while others (Italy, for one) were forced out. Largely forgotten in the criticism of Bundesbank policy was the fact that the United States had already in 1991 launched a policy of benign dollar neglect. With the dollar hitting historic post–World War II lows in September 1992 and U.S. Treasury secretary Nicholas Brady putting continued pressure on Germany to lower interest rates, Germany's resolve stiffened—at the expense of the EMS.

By August 1993, the EMS had been hollowed out, or as *Financial Times* correspondent Lionel Barber has suggested, a "boulevardization" of the trading margins to 15 percent within the ERM had occurred. This hollowed-out version of the EMS operates today, although some members of the EMS have voluntarily sought to retain their currencies with the older 2.5 percent margins of the old system. It is not surprising that these members are the same that had little difficulty in doing so before 1993 (Benelux, Denmark, and Austria, Sweden, and Finland as new members[21]). France, largely for political reasons, has also held firm, although doubts remain as to France's political will and the economic conditions supportive of French adherence to the convergence criteria. The other former EMS members have either remained out on their own conviction or have experienced serious difficulties in adhering to a smaller trading margin or standing firm to the convergence criteria. Moreover, steps in the period through 1994–1996 in filling in some of the details of Maastricht have continued to impress on everyone the dominant German role: the name of the new currency, "Euro," proposed by Germany; the location of the European Central Bank's forerunner, the European Monetary Institute, in Frankfurt; the German insistence that the convergence criteria not be negotiated; and the German-influenced "stability pact" on budgetary discipline agreed upon at the Dublin summit of December 1996.

As this brief history shows, decisive junctures in the evolution of the EMS indicate the importance of external or international monetary pressures and constraints. At the founding of the EMS, at its important restructuring and political decisions (the French decision to follow the German monetary norm in March 1983, the Gleneagles strategy, the Basel-Nyborg agreements, and the Maastricht Treaty) as well as the turmoil of the last years, the triangulation of Europe's monetary affairs has revealed a mixed record of success. On the one hand, Europe has moved farther ahead on monetary integration than ever imagined. On the other hand, the actual operation of the EMS has reinforced internal asymmetry and German leadership. This triangulation has placed the decisions surrounding the IGC negotiations and the debate over the final steps toward EMU in a difficult position. This means that the Europeans will have to fundamentally agree to restructure the process of European monetary integration once and for all. This also suggests reining in German power and leadership and securing, at last, a zone of monetary stability in Europe. It is to these points that this chapter now turns.

The Challenges Facing European Monetary Integration

The 1996 negotiations over EMU have become a critical defining point in the nearly thirty-year process of European integration. A difficult set of issues remains unresolved,[22] with the Germans and Europeans locked in complicated negotiations surrounding entry requirements, stability pacts, timetables, and such. But I want to suggest that however important these may be, they are mere details to something larger that I believe scholars examining and politicians negotiating EMU overlook. Why was European monetary integration so important in the first place? What was the original overriding objective of the EMS? Certainly, enhancing the role of the market and furthering political integration played a role. But from the design set out in the Werner Plan and cemented in the ideas of Schmidt and Giscard with the creation of the EMS, a critical motive of EMS and EMU architects—along with making the single market work—was to establish a more powerful European voice in international monetary affairs. The global pull of the international monetary system exerted at the time (and still does) an irresistible but differential pull on EC currencies. As a result of this tension and turmoil among EU currencies (especially France and Germany, tracing back to the Franco-German monetary crisis of October 1968), the desire to create common monetary institutions, a common monetary voice, and a common political counterweight to U.S. pressure must be more forcefully conveyed; the Europeans must refocus on the original intent of monetary integration: to develop a common European voice in global monetary affairs.

Therefore the primary problem facing Europe's drive toward monetary union is not the weak support among the public (problematic, yes; impossible to overcome, no) in some countries or even the difficulty of member states in attaining the convergence criteria, admittedly a laborious task. Rather, the primary problem of European monetary integration today is the lack of an external focus that can continue to drive pressures for integration and that can refocus energies on the original objective of the founders of European monetary integration. Dollar volatility, as we have seen, played a dual role in European monetary integration. First, it led to increased conflict within the EMS. Second, this conflict within the EMS would help focus European energies upon the task of solidifying a European monetary voice and encouraging compromises from EMS members, including Germany. Today, with less instability coming from the United States, the powerful external driving forces of EMU are no longer there. Of course the continuing forceful element of Franco-German reconciliation remains, as do the driving forces of financial capital market integration. However, the outside factors that kept the Germans and Europeans intent on monetary affairs have dissipated.

As a result, it is imperative that EMU negotiators give renewed attention to the original goal of developing this common European voice on monetary policy and exchange rate management. The Maastricht Treaty alludes to this policy in Article 105, although it is ambiguous as to who or what would determine exchange rate policy. Article 105 delegates authority to the European System of Central Banks (ECSB), not only to control monetary policy but also to manage exchange rates. However, this provision is qualified—if not contradicted—by Article 109, paragraph 1, which declares that the Council of Ministers, comprising relevant government ministers from the member states, may (acting unanimously) conclude formal arrangements for an exchange rate system for the Euro (the new single currency) with respect to non-Community currencies. Paragraph 2 goes on to declare that the Council (voting by qualified majority) may "formulate general guidelines for exchange rate policy vis-à-vis these currencies." It is entirely unclear how the tension between monetary policy, controlled by the ECSB, and exchange rate policy, determined by the Council of Ministers, will be resolved.

As it has functioned up until today, Germany has more or less determined Europe's external exchange rate policy through the relationship of the DM and the dollar. This, as we have seen, has been the source of many of the problems and turmoil within the EMS and its operation. Until Germany relinquishes this role or the DM disappears, nothing will change. That is why it is so important at this juncture to reexamine the components of the Maastricht Treaty that focus on external exchange rate management, clarify them, and suggest an early process of a more formal exchange rate policy for the EMS. If the Europeans cannot determine how to resolve the problem of German leadership today, they will not be able to resolve the tension that exists between Articles 105 and 109 when the system is supposed to be up and operating. The same problem in terms of clarifying leadership on European exchange rate policy that exists today will certainly reoccur later. Similar to the tension between the Bundesbank and German federal government over defining Germany's exchange rate strategy,[23] the lack of clarity on European exchange rate management will likely cause non-Europeans interested in monetary cooperation much consternation. Should the United States and the Japanese negotiate with the ECSB or the Council of Finance Ministers or the Germans?

Europeans have generally been fortunate that the monetary conditions both in the United States and Germany in 1996–1997 have been favorable for the relative stability within the EMS. As suggested, the fact that dollar neglect (which briefly resurfaced in the winter and spring of 1995 as the dollar slid to historic lows) did not unleash more turmoil within the EMS can largely be attributed to a Bundesbank policy that has steadily lowered interest rates. This has provided the EMS with the breathing room necessary to more easily adjust to any external pressures. This rather uneasy state will not continue uninterrupted. Unless EMU is completed, the Bundesbank will find it in its own interest at some point in the near future to pursue a tighter monetary policy for Germany. Moreover, external pressures brought on by U.S. policy will undoubtedly resurface in some more malign form in the near future. These two conditions—a volatile international monetary situation and a less European-friendly Bundesbank policy—will undoubtedly unleash further strains upon European monetary stability. In one sense, it may help Europeans refocus on the goal of European Monetary Union. However, the Europeans must be prepared for such conditions.

Within this context, completing the IGC and enhancing monetary cooperation in Europe will remain problematic. On the one hand, the coexistence of different currencies and monetary authorities and the continued monetary autonomy of the EU member states will persistently lead to conflicts of interests and aims. On the other hand, the implementation of the single market, the liberalization of capital movements, and the integration of the financial markets have increased the interdependence among member states. This necessitates growing monetary policy cooperation. Whether cooperation will be forthcoming will depend on the political will of member states.

As it stands today, France and Germany are dead set on meeting the deadline for EMU. A "hard core" of six to nine members—the Benelux countries (if Belgium's debt can somehow be overlooked), Austria, France, Germany, and possibly Ireland, Sweden, and Finland—are still publicly bent on forging ahead with the 1999 EMU timetable. As a result, important EU members such as Britain, Spain, and Italy, to say nothing of the other members, may be left behind. In this sense, deepening EMU to a hard core of countries would necessarily leave these members out of the core (Italy and Spain have pledged budgetary austerity for 1997 in order to meet the criteria). While the concept of a hard core of EMU runs counter to the spirit of a united Europe, it does draw upon deep historical movements within the two main founding members, Germany and France. Moreover, it should be recognized that the idea of a hard-core or two-speed Europe was agreed upon by all EU members in the Maastricht Treaty. While one could have hoped that all twelve members (at the time) would meet the criteria for membership, it was also clear that some might require more time to join. In part the IGC has dealt with the issue of those left out of the core group of EMU. In April 1996 in Verona, Italy, the EU's finance ministers and central bankers agreed to set up a new exchange rate mechanism to link the planned single currency, the Euro, to currencies that do not join. Moreover, the future European Central Bank will be empowered to demand alignments of currencies in the new ERM rather than waiting for countries to ask for a devaluation. What this suggests is that each individual country outside the core will be interacting within some form of system governed by the ERM and European Central Bank. Germany's singular position as leader will be reduced.

Although predicting the outcome of the IGC and the likelihood of a single currency's arriving in some European capitals by 1999 is a thankless task, I believe that the EMU negotiations will cement the two-track, hard-core approach envisioned by the Germans. The convergence criteria will remain unchanged, albeit perhaps loosely interpreted for key members (Belgium, Germany, and France), and the timetable will be held firm until the fateful decision date in early 1998. If a core group of countries (France and Germany—with Helmut Kohl likely still at the helm in Germany— must be part of this group) meets the criteria for launching the union, we can expect the movement toward EMU to proceed. Such movement should be welcomed and encouraged. Europe's international monetary power and influence will be enlarged, and the Euro may indeed truly balance the dollar's role in international monetary affairs.

EMU and Enlargement: The Link to the IGC

The relationship between EMU and the question of enlargement being discussed at the IGC is also quite complex yet inextricably linked. Real fears remain among existing and potential EU members. Jan Kryzstof Beilecki, the former Polish prime minister, has suggested that "if a monetary union is launched on schedule, it will touch off a chain reaction that will halt integration"[24] of Spain, Portugal, and Italy as well as the enlargement of the EU to Poland, Hungary, and the Czech Republic, the three most likely EU candidates in the next decade. EMU among a core group of countries would further demand difficult adjustments for those economies in transition at a time that would distract political and economic energies of the economies with weak currencies. Potential deflationary policies to meet the criteria for monetary union might further embolden former communists (who are already in power in Poland and Hungary) to renege on their commitments to market liberalization. Moreover, the Western European countries might be distracted with the necessity to integrate Spain, Italy, and Portugal into EMU and therefore will be less inclined to seek the formal integration of Central Europe for many years to come.

This chapter suggests that how Europe addresses and resolves these issues will determine its future viability as an actor with international influence. Europe should therefore consider its own history of monetary deepening and enlargement. In the early 1970s, fundamental political and economic considerations prevented agreement on what the purpose and meaning of monetary union would be, except for the reason that it might provide an escape from U.S. monetary policy. In its desire to shield Europe from disruptive dollar policies, West Germany demanded that its partners conform to German economic and monetary preferences. France also wanted a common currency to guard against the powerful influence of the dollar in European monetary affairs and to restrain rising German economic and political power. The Werner Plan ultimately failed because of the inability, primarily on the part of France and Germany, to agree on how to deal with the dollar as the global monetary crisis of 1971 erupted. Had the Werner Plan been fully implemented, it would have required the harmonization of a wide variety of monetary and fiscal policies. Deepening was put off for another twenty years.

The consideration of enlarging the EC was dealt with more successfully in the early 1970s. The impending enlargement of the EC to include Britain, Ireland, and Denmark depended primarily on Britain's relinquishing the reserve role of the sterling. Monetary issues were thus intricately involved in the debate over enlargement. However, Britain agreed to do away with the reserve role of the sterling. Moreover, Ireland's weaker and largely agricultural-based economy would require increased transfers of regional funds to sustain its entry into the EC. The potential also existed that Britain might require transfers to alleviate industrially depressed regions. Difficult issues thus confronted the EC members on the terms of enlargement. Nonetheless, both the new members and the existing EC members found room to compromise. The enlargement of the EC was completed.

Today there are reasons to be optimistic about the enlargement of new members into the EU, even with EMU deepening among a possible core groups of states. First, EU Commission president Jacques Santer has given his strong support to enlargement. Germany has also shifted its weight in favor of enlargement, especially in support of Poland's entry. At the 1996 World Economic Forum, Polish president Aleksander Kwasniewski declared it his personal task "to see Poland inside the EU by the year 2000."[25] His words are backed up by action as many states are working full

time to bring national laws and regulations into conformity with EU standards. The desire to join the EU and eventually EMU is driving many
aspects of policymaking throughout East and Central Europe.[26] Already in
October 1992, the Visegrád members (before the split of Czechoslovakia)
presented a memorandum to the Union that set out along similar lines the
convergence philosophy of the Maastricht Treaty: liberalization of financial
flows, controls on inflation, and convertibility of currencies. More important, several East European countries, notably the Czech Republic and
Poland, have tied their currencies to strong Western ones, either the
Deutschmark or a basket of the dollar to the mark.[27] The pegging of these
currencies to a stable currency or set of currencies has produced results
complementary to the goals of EMU: relative steady prices, reduced inflation (the Czech Republic's annual rate is under 10 percent), stable
exchange rates (with the use of crawling pegs), GDP growth, and tighter
controls on budgetary deficits.[28] While difficulties remain, most notably in
terms of continued privatization and agricultural supports, many East
European countries are headed in the proper macroeconomic direction.

Difficult reforms of the EU, much like those undertaken in earlier
efforts to enlarge the EC in the 1970s and 1980s, are still necessary. In a
widely cited study, Richard Baldwin has stated that bringing in Poland,
Hungary, the Czech Republic, and Slovakia under existing rules would
boost EU spending by $80 billion annually, requiring a 60 percent increase
in member state budget contributions.[29] Such contributions would be
impossible given the existing Maastricht monetary requirements for EMU.
Moreover, reform of the CAP, structural policies, and regional transfer programs have strong support among some EU states, and CAP retains the support of EU agricultural commissioner Franz Fischler of Austria. Additional
reform of EU decisionmaking procedures, trade in sensitive products, and
migration policy must also be accomplished. General inequality between
the East and the EU remains. The Czech Republic, the richest of the applicants, has a GDP per head that is only 45 percent of the EU average. An
alliance among potential new members in the East and those members of
the EU that may not be part of a first stage of EMU might prove effective to
develop a coherent strategy for eventual EMU inclusion.

Conclusion: Widening and Deepening EMU

What final lessons for today, if any, can be drawn from the earlier periods
of enlargement and deepening? First, for France and Germany, a historic
opportunity in the early 1970s to develop a balanced program on monetary
integration and union was lost. The failure of the Community's efforts to
achieve a consensus on harmonizing monetary policies thus deprived it of

the first opportunity to deepen its integration. The lesson for the late 1990s should thus be clear. Deepening the EU's monetary arm through the program for EMU should be paramount. Without such deepening, Germany's leadership role in the EMS will be extended indefinitely and would merely reinforce the asymmetrical operation and unequal adjustment of the ERM based on the triangulation of European monetary policy examined above. Germany and the Europeans must therefore return to the original goals and objectives of monetary integration: to speak with one voice in global monetary affairs.

Moreover, the EU could help potential EU members by setting firmer targets concerning what the 1993 Copenhagen summit referred to as a "functioning market economy." These criteria could include limiting the state sector to no more than 20 percent of GDP.[30] Targets could be set for inflation and for budget deficits that would exceed the EU average by no more than an agreed proportion. Flexible interpretation of the criteria would be used as well. A negotiated arrangement between the EU and associate members on such a target plan and agenda would prove useful for setting a firm timetable for more serious entrance negotiations to follow the decision to proceed with EMU in the West in 1998. Deepening monetary integration in the West need not suggest that the East be forever locked out.

Second, enlargement must continue in tandem with deepening. If enlargement is put off indefinitely, Europe, especially Germany, may lose a historic opportunity permanently to bind and institutionalize relationships within the multilateral confines of the EU. Enlargement versus deepening should not be seen in a zero-sum context. I remain unconvinced that one goal has to be sacrificed at the expense of the other. Both are compatible in a larger, long-term vision of European integration. Deepening monetary union can stimulate the necessary reforms of the decisionmaking structure and agricultural policies of the EU, both in dire need of reform before enlargement can occur. In fact deepening EMU could provide an easier transition for the entry into the EU of possible new members. As noted, many East and Central European countries are already adjusting their policies to conform with the Maastricht convergence philosophy. With a firm timetable for the transition to EMU, ministers and heads of state will be hard pressed *not* to consider streamlining EU decisionmaking, reforming agricultural policy, and accepting associate EU members. Deepening EMU, enlarging the EU, and reforming the EU would make the EU a world-class economic and political actor, globally competitive and politically influential. Without progress on EMU or such policy reforms, the EU will remain fractured and without international influence. Enhancing Europe's international monetary power means completing Europe's drive toward a single currency.

Notes

1. "Club Europe's Tough Doorman," *New York Times,* 29 November 1995.

2. See Chapter 14 of this volume.

3. The concept of the tripartite framework, or triangulation, of Germany monetary policy has a long and distinguished history in analyses of German foreign policy and Germany in general. I am particularly indebted to the work of the late Wolfram Hanrieder, *Germany, America and Europe* (New Haven: Yale University Press, 1989).

4. Henning's argument is similar to mine, but I build on Henning's points by further defining the role of Germany in the development of Europe's external monetary role. C. Randall Henning, "System, Power, and European Monetary Integration," draft manuscript, Institute for International Economics, Washington, DC, July 1995.

5. For one account, see Benjamin J. Cohen, "An Explosion in the Kitchen? Economic Relations with Other Advanced Industrial States," in Kenneth A. Oye, Robert Lieber, and Donald Rothchild (eds.), *Eagle Defiant: United States Foreign Policy in the 1980's,* (Boston: Little, Brown, 1983).

6. Commission of the European Communities, *Economic and Monetary Union: The Economic Rationale and Design of the System* (Luxembourg: Office for Official Publications of the European Communities, 1990), pp. 5–6.

7. *One Market, One Money,* special issue of *European Economy* (published by the Commission of the European Communities), 44 (October 1990).

8. Hans Tietmeyer, "National Monetary Policy and European Monetary Union," *Occasional Paper Series* 23-93 (Washington, DC: Konrad Adenauer Stiftung, 1993), p. 10.

9. That is to say nothing of the negative consequences of monetary cooperation. Such consequences include the loss of monetary autonomy and the ability of each nation to unilaterally adjust to negative economic circumstances. The economic and political costs of attaining monetary union through cooperation have been large: high unemployment, social unrest, and public unease over the process of European integration. Moreover, the potential economic benefits—enhanced trade, competitiveness, productivity, and job growth—may turn out to be minimal. Nevertheless, the argument presented here emphasizes the external political configuration of factors pushing EMU forward.

10. Hugo Kaufmann, "The Deutsche Mark Between the Dollar and the European Monetary System," *Kredit und Kapital* 18 (1985); also Hugo Kaufmann, *Germany's International Monetary Policy and the European Monetary System* (New York: Brooklyn College Press, 1985).

11. A partial and inevitably deficient list would include Hanrieder, *Germany, America, and Europe,* and Otmar Emminger, *Dollar, D-Mark, und Währungskrisen* (Stuttgart: Deutsche-Verlags Anstalt, 1986). More recent works include Ellen Kennedy, *The Bundesbank* (London: RIIA, 1991); David Marsh, *Die Bundesbank: Geschäfte mit der Macht* (Munich: Bertelsmann, 1992); and in comparative perspective, John Goodman, *Monetary Sovereignty: The Politics of Central Banking in Western Europe* (Ithaca, NY: Cornell University Press, 1992). An excellent source is C. Randall Henning, *Currencies and Politics in the United States, Germany, and Japan* (Washington, DC: Institute for International Economics, 1994).

12. Kaufmann, *Germany's International Monetary Policy,* p. 83.

13. For the problems associated with international policy coordination and the weak record of G7 coordination, see Benjamin J. Cohen, "The Triad and the Unholy Trinity," in Richard Higgot, Richard Leaver, and John Ravenhill (eds.), *Pacific*

Economic Relations in the 1990's: Cooperation or Conflict? (London: Allen and Unwin, 1993).

14. Such a policy would be envisioned if the protocols of Maastricht are ever implemented. Article 105 of the Treaty designates the European System of Central Banks to manage external rates, presumably against the dollar.

15. The most important issue is what happens when the dollar is in decline: The dollar is sold for DM, driving a wedge between the DM and other EMS currencies and forcing these others to defend their currencies' link to the DM via tight monetary and fiscal policies. The burden of adjustment weighs heavy on the other EMS members.

16. This period is deftly handled by Henning, "System, Power," pp. 45–47.

17. "European Finance Ministers Meet," *New York Times,* 22 September 1986.

18. A very thorough review is in Daniel Gros and Niels Thygesen, *European Monetary Integration* (New York: St. Martin's Press, 1992). See also Wayne Sandholtz, "Choosing Union: Monetary Politics and Maastricht," *International Organization* 47, 1 (Winter 1993). As these authors, among many, have noted, Maastricht was uniquely influenced by the end of the Cold War and German unification.

19. These included limitations on budget deficits, overall public debt, inflation, and exchange rate instability. As of mid-1997, only Luxembourg had sufficiently met all the conditions. To its embarrassment, Germany overshot the 3 percent barrier on public debt in 1996.

20. Informally, the Europeans, including Britain and France, had more or less already willingly internalized this German macroeconomic norm enshrined in the Maastricht convergence criteria.

21. Again, the three new members to the EU had already internalized the Maastricht criteria as domestic policy goals in order to ease their transition into the EU.

22. See Chapters 14 and 15 in this volume.

23. The Finance Ministry is formally given the role of setting exchange rate policy.

24. Quoted in Peter Passell, "Economic Scene," *New York Times,* 16 May 1996.

25. Barry Wood, "EU Eastward Expansion," *Europe,* May 1996.

26. For a strong argument in favor, see Jacek Saryusz-Wolski, "The Reintegration of the 'Old Continent': Avoiding the Costs of 'Half Europe,'" in Simon Bulmer and Andrew Scott (eds.), *Economic and Political Integration in Europe* (Oxford: Blackwell, 1994).

27. For an interesting study of how East European countries should peg their currencies to the ECU, see Jeffrey Frankel and Charles Wyplosz, "A Proposal to Introduce the ECU First in the East," manuscript, Institute for International Economics, Washington, DC, 1995. For a critique of this approach, see "Peddling the Ecu in the East," *Economist,* 25 March 1995.

28. For a general review of the economic conditions of Poland, Hungary, Slovakia, and the Czech Republic, see "Survey of Central Europe," *Economist,* 18 November 1995.

29. Richard Baldwin, *Towards an Integrated Europe* (London: Center for Economic Policy Research, 1994).

30. For this and other possible ideas, see "An Agenda for Accession," *Economist,* 5 November 1994.

14

Explaining the Dominance of German Preferences in Recent EMU Decisions

Dorothee Heisenberg

On 12 October 1993, the German Constitutional Court ruled that the Treaty on European Union (Maastricht Treaty) was constitutional and that President von Waizsäcker could sign the Treaty at last. With the final member state's assent, the TEU entered into force on 1 November 1993 and committed the member states to creating a common currency by 1999 at the latest. The path to Economic and Monetary Union was clear and codified, or so it seemed. In reality, although the large issues certainly had been settled (and settled mainly in accordance with the German Bundesbank's preferences), many of the smaller issues regarding the implementation of EMU had either been left deliberately vague in the Treaty in order to facilitate agreement or not specified at all. Once the Treaty entered into force and moved out of the spotlight, decisions about EMU continued to be made in the EU's institutional forums, the Monetary Committee, the Committee of Central Bank Governors, and the finance ministers meetings.

The focus of this chapter is the role of Germany in negotiations on the implementation of EMU after the TEU was signed. The emphasis on Germany is deliberate and results from two factors: Many accounts of the EMU negotiations[1] demonstrate that Germany was instrumental in structuring the details of the final agreement, and the role of the recently unified Germany in the European Union generally is of interest to many scholars, not simply those who study Germany. An analysis of Germany's negotiating style in the EMU implementation discussions sheds light on Germany's actions in other negotiations when it believes its vital national interests are at stake. Whether the outcome of negotiations on other issues will be similar to those of the EMU implementation negotiations remains to be seen. It is clear, however, that in this case German preferences were predominantly institutionalized. A closer view of Germany's role is therefore instructive in how a unified Germany *can* act, not necessarily how it *will* act in other negotiations.

This chapter documents some of the issues that were divisive in EMU negotiations from 1993 to 1996 and how they were resolved. It immediately becomes apparent that in most of the issues the German, or more precisely the Bundesbank's, conservative preferences continued to be institutionalized as they had been before the signing of the TEU. This outcome, I argue, is due to the 1993 Constitutional Court decision that stipulated that before Germany entered into monetary union, the Bundestag and Bundesrat had to vote again, confirming that all of the convergence criteria in the TEU had been met. Because of the Bundesbank's domestic reputation as a nonpartisan and strictly technical institution, the opinions of the Bundesbank about the economic convergence would be a significant piece of information for the members of parliament when deciding how to vote in 1998. The Constitutional Court decision thus created a way to make the Bundesbank continue to behave as a domestic ratifier[2] in the international negotiations about EMU implementation. As other studies have shown,[3] the more constraining the domestic ratifier, the greater its leverage in international negotiations.

The second section of the chapter focuses on the popular opposition in Germany to EMU and the lack of party support for anti-EMU initiatives. Even though surveys consistently find the German public to be more negatively predisposed to EMU than the public of every other member state except perhaps Britain, German mainstream political parties have continued to avoid making a political issue of EMU. This somewhat surprising fact demonstrates that in German political dialogue the commitment to Europe continues to be sacrosanct and that any real or perceived retreat from European commitments is politically incorrect. Therefore, despite comments that Germany is the only state that could propose a delay in EMU without losing face,[4] Germany is unlikely to make such a proposal, although it would probably agree to it.

Germany's Influence on Post-Maastricht EMU Decisions

Like other contributors to previous volumes in this series,[5] I assume that Germany is *bargaining* with other member states, and the outcomes of those negotiations are not preordained by a structural power configuration. It is therefore somewhat unexpected that most of the decisions of the EU committees were made in accordance with Germany's preferences. It is essential that I be clear about what I mean by "Germany," since institutionally several different voices exist in monetary issues. This chapter focuses on the Bundesbank and the Finance Ministry, which often took the same positions during this post-Maastricht period.[6] Although their positions on the issues tended to be similar, these two institutions have very different abilities to defy the chancellor: Whereas the Bundesbank is statutorily independent in many areas, the Finance Ministry must adhere strictly to the wishes of the government. Moreover, the Bundesbank's domestic reputation as a nonpolitical actor is in contrast to the very political role of the finance minister. For these reasons, even though Finance Minster Waigel often fought important battles in EU finance ministers meetings (e.g., the stability pact), the Bundesbank is considered the more significant actor.[7] The following section reviews some of the key decisions made after November 1993 to establish the fact that Bundesbank preferences were incorporated more often than those of other member states, notably France.

The Calm After the 1993 EMS Storm

The EU member states spent the months of August and September 1993 reappraising the EMS and reassessing plans for monetary union.[8] Initially it was uncertain whether or not the EMS still really existed, given that a 30 percent fluctuation margin was equivalent to floating for most currencies. There were also questions about how quickly France and other member states with depressed economies would lower interest rates and what effect that would have on exchange rates. Finally, the question remained what the widening of the bands meant for Article 109j of the TEU, which stipulated that each member state had to observe the "normal" fluctuation margins of the EMS for at least two years without devaluing.[9] Given that the bands were only "temporarily" widened, it was uncertain how long exactly the bands were to be held at ±15 percent. It seemed clear in 1993; however, that eventually the members would return to the narrow ±2.25 percent bands, since the other state could not be described as "normal" by any stretch of the imagination.

The EU finance ministers took the first step toward the status quo ante by vowing at their 14 September 1993 meeting to continue with the Maastricht timetable. After the December 1993 European Council summit, Henning Christophersen, commissioner for economic affairs, stated that EMU did not depend on the member states' returning to the EMS's narrow bands, a position the Bundesbank strongly advocated. The Bundesbank had been the driving force behind the widening of the bands during the August 1993 crisis,[10] and Bundesbank president Tietmeyer continued to support the wider bands because it deterred currency speculators and effectively eliminated the Bundesbank's intervention obligations. By stating that EMU did not require a return to the smaller bands, Christophersen broke with European Monetary Institute president Lamfalussy's position and made the status quo politically viable at a time when no member state (with the possible exception of Denmark) was anxious to return to the former bands.

The issue of a return to the narrow bands was raised several times in 1994; in February eleven of the EU finance ministers voted against a

Danish proposal to return to the narrow bands, and in April Lamfalussy told
the European Parliament that he had changed his mind about the need to
revive the former bands, thus solidifying and legitimizing the status quo.
The conversion of the EMI president to the position of the Bundesbank
may be just a coincidence in this particular case, but it remains to be seen
how well equipped the institutions of the EMI and the European Central
Bank are to resist Bundesbank pressure.

At their December 1994 meeting, the EU finance ministers officially
endorsed an EMI proposal that member states could enter EMU without
having been in the narrow EMS bands for the required two years. The decision marked the complete legitimization of the status quo and represented a
victory for the Bundesbank's position that a return to the narrow bands
before the economies had converged would invite currency speculation.
The finance ministers avoided calling the wider bands "normal" as the
Commission had wanted, but one minister indicated after the meeting that
if monetary union were to occur on 1 January 1997, the wide bands could
retroactively be deemed normal.[11]

Location of the European Central Bank

Negotiations on the location of the EMI, the ECB's precursor, had been
ongoing since the signing of the Maastricht Treaty. Behind the scenes,
Chancellor Kohl pressured all of the member states to allow it to be located
in Frankfurt or, failing that, Bonn. The decision to locate the EMI in
Frankfurt had been blocked by the British at the June 1992 Lisbon summit,
but Kohl continued to insist that locating the ECB in Germany was essential to receiving the German public's support for EMU, which was falling
precipitously. According to a confidential Dutch memo, Kohl went beyond
cajoling his partners: He threatened to block the candidacy of Dutch prime
minister Ruud Lubbers for Commission president unless Lubbers dropped
his opposition to Frankfurt.[12] At the 29 October 1993 Brussels informal
summit, the decision was made to locate the EMI in Frankfurt.

What's in a Name?

The extent of Germany's dominance of the EMU-implementation process
is nowhere more apparent than in the question of what the single currency
should be named. On the face of it, the question seems trivial, and indeed
some member states thought that the issue had been resolved in 1978 when
Chancellor Helmut Schmidt agreed with French president Giscard
d'Estaing that the currency basket be called the "ecu." Kohl and Finance
Minister Waigel first raised the issue after the signing of the TEU in
December 1991, saying that the final decision on whether the single curren-

cy would be called "ecu" had not yet been made.[13] The Bundesbank fully
supported this position, believing the German public would not have faith
in the single currency if it were named "ecu," since the value of that currency basket had depreciated over time against the DM. The Bundesbank
maintained that in order to inspire confidence that the new single currency
was as stable as the DM, the new currency must be named something other
than "ecu." It is far from clear that Germans were really against the name; a
December 1994 *Spiegel/Financial Times* poll showed that of the respondents who favored a single currency, the top name suggested was "ecu" in
Germany (40 percent), followed only distantly by "Euromark" (21
percent).[14]

The French were indignant that Germany was suddenly against the
name, since it had deep roots as a historical compromise to which Germany
had agreed. Former prime minister Balladur publicly complained, "I think
that the discussion [in Germany] is infantile. I don't see why one should
change the name under a German pretext. It's a French word corresponding
to an English acronym. I don't want to put the name into question."[15] The
question of the name of the currency was to be decided by the end of 1995,
and throughout the year Kohl and Waigel stepped up the pressure on their
European counterparts to consider another name. In February Waigel publicly supported claims by the Bundesbank that the German electorate would
find it difficult to accept a currency called the "ecu." The strategic use of
the Bundesbank and the electorate's opposition to EMU for negotiating
leverage is again evident in this case.

In May 1995 the Commission published a green paper of its recommendations on the introduction of the Eurocurrency.[16] The paper contained
several ideas that closely followed German thinking on the process; among
them was the parenthetical mention that the question of the name was not
entirely settled.[17] In a 22 June speech to the Bundestag, Waigel praised this
particular element of the green paper: "The Green paper also rightly considers the question of the name of the new currency to be open. The question of the name is a very decisive point for us. The technical term, ecu, is
not possible to convey to our citizens. We should agree on a solid name
which will receive the acceptance of our citizens."[18]

At the 15–16 December 1995 Madrid summit, EU leaders finally confirmed the new name of the currency—the "Euro." Throughout the fall,
France had held fast to the name "ecu," and former president Giscard "was
said to be furious about the German-led campaign to kill the Ecu."[19] Right
before the summit, however, French president Chirac changed his tactic
and campaigned for an EU-wide referendum on the name. Kohl countered
with the argument that 80 million Germans would vote for "Euro," so why
bother to go through the exercise?[20] Kohl's argument carried the day, and
the Euro was created.

The Commission's Green Paper on the Practical
Arrangements for the Introduction of the Single Currency

The Commission's green paper provided the Commission's view of a blue-print for how the actual changeover to the single currency was to occur. The Commission proposed several features to which the Bundesbank was opposed, including the one that the changeover should have a short transition period for most financial transactions.

The 19 June 1995 finance ministers meeting proved divisive on several of the paper's points. France and the southern states all supported the Commission's emphasis on the irreversible move to monetary union and the need to enhance the credibility of the Euro by having business and banks use it early in the timeline. But Austria, Germany, and Britain resisted that proposal. Germany in particular wanted the single currency to become sole legal tender only once the Euro was minted and used by everyone at the end of the transitional phase. Before that, Germany insisted that businesses, banks, and the federal government be able to use the DM. In October of the previous year, President Tietmeyer had already confidently stated, "I am convinced that we will still be able to pay in DM in the year 2000."[21]

In November 1995 the EMI weighed in with its proposal, which was approved by the heads of state at the December Madrid summit. The EMI proposal reflected a great deal of German input—an unsurprising result not only because of the Bundesbank's membership on the EMI Council but also because of the composition of the EMI staff: Sixty-one of the 192 staff members were German (32 percent), twenty-nine British (15 percent), and eighteen French (9 percent).[22] Tietmeyer expressed his approval of the EMI proposal before it was even announced publicly: "Without wanting to pre-empt [the EMI's announcement], I may state that the recommendations will take account of significant German concerns."[23]

The document proposed a four-step timetable. During the first stage, which could start as early as 1998, governments would decide which countries were going to join EMU. The EMI would oversee production of the new Euro banknotes and coins. In the second stage, beginning 1 January 1999, the Euro would be introduced for noncash transactions. New public debt would be issued in Euros, and conversion facilities would be established to change national currencies to Euros.[24] Member states would have the choice of continuing to transact business in the national currencies or the Euro. Stage three would begin by 1 January 2002 at the latest and would involve the introduction of the Euro coin and banknote to the public. The final stage would begin 1 July 2002 at the latest and would require the removal from circulation of all national currencies.

The EMI's proposal reflected the Bundesbank's primary concern that the DM be allowed to be used during the transition period. In essence, the

EMI proposal bought the DM three more years before its extinction. France, which maintained that a long transition phase exposed its currency to speculation, argued to no avail against the EMI's plan at the EU finance ministers meeting on 27 November 1995. The ministers endorsed the EMI's proposal, and the heads of state formally approved the plan at the Madrid summit.

EMI Excessive Deficit Recommendations

Of the major implementation issues, the exemption for Ireland and Denmark from the EMI's excessive deficit recommendations is perhaps the only setback for the Bundesbank's position, and arguably only a minor one. At their 10–11 September 1994 informal meeting in Lindau, the EU finance ministers considered the questions of (1) which member states should receive a warning about their budget deficits and debts as stipulated by the Maastricht Treaty and (2) whether or not to make the EMI's recommendations public. The first order of business was to decide whether to agree to the Commission's recommendation to consider Ireland in compliance with the convergence criteria despite its debt ratio. According to the Maastricht Treaty, member states must keep their annual budget deficits to less than 3 percent of GDP and their total government debt to less than 60 percent of GDP. Ambiguity in the Treaty, however, allows member states to join EMU even if their ratios are not at those levels. The precise text of Article 104c is worth quoting at length:

> [The Commission] shall examine compliance with budgetary discipline on the basis of the following two criteria:
>
> (a) whether the ratio of the planned or actual government deficit to gross domestic product exceeds a reference value, unless
>   • either the ratio has declined substantially and continuously and reached a level that comes close to the reference value;
>   • or, alternatively, the excess over the reference value is only exceptional and temporary and the ratio remains close to the reference value;
> (b) whether the ratio of government debt to gross domestic product exceeds a reference value, unless the ratio is sufficiently diminishing and approaching the reference value at a satisfactory pace.[25]

The ambiguity of the TEU, which had helped to get the Treaty signed and ratified by member states, thus required interpretation in its implementation. How would a judgment about whether a ratio was "sufficiently diminishing" or "close to" the reference value be made? The Bundesbank used every opportunity to stress the importance of a strict interpretation of the ratios; in fact, the Bundesbank preferred to disregard entirely the caveats in Article 104c and to use only the ratios as the final determinants. At the

Lindau meeting, the finance ministers were well aware that granting an exception to the most conservative interpretations of the ratios for Ireland would create a precedent for such exceptions; the negotiations were therefore quite heated.

At issue was whether Ireland should be one of the states to receive a warning—an "excessive deficit recommendation"—from the EMI or whether it, like Luxembourg, met the Maastricht criteria. The case for a generous interpretation of Ireland's condition had merit: Ireland had kept its budget deficit below 2.5 percent and had reduced its government debt from 114 percent to 90 percent of GDP in the previous two years. Moreover, the exemption for Ireland had been approved by the Monetary Committee. However, in that committee France had supported the Bundesbank's reservation about considering the convergence criteria flexible.

At Lindau the ministers followed the lead of the Monetary Committee and agreed not to sanction Ireland. Germany conceded on the condition that in the future EU Monetary Committee and Commission members would be more explicit about why they chose to censure certain states and not others.[26] Tietmeyer responded that "from my point of view it is to be welcomed that the Council of Finance Ministers has resisted a general softening of the budgetary criteria although I have some difficulties in understanding why the Irish case was not addressed critically."[27]

Germany's representatives had a similar reaction to the question of Denmark's not receiving an excessive deficit recommendation in June 1996. At the finance ministers meeting in Luxembourg, Germany formally objected to allowing the Danes to join Ireland and Luxembourg as states that met the criteria because Denmark's debt ratio was 71.9 percent.[28] Germany was again outnumbered in the committee.

A second question arose at the Lindau meeting about the excessive deficit recommendations the EMI made for all member governments that did not meet the convergence criteria. Although the Maastricht Treaty stipulated that they would remain private during the second stage, some finance ministers wanted to make them public. Waigel (with the full support of the Bundesbank) was among those advocating this course on the grounds that public pressure was helpful in getting the member governments to take unpleasant corrective action. This point of view prevailed, and the finance ministers agreed informally that the EMI's recommendations be published in November in time for the first EMI Council meeting.[29]

Waigel's "Stability Pact"

In an interview in September 1994, Waigel called for the "installation of additional measures to secure budget discipline" and revealed that proposals for enhancing the Maastricht Treaty had been discussed within the Bundesbank and in EU finance ministers meetings for six months.[30] Two proposals emerged from the discussions: a Commission proposal that countries that run excessive deficits should lose some of their regional aid, and Waigel's stability pact. In a 10 November speech to the Bundestag, he described his concept: After 1999, any state that had a budget deficit of greater than 3 percent of GDP would be required to place a non-interest-bearing deposit of .25 percent of GDP for each additional 1 percent of budget deficit with the ECB. If the deficit were still above 3 percent after two years, the deposit would become a fine and be paid into the EU budget.[31]

Although the French government supported the need for a penalty against governments that run excessive deficits once in the single currency, it was reserved about Waigel's proposal. Several member states objected to the harsh nature of Waigel's sanction, however, and interpreted the proposal as Germany's unilaterally raising the hurdles for weaker-currency states to join EMU. Perhaps more troubling, the Waigel proposal reflected the degree to which Germany distrusted its partners to maintain correct economic policies once the Maastricht criteria had been met.

By March 1996 Waigel's stability pact had been opposed on both legal and political grounds by all of the EU member states except France and the Netherlands in the Monetary Committee.[32] When the issue arose again at the Luxembourg meeting of finance ministers in June 1996, Germany was isolated in its position that the disciplinary procedures begin as soon as an excessive deficit "exists." The other fourteen states wanted action only when "an excessive deficit *persists*."[33] The other states did, however, concede to Germany the inclusion of time limits that would give a delinquent state a finite amount of time to rectify its problems.[34]

In August 1996, state secretary for finance Jürgen Stark suggested a softening of Germany's position. He proposed that in exceptional circumstances a state could be allowed to exceed the excessive deficit criterion.[35] This led to a tentative agreement, announced after the 10 September 1996 Monetary Committee meeting and endorsed by the finance ministers in their 21 September meeting, that the member states would have nine to twelve months to correct their fiscal imbalances. Thereafter, sanctions would be automatic but would be imposed only by a "stability council" of other EMU participants, first in the form of non-interest-bearing deposits and then as fines.[36] The final terms of the stability pact were not, however, settled until a marathon negotiating session during the Dublin summit of 13–14 December 1996. Kohl remained isolated in his position that the fines be automatic, and he rejected the French position that some political intervention mechanism was necessary to make the sanctions practicable. "The negotiations on the stability pact were driven by concern about domestic public opinion, and that's a new phenomenon," said a German diplomat.[37] Waigel finally conceded that automatic fines would require rewriting the terms of the Maastricht Treaty's criteria, which Germany believed would be counterproductive. In the end, Kohl settled for a stability pact less strict than the one Waigel had originally proposed.[38] It should be remembered, however, that a fiscal stability pact was not in the Maastricht Treaty, and thus the Germans ultimately added to the requirements of EMU.

"Trust but Verify": Financial Statement Dates

The final issue was again a minor one, but it also illustrates the level of German distrust of its partner governments. At issue was the date of financial statements that would be used to gauge fitness for entry into the single currency. This became the subject of discussion at the 27 November 1995 finance ministers meeting when Waigel insisted that the decision by the member states on EMU entry be made on the basis of *actual* 1997 data rather than 1997 forecasts or quarterly reports. The implicit rationale for this course was to prevent states from optimistically projecting that they met the criteria when in fact they did not. However, in practice this also meant that the selection of countries would be made as late as May 1998. The French, in particular, objected to the German proposal because they wanted the decision made well before that date. With parliamentary elections due in March 1998, French leaders did not want EMU entry to become a campaign issue. At their Madrid summit, however, EU leaders acceded to Germany's demands that the decision be made "as soon as possible in 1998" on the basis of actual performance in 1997. Once again, the most conservative position had been accepted.

The Roles of the Political Parties and the Public

While the German government was bargaining with the other EU member states about the specific implementation of the Treaty, German public support for giving up the DM for a single European currency continued to decline. The *Eurobarometer* surveys leave no doubt as to where Germans stood on relinquishing the DM: As early as 1983, Germans had a net negative (–40 percent) response to the question, "Would you be for or against replacing your national currency by one common European currency?"[39] But when discussions of a common currency began at the elite level, in the fall of 1988, Germans were slightly (+6 percent) in favor of "a single European currency, the ecu."[40] By fall 1990 (West) German net support for the single currency peaked at +23 percent.[41] In the fall before the signing of the Maastricht Treaty, net support fell to +10 percent,[42] and by June 1992 (after the failed Danish referendum) net German support was negative again (–15 percent) and has remained so.

It is therefore clear that the German public has been against the single currency almost since the signing of the Maastricht Treaty. As mentioned, however, no mainstream party has been willing or able to capitalize on this fact, despite numerous attempts by various party leaders.[43] Even before the Maastricht Treaty had been signed, Bavarian minister of the environment Peter Gauweiler of the Christian Social Union (CSU) spoke out against the single currency, calling it "esperanto-money." In November 1993 Bavaria's minister-president Edmund Stoiber (CSU) criticized the treaty and accused his fellow politicians of suffering too long from guilt over their national identity. As both of these leaders were from a party closely linked to Kohl's, it is perhaps understandable that the party would not take up the anti-EMU cause. However, neither the opposition Social Democratic Party (SPD), which had argued vigorously against the Maastricht Treaty in the Bundestag and Bundesrat,[44] nor the Greens, who had brought a constitutional challenge to the Maastricht Treaty,[45] made an issue of EMU in the 1994 election. Moreover, when the SPD's economics spokesperson, Gerhard Schröder, said in November 1995 that the party would make Germany's EMU commitment an electoral issue, SPD-leader Scharping called Schröder's comments "irresponsible" and added that "we also don't make the death penalty an electoral issue."[46]

Conclusions

How can one explain that in most of the major EMU decisions after Maastricht, the German Bundesbank's preferences were institutionalized? This fact is all the more surprising given that during this period the economic performance of most of the member states—including Germany—indicated that meeting the convergence criteria would be difficult at best. Yet in decision after decision, the strictest interpretation of the TEU was applied, making the achievement of a single currency more difficult. If it is true that "formally, the views and opinions of the Bundesbank are no more important than those of the Central Bank of Greece and barely more important than those of the Bundespost or the Bundesliga,"[47] how can the Bundesbank influence the other member states to accede to its position more often than the other member states can get the Bundesbank to agree to theirs?

The answer lies in the 1993 ruling of the Constitutional Court on the TEU, which stated that Germany would not "automatically" give up sovereignty and required both houses of parliament to vote again in 1998 that the conditions in the TEU had been met before Germany could join the single currency. What factors might a legislator consider when making that determination? A leader would probably not base a decision solely on popular sentiment, which has been consistently anti-EMU and which politicians have heretofore ignored. More likely, the Bundesbank's recommendations would carry significant weight. A negative assessment by the Bundesbank of the economic convergence would be influential with many legislators, especially since it would give them political cover to do the popular thing, that is, vote against entering the single currency.[48] The Bundesbank seemed to be laying the groundwork for just such a scenario. In January 1996, Tietmeyer indicated that when the EMI votes in 1998 about which members meet the criteria, dissenting views would also be published. "This means there will be a transparency of opinion in the EMI for the public," he asserted.[49] Allowing the Bundesbank to publish its views on whether the convergence criteria have been met promotes the possibility that the German members of parliament will vote against entering the single currency on the basis of the Bundesbank's objections. The importance of the Bundesbank's preferences in international negotiations therefore stems from the other member states' wish to ensure the Bundesbank's agreement in 1998 that all the convergence criteria have been met as exactly as possible.

Why would German political leaders give more weight to the opinions of an undemocratic, technocratic institution than the public on the avowedly political issue of EMU?[50] The most important reason is an aversion, based on historical experience, to pandering to populism, or "lowest-common-denominator" politics. The clearest expression of this conceptualization of politics was Chancellor Kohl's statement about the "sentiment among the 'well-educated and informed' Germans. He had 'no doubt' they would 'opt for' a single currency in the unlikely event that he offered them a referendum."[51] Especially when essential principles are at stake, popular opinion will not be processed through the parties to the leadership if it is contrary to the government's ideas of what Germany's real interests are. Germany's commitment to Europe and Kohl's personal commitment to further integration—both widening and deepening—ensure that popular opposition to EMU is unlikely to make a mark on policy. Indeed, recent polling data suggest a deep schism between elite and mass public support for EMU.[52]

But this raises an intriguing question. If the parties are unwilling to countenance dissent on the issue of EMU, why do Germany's EU partners perceive a threat of a no vote by the parliament in 1998? This perception is probably based on a (correct) analysis of the Bundesbank's institutional role in Germany and the function it fulfills as the technocratic or nonpartisan defender of German stability. Although the Bundesbank is far from unassailable on the domestic front, in international matters the Bundesbank's opinion has a legitimacy not shared by other institutions.[53]

The link between the Bundesbank's opinions and the vote of the legislators elevates the Bundesbank to the position of dominance in the international bargaining on EMU. While the position of the Bundesbank is generally the most conservative interpretation of the Treaty criteria, the exceptions to this (for example, not returning to the narrow EMS bands or the name of the currency) show that it is the Bundesbank's *preferences* rather than economically defined positions that prevail. Allowing the Bundesbank's preferences to prevail a disproportionately large number of times is part of the price the other member states have had to pay for EMU. Would the other member states have been quite so generous had the German Constitutional Court not given the German parliament the right to veto entry into the single currency? That, I would argue, is unlikely.

Notes

The author would like to thank David Cameron, Sean Duffy, Soo Yeon Kim, Amy Richmond, Thomas Risse-Kappen, and Adam Sheingate for their helpful comments on this chapter.

1. See, for example, Daniel Gros and Niels Thygesen, *European Monetary Integration* (New York: St. Martin's Press, 1992), and Kenneth Dyson, *Elusive Union: The Process of Economic and Monetary Union in Europe* (London: Longman, 1994).

2. The term is from Robert Putnam, "Diplomacy and Domestic Politics: The Logic of Two-Level Games," *International Organization* 42 (Summer 1988): 427–460. See also Kenneth Shepsle and Barry Weingast, "The Institutional Foundations of Committee Power," *American Political Science Review* 81 (March 1987): 85–104.

3. See Peter Evans, Harold K. Jacobson, and Robert D. Putnam (eds.), *Double-Edged Diplomacy: International Bargaining and Domestic Politics* (Berkeley: University of California Press, 1993); Dyson, *Elusive Union;* Dorothee Heisenberg, "The Mark of the Bundesbank: Germany's Role in European Monetary Cooperation," Ph.D. diss., Yale University, 1996.

4. See Douglas Hurd in *Financial Times,* 31 January 1996.

5. See Hugo Kaufmann and Stephen Overturf, "Progress Within the European Monetary System," in Leon Hurwitz and Christian Lequesne, (eds.), *The State of the European Community,* vol. 1 (Boulder: Lynne Rienner, 1991); Wayne Sandholtz, "Monetary Bargains: The Treaty on EMU," and David Andrews, "The Global Origins of the Maastricht Treaty on EMU: Closing the Window of Opportunity," both in Alan Cafruny and Glenda Rosenthal (eds.), *The State of the European Union,* vol. 2: *The Maastricht Debates and Beyond* (Boulder: Lynne Rienner, 1993); David M. Andrews, "European Monetary Diplomacy and the Rolling Crisis of 1992–1993," and Michael E. Smith and Wayne Sandholtz, "Institutions and Leadership: Germany, Maastricht and the ERM Crisis," both in Carolyn Rhodes and Sonia Mazey (eds.), *The State of the European Union,* vol. 3: Building a European Polity? (Boulder: Lynne Rienner, 1995).

6. In other international monetary negotiations, the finance ministry and the Bundesbank were often at odds, and so one cannot assume the two institutions have identical preferences. Of the two institutions, the Bundesbank's preferences have been more stable, although even within the Bundesbank there has been institutional evolution. For more detail, see Heisenberg, "The Mark of the Bundesbank."

7. For more on relations between the Bundesbank and the German federal government, see David Marsh, *The Bundesbank: The Bank That Rules Europe* (London: William Heinemann, 1992); Ellen Kennedy, *The Bundesbank: Germany's*

Central Bank in the International Monetary System (London: Pinter, 1991); and Heisenberg, "The Mark of the Bundesbank."

8. For more on the 1993 EMS crisis, see Paul Temperton (ed.), *The European Currency Crisis: What Chance Now for a Single European Currency?* (Cambridge: Probus Europe, 1993); Smith and Sandholtz, "Institutions and Leadership"; Dyson, *Elusive Union,* pp. 162–167; and Heisenberg, "The Mark of the Bundesbank," chapter 7.

9. Council of the European Communities/Commission of the European Communities, *Treaty on European Union* (Luxembourg: Office for Official Publications of the European Communities, 1992), Article 109j.

10. *Financial Times,* 23 December 1993.

11. Ibid.

12. Ibid., 26 October 1994.

13. Ibid., 12 December 1991.

14. Ibid., 5 December 1994. However, the percentage of respondents supporting a single currency was quite low in Germany (24 percent) compared to that opposing the single currency (53 percent).

15. *Financial Times,* 23 June 1992.

16. "Green Paper on the Practical Arrangements for the Introduction of the Single Currency," 31 May 1995, COM (95) 333 final.

17. See the "Green Paper," chapter 3, section 2(106).

18. *Auszüge aus Presseartikeln* 46, 26 June 1995.

19. *Financial Times,* 17 December 1995.

20. Ibid.

21. *Süddeutsche Zeitung,* 20 October 1994.

22. *Financial Times,* 15 November 1995.

23. Ibid., 14 November 1995.

24. At the Madrid summit, the heads of state allowed an exception to the government debt rule in deference to Germany. During the transition, nontradable debt will be allowed to be denominated in national currencies. See Conclusions of the Presidency, Madrid European Council, *Bulletin of the European Community* (12-95) December 1995.

25. Treaty on European Union, Article 104c(2).

26. *Irish Times,* 12 September 1994.

27. *Auszüge aus Presseartikeln* 72, 30 September 1994.

28. *Financial Times,* 4 June 1996.

29. These were published as European Monetary Institute, *Progress Toward Convergence,* November 1995.

30. *Financial Times,* 12 September 1995.

31. Ibid., 11 November 1995.

32. Ibid., 28 March 1996.

33. Ibid., 4 June 1996.

34. Ibid.

35. Ibid., 30 August 1996. The finance ministers, however, were unable to agree on how "exceptional" circumstances should be defined. See *Financial Times,* 23 September 1996.

36. *Financial Times,* 11 September 1996 and *New York Times,* 11 September 1996.

37. *Financial Times,* 14 December 1996.

38. The final version of the stability pact (renamed the "stability and growth pact") was a compromise between the French and the German positions. A drop in GDP of 2 percent or more per year would automatically be classified as exceptional

circumstances and the sanctions would not apply. A fall of between .75 percent and 2 percent of GDP would enable that member state to petition the Council of Ministers for special status. The Council would vote by qualified majority on whether or not to apply the sanctions. Bundesbank director Otmar Issing expressed disappointment with the pact, saying, "Unrestrained automaticity would not have been possible, but one cannot be satisfied with a decision mechanism in which potential sinners pass judgment on actual sinners." See *Financial Times,* 17 December 1996.

39. Survey Research Consultants International, *Index to International Public Opinion, 1983–1984* (Westport, CT: Greenwood Press, 1985), p. 576. A net negative response means that a greater percentage of people responded against than for, that is, in this survey, 27 percent responded for and 67 percent responded against.

40. *Eurobarometer,* November 1988.

41. Ibid., Fall 1990.

42. Ibid., Fall 1991.

43. For more on the parties' response, see Dorothee Heisenberg, "Loud and Clear: Germany's EMU Agenda-Setting After Maastricht," paper presented at the Conference of Europeanists, 14–16 March 1996, Chicago.

44. See Smith and Sandholtz, "Institutions and Leadership," pp. 253–254.

45. See *Financial Times,* 18 May 1993 and 6 October 1993. The Greens who brought the challenge were members of the European Parliament.

46. *Der Spiegel* 45 (6 November 1995).

47. *Financial Times,* 20 February 1996.

48. See Kent Weaver, "The Politics of Blame Avoidance," *Journal of Public Policy* 16 (October 1986).

49. *Financial Times,* 18 January 1996.

50. Since there are no elite surveys of members of the parliament in Germany, it is difficult to obtain evidence that the members of parliament defer to the Bundesbank's views on international monetary cooperation. However, a historical example, the Franco-German Economic Council of 1988, showed this to be the case. For more on that issue, see Kennedy, *The Bundesbank.* In the present case, I am currently conducting a survey that may show this deference more clearly.

51. *Financial Times,* 30 April 1996.

52. See *Süddeutsche Zeitung,* 25 July 1996. According to this poll, the elite is 83 percent in favor of EMU, whereas the mass public is 58 percent against it.

53. On domestic politics, see examples in Marsh, *The Bundesbank;* Kennedy, *The Bundesbank;* and Rüdiger Robert, *Die Unabhängigkeit der Bundesbank* (Kronberg: Athenäum Verlag, 1978). The Bundesbank's legitimacy has also been reinforced by the successes of the EMS, which established Bundesbank principles as the norms of the EMS. See Heisenberg, "The Mark of the Bundesbank."

15

A Two-Speed Europe?

Alison M. S. Watson

When the signatories to the Maastricht Treaty "resolved to achieve the strengthening and the convergence of their economies, and to establish an economic and monetary union including . . . a single and stable currency," they were embarking upon one of the most significant episodes in European financial history. This was a significance not lost on the Commission president at the time, Jacques Delors, when he noted that "economic and monetary union is the political crowning of economic convergence. It is a perfect illustration of the joint exercise of sovereignty. . . . Without such a policy, we would be prey to international speculation and the instability of dominant currencies."[1]

The timetable for the achievement of this "crowning of economic convergence," laid down in the Maastricht Treaty, set out in great detail the procedures that were to be followed for the realization of Economic and Monetary Union in Europe. As had the earlier Delors Report, the Treaty defined three stages, the first of which was already under way at the time of the Treaty signing. Since then, the EU member states have embarked upon Stage II of EMU, the principal goal of which is to secure broad convergence among the economic policies of the member states before Stage III begins (at the very latest on 1 January 1999). This chapter analyzes the process of EMU as the deadline for its establishment looms closer. In particular, uncertainties about the policy remain as the realization dawns that not all countries will qualify to proceed to the third stage. A combination of economic recession and unstable currency markets (arising partly from Germany's high interest rates maintained as a consequence of German reunification) has cast doubt on the feasibility of EMU. Under these circumstances, it is becoming increasingly obvious that before there can be any hope of a further deepening of the European integration process, the needs of three sets of actors must be reconciled: those member states who meet the so-called convergence criteria and may proceed toward the introduction of Economic and Monetary Union; those member states who do not (or do not want to) meet the convergence criteria and cannot therefore proceed with EMU; and those states who are external to the process but will be greatly effected by it. This chapter concentrates on the latter two sets of actors. The first section describes the process up to and including the transition to EMU, including an examination of the convergence criteria. It sets the scene for the analysis that follows in the next two sections, where I discuss the implications of EMU on "EU, non-EMU" and "non-EU, non-EMU" actors.

The EMU Process

Monetary union can exist in either a strong or a weak version. In its weak version, the members of a monetary union agree to irrevocably fix their bilateral exchange rates (either rigidly or within bands) while at the same time allowing the national monetary authorities of each of the member states to undertake the necessary monetary policy in order to defend this exchange rate. In its strong version, monetary union implies that the individual currencies of the member states are replaced by a single currency, which will be in use throughout the union, and national monetary authorities are replaced by a single, central monetary authority. The national monetary authorities thus effectively relinquish their control of national monetary affairs. It is the strong version of EMU with which the European Union wishes to proceed.

The process of Economic and Monetary Union as stated at Maastricht is the latest in a line of efforts toward European monetary integration that began in earnest in the late 1960s, as the Bretton Woods system began to collapse and the European countries recognized the need for closer monetary cooperation and coordination. The support for this latest effort, however, proved initially to be stronger than even the authors of the earlier Delors Report could have hoped for. The European industrial sector expressed strong interest in a single currency (now named the "Euro"), and European policymakers accepted that EMU's long-term institutional arrangements provided a definite chance for future success. Moreover, the collapse of communism in Central and Eastern Europe persuaded the Community of the need to become a more significant actor on the international scene, particularly given Germany's possible reunification, a wish echoed by a Germany keen to emphasize its European credentials and willingness to continue to operate in partnership with the other member states.

Despite this initial approval, however, it was not long before doubts began to be expressed about the feasibility of EMU, particularly given the Danish rejection of the Maastricht agreement, the close vote on the agreement in France, and the subsequent ERM crises of September 1992 and

July 1993. These events prompted concern over the future implementation of the Treaty. In particular, doubts surfaced over how widespread the support for EMU actually was and how useful the convergence criteria were at determining a country's suitability to embark upon the process.

The momentum of popular support that EMU had initially enjoyed appeared to have been lost. For example, although the populations of most of the EU states are generally supportive of a single currency, there were three important exceptions. In a 1995 poll, only 29 percent and 40 percent, respectively, of the populations of Denmark and the UK supported EMU. This was not really surprising, given that Denmark has the right to a referendum over EMU and the UK has its much-discussed opt-out clause. What *was* perhaps surprising was that only 45 percent of the German population supported a single currency.[2] Most Germans regard the Deutschmark as a symbol of their economic strength and are not keen to see it replaced. In addition, many German economists and bankers believe the convergence criteria to be too weak and the planned structures of the ECB and the ESCB to be such that EMU could increase inflation in Germany.[3] It is not an exaggeration to say that there could be no EMU without widespread German support, and for this reason, in any referendum the German electorate would likely be subjected to a large amount of pro-EMU campaigning by the main political parties in Germany. German support could also be increased if concessions were made, for example, in the form of additional guarantees concerning the monetary credibility of the ECB. This might go some way toward tackling German concerns over the planned structures of the ECB and the ESCB. Nevertheless, doubts would still remain regarding the fundamental difficulties in applying the convergence criteria.

Article 109j of the Maastricht Treaty outlines the four convergence criteria countries must meet in order to proceed with EMU. In short, they require that each prospective EMU member achieve a high degree of price stability (i.e., an average rate of inflation of not more than 1.5 percent above the average of the three best performing states in the previous year); a sustainable financial position (i.e., budget deficits should not be more than the reference value of 3 percent of GDP, and general government gross debt should not be more than the reference value of 60 percent of GDP); exchange rate stability (i.e., a currency must have remained within the "normal fluctuation margins" for at least two years, a criterion drafted before the ERM crises, when a normal margin was 2.25 percent); and long-term interest rate stability (i.e., a rate that does not exceed by more than 2 percent the average of the three best performing states in terms of price stability).

These convergence criteria have stimulated a considerable amount of debate among policymakers and academics alike. Their negotiation was delegated to the EC Monetary Committee, where there was a high degree of conflict among the member states' positions. German officials of course took the lead in negotiations, their policy position facilitated by the fact that the German economy would suffer if it entered into a monetary union without a firm monetary policy stance (see Chapter 14 in this volume for a fuller analysis of Germany's subsequent policy position on EMU). It was therefore in Germany's national economic interest to ensure that the potential members of EMU were similarly committed to the same kind of low-inflation stance. In particular, the Bundesbank was not prepared to accept an EMU that could threaten Deutschmark stability. Yet Germany was determined to achieve closer political integration in Europe and was willing, at times, to make concessions—hence the feeling among some in Germany that the convergence criteria were too weak.[4]

Other countries, however, were not so sure that tough convergence criteria were the answer. The Italian government, for example, suspected that such harsh conditions were a way of reducing the chance of Italian eligibility for EMU, given Italy's unstable domestic political situation. The UK was even more dissatisfied with the nature of the criteria, insisting on the protocol that gave it the famous "opt-out" clause. Later, at the Edinburgh European Council of December 1992, Denmark as well expressed dissatisfaction with the nature of the criteria and made the definitive decision not to participate in the third stage. The convergence criteria debate has, of course, not been limited to policymakers. Academics, too, argue that the convergence criteria raise some fundamental concerns.

For example, there is at least one problem with the notion of price stability as conceived in the Maastricht Treaty: the choice of an appropriate price index. In order to make the concept of price stability operational, it is necessary to specify what price index is to be stabilized. The Maastricht Treaty states that "inflation shall be measured by means of the consumer price index on a comparable basis, taking into account differences in national definitions."[5] However, nowhere does the Maastricht Treaty define "price stability." In effect the central bankers will be left to define their own objectives.[6]

With regard to the exchange rate criterion, some economists have argued that nothing can be gained by requiring a country to achieve exchange rate stability when the whole convergence operation is aimed at deciding whether or not a country is ready to join a monetary union in which it will have no exchange rate of its own.[7] Although the criterion may have been designed to reduce the risk of realignments during Stage II in order to bestow credibility on the process of locking exchange rates at the beginning of Stage III and hence guard an embryonic EMU from exchange rate crisis before use of the Euro has been established, "concerns of that sort cannot really justify using the exchange rate test as a measure of convergence."[8] Similarly, concern has been raised over the usefulness of viewing long-term interest rate stability as a measure of convergence, because changes in a country's long-term rate relative to other countries' rates may arise for a number of reasons (e.g., because of market expectations over the

country's short-term interest rate or over the likelihood of a currency devaluation), not all of which would be relevant in assessing a country's suitability for EMU.

Of all the convergence criteria, however, the role of the fiscal criterion
(i.e., the requirement on government deficit and debt levels) has led to the
most heated debate. For example, there has been concern over the arbitrary
nature of the numbers chosen for the debt and deficit targets. Buiter,
Corsetti, and Roubini argue that "the wording of the Treaty is sufficiently
vague that irrelevant or even harmful political considerations may affect
the assessment of whether the fiscal convergence criteria have been met."[9]
Others have argued that the figure for the debt (GDP ratio of 60 percent)
has no economic rationale or any historical relevance but just happened to
be the Community's average in 1991.[10]

Further concerns centered on the attempt by EU countries drastically to
reduce their budgetary deficits in the hope of achieving the convergence
criteria by applying strenuous fiscal and monetary restrictions. These
efforts probably intensified the European recession, leaving serious concerns that the fiscal provisions laid down in the Maastricht Treaty will actually prevent a number of states from embarking upon the final stage of
Economic and Monetary Union.

Table 15.1 sets out how EU member states are currently meeting the
price, interest rate, and budgetary criteria. Results for the exchange rate criterion are not depicted because that criterion was drafted on the assumption
that the ERM would continue to observe its original margins of 2.25 percent. Following the ERM crisis of 1993, however, the band was widened to
15 percent on either side. Thus any decision about whether or not a member
state has achieved the exchange rate criterion is dependent upon the
European Council's interpretation. The European Council could interpret it
as meaning that a currency must be within a reasonably stable relationship
with its peers for two years before a decision is made about Stage III,
although it is far from certain that Germany, for one, would accept less
rigor than was originally envisaged. In terms of inflation, the recent recession has made the exchange rate criterion relatively easy to meet for a
majority of countries. Only three of the fifteen member states (Greece,
Portugal, and Spain) were forecast to fail this criterion. Similarly, only
three of the fifteen member states (Greece, Italy, and Sweden) were forecast to fail the convergence criterion on interest rates. At the very least,
these two results taken together would suggest that ten (i.e., a majority) of
the countries could proceed toward Economic and Monetary Union. The
scenario is different, however, when we consider the results for the budgetary criterion: As things stand, only Germany, Luxembourg, and the UK
are forecast to fulfill both the deficit and debt criteria by 1996. Moreover,
in eight member states debt/GDP ratios will probably be rising. Thus,
although the European Commission optimistically forecasts that a significant number of member states will be capable of meeting the criteria by the

Table 15.1   The EMU Convergence Criteria (percent changes)

	Inflation	Interest Rates	Government Deficit	Government Debt	Debt Trend
Austria	3.1	7.5	4.2	61	rising
Belgium	2.6	8.0	4.0	136	falling
Denmark	2.4	8.7	2.2	78	stable
Finland	2.7	8.7	2.5	86	rising
France	2.1	7.5	3.9	56	rising
Germany	2.4	7.3	2.0	59	stable
Greece	9.0	17.5	12.9	128	rising
Ireland	2.7	8.5	1.5	79	falling
Italy	3.5	11.7	7.9	129	rising
Luxembourg	2.7	7.5	+2.0	10	stable
Netherlands	2.5	7.3	2.7	78	stable
Portugal	4.4	8.5	4.8	72	rising
Spain	4.4	8.8	4.7	66	rising
Sweden	3.1	10.8	7.3	111	rising
UK	3.3	8.1	2.1	49	stable
Target	3.8	9.8	3.0	60	
EC 12	3.1	8.4	3.9		
Three Best	2.3	7.8			

Source: Federal Trust (1995).
Note: Inflation is measured by the consumer price deflator (1996); interest rates by the government long bond interest rate (1996); government deficits by the ratio of gross government deficit to GDP (1996); government debt by the ratio of gross government debt to GDP; and the debt trend by the government debt ratio trend (1994–1996).

time the European Council takes its decision, it looks increasingly likely that a number of member states will be unsuccessful in their bid to join EMU and that the path toward EMU will inevitably be a two-speed one.[11] With this in mind, let us turn to the issue of how the European Union might cope with such a scenario and the difficulties it might cause.

The Unsuccessful EMU States

Three issues are of particular concern with regard to the reality of a two-speed EMU: the nature of the institutions that would deal with such a scenario, the matter of the arrangements to ensure exchange rate stability, and the question of whether a one-speed monetary union could or would actually take place.

The Institutional Framework

The Maastricht provisions on EMU embody two principles. The first is that the transition to monetary union should be gradual in order to allow states time to meet the convergence conditions. The second is that not all EC countries have to join a monetary union at the same time: Their accession to the union is made dependent on satisfying the convergence criteria. An EMU without all of the member states has thus always been considered possible, particularly given the British and Danish positions laid down in the Treaty. The debate at Maastricht was how this position was going to be solved institutionally, particularly given the care that was taken in designing institutions that would lend the future Economic and Monetary Union a high degree of credibility.[12]

This debate centered on two basic points of view. On the one hand, those governments for whom the slow track was more than a possibility were concerned lest they be left out of future EMU decisionmaking. If indeed a two-speed EMU took place and they were to proceed at a slower speed, they wanted their national central bank governors to continue to participate in the deliberations of the Governing Council of the ECB, even if they could not vote on policy matters.[13] On the other hand, those governments who saw themselves proceeding toward EMU at a faster speed wanted the slower states to be excluded from any formal role in the decisionmaking process.

In the end, the Maastricht Treaty reflected a compromise. Article 109l basically states that if a two-speed Europe is to take place, a "General Council" will be established as a third decisionmaking body of the European Central Bank, its membership to include the president and vice president of the ECB and the governors of all the member states' national central banks. The role of this General Council would be to take over the function of the European Monetary Institute for those countries that have not yet attained the convergence criteria. The General Council would therefore be required to continue to aid in the transition process of the non-EMU states, for example, in strengthening the coordination of monetary policies with a view to ensuring price stability and in monitoring exchange rate stability. However, at the same time, the role of the General Council would be limited in that it would not have the authority to make any policy recommendations to individual countries or indeed to be consulted in advance about the future course of monetary policies in the Economic and Monetary Union.

The practical importance of this institutional framework to the future European policy landscape is, naturally, very much dependent upon how many non-EMU participant countries there actually are and indeed how important those countries are to the EC decisionmaking process. If there are few nonparticipants and they are minor actors in European policymaking, then there will be the need for consultation over monetary and exchange rate policies, but in general they will have to adapt their policies to those of the ECB and peg their currencies to the Euro if they wish to qualify for eventual EMU participation. If, however, there are a significant number of non-EMU states and some are major actors (as is a more likely scenario, given that the UK, for one, is highly unlikely to be among the fast-speed EMU participants), then the issue of policy coordination is far more significant, not only to the non-EMU participants but also to the EMU participants.[14] Under these circumstances, the ECB would need to consult closely with the non-EMU national central banks, and they in turn would want to be consulted by the ECB. Despite this institutional framework, however, questions still remain as to the manner in which exchange rates should be managed in this probable two-speed Europe.

Exchange Rate Management

If there was one economic issue more than any other that gave impetus to the political moves toward European monetary integration, it was that of creating a stable exchange rate regime in Europe.[15] The Treaty of Rome set the fixity of currency parities as a fundamental objective, and Article 107 qualified the exchange rate policy of each member state as a "matter of common interest." Later, in the 1970s, Dutch prime minister Duisenberg noted in a letter to his colleagues: "We are worried about the exchange rate developments in the Community. There is at present no effective Community framework for the coordination of policies in this area among all members, while recent developments have surely indicated the urgent need for common action."[16]

The drive toward exchange rate stability was apparent in the exchange rate mechanism of the European Monetary System and later in the proposals for Economic and Monetary Union itself. It is surprising, therefore, given the degree of concern the EC has historically expressed over exchange rate management, that the issue of such in a two-speed Europe should be covered so ambiguously. Indeed, even though the General Council is appointed to contribute to the preparations for irrevocably fixing the exchange rates of the non-EMU states against the participant EMU states, the Treaty is unclear as to how exactly this should be done. Article 109k does state that unsuccessful EMU states cannot enter Stage III until they meet the conditions that call for "the observance of the normal fluctuation margins provide for by the exchange-rate mechanism of the European Monetary System" (and from this it can be argued that non-EMU states will still be expected to assume an exchange rate obligation of some form), but nowhere does the Treaty impose any complementary obligation on the ECB to manage exchange rates between the Euro and non-EMU currencies.

There are basically two ways of managing such rates. The first is to have non-EMU participants unilaterally peg their currencies to the Euro and have them take responsibility for maintaining their exchange rates within predetermined bands. To do this, they would intervene using their own currency reserves and would set their interest rates at levels that would maintain exchange rate stability. Assuming such responsibilities, however, might also lead them to insist on the right to change their exchange rates as and when they felt it necessary and without the permission of the European Central Bank, which would be contrary to the spirit of increasing monetary integration in Europe.

Exchange rates could instead be managed in such a way that decision-making could be shared between the ECB and the non-EMU national central banks. This is the so-called residual EMS framework in which both the Euro and the non-EMU states' currencies would participate. Central rates would then be chosen on a collective basis and the ECB would intervene whenever the Euro reached its margins and would be expected to adjust interest rates in order to maintain exchange rate stability.

Although policymakers and academics have expressed support for a residual EMS in the face of a two-speed Europe (most notably in a recent speech by the president of the EMI, Alexandre Lamfalussy),[17] there is always the possibility that a residual EMS might interfere with the pursuit of price stability by the ECB,[18] as well as the issue of whether or not such an arrangement would place undue stress upon the economies of the non-EMU participants. For example, it is unlikely that if a country fails to satisfy the exchange rate criterion for entering Stage III (while participating in the exchange rate mechanism with the rest of the member states) it would find it any easier to satisfy the criterion after some of the other states had already embarked upon the third stage. Moreover, the EMS crises have only complicated the scenario. In particular, and given the British and Italian ERM withdrawals, the 1992–1993 crises have made it more likely that there will be several countries unable to achieve EMU at the faster speed. This would have repercussions not only on the non-EMU participants but also on the EMU participants. Again, the impact depends upon the number and importance of the non-EMU participants. If the nonparticipants are all small countries, then the monetary policy of the ECB will not be effected significantly. But if some of the non-EMU countries are large (as is more likely), then the European Central Bank may find its position in monetary policy decisionmaking compromised. With such difficulties in mind, it becomes even more important to consider the issue of whether a one-speed monetary union could or would actually take place.

A One-Speed European Monetary Union

The process of Economic and Monetary Union in Europe is at a stage when many obstacles must still be overcome. Once, as is likely, a two-speed Europe is embarked upon, those obstacles will increase rather than subside, as concerns mount over the need to draw the non-EMU states into the participating fold. Two possible scenarios pose a particular threat: first, that a non-EMU country might have an incentive never to participate; second, that the EMU countries might never admit those countries that stayed outside.

The first scenario stems from the possibility that those countries who traditionally take a low-inflation policy stance (such as Germany) may not invite a high-inflation non-EMU state to participate until it has sufficiently diminished its inflation bias.[19] However, if the EMU participants wait too long before admitting additional members (i.e., until after a country has been enjoying the benefits of low and stable inflation for a significant period of time), then the non-EMU participant will be gaining from its new low, stable inflation stance without the policy limitations of being a member of the Economic and Monetary Union—that is, the non-EMU state will be free-riding. Casella, in an analysis of small countries in a currency union, comes to the conclusion that it might be in a non-EMU participant's best interests to remain outside of a one-speed EMU.[20] Casella argues that unless a country can exercise substantial influence upon the monetary union, it may prefer to remain outside of the decisionmaking process. In this way, its nonparticipation may actually allow it to have more influence on policymaking than its size warrants.

With regard to the scenario that EMU participant countries might never admit those countries that stayed outside, the first question to consider is why a country with a low and credible inflation stance (e.g., Germany) would agree to help other countries without such economic attributes achieve them. The answer is that the low-inflation countries have a lot of bargaining power because of their superior economic position. If, however, they are to maintain this power, they must ensure that when Economic and Monetary Union takes place they are at the heart of the institutional process. In particular, they must have dominance within the European Central Bank.[21]

Following Alesina and Grilli, if we assume that in 1999 three countries make the transition to EMU in Europe, they must subsequently resolve the issue, by majority rule, of whether or not to admit additional members. Given such a situation, it is possible that those first three countries would never choose to admit subsequent members (for example, because of their fear over the future monetary policy stance of the enlarged EMU) and a one-speed EMU would never take place. Under such circumstances, embarking upon a two-speed EMU would appear to put the whole integration process in jeopardy. What would therefore be important in such a situation is whether or not the EMU participants can be compensated for their fears over future monetary policy stance in return for admitting additional members and safeguarding the integration project. For example, it is often stated that Germany has nothing to gain economically from EMU but has something to gain politically in that monetary union is a necessary step toward the future political integration of Europe, which Germany desires.

An additional issue is whether it might be in the interests of the non-EMU countries to form their own union, a question that goes to the heart of the differentiated integration debate.[22]

This section has outlined the possible difficulties a two-speed EMU might face, difficulties that are magnified depending upon whether the non-EMU participants are many or few and important or unimportant in terms of political leverage. The fact that the UK and Denmark are likely to be two of those nonparticipants suggests that the troubles a two-speed EMU would bring with it would be significant. Moreover, one consideration not yet discussed is that the EU may admit more members. Indeed, an EU enlargement would likely present far greater problems with regard to the appropriate institutional arrangements and entry times for new EMU members (see Chapter 13 in this volume for a fuller consideration of the enlargement issue). For example, the prospective accession of Poland, Hungary, the Czech Republic, and other Eastern European states—poorer, more agricultural, and a threat to the voting weight of smaller existing members—may make a complex multispeed design even more likely. Whether we are considering non-EMU states from the existing membership of fifteen or future non-EMU members from an enlarged Europe, relations among EMU participants, EMU institutions, and the nonparticipant countries are likely to require close attention for many years to come.

EMU and the Rest of the World

Most discussions of EMU focus upon the costs and benefits that Europeans are most likely to experience from the process. Even in terms of EMU's relationship to the outside world, such analysis tends to look inward to European implications rather than outward to the impact of EMU elsewhere. For example, EMU supporters argue that EMU will facilitate policy coordination among the major industrial countries and will give the member states the chance to reestablish European control over European monetary conditions. This stems from the notion that under EMU Europe will be more insulated from changes in international exchange rate conditions because it will be in control of its own monetary destiny, and thus the individual member states will be less likely to be affected by changes in international monetary conditions in the way they were in the 1960s and 1970s. This echoes the statement quoted above by Jacques Delors, who saw one important feature of EMU as being the insulation it would give European currencies from the instability of their non-European counterparts. However, EMU's impact on external actors must also be considered. In this regard, there are two main issues: first, the international role of the Euro and its effect upon the stability of international foreign exchange markets;

second, how the changing policy mix in Europe will affect policy coordination and exchange rate management internationally.[23] This section briefly discusses these issues.[24]

In 1990 the Commission noted that "due to its weight in the world economy, EMU will necessarily have far-reaching implications for the international economic and monetary system."[25] Indeed, the Commission estimated that the Euro would be held in significant amounts in the international market: as a numeraire for trade and contracts and as a means of payment and store of value in the denomination of assets and liabilities.[26] Alogoskoufis and Portes claim that the Euro will be widely held as a reserve asset as a result of traders' switching from previously held European currencies to the Euro on the day that it is introduced.[27]

However, although the majority of economists agree that the Euro will be an important international currency, they do not agree about the implications of such importance, particularly given the increasingly obvious scenario that EMU will take place at two speeds. Supporters of EMU claim that EMU will make for a more balanced international monetary system because the dominant role of the dollar will be reduced. Policymakers in the United States will be under increasing pressure to practice better fiscal and monetary policy management in order to ensure that the dollar is not weakened by currency movement from it into either the Euro or the yen. Of course the same is true, at least up to a point, for Japanese policymakers. Any further weakening in the Japanese economic situation would lead speculators to move funds from the yen into either the Euro or the dollar. Thus, by emphasizing the need for economic stability in the minds of U.S. and Japanese policymakers, EMU could lead to a more balanced international monetary system. Then again, both Japanese and U.S. firms operating within the EU are likely to benefit from the greater financial freedom EMU would facilitate. They will be able to enjoy the same gains from a Single European Market as any European firm operating within the European Union, and they will benefit from the greater financial stability that EMU should engender (assuming, of course, that the probable two-speed nature of that union is not in itself destabilizing). Such freedom, however, would also create a higher degree of interdependence among Europe and the United States and Japan, as their economies become increasingly linked. In this case, EMU would mean that coordination of economic policy would depend on fewer players, but their interdependence would keep them sensitive to each other's actions.

Despite these implications that the Euro might have as an international currency, the move toward EMU does not imply that the introduction of the Euro will cause sudden shifts in international financial relations. Kenen notes that although the developing countries began diversifying their currency reserves in the early 1970s (soon after the collapse of the Bretton

Woods system of macroeconomic management), unless the Euro's introduction affects the pricing of major commodities such as oil, it will be
unlikely that an ERM will induce another round of currency diversification
in the developing countries.[28] Similarly, the large industrial countries such
as the United States and Japan will obtain Euros in exchange for the EC
currencies of EMU participant states held as reserves at the beginning of
Stage III, and they will add to the holdings of Euros when they buy them on
the foreign exchange market. However, they are not likely to buy many
Euros in the early stages of EMU, because the Euro is actually more likely
to be strong than weak.[29] Moreover, for the EU countries themselves, who
at the moment hold large amounts of the current "European currency," the
ecu, and national currency reserves, the former will turn into dollars and
gold on the first day of Stage III, whereas the latter will become domestic
currency claims on the central bank. For example, any Italian lira held in
the Bank of England will become Euro claims on the European Central
Bank. But these lira reserves were used previously to stabilize the
lira–pound sterling exchange rate and will be in excess of what is required
for interventions in the international financial markets. There has thus been
a once-and-for-all reduction in the demand for Italian lira, which, in turn,
will be destabilizing to the economies of the European Union as a whole.[30]
Such findings tend to support the view that the international role of currencies changes only slowly because new financial markets and instruments
develop gradually.

In terms of how the changing policy mix in Europe will affect international policy coordination and exchange rate management, Henning identifies one major issue as the level of central bank independence present within an Economic and Monetary Union. Indeed, Henning notes that "the
degree of legally sanctioned independence would be extraordinary by international standards."[31] Once again, Article 109 is the crucial part of the
Treaty in this regard in that it lays down the legal relationship between the
ESCB and the Council of Ministers on exchange rate policy. Representatives of the Council would hold the authority to negotiate formal and informal exchange rate agreements with foreign governments (under consultation with the ESCB). Formal agreements that peg the Euro to the dollar or
yen, however, would require a unanimous vote within the Council after it
consulted the European Central Bank, the Commission, and the European
Parliament. This is an especially arduous requirement, particularly in light
of a possible future enlargement of the European Union. Institutional
arrangements such as these are then basically a recipe for a policy of
exchange rate flexibility with respect to currencies outside the European
region because any other policy would probably not meet with the unanimous approval of the Council. Moreover, this predisposition toward
exchange rate flexibility would be further reinforced by structural changes

in the monetary union's relationship with the United States and Japan, which would make Europe less vulnerable to fluctuations in the Euro-dollar and Euro-yen bilateral exchange rates.

Conclusion

"By the end of the century, Europe will have a single currency. It will be strong and stable. This is the wish of the leaders and peoples in signing and then ratifying the Treaty on European Union."[32] These opening lines of the "Green Paper on the Practical Arrangements for the Introduction of the Single Currency" demonstrate the confidence the European Commission has in the viability of the EMU project. Meeting the convergence criteria is of primary importance in achieving this long-term goal. Just how strong the belief in these criteria is can be seen in the introduction to the green paper, which reads in part, "The need to raise awareness of the technical issues involved does not in any way weaken the primary importance of economic convergence. This is at the heart of the Treaty and the indispensable condition for a strong and stable single currency, at least as strong as the strongest national currency."

We have seen, however, that the hope that all fifteen member states will join the process as a one-speed Europe is a vain one. Not only does this cause practical difficulties for the realization of EMU, but failure to achieve the Maastricht objectives would pose serious dangers for the Single European Market and for the Union itself. Economic and Monetary Union was by far the most ambitious objective of Maastricht. All EU governments except Britain and Denmark have bound themselves to the aim of EMU. If the objective were now to be abandoned or postponed indefinitely, contrary to the Treaty's terms, it would be the most serious failure since the founding of the Community. A return to devaluations of EU currencies would weaken the single market more than if the goal of EMU had never been declared. Protectionism could resurface. The setback to the process of closer political union would also prove divisive to an extent that would greatly damage the European Union.

In order, then, to address the problems such a far-reaching policy as EMU will encounter, member states not only must have the political will but must reconcile the needs of three sets of state actors: those member states who meet the convergence criteria and may proceed toward the introduction of economic and Monetary Union; those member states who do not meet the convergence criteria and cannot therefore proceed with EMU; and those states who have not yet or never will join the European Union. It is therefore in the process of EMU that the incompatibility of deepening and widening the European Union of the future can most clearly be seen.

Notes

1. Address by J. Delors, president of the Commission of the European Communities, Bruges, 17 October 1989.

2. Robert Waller, "Taxing Polls," *New Statesman and Society,* 26 May 1995.

3. Alfred Steinherr, *30 Years of European Monetary Integration: From the Werner Plan to EMU* (London: Longman, 1994), "Appendix 2: Against and for EMU: Two Manifestos for 1992."

4. P. Jacquet, "The Politics of EMU: A Selective Overview," in *The Monetary Future of Europe* (London: Centre for Economic Policy Research, 1993).

5. "Protocol on the Convergence Criteria Referred to in Article 109j of the Treaty Establishing the European Community," Article 1.

6. Eurostat and the national statistical institutes of the member states are in the process of working out new ways of comparing inflation in order to facilitate the European Council's decision on which countries have met the inflation criterion.

7. Peter B. Kenen, *Economic and Monetary Union in Europe—Moving Beyond Maastricht* (Cambridge: Cambridge University Press, 1995), p. 129. Others, however, take a different view, aspiring to the notion that the exchange rate criterion is the only one to which attention be paid. These observers believe that the success of the EC countries in avoiding realignments in the run-up to Stage III is a sufficient test of their ability to bear the costs of reducing inflation in Stage III itself. For example, see David Begg, Francesco Giavazzi, Luis Spaventa and Charles Wyplosz, "European Monetary Union—The Macro Issues," in *Monitoring European Integration: The Making of Monetary Union* (London: Centre for Economic Policy Research, 1991).

8. Kenen, *Economic and Monetary Union,* p. 130.

9. Willem Buiter, Giancarlo Corsetti, and Nouriel Roubini, "Excessive Deficits: Sense and Nonsense in the Treaty of Maastricht," *Economic Policy* 16 (1995): 61.

10. Begg et al., "European Monetary Union," p. 24.

11. European Commission, "Preparing for EMU Stage 3," *Week in Europe,* 13 June 1996.

12. For an excellent discussion of this issue, see John T. Woolley, "Policy Credibility and European Monetary Institutions," in Alberta M. Sbragia, *Europolitics* (Washington, DC: Brookings Institution, 1992).

13. The responsibilities of the Governing Council are defined in Article 12 of the Statute of the ESCB, in that it: "shall adopt the guidelines and take the decisions necessary to ensure the performance of the tasks entrusted to the ESCB under this Treaty and this Statute. The Governing Council shall formulate the monetary policy of the Community including, as appropriate, decisions relating to intermediate monetary objectives, key interest rates and the supply of reserves in the ESCB, and shall establish the necessary guidelines for their implementation."

14. Kenen, *Economic and Monetary Union,* p. 147.

15. For a more detailed discussion, see J. A. Frieden, "Exchange Rate Politics: Contemporary Lessons from American History," *Review of International Political Economy* 1, 1 (1994): 93–97.

16. D. Gros and N. Thygesen, *European Monetary Integration* (New York: St. Martin's Press, 1992), p. 39.

17. Mark Milner, "ERM Mark 2 Second-Best Plan, Says Lamfalussy," *Times* (London), 20 June 1996, p. 19.

18. This factor received much attention at the Maastricht summit. See Article 109 of the Treaty on European Union.

19. Phillippe Martin, "Free-riding, Convergence and Two-Speed Monetary Unification in Europe," *European Economic Review* 39, 7 (1995): 1345–1364.

20. Alessandra Casella, "Participation in a Currency Union," *American Economic Review* 82, 4 (1992): 847–863.

21. Alberto Alesina and Vittorio Grilli, "On the Feasibility of a One-Speed or Multispeed European Monetary Union," *Economics and Politics* 5, 2 (1993).

22. See, for example, B. Langeheine and U. Weinstock, "Graduated Integration: A Modest Path Towards Progress," *Journal of Common Market Studies* 23 (1985): 185–197; H. Wallace, with A. Ridley, *Europe: The Challenge of Diversity* (London: Chatham House, 1985); and Alexander C. G. Stubb, "A Categorisation of Differentiated Integration," *Journal of Common Market Studies* 34, 2 (1996): 283–295.

23. A. J. Hughes Hallet and Maria Demertzis, "Economic and Monetary Union in Europe: Some Unresolved Issues," University of Strathclyde International Centre for Macroeconomic Modelling Discussion Paper, no. 31 (1994).

24. In addition see G. Alogoskoufis and R. Portes, "The International Costs and Benefits from EMU," in *The Economics of EMU, European Economy* special edition 1 (1991); and K. H. Johnson, "International Dimensions of European Monetary Union: Implications for the Dollar," International Financial Discussion Paper 496, Board of Governors of the Federal Reserve System, 1994.

25. One Market, One Money," special issue of *European Economy* 44 (October 1990).

26. Ibid., pp. 24–25.

27. Alogoskoufis and Portes, "International Costs and Benefits."

28. Kenen, *Economic and Monetary Union,* p. 113.

29. Ibid., p. 116.

30. See Hughes Hallett and Demertzis, "Economic and Monetary Union," pp. 28–29 for a fuller analysis.

31. C. Randall Henning, *Currencies and Politics in the United States, Germany and Japan* (Washington, DC: Institute for International Economics), 1994, pp. 365–366.

32. "Green Paper on the Practical Arrangements for the Introduction of the Single Currency" (Luxembourg: Office for Official Publications of the European Communities, 1995).

PART 5

EXTERNAL RELATIONS

16

U.S.-EU Relations: The Commercial, Political, and Security Dimensions

Roy H. Ginsberg

U.S.-EU relations improved in the mid-1990s as the partners began working through the implications of the end of the Cold War for their common security, facing together the global challenges and threats originating outside the North Atlantic, and responding to the growing impact of domestic politics on transatlantic policies. Relations during the first half of the decade were seriously strained over very different approaches to ending the war in the former Yugoslavia. The EU was itself split over how best to promote peace, given its members' varying historical ties with the belligerents and the EU's underdeveloped capacity for Common Foreign and Security Policy actions.

The commitment to work together in areas of common interest was translated into the New Transatlantic Agenda and the Joint Action Plan signed by Presidents Clinton, Gonzalez (EU Council), and Santer (EU Commission) at the December 1995 U.S.-EU summit in Madrid.[1] The NTA commits the two to act jointly in each of four pillars: peace, stability, democracy, and development worldwide; global challenges; expansion of global and bilateral trade; and closer bilateral ties between civil societies. The NTA builds on the framework of foreign policy consultations established by the November 1990 Transatlantic Declaration and represents the first document of its kind, bringing together the commercial, political/diplomatic, and societal dimensions of bilateral relations under one rubric.[2] However, cooperation in monetary affairs and in joint task forces between the North Atlantic Treaty Organization and the Western European Union, the EU's defense arm, were left outside the NTA even though they represent critical elements of bilateral relations.

Differences and disputes across all dimensions of bilateral relations remained—as they always have—but overall improvement occurred as a result of the belated and much-needed decisions taken to transform the General Agreement on Tariffs and Trade (GATT) and NATO into fora better able to face the new realities of global interdependence and post–Cold War security challenges. U.S.-EU relations have always depended heavily on these bodies to provide an institutional framework for mutual trade and security. This chapter reviews and assesses bilateral relations in each of three major dimensions—commerce, politics, and security—during 1995 and 1996.

Commerce remains the bedrock of U.S.-EU relations. Each is the other's largest commercial partner, and together they dominate world trade and investment flows. Political relations are being transformed from the practice of foreign policy consultations to the promise of coordination and joint action in areas where the two can and wish to act together in the face of global challenges. Security defined in terms of NATO collective self-defense and an integrated military command keeps U.S. troops in Europe, maintains the U.S. defense guarantee for the largest EU members, and enables the United States to remain a force for balance and a provider of security within the EU and across Europe. A rounded view of U.S.-EU relations requires an understanding of their different but interrelated dimensions.

There are certainly difficulties in each of the three dimensions of bilateral relations, which this chapter outlines, but no one difficulty threatens adversely to affect overall relations. Relations are presently in good shape given the rhetoric and actions of leaders on both sides who stress adaptation and renewal, and in spite of the inevitable disputes that arise between interdependent partners. In the longer run, as this chapter shows, the commitment to the common security is something that will have to be revitalized to ensure support within U.S. and European civil societies now that the Cold War and the common enemy are gone. The commitment to joint foreign policy action will have to be cultivated over the longer run as well. Given the EU's limited capacity to carry out Common Foreign and Security Policy actions, there are constraints on how far U.S.-EU cooperation can go in areas where the EU has yet to develop competence to act on behalf of its members. For their part, Congress and the White House need to work in less partisan ways to conduct U.S. foreign policy, otherwise the United States will be seen as a constraint on the renewal of U.S.-EU relation as well.

The State of the Commercial Relationship

U.S.-EU commerce (two-way trade in goods and services, foreign direct investment, and sales generated by investment) continued to grow in volume and value and remained the world's largest commercial relationship in 1994. Continued growth was assured and commercial relations were strengthened by the conclusion in late 1994—and implementation in

1995—of the Uruguay Round of multilateral trade negotiations (MTNs). The MTNs resolved most of the nagging bilateral trade disputes and reinforced the multilateral framework of rules by which the United States and the EU trade with each other and the world. Another milestone in 1995 was the completion of difficult negotiations to renew the U.S.–European Atomic Energy Community accord on nuclear trade and safety.

Admittedly, there was disappointment in 1996 over the failure of negotiations to conclude multilateral trade liberalization pacts in sectors that eluded such efforts during the MTNs (global telecommunications, maritime transport services, and information technology). Running disputes over broadcasting, beef hormones, and other areas of concern ruffled feathers. Nevertheless, the vast volume and value of two-way commerce remains dispute-free.

U.S. and EU businesses formed the Transatlantic Business Dialogue (TABD) in 1995 to influence the two sides to continue to work together to reduce and eliminate trade barriers. As discussed below, TABD has been a force for innovation in U.S.-EU trade negotiations.[3]

Trade and Investment

Commercial relations in the mid-1990 were "robust."[4] Transatlantic commerce remains more balanced and transparent than transpacific commerce. U.S.-EU trade disputes as a percentage of total trade value tend to be small relative to transpacific disputes.

Two-way total commerce exceeded $1.7 trillion in 1994, of which $232 billion was in merchandise and $100 billion in services.[5] The United States is the EU's largest trading partner, taking 17 percent of total EU imports and 18 percent of exports. The EU is the second largest trading partner of the United States (following Canada), taking 20 percent of U.S. exports and 17 percent of imports. Although the United States had a $17 billion trade deficit with the EU in 1994, the second year in a row,[6] the United States has also had trade surpluses with the EU in recent years. As robust as U.S.-EU trade is, it is declining as a percentage of world trade, reflecting the growing importance of Asia and Latin America.

The United States is the largest destination of the EU's foreign direct investment (FDI), accounting for 53 percent of total outward investment of the EU. According to the European-American Chamber of Commerce, EU companies are now the leading international investors in thirty-nine U.S. states, and one-half of the jobs in the United States created by EU companies are in the high-wage manufacturing sector.[7] The EU is the largest destination of U.S. FDI, accounting for 42 percent of total outward investment of the United States.

U.S. and EU dependence on trade with other partners and thus on the multilateral order were reinforced and improved as a result of the conclusion and implementation of the MTNs. The Uruguay Round eliminated most of the trade disputes between the United States and EU that had been simmering since the 1970s or so. The two can look forward to such benefits as substantial tariff cuts on industrial and farm products and cuts in the volume and expenditures of subsidized farm exports; replacement of variable levies and quantitative restrictions on farm products with import tariffs; the extension of most-favored-nation treatment to trade in services; and improved dispute settlement mechanisms. The cuts in subsidized farm exports, the EU's own farm reform process, and the pressure of EU Eastern enlargement as a spur to continued farm spending reform all bode well for U.S.-EU trade relations, which have been plagued by subsidies wars since the 1980s.

The TABD met in Seville in November 1995 to prepare recommendations for new trade liberalization negotiations to the U.S.-EU summit in Madrid the following month. Its recommendation for a New Transatlantic Marketplace (NTM) was accepted at the Madrid summit and incorporated into one of the four pillars of the NTA and Joint Action Plan. In the commercial pillar of the NTM, the United States and EU committed themselves to reduce or eliminate bilateral trade barriers and then seek to "multilateralize" those actions at the World Trade Organization, successor to the GATT, by making those benefits available to all WTO members on a most-favored-nation basis. The NTM commits the two to:

- further reduce tariffs on industrial goods;
- negotiate global liberalization accords on telecommunications, information technology, and maritime transport services;
- remove or eliminate nontariff barriers to trade such as conflicting standards and duplicative testing and certification procedures;
- consider negotiations for a new antitrust cooperation accord;
- complete negotiations for multilateral accords to liberalize trade in telecommunications, maritime transport, and other services; and
- conclude a Customs Cooperation and Mutual Assessment Agreement to simplify customs procedures and exchange enforcement information.[8]

Since the NTM was announced, the two sides have not been able to reach agreement on telecommunications and maritime transport services but have made progress in negotiations for mutual recognition accords (MRAs) by which all products certified or inspected in one of the partner countries would be recognized automatically in the other, resulting in huge savings for producers. The two sides have begun negotiations to cover standards and norms for such sectors as telecommunications, medical equipment, pharmaceuticals, and chemicals. According to the American Chamber of Commerce in Belgium, MRAs directly affect about $80 billion in U.S.-EU trade each year.[9] Negotiations also progressed for a Customs Cooperation Agreement.

Trade Frictions

Trade discord is an old story in bilateral relations. Whether the chicken war of the 1960s or the pasta war of the 1980s, trade discord has been a concomitant of U.S.-EU commercial interdependence.[10] In 1995 the EU engineered a multilateral trade liberalization pact on financial services without the United States, which has since remained outside the agreement. The United States claimed inadequate offers from other countries. Conclusion of talks for a trade liberalization pact in global telecommunications eluded Uruguay Round negotiators, as did an accord on maritime transport services, despite pledges the United States and EU made to complete the pacts in 1996 within the context of the NTM and the WTO. European and other trading partners cited the presidential election year as a chief constraint on Clinton's ability to press for agreement in light of industry opposition. The United States cited inadequate offers from countries outside the EU, given how far the United States has already deregulated its own market. However, since the United States and EU are not far apart on a telecommunications pact, prospects for a pact were still good in 1997. Talks on trade in other services continued in 1997 as well.

Certain import levies of Austria, Finland, and Sweden (who acceded to the EU in 1995) rose to meet the EU's higher tariff on some products, (e.g., chemicals and computer parts), thus entitling the United States and others to compensation under WTO rules. Negotiations led to a fixed amount of compensation owed the United States under a 1995 agreement, thus sparing the two sides from the trade war that followed Iberian accession in 1986.

The United States continued to complain about the EU broadcast directive requiring member states to guarantee "when practicable" that a majority of broadcast time be reserved for EU operations. Whereas the EU argues that it needs to maintain national and European cultural identities in light of United States dominance of the global entertainment industry and thus must reserve broadcast time for European producers, the U.S. industry claims overt trade discrimination. The General Agreement on Trade in Services (GATS) covers the audio-visual sector, but the EU sought an exemption from offering national treatment status to non-EU producers, thus, according to the European Commission, effectively excluding this sector from GATS provisions.

Throughout 1995 and 1996, the Commission opposed the conclusion of various "open skies" accords between the United States and individual airline carriers in the member states, claiming it was in the members' interest for the EU and United States to conclude an open skies accord since the EU could conclude a better deal with the United States than could individual carriers. However, after receiving a mandate from the EU transport ministers in June 1996, the Commission and the United States were scheduled to begin talks on an EU-U.S. accord to liberalize transatlantic civil aviation.

The EU ban on growth hormones in livestock continued in 1995–1996, as did previous U.S. retaliatory measures. The EU is considering counter-retaliation, claiming the U.S. action violates WTO rules. Last, the United States has pressed the EU to reverse its 1994 decision to increase import levies on bananas from non–Lomé convention states as part of the new EU banana regime. Claiming that increased levies harmed banana exports to the EU from Hawaii and from U.S. subsidiaries in Central America, the U.S. industry filed a petition with the U.S. Trade Representative requiring a Section 201 investigation. In April 1996 the EU blocked moves to obtain a WTO dispute panel on the charges.

Analysis

Of the three dimensions of bilateral relations, commercial ties are the oldest and strongest. Commercial links predate the military alliance by two centuries.[11] Thus, although the end of the Cold War throws open questions about NATO's future, it will not diminish the importance of bilateral commerce.[12] Those who warn of the coming clash of trade blocs now that the Cold War is over[13] seem to have forgotten the bitter trade and foreign policy disputes between the United States and EU during the Cold War over East-West détente, North-South relations, oil politics, and agricultural export subsidies. U.S.-EU commercial relations are enduring features of the global economy.

Overall the tenor of bilateral trade relations is positive. The Uruguay Round agreements on farm export subsidies removed one of the longest, costliest, and most self-defeating disputes in the history of bilateral relations. The NTM opens the door to further reduction and elimination of trade barriers that, if successful, will serve as a bilateral spur to further global multilateral trade liberalization efforts. Bilateral commerce is relatively balanced and pacific when compared to U.S. and EU trading relationships with East Asian countries. Although bilateral trade frictions remain, they are still small in relation both to total two-way commerce and to U.S. and EU trade disputes with Japan and other East Asian countries. U.S. and EU trade with other parts of the world where economic growth is far outpacing the Atlantic world is developing at a rapid rate. Although this trade lacks the political-security framework of U.S.-EU relations and tends to be much less balanced, the United States and EU are increasingly dependent on new markets in Asia and Latin America. To avoid carving up the world into competitive regional trade blocs and destroying the global trading system, the NTM commits the United States and EU to work together to uphold multilateral trade structures and support global liberal-ization.[14]

The State of the Political Relationship

Whereas commercial relations constitute trade and investment, political relations comprise diplomatic interactions, foreign policy agreements and disagreements, and consultations in international politics. Despite policy disputes and differences, the two have clearly aimed to transform their for-eign policy consultative mechanisms that originated in the TAD (and in ear-lier incarnations) into joint problem-solving actions as outlined in the NTA and its Joint Action Plan. High hopes held by U.S. and EU negotiators accompanied the announcement of the NTA in 1995. However, by 1996 progress in beginning to implement the goals of the Joint Action Plan was modest. It is obvious that U.S.-EU joint actions must first overcome a wide variety of hurdles, whether they be presidential election year politics in the United States, the EU's underdeveloped competencies in such areas as antiterrorism and crime prevention, or the clash of bureaucracies within and among EU states and within the United States.

Foreign Policy Cooperation and Action

The TAD set out the mechanisms for foreign policy consultations. Although the goal of the TAD was to exchange diplomatic information and to avoid working at cross-purposes as the Cold War was coming to an end and the Germanies were unifying, in practice the United States and EU had already begun to act in complementary and coordinated ways in certain areas of international relations. The two found it necessary to justify the substantial use of time, energy, and resources that joint foreign policy consultations required by bringing home tangible outcomes.

The repertoire of EU-U.S. foreign policy activity had by 1994 already assumed a complex and far-reaching character that encompassed the world's major regions and key issues (e.g., Asia, human rights, terrorism, weapons proliferation); assumed different forms (economic/diplomatic sanctions, diplomatic recognition); was organized by scheduled as well as ad hoc consultations (from civil servants to foreign ministers to presidents); drew on a dense web of bilateral links and communications between the EU and the United States and between the EU member states and the United States; and has been acted out in Washington, New York, Brussels, other EU member capitals, and third-country capitals, and at the margins of meetings of international organizations and conferences.[15] One study iden-tified four variants of U.S.-EU cooperation linked to the TAD and thirty-one examples of such cooperative acts between 1990 and 1994,[16] including:

- coordinated action in pursuit of common objectives, either jointly (e.g., establishment of the Gulf Crisis Financial Coordination Group and the Regional Environmental Center in Budapest) or separately (sanctions against Serbia);
- complementary action taken separately but in pursuit of common objectives (sanctions against Nigeria);
- coordinated declarations in which statements were issued in pursuit of common objectives either jointly ("Joint Statement on UN Conventional Arms Transfer Register") or separately (Sudanese repression); and
- complementary declarations in which statements were issued separately in the pursuit of common objectives (Burmese repression).

Building on the success of the TAD and aiming to reconnect the U.S.-EU relationship to firmer political and security moorings just ahead of EU institutional reform and membership expansion, leadership on both sides considered how best to notch up the bilateral political relationship to prepare for change. At the June 1994 U.S.-EU summit in Berlin, the two sides charged ad hoc working groups to make recommendations for how coordination in each of three areas should occur in advance of the December summit. Working groups on international crime prevention, humanitarian assistance and aid coordination, and Central and Eastern Europe met to discuss what the two sides might do together. The extent to which the two could work together depended on how clear the EU competence to act was. Thus progress was made on humanitarian aid coordination (where the EU is competent) but not on crime prevention (where the EU is still developing competence). The groups disbanded by the December summit, but their work served as the basis for recommendations for the NTA and Joint Action Plan of the following year.

The EU Spanish presidency made transatlantic relations a top priority during the second half of 1995, and such leaders as U.S. secretary of state Warren Christopher[17] and European Commission president Jacques Santer[18] among others articulated ideas on how to upgrade political and commercial relations throughout 1995. Both sides were concerned about how to avoid the perceived drift in transatlantic relations in the post–Cold War era and to ease tensions over three years of painful policy differences over how to deal with the former Yugoslavia.

The United States sought to engage the EU as an interlocutor, however imperfect, to help solve problems too big and too costly for the United States to contemplate alone. The United States recognized that cooperation would be substantial in areas where the EU had clear competence (development and humanitarian aid) and less extensive in areas where the EU was either developing or had not yet developed competence (Europol, the embryonic EU police organization). Thus, although it was not the intent of the United States to stimulate integration, the NTA put pressure on the EU to develop the capacity to act internationally. The EU supported the NTA because the Commission saw opportunities to expand its jurisdiction in Pillars II (CFSP) and III (justice and home affairs) of the Treaty on European Union. The member governments in general and the Spanish presidency in particular felt the need to reassert and revitalize the EU's relationship with its most important bilateral partner at a time of significant flux in Europe.

The principals at the June 1995 U.S.-EU summit in Washington charged a senior-level group of officials to make proposals for consideration at the next summit aimed at strengthening bilateral cooperation. The December 1995 Madrid summit approved the senior-level group's recommendations for a NTA and Joint Action Plan. In foreign policy, the NTA committed the two sides to work together to respond to global challenges, including international terrorism, crime, environmental degradation, humanitarian affairs, and disease, by

- holding assistance coordination meetings between U.S. missions and Commission delegations in capitals of Central and Eastern European and newly independent states of the former Soviet Union;
- establishing a High-Level Consultative Group on Development Cooperation and Humanitarian Assistance to extend operational coordination and information sharing;
- establishing mechanisms for the exchange of information between the United States and EU and its member states in law enforcement and criminal justice;
- establishing a U.S.-EU task force to develop and implement a global early warning system and response network for communicable diseases;
- supporting the Korean Peninsula Energy Development Organization to assist North Korea in nonnuclear energy sources;
- facilitating Europol-U.S. relations; and
- seeking agreement on the shipment of essential and precursor chemicals used in the production of illegal drugs.[19]

Only modest progress to date has been achieved on meeting the objectives set out in the Joint Action Plan. For example, the two sides:

- made progress in talks that led to a small but first EU contribution to KEDO and to the possibility of EU accession to KEDO;
- made progress in talks on an accord to enhance cooperation in preventing the shipment of essential and precursor chemicals used to produce illicit drugs;

- worked closely together in preparing for the UN workshop on counter-narcotics cooperation in the Caribbean;
- set up a U.S.-EU Joint Task Force on Communicable Diseases to build a global early warning and response network for such diseases in cooperation with the World Health Organization;
- cooperated to ensure a successful outcome of the April 1996 Bosnia Donors' Conferences in Brussels;
- worked together at the Sharm el-Sheik summit in March 1996 and its follow-up meeting in Washington;
- worked together in the Regional Economic Development Working Group of the Middle East peace process;
- continued to work together on assistance programs in Central and Eastern Europe;
- participated in a summit of the United States, EU, and the largest international humanitarian aid organizations;
- agreed to hold their first trilateral consultations with the UN High Commissioner for Refugees in June 1996; and
- sent a joint mission to Rwanda and Burundi to assess refugee needs.[20]

The two partners at their June 1996 summit were more subdued about the speed with which common actions will occur. The room for more resolute joint problem solving was clearly constrained by the Helms-Burton legislation discussed below, the need to continue negotiations for new trade pacts on global telecommunications and other sectors, and the preoccupation of the White House with the presidential election and of the EU with the intergovernmental conference on institutional reform and the EU's difficulties in developing its internal coordination for CFSP and for Europol. U.S.-Europol cooperation fell short of U.S. expectations, reflecting opposition within the EU, mostly from France, for EU support of cooperation with the United States on antiterrorism. Still, the above examples of actual, ongoing, or potential coordinated actions are the first steps in implementing the ambitious goals of the NTA and Joint Action Plan.

Foreign Policy Discord

Whether over divergent responses to the oil cartel of the 1970s, construction of the Siberian natural gas pipeline in the 1980s, or war in the former Yugoslavia in the 1990s, the United States and EU have had foreign policy frictions. In recent years the two sides have sparred over

- whom to name as director-general of the WTO, revealing the capacity of the United States and EU to bicker over relatively small issues;

- whether to maintain the UN arms embargo on ex-Yugoslavia;
- the U.S. lead in defusing the Greco-Turkish dispute over the Imia islet, revealing severe limits to the CFSP;
- the projected speed of NATO enlargement, which the United States tended to press more quickly than the EU states; and
- the speed with which the United States put together and pressed the allies to accept a multilateral bailout of the Mexican peso, with the EU states complaining that the United States was expecting too much of others.

One of the most serious foreign policy disputes between the United States and the EU has always been over how to deal with rogue states, dictatorial states whom other states consider a threat to international peace and security or in violation of basic human rights. Should the United States and EU favor economic sanctions against rogue states—the U.S. proclivity—or "critical dialogue" while maintaining open commercial ties—the EU proclivity?

In the era of *Ostpolitick* in the 1970s, for example, the European Community was forging trade and political ties with Communist states in the East in advance of the United States. When in 1979 the Soviets invaded Afghanistan, the United States sought a strong united allied policy of economic and political sanctions against the Soviets but failed when the EC was willing to impose only mild sanctions, instead wishing to retain *Ostpolitik* while détente withered.

Similarly, when in response to the Soviet clampdown in Poland President Reagan extended the 1981 embargo on U.S. exports of parts and equipment for the construction of the Soviet natural gas pipeline to subsidiaries of U.S. firms abroad, the EC bitterly fought against Reagan's action and condemned the unilateral and extraterritorial extension of U.S. law to foreign firms subject to the laws of their host states. When in 1986 the United States again sought a strong united allied policy of sanctions against Libya for involvement in international terrorism, it again failed.

Throughout the 1980s and 1990s, the United States urged the EU and the member states—to no avail—to limit trade ties with and loans for Iran as a means to press for change in the country's policies that promote international terrorism. Indeed Germany, for example, one of the United States' closest allies in the EU, has become Iran's largest trading partner, and the German government underwrites approximately $10 billion in sales of and investment by German companies in Iran.[21] The EU maintains that "critical dialogue" with Iran is preferable to isolation. The United States faults German and EU policies in Iran, maintaining that "critical dialogue has utterly failed to produce any positive changes in Iranian behavior."[22] The clash of policy preferences over how to respond to rogue regimes came to a head in 1996. Although it deals a blow to prospects for foreign policy cooperation, that blow it is by no means fatal.

Even before Cuba shot down two civilian planes piloted by anti-Castro Cuban Americans in international airspace in 1996, the United States was at odds with the EU's evolving Cuba policy. The United States is concerned that the EU's policy of trade with and investment in Cuba might "reward the Castro regime without sufficient signs of genuine political and economic changes."[23] The United States has pressed its allies to join in a united effort to isolate Cuba but, as in the case of Iran, with no success. Although in 1996 the EU broke off negotiations for an economic cooperation accord with Cuba because of the government's worsening human rights record, Germany in the same year signed an investment accord with Cuba.

In response to Cuba's shooting of two civilian planes, Congress passed the Cuban Liberty and Democratic Solidarity Act of 1996, also known as the Helms-Burton Bill, which the president signed in March. The legislation, which entered into force in August 1996, tightens the U.S. embargo of Cuba; provides for legal action in the United States against foreign companies and their executives who "traffic" in property owned by U.S. citizens but confiscated by the Cuban government after the 1959 revolution; and prohibits entry into the United States of sugars, syrups, and molasses unless they are certified to be of non-Cuban origin.

Although the EU does not differ with the United States over the need to press the Cuban government to introduce democratic reforms, the EU issued strong demarches to the president and Congress concerning its opposition to the Helms-Burton Bill. The EU maintains that the bill is illegal in its extraterritorial application of U.S. jurisdiction and for attempting to expose foreign incorporated companies to conflicting legal requirements; runs counter to U.S. obligations under the WTO; and will result in legal chaos for EU firms doing business in Cuba and thus harm EU commercial interests. The EU has threatened retaliation and has taken its case to the WTO. If the EU retaliates, Congress will be expected to counterretaliate; thus the conflict has the potential to balloon.

In April 1996 the EU took the first steps toward calling a WTO dispute panel to review the Helms-Burton law. At the June 1996 U.S.-EU summit in Washington, the European Commission asked President Clinton to use his presidential waiver to nullify Title 3 of the Helms-Burton legislation. The president may suspend the right to sue in six-month intervals if he maintains that it is in the security interests of the United States or if it will speed a democratic transition in Cuba. In order to postpone a difficult decision, placate the EU yet retain the voting support of Cuban Americans, and protect investors from being sued—thus to buy time until after the November 1996 presidential elections—President Clinton waived the part of the law regarding lawsuits against foreign companies who "traffic" in expropriated property for up to six months effective August 1996 (until February 1997), allowing time for tempers to cool and a resolution to be found.

The potential for a crisis in U.S.-EU relations increased when in July 1996 Congress passed legislation requiring the president to impose sanctions on foreign companies that invest in the energy industries of Iran and Libya. President Clinton signed the so-called D'Amato Bill into law in August. The EU has opposed the bill for the same reasons it opposed Helms-Burton, and it has asserted its right and intent to react in defense of its interests in respect to the bill and to any other secondary boycott legislation that has extraterritorial effects.

Analysis

Although many consider the U.S.-EU relationship to be largely commercial, its political dimension has grown and taken shape since the 1980s. In general, the United States and EU share many of the same foreign policy goals as outlined in the NTA but often differ over the means to meet those goals. The EU itself is at times divided over foreign policy, thus making U.S.-EU cooperation even more difficult. For example, the EU was split over France's diplomatic efforts in southern Lebanon in April 1996 to press for a cease-fire between Israel and the pro-Iran Hezbollah guerrillas. Not only was Chirac's effort outside the CFSP framework, but it ran counter to U.S. diplomatic efforts, which in the end ensured a cease-fire. Another example of divisions among the Europeans came in May 1996, when the European commissioner for external affairs, Hans van den Broek, stated that he believed the EU should play the main role in assembling a military force for Bosnia in 1997, only to be quickly overruled and chastised by the EU member foreign ministries for imagining the EU will have the capability to handle such an action.

The NTA and Joint Action Plan reconfirm U.S.-EU foreign policy cooperation and set out an agenda for what the two would like to do together. It is an evolving framework. In areas where the EU Commission has competence (e.g., humanitarian affairs, development and emergency assistance, and migration) cooperation will intensify. In areas where the Commission's competence is either shared or nonexistent and where the EU itself has not yet developed internal coordination sufficiently to interact with the United States (e.g., police affairs, crime prevention, and antiterrorism), cooperation will have to depend on internal EU developments.

The NTA is an umbrella for the many dimensions of bilateral relations, but it is weakened by the absence of sections on cooperation in two critical areas: monetary and security issues. With the expected entry into force of the European monetary union at the turn of the twentieth century and the impact of the future Euro on the U.S. dollar and the G7, it does not take a vivid imagination to expect some acknowledgment of that impact in the NTA. Because of the impact of exchange rates on trade and investment flows, it would have been logical to include some language in the NTA in support of monetary cooperation. The same can be said for security. Given the negotiations between the WEU and NATO for Combined Joint Task Forces enabling the EU to use NATO command and assets in peacekeeping operations without U.S. ground troops, it would follow that the NTA should have contained some language in support of that endeavor. Why, then, the silence?

Both issues have clearly fallen outside the traditional realm of commercial relations between the United States and EU. The U.S. Treasury Department continues to prefer to work through the G7 on monetary issues and insists that such issues not be placed within the U.S.-EU orbit despite what many see as the coming of EMU and the Euro. Of course defense and security have always been the purview of defense ministries and NATO. No one seriously equates the EU with defense, and there is universal agreement that the EU is not going to develop its ESDI any time soon. However, the NTA addresses cooperation to fight terrorism and international crime, which are security issues, and the EU itself has as a treaty goal the development of a common security and defense identity. With the WEU and NATO negotiating the modalities of CJTFs in 1995–1996, it would have been logical to include some language in the NTA in support of closer alliance relations. Whatever the reasons for keeping monetary and security issues out of the NTA, the NTA and Joint Action Plan cannot be said to cover the entirety of bilateral relations.

Bilateral cooperation in international politics, humanitarian affairs, support of democratic and market reforms, and the fight against terrorism and international crime depend on the ability of both sides to make good on their promises to work together. The EU must develop Pillars II (CFSP) and III (justice and home affairs) of the TEU in order to act as an effective interlocutor of the United States. For its part, the White House and Congress must find a way to avoid paralysis in foreign policy making even as each is controlled by the opposition party.

When it comes to dealing with rogue states, the truth of the matter is that neither critical dialogue through trade and loans nor total economic isolation works, and the United States and EU will work at cross-purposes, and thus defeat each another, if they do not find a middle way. As serious as these disputes are, they do not threaten to upset the overall political relationship. The two have always differed over the U.S. proclivity to use trade measures to pursue foreign policy goals. Nevertheless, political relations are maturing in terms of the potential for real cooperation to solve global problems. In many respects the political cooperation dimension is a growth area of bilateral relations because it is relatively new and full of potential. It gives civil servants and diplomats deeper stakes in transatlantic relations and provides the potential for economies of scale as the two sides attempt to solve the world's problems with fewer resources than ever before. It also gives political leaders something tangible to point to when they attempt to show their citizens the value of transatlantic cooperation.

The State of the Security Relationship

Bilateral commercial and political relations are embedded in NATO, which provides for the common security and is the chief transatlantic institutional bridge. Many questioned NATO's place in transatlantic relations once the Cold War ended. However, NATO has shown itself to be indispensable to the security and stability of Europe. It thus remains vital to U.S.-EU relations, given (1) the dependence of the EU on NATO's continued existence; (2) the failure of the EU through the WEU to develop the European Security and Defense Identity as envisaged by the TEU; and (3) the unprecedented role of NATO in ending military hostilities in Bosnia in light of the inability of both the EU and the UN to broker peace. In addition, NATO agreement in June 1996 on the modalities for use of NATO-WEU CJTFs ended two years of difficult negotiations and provided for the potential use by the WEU of NATO command structure in pursuit of WEU-led peacekeeping and other soft security undertakings. Although NATO is attempting to adapt to the post–Cold War international order, publics on either side may be drifting from each other. Renewing the Atlantic Alliance will require support from civil societies, without which the organization will decline. Although strengthening the European pillar of NATO through the WEU and CJTFs is a step in the right direction—it shows Congress and the U.S. public that the Europeans take defense seriously—declining defense budgets throughout the European NATO member states give the opposite impression.

NATO's Transformation

During the first half of the 1990s, the NATO allies were torn over how they could together help end the war and ethnic cleansing in what was once Yugoslavia. The EU itself was also divided. It initially wanted to take the lead in peace negotiations but in the end did not have the unity and capability to enforce a peace. The United States initially wanted to yield leadership to the EU but in the end employed its own and NATO military power to press for a peace settlement (the Dayton peace accords) because it *did* have the unity and capability. It then went on to organize the UN-sanctioned NATO force (IFOR) to enforce the peace.

U.S. and EU leaders were jittery throughout 1996 over how to implement the civilian aspects of the Dayton peace accords, for which the EU has assumed responsibility, and over IFOR's future should the United States pull out by the end of 1996, as it originally planned to do. They did not, and the Clinton administration officials suggested in summer 1996 that under certain circumstances the United States could remain in IFOR beyond the projected December pullout date. The departure of U.S. troops would likely force the collapse of IFOR and the resumption of military hostilities.

Allied relations within NATO passed through a difficult set of negotiations from 1994 to 1996. The result has been the potential strengthening of NATO and thus of the security context of U.S.-EU relations. At its January 1994 council summit, NATO approved the concept of CJTFs to facilitate the dual use of NATO forces and command structures for either NATO or WEU operations and encourage WEU states to undertake peacekeeping missions with forces that are "separable but not separate" from NATO within the context of the ESDI and CFSP. At their June 1996 Berlin meeting, NATO foreign ministers finally agreed to the modalities for CJTFs. NATO may supply military forces and equipment to the WEU. A CJTF allows the WEU to undertake a mission in which the United States does not want to participate directly but that needs U.S. equipment and logistical support at NATO's disposal. All CJTFs require the approval of the NATO Council.

For the EU, it is a mixed blessing. On the one hand, it is a blow, at least for many years to come, to the dream of an independent ESDI, as initially envisioned by France and provided for in the TEU. The United States through the NATO Council will hold veto power over all CJFTs. On the other hand, CJTFs open up possibilities for the strengthening of the European pillar of NATO and for the Europeans to undertake missions they previously could not consider. What made the accord on CJTFs feasible in part was France's decision to allow its military officers back into NATO's military command after a thirty-year absence, thus making CJTFs more operationally feasible given the likelihood that France would shoulder significant responsibility in future WEU operations. In short, France's return helps allied forces work better together. Although the arrangements reconfirm U.S. leadership—and the centrality of NATO—in transatlantic relations, they also confirm the EU's failure to date to develop an independent ESDI.

A remaining question in security relations is NATO enlargement and Russia. Whereas some in the United States prefer to press for Eastern enlargement of NATO regardless of Russian objections, many in the EU prefer a more cautious approach, fearing the impact of a precipitous NATO move on the delicate democratization process in Russia. The EU, joined by Russia, views EU enlargement to the east in favorable terms relative to NATO enlargement. Coordinating NATO and EU enlargements to foster an orderly integration of East into West and to take into account Russia's needs will test U.S.-EU resolve in making a foreign policy partnership a reality in the immediate years ahead.

Analysis

Despite the breakthrough over IFOR and CJTF, which point to NATO's adjustments to post–Cold War change, the future of the security relationship is still problematic. Commercial relations predate NATO, so they are not affected by geostrategic change. There have always been political conflict and cooperation among like-minded states, and because U.S.-EU foreign policy cooperation is driven in part by economies of scale, it is not controversial and should continue to develop. However, in security, civil societies on each side have to feel they have a stake in the other's security to make the necessary sacrifices in money and, potentially, in blood.

A worrying degree of drift[24] among civil societies has caught the attention of U.S. and EU policymakers. "Building bridges" across the Atlantic is one of the pillars of the NTA, and the two sides have begun to finance joint projects among universities and nongovernmental organizations. The work of TABD and the promise of a transatlantic labor dialogue in the future are also examples of how civil societies can connect. The efforts are still modest, but the two have identified the problem and made a start. Basic education of what the EU and NATO are and what they mean to U.S. interests is prerequisite to stem the tide of neglect in the United States. Basic education of what the United States and NATO are and what they mean to EU interests is needed as well.

On the U.S. side, a growing domesticization of foreign policy puts local politics before international obligations. A massive generational and ideological turnover in Congress as a result of the November 1994 elections brought to Capitol Hill scores of new members with no or little foreign policy experience and understanding. With Republican control of both Houses, the Democratic administration was beleaguered in 1995 and then faced a presidential reelection campaign in 1996, constraining the president's hand in foreign policy, including European policy. On the EU side, a renationalization of the integration process has hampered problem solving at the European level and may derail the quest to achieve common foreign, security, and antiterrorism policies.

On both sides, fiscal constraint demanded by the pressing need to reduce the federal budget deficit in the United States and to meet the convergence criteria for EMU in the EU are drawing down budgets for collective self-defense via NATO and the WEU, Third World development, and UN peacekeeping.

A perennial problem in U.S.-EU relations is that the United States and EU are not governmental equals. One is a superpower whose government, despite executive-legislative infighting, has a single foreign and defense policy. The other is a partially integrated union of states that is attempting, without much success, to unify the foreign and security policies of its fifteen member governments. Whether internally divided over how to deal with crises from Bosnia to Imia and from southern Lebanon to the southern Pacific, or lacking the institutional basis for common foreign policy making, the EU is a very difficult interlocutor for such partners as the United States. Still, there are areas where the EU either has clear competence and may act as a unit or is beginning to develop new internal bases for coordination, and thus there is reason for the United States to work with the EU in the first category and to pressure it to develop capabilities in the second.

Conclusions

The general health of U.S.-EU relations as 1997 began was good, but the long-term prognosis in the security dimension requires a steady diet of confidence-building measures to ensure that civil societies outside of the commercial world stay healthily engaged. Commercial relations are relatively balanced and pacific. The work of the TABD is a new innovation in bilateral relations and a force for bilateral and multilateral trade liberalization. The more the private sector engages in influencing official relations and negotiations, the more policymakers can address the needs of civil societies. Political relations hold out the promise of joint problem solving. Despite the potential for damage to political relations over U.S. legislation concerning Cuba, Iran, and Libya, foreign policy cooperation is likely to continue to mature. Joint actions will take longer to evolve given the vicissitudes of international and domestic politics and the EU's own development in areas subject to joint action. In security, NATO passed through very difficult times in the early 1990s. The success of the Dayton peace accords and of IFOR will have a heavy impact on NATO's future and thus on U.S.-EU relations, given the latter's dependence on the former.

Finally, the United States has deep stakes in the outcome of the intergovernmental conference that began in Turin in March 1996. If the EU can make pragmatic adjustments in Pillar II, the CFSP, by increasing the opportunity of qualified majority voting; improving forward planning and analysis; better organizing itself vis-à-vis the outside world; and easing strains among the Commission, Council, and Parliament over foreign policy responsibilities and resources—and if the members can summon the political will to operationalize their CFSP—then the EU will be more likely to implement the Joint Action Plan. In short, the United States needs the EU to be a more effective international actor. Thus all eyes are on the IGC for needed reforms and on NATO for continuing to maintain order in the former Yugoslavia and recapturing public support to stem the tide of indifference.

Notes

1. Bureau of Public Affairs, "The New Transatlantic Agenda," *U.S. Department of State Dispatch* 6, 49 (3 December 1995).

2. For an analysis of the TAD, see Kevin Featherstone and Roy H. Ginsberg, *The United States and the European Union in the 1990s: Partners in Transition* (New York: St. Martin's Press, 1996), and John Peterson, *Europe and America in the 1990s: The Prospects for Partnership* (London: Edward Elgar, 1993).

3. The Transatlantic Business Dialogue consists of representatives from major businesses on both sides of the Atlantic who met in 1995 and 1996 to recommend trade policy to the United States and EU in advance of their biannual summits.

4. Bruce Stokes (ed.), *Open for Business: Creating a Transatlantic Marketplace* (New York: Council on Foreign Relations, 1996), p. 4.

5. Ibid., p. 23.

6. United States International Trade Commission, *Operation of the Trade Agreements Program—46th. Report* (Washington, DC: United States International Trade Commission, 1995).

7. Nancy Dunne, "Study Highlights U.S.-EU Links," *Financial Times,* 27 April 1995, p. 8.

8. "Senior Level Group Report to the U.S.-EU Summit," U.S. Department of State, 12 June 1996.

9. "Negotiations Continue on a Mutual Recognition Agreement," *Agence Europe* 3 July 1995, p. 8.

10. A catalogue of EU trade disputes with the United States appears in the EU's annual *Report on U.S. Barriers to Trade and Investment* (Brussels: European Commission, 1995).

11. Miles Kahler, *Regional Futures and Transatlantic Economic Relations* (New York: Council on Foreign Relations Press, 1995), p. 2.

12. For further discussion of the endurance of bilateral relations in the post–Cold War era, see chapter 1 in Featherstone and Ginsberg, *The United States and the European Union.*

13. Lester Thurow, *Head to Head: The Coming Economic Battle Among Japan, Europe, and America* (New York: Morrow, 1992).

14. For an analysis of the impact of regional trade blocs on U.S.- EU relations, see Kahler, *Regional Futures.*

15. See Thomas Frellesen and Roy H. Ginsberg, *EU-U.S. Foreign Policy Cooperation in the 1990s: Elements of Partnership* (Brussels: Centre for European Policy Studies, 1994).

16. Ibid., p. 2.

17. Warren Christopher, "Charting a Transatlantic Agenda for the 21st Century," *U.S. Department of State Dispatch* 6 (2 June 1995).

18. As quoted in Lionel Barner, "Niggling Trade Disputes Threaten U.S.-EU Relations," *Financial Times,* 13 March 1995, p. 2.

19. Excerpted from Delegation of the European Commission, "The New Transatlantic Agenda and Joint Acton Plan" (Washington, DC: Delegation of the European Commission, 1995).

20. Excerpted from the Senior Level Group Report to the U.S.-EU Summit, U.S. Department of State, 12 June 1996, and "Press Conference by President Clinton, President Santer of the European Commission, and Prime Minister Prodi of Italy," Office of the Press Secretary, White House, 12 June 1996.

21. "Warning on Iran Sanctions," *Financial Times,* 24 May 1996, p. 4.

22. Stuart Eizenstat, "Farewell Remarks to the EU Committee of the American Chamber of Commerce," U.S. Representation to the European Union, Brussels, 8 February 1996, p. 4.

23. Ibid., p. 4.

24. Drift in a declining relationship is one of the three directions relations might take, according to a study for the Forward Studies Unit of the European Commission in advance of the U.S.-EU summit in December 1995. See Wolfgang Reinicke and Reinhardt Rummel, *Perspectives on Transatlantic Relations* (Washington, DC: Brookings Institution, 1995).

17

The EU and the WTO Global Trading System

Mary E. Footer

The World Trade Organization came into existence on 1 January 1995.[1] The role of this new international economic organization is to oversee the implementation of the trade agreements annexed to its charter (the WTO Agreement), to provide a common institutional framework for the liberalization of trade through a rule-based system, and to act as a forum for ongoing trade negotiations and the work program of the organization.[2]

The Multilateral Trade Agreements annexed to the WTO Agreement form a single undertaking to which all WTO members are bound. They include the various agreements on trade in goods (including an updated version of the 1947 GATT and associated legal instruments), the General Agreement on Trade in Services, and the Agreement on Trade-Related Aspects of Intellectual Property Rights (TRIPs).[3] There is also provision for a single, integrated dispute settlement mechanism to cover all trade disputes arising under the WTO Agreement and a trade policy review mechanism.[4]

The European Union is not a member as such of the WTO. Instead, the European Communities and its member states are original founding members of the WTO.[5] This marks a departure for the European Communities in world affairs since there have been few precedents for their membership in other international organizations. The reason for this is twofold. First, many of the key international organizations were formed in the aftermath of World War II and predate the Treaty of Rome. Second, the classical type of international organization admits only states as members, although this has not necessarily proven to be a drawback to EC participation in such organizations.[6] Sometimes such participation has been restricted to observer status; at other times it has included active involvement in the affairs of international organizations of which it is not a member but that brings with it the conclusion of secondary legislation that binds the member states.[7]

It is significant that for EC membership of the WTO there is no explicit provision in either the Treaty of Rome (EC),[8] the Euratom treaty, or the ECSC treaty empowering the EC to accede to another international organization. Accession by the EC to an international organization foresees accession of the Community to an international agreement and remains essentially a question of compatibility of the agreement with the Treaty of Rome.[9]

However, EC membership in the WTO reinforces the underlying basis of the European Union. The European Union, despite the introduction of two new pillars (the CFSP and justice and home affairs), is primarily an economic community, and WTO membership accentuates the importance of the EC's external trade relations with the rest of the world. At the same time, an increased potential for conflict between the member states and the EC arises from the existence of a duality of competences and their exercise by the member states and the EC in the field of external trade law and policy.

EC and Member States' Participation in the WTO

Post-Maastricht: "Common Position" or "Joint Action"?

The Treaty on European Union (the Maastricht Treaty) offers various legal possibilities for the EC to exercise competence on the external plane and to participate in other international organizations, including the WTO, dependant upon two factors. One is the presence of dominant, political considerations; the Maastricht Treaty carries forward the concept of coexistence of intergovernmental action, in the form of European Political Cooperation, into a Common Foreign and Security Policy in conjunction with action taken by the EC.[10]

As a result, EC participation in external trade policy may be considered one that calls for a "common position" of the member states (Article J.2 of the TEU). Alternatively, it may require "joint action" by the EC and member states (Article J.3). In practice, developments within the European Union generally reflect the previous position of the EC and the member states in the conduct of external trade as developed under the Common Commercial Policy (CCP). Much depends on whether the EC's competence in a particular area of trade policy, including the conclusion of international trade agreements, is exclusive or nonexclusive.

EC Exclusive Competence

Under EC Article 228 the Council of the EU is the competent institution to conclude all international agreements entered into by the EC after consulting the European Parliament. Where the envisaged agreement establishes a specific institutional framework or has important budgetary implications for the Community, the additional assent of the European Parliament is required.[11] The only exception to this rule is those agreements which have been concluded by the European Commission on behalf of the Community under the CCP provisions of Article 113.

It is in this latter domain that the Community's competence extends to the adoption of autonomous and conventional trade measures that include the negotiation and conclusion of agreements with "one or more States or international organizations," on the basis of negotiation by the Commission and conclusion by the Council.

Mixed EC and Member States' Competence

However, the competence to enter into international agreements may be shared by the Community with the member states, for example, in the conclusion of association agreements under Article 238. This is because those agreements have an important dimension that extends beyond the scope of trade and economic relations and encompasses a political dialogue or addresses the basic protection of human rights.[12] Likewise, where the subject matter of the agreement includes other elements not essentially trade-based, as with the protection of intellectual property rights or the environment,[13] the competence is shared between the Community and the member states and is variously based on EC Articles 100, 100a (approximation or harmonization of national laws), and 235 in addition to Article 113 (action necessary to attain a Community objective). In these latter cases, the "mixed competence" is more along the lines of "joint action" foreseen in Article J.3 of the TEU.

The EC's participation in international economic organizations under Article J.2(3) of the TEU[14] calls for member states to "co-ordinate their action in international organizations and at international conferences." Under the Maastricht Treaty, they are urged to maintain "common positions in such fora," and this applies even where not all member states participate. Thus the prerequisite for action by the Community and member states is a "common position," as foreseen in Article J.2. The WTO Agreement also paves the way for the mixed participation of the EC and the member states in new institutional structures, namely, the different WTO councils to oversee trade in goods and services and intellectual property protection.

On 6 April 1994, just prior to signature of the Final Act of the Uruguay Round, the European Commission requested an opinion of the Court on the competence of the Community and the member states to conclude the WTO Agreement and to participate in the WTO.[15] In response, the ECJ confirmed that the European Community has exclusive competence on the basis of EC Article 113 to conclude multilateral agreements relating to trade in goods.

On the matter of trade in services, the Court confirmed that the powers of the Commission under the CCP of Article 113 are not exhaustive.[16] While in principle it found that trade in services falls within the Community domain, it made a further distinction. The simple cross-border supply of services is synonymous with a simple exchange of products and therefore falls within the exclusive competence of the Community.[17] However, where the consumer or supplier of the service moves across a border or where the provision of a service requires a foreign presence, the Community and the member states are jointly competent, that is, joint action is called for.

As to trade-related aspects of intellectual property rights, the Court found that the Community has exclusive competence on the basis of Article 113 only when the enforcement of intellectual property rights is related to counterfeit goods because of the relationship to the measures taken by customs' authorities at the Community's external borders.[18] The "trade effects" of all other intellectual property rights do not touch specifically upon the international exchange of goods and services, but where they do the effect is greater internally than externally. Besides, the prime objective of the TRIPs agreement is to strengthen and harmonize intellectual property rights protection on a global basis, and this is realizable only on the basis of joint action between the Community and the member states.[19]

Consequences of Joint EC and Member States' Participation in the WTO Agreement

From a legal standpoint, the conclusion of international agreements with the mixed participation of the EC and the member states means that both sets of parties are responsible for performance, including liability for any breach. A third party can choose to address either the EC, the member state(s), or both.[20] There have been other instances in international affairs where the EC has been required to specify its competence and that of the member states with respect to the subject matter of the convention, as in the case of the 1979 convention on the physical protection of nuclear materials,[21] but no specific criteria were set by other WTO members for the mixed participation of the EC and member states in the new organization.

The practical difficulty of mixed participation of the EC and member states in international affairs is not unique. It has also arisen in agreements that establish a regime for the international management of natural resources (the exploitation of the continental shelf or the regime of the deep-sea bed) or extend to environmental protection.[22] Sometimes the inclusion of a "participation" clause in such an agreement, providing for the specific competence of the EC or the member states, can contribute to an equitable solution with respect to the management of the regime.

Where no such participation clause exists, as in the case of the WTO

Agreement (other than provisions on voting),[23] the picture is less clear. Besides, the WTO Agreement is also the charter for a brand new international economic organization with a set of institutions. It is to this aspect that we next turn.

Practice of EC and Member States in GATT and Other International Agreements with Institutional Structures

After the end of the transitional period on 1 July 1968, the European Economic Community succeeded to the rights and duties of the member states in the GATT.[24] The practice of the GATT contracting parties thereafter was to accept that the EEC should act on behalf of the member states in trade matters. Within the GATT framework, this extended to EEC participation in all the GATT multilateral trade negotiations, beginning with the Dillon Round (1960–1961) through to the more recently concluded Uruguay Round (1986–1993).

Similarly, the EEC participated in GATT institutions, the most important being the GATT Council of Representatives, where it was represented by the Commission. Earlier commentators classified EC participation in the GATT as a sign of "new principles of representativity" and as marking "a whole new concept" in the law of international relations.[25] The Community's authority to negotiate on behalf of the member states in GATT MTNs is derived from its explicit competence under the CCP of EC Article 113. In the case of its participation in GATT institutions, the legal basis is less obvious.

The earlier practice of Community participation in other international agreements with organizational and institutional mechanisms, particularly commodity organizations,[26] required member states to coordinate their actions and uphold "common positions" in such fora, even where not all member states participated. As already noted, this continues through the exercise of Article J.2(3) of the TEU and thereby reinforces the guiding principle of consistency to be found in the Maastricht Treaty.[27]

Similarly, EC Article 229 calls upon the Commission to ensure the maintenance of "all appropriate relations" with the UN, its specialized agencies, and the GATT. The situation is now on firmer footing with the establishment of the WTO, but it is virtually unique in the law of international organizations.

Although the EC is an original WTO member, it derives recognition of its separate existence as a regional economic entity from an existing GATT provision permitting the formation of customs unions and free trade areas.[28] As a result, current EC participation in the WTO owes more to established practice under the GATT over a period of more than twenty years than to any formal participation clause. The experience is relevant in the context of the new WTO, since the WTO Agreement establishes a number of institutional bodies that call for the mixed participation of the EC and the member states.

The main WTO institution is the ministerial conference, which meets every two years.[29] There is also a General Council, which carries on the work of the ministerial conference in between its sessions,[30] supplemented by individual councils on goods (Annex IA), services (Annex IB), and intellectual property rights (Annex IC). These operate under the guidance of the General Council and are charged with overseeing the implementation of the relevant annexes.[31]

So far only the matter of voting rights, as part of the broader spectrum of WTO decisionmaking, has been specifically regulated in the WTO Agreement, where it has been decided to continue the established GATT practice of decisionmaking by consensus.[32] Where this cannot be achieved, the issue is to be decided by voting, as when amending certain provisions of the WTO Agreement or the annexed multilateral agreements or dealing with future accessions to the WTO at ministerial conferences.[33] The WTO Agreement specifically states that "where the European Communities exercise their right to vote, they shall have a number of votes equal to the number of their member States which are members of the WTO."[34]

The ECJ was not asked to rule upon the internal division of competences between the EC and the member states in the work of the WTO institutions, such as the individual councils that oversee the main WTO agreements. However, during oral hearings, the European Council drew attention to the need for a solution that would be "fully consistent with the Treaties and the *acquis communautaire.*" It emphasized the need for a common voice "even in matters not falling wholly or at all within the competence of the Community," for decisions generally to be taken within the Council "even in non-Community matters, in order that it may fully perform the role assigned to it by the Treaty on European Union," and the need to adopt the "principle of a single 'post-box,'" in order to spare the other WTO members the burden of determining whether competence lies with the Community or the Member States."[35]

To date, no specific arrangement has yet been concluded. According to Articles C, para. 2, and J.1(4) of the TEU as well as Article 5 of the EC treaty, the EC and the member states are responsible for ensuring that there is cooperation and coherence in the exercise of the external relations on the international plane. Its opinion on *Convention No. 170 of the International Labour Organization* stresses that where competence is shared between the EC and the member states, negotiation and implementation of the agreement require "joint action" by the EC and the member states.[36] The member states were in common agreement on these points.[37]

How should this mixed participation be effected in practice? Who will act as spokesperson for the Community and the member states in WTO affairs within the WTO's organizational and institutional framework? Should there be a single representative and, taking its cue from the Uruguay Round, should this be the European Commission, irrespective of whether a Community or member states' competence is at issue? An alternative might be for the EC to have two representatives, the European Commission's spokesperson for matters within its exclusive domain and both the Commission spokesperson and a spokesperson for the European Council in cases of mixed competence. This would represent a step backward in the direction of the UN Conference on Trade and Development (UNCTAD) formula used in some commodity agreements, and yet it is not entirely compatible with the current objectives of the European Union.[38]

The question of a WTO spokesperson is separate from the question as to what "internal" procedures may be reached for the determination of the EC's viewpoint within the European Union. The voting procedures in the new WTO call for careful consideration. The European Union consists of a single institutional framework (Article C of the TEU); thus the positions it must take within the WTO, whether they concern EC or member states' competence in the area, must be decided by the Council of the European Union.

As for voting in the WTO, it has been suggested that a qualified majority vote apply for EC questions and where specifically laid down in the Treaty of Rome; otherwise, unanimity for questions exclusively within the domain of the member states' competence and likewise for those in the realm of exclusive EC competence or where the Treaty specifically calls for this (for example, in the field of fiscal harmonization). At the beginning of the 1996 IGC, qualified majority voting in the Council was viewed as the normal method of voting on most legislative matters under the Treaty of Rome, although there were still some areas where unanimity was required. It is anticipated that the IGC will expand the scope of qualified majority voting still further.[39]

The adoption of a fully integrated dispute settlement mechanism in accordance with the Understanding on Rules and Procedures Governing the Settlement of Disputes (DSU) in Annex 2 of the WTO Agreement calls for a new Dispute Settlement Body (DSB) to administer the rules and procedures contained therein.[40] The scope of the DSU extends to all of the multilateral trade agreements. It also includes coverage of the plurilateral agreements—the agreements on trade in civil aircraft, government procurement, as well as the international dairy and bovine meat agreements—found in Annex 4 to the WTO Agreement.[41]

The issue of mixed EC and member states' participation in the WTO may lead to some bizarre consequences when it comes to the exercise of any remedies set out in a panel report adopted by the DSB (or a report adopted by the new appellate body in the case of appeal against a previous panel decision). Under the DSU, the available remedies extend not just to compensation but to the possibility of retaliation in the form of suspension of concessions under the "covered agreements."[42] In fact Article 22 of the DSU opens the way not only for retaliation but also for cross-retaliation. Difficulties may arise for the EC and the member states in implementing panel, or appellate body, decisions where cross-retaliation has been authorized.

On a simple division of competences between the EC and the member states, a member state that begins and wins a panel in the area of trade in services or intellectual property rights protection and thus involving mixed competence may, in the event that it is unable to take a cross-retaliatory measure in either of those fields, be precluded from doing so in the area of trade in goods, as this is the exclusive competence of the EC under Article 113. Conversely, the EC may find its hands tied if it tries to seek cross-retaliation under the trade in services agreement (GATS) or the agreement on intellectual property rights (TRIPs) in situations where it is unable to exercise the right of retaliation in the goods sector (except in the GATS and TRIPs area where it is able to limit itself to cross-border trade in services or trade in counterfeit goods).[43]

Likewise, unfair situations may arise for the EC or the member states in the context of cross-retaliation where another WTO member wins the right to retaliate against the EC for an infringement of any of the agreements on trade in goods but is authorized by the DSB to retaliate against one or more member states under the GATS or TRIPs. The same situation could arise for the EC because it may be struck by a retaliatory measure in the goods sphere for an infringement by a member state of the GATS or TRIPs agreements. The ECJ chose not to address this point other than to urge a duty of close cooperation on the EC and the member states.

A Selected Review of Some Vital
EU Commercial Relations Under the WTO

The process of completing the internal market program in 1992, coupled with the entry into force of the Maastricht Treaty in November 1994, largely overshadowed the closing stages of the Uruguay Round and left their imprint on the EC and member states' participation in some of the ensuing agreements. Not only in the field of institutional competence under the WTO have issues arisen but also the subject matter of some WTO agreements bears the hallmark of the Community's internal market policies. In view of this, certain areas of substantive trade coverage call for closer examination. These include financial services under GATS, the protection of intellectual property rights under the TRIPs agreement, and the new Agreement on Government Procurement (one of the plurilateral agreements in Annex 4 to the WTO Agreement).

The General Agreement on Trade in Services

The GATS is a major achievement of the Uruguay Round MTN. It covers all service sectors, including financial services, and is composed of two main parts. The first is a framework agreement consisting of a set of general concepts, basic principles, and rules that apply to all WTO members across all service sectors. These general concepts include definition and scope of services, the application of the most-favored-nation principle, transparency, provisions for increased participation of developing countries, the administration of domestic regulations, and obligations on mutual recognition requirements. The operative part of the agreement contains provisions on the application of national treatment and market access principles to the laws and regulation of each country, on a sector-by-sector basis.

The second part of the GATS contains the WTO members' "schedules of specific commitments." These are the commitments on an individual-country basis (there is a single one for the EC) to grant access to specific service sectors and subsectors. They are subject to sector-specific qualifications, conditions, and limitations and a continuing process of liberalization in the same way as are tariff concessions in the goods sphere.

The application of MFN is supposed to ensure that a WTO member will not discriminate among members supplying a service; where this is not possible for a particular service activity a so-called MFN exemption must be filed. Where full national treatment cannot be granted or other limitations on market access are imposed (e.g., number of providers is limited or qualitatively assessed), this fact must be listed in the relevant WTO member's country schedule.

The annex on financial services forms one of the technical annexes appended to the GATS that adapts the basic provisions of the GATS to the specifics of financial services, including banking, investment, securities trade, and insurance. One of the most contentious elements of the negotiations was the question of how the GATS should apply to government laws and regulations in the financial sector.

The EU and Financial Services

The EC's negotiating stance throughout the Uruguay Round had been to get a services agreement that was in terms of both general scope and sectoral coverage able to maximize the potential for "effective" market access and encourage wide participation. Two key factors emerged in the negotiating stage. First, the EC favored an agreement with "soft" obligations, that lacked binding obligations yet included the principle of national treatment.[44] Second, the EC placed strong emphasis on the sectoral approach in what it termed "sectoral appropriateness."[45] In concrete terms, the EC sought progressive liberalization on the key issue of market access, which rests upon respect for policy objectives and the "appropriateness" of regulations in each sector.

Among member states there was a greater lack of uniformity and agreement over the regulation of services trade than might have been supposed.[46] This was further accentuated by the Community's preoccupation with its policy of completing the internal market by 1992, which led to services negotiations at the global level being viewed as part of the overall aim of the EC to achieve "services-friendly" policies in the home market and to develop "an institutional, regulatory and fiscal environment in accord with those needs."[47]

The EC, already in a dominant position in world service exports by the mid-1980s, saw a shift to the service sector as investment-led[48] and was keen that adequate consideration be given to both services and investment issues, especially where a commercial presence is needed. The field of banking and investment services is illustrative in this respect.

Set against this background of multilateral negotiations on financial services, the original proposal for the EC's second banking directive embraced the concept of a universal banking model, under which banks would be able to conduct a wide range of activities within the parent bank or its branches. Within that context, Article 9, Section 4, of the proposed directive gave rise to the most concern when negotiating with third countries, in particular the United States. This was because its intended operation sought to restrict, on a reciprocal basis, foreign bank entry by limiting or suspending the authorization or acquisition of a new subsidiary in the EC.

The call for "mirror-image" reciprocity angered the United States since U.S. banks, limited by the Glass-Steagall Act and home-country regulation, would be forced to restrict their operations in the Community's internal market. Eventually, the EC, under pressure from the United States, amended its proposal, relinquishing mirror-image reciprocity. Instead, the EC proceeded with the principle of national treatment, combined with a new Article 7, under which the Commission can propose to the Council the opening of negotiations with third countries, provided the latter grant "effective market access" comparable to that enjoyed by those countries' banks in the EC.[49]

If the EC and United States had managed satisfactorily to resolve the issue of market access, the same was not necessarily true of negotiations with other countries. The adoption of a second annex on financial services at the last minute in the original Uruguay Round MTN was an attempt to redress what some developed countries, especially the United States, saw as unfair balance in negotiations on financial services. They argued that in the absence of substantial market access commitments by developing countries, the MFN obligation in the financial sector might work to the disadvantage of countries like the United States, or even the EC, with relatively open markets in financial services. The latter would be required, under the MFN obligation, to maintain current high levels of market access and would have no leverage in subsequent rounds of negotiations with developing countries. As a result, the second annex on financial services operated as an interim set of financial services obligations for a six-month period from the commencement of the WTO (i.e., between 1 January and 30 June 1995). That six-month period was used to negotiate further commitments, based on the notion that at the conclusion thereof, any country that considered its overall set of market access commitments to be insufficient would be free to reduce or retract its own commitments or to exempt itself, fully or partially, from an MFN obligation in the financial services sector.[50]

By the end of the process, most of the seventy-six WTO members involved in financial sector negotiations had improved their market access commitments and had appended them to a "protocol" to the GATS.[51] The notable exception was the United States, which despite noting the improvement in market access commitments that some countries had made nevertheless felt the overall package of commitments to be insufficient to warrant a full MFN undertaking. This essentially means that it would remove most of its offer on financial services and take an MFN exemption for the whole financial services sector. Accordingly, existing financial services investments in the United States are assured continued national treatment, but there is no guarantee of MFN treatment for foreign firms seeking to establish new financial services business or to expand existing operations in the United States.

All WTO members separately agreed to set up an additional negotiating round on financial services on 1 November 1997 for a sixty-day period in order to allow countries to modify their market access commitments and MFN undertakings anew in the financial services sector.[52] The hope was that a second period of "extended negotiation" would speed up the process of liberalization of trade and investment rules in the financial services sector and in the process draw the United States back into the fold. The period for ongoing negotiations was extended into 1997.

Protection of Intellectual Property Rights Under TRIPs

The Agreement on Trade-Related Aspects of Intellectual Property Rights is the most comprehensive multilateral agreement on intellectual property and was considered absolutely essential to the completion of the Uruguay Round. This is because the number of goods embodying intellectual property rights, such as patents, trademarks, or copyright, has increased markedly in recent decades. Many industrialized countries have seen their competitive position in the marketplace eroded because of inadequate protection of intellectual property in less-advanced, technology-importing countries where counterfeit and infringing goods, particularly in the high-tech and pharmaceutical industries, have been branded as theft and piracy.[53] Whereas disputes on inadequate property protection previously tended to be addressed through intergovernmental channels involving either bilateral agreements or unilateral imposition of trade sanctions (for example, U.S. measures under Section 337 of the 1930 U.S. Tariff Act and Section 301 of the 1974 Trade Act, as amended), such action was open to challenge.[54] It was considered wiser to aim for an all-inclusive protection of the key intellectual property rights—patents and trademarks, copyright and neighboring rights, industrial designs, trade secrets, marks of origin (appellations for wines and spirits), and integrated circuit designs—through a new international agreement with tough enforcement clauses.

There are two key aspects of the EU's participation in TRIPs. The EC's internal market in the field of intellectual property rights protection is incomplete. As a result, the desirability of achieving this through Community action on the external plane, within the framework of a multilateral convention like TRIPs, is equivocal. This is evident in the ECJ's ruling that only the provisions in the agreement on TRIPs dealing with the prohibition on counterfeit goods fall within the exclusive domain of the Community. Recall that in all other areas the Court ruled that the EC and the member states were jointly competent to conclude the TRIPs agreement, since the prime objective of the agreement was to strengthen and harmonize intellectual property rights protection on a worldwide scale.

The EC is competent internally to legislate in the field of intellectual property and to harmonize national laws on the basis of Articles 100 and 100a, or alternatively on the basis of Article 235, in order to create new rights, superimposed on national rights as it has done in the case of the Community trademark. To assign sole competence to the Community to enter into agreements with third countries, aimed at harmonizing intellectual property both on the external and coincidentally on the internal plane, would mean that the Community's institutional practices on internal voting and consultation procedures would effectively be bypassed.[55]

As a result of this, and of more immediate importance, work is due to commence in the TRIPs council on certain revisions to the TRIPs agreement. First, in order to enhance protection of geographical indications for wines, negotiations are planned for the establishment of a multilateral system of notification and registration of geographical indications for wines, eligible for protection in those member states participating in the system. Second, the provisions on patentability of plants and plant varieties are reviewable within four years of entry into force of the WTO (i.e., before the end of 1998). Third, there is a general review clause for the TRIPs agreement five years after its entry into force (i.e., as of 1 January 2001).

In view of the ECJ's opinion, it would appear that current and future practice under the WTO must mean that EC member states will participate in the work of the TRIPs council and any of its committees. Additionally, they must be fully consulted and advised of formal and informal contacts and discussions, even allowing at times for a member state to intervene where justified and in accordance with a previously agreed arrangement on a matter that relates specifically to trade aspects of intellectual property within its national competence, always provided that there has not been or that there is insufficient Community harmonization on the matter.

Government Procurement

The incomplete CCP in the field of government procurement has had direct effects both on the course of negotiations for a new agreement and on the contemporary development of EC-U.S. commercial relations. The EC's program for completion of the internal market resulted in major revisions of the Community's public works and public supplies directives, as well as the award of public works contracts, but it failed adequately to address the external aspects of its internal procurement laws and policy.

The EC and the member states are parties to the new multilateral Agreement on Government Procurement that was concluded within the framework of the Uruguay Round MTN and that builds upon and extends the scope of the 1979 and 1988 agreements.[56] The new agreement covers services, including construction services, and certain activities in the utilities sector and embraces subfederal and local entities as well as certain public undertakings for the first time. On the procedural side, it introduces improved legal remedies that extend to bid challenge procedures in WTO members' domestic fora.[57]

The agreement sets out a number of general principles to be applied by all the parties, including the application of the principle of nondiscrimination and national treatment.[58] It also provides for detailed award procedures, with four basic methods of tendering (open, selective, limited, and competitive negotiations).[59] Other key provisions include enhanced transparency requirements, rules governing the opening of procedures, with detailed coverage of qualification of suppliers and service providers, publication of procurement notices, treatment of information prior to notice, and more stringent time limits and delivery.[60]

Notwithstanding its participation in the Agreement on Government Procurement, the Community also has an extensive system of bilateral agreements and autonomous measures in place in the field of government procurement with respect to third countries.[61] The most significant set of agreements in the bilateral sphere are those that were reached between the EU and the United States during the Uruguay Round and after its conclusion in April 1994. The two council decisions of 1993 both form part of the agreement, drawn up as a memorandum of understanding, that was reached between the United States and the EC in 1993, after months of disagreement over Article 29 of the newly implemented utilities directive (Article 36 under the consolidated version).[62]

Essentially, the Community had agreed to disapply the exclusion and preference rules of Article 29 (Article 36 under the consolidated directive) with respect to tenders comprising products of U.S. origin in the Community's electrical equipment markets (but excluding telecommunications equipment) in exchange for access by Community tenderers to five of the publicly owned federal utilities and the Tennessee Valley Authority in the United States. The United States also agreed to seek to gradually eliminate "Buy America" provisions on subfederal funding authorities.

The memorandum of understanding was used to break the virtual deadlock between the EU and the United States in negotiations for a new government procurement pact. It was also a term agreement with an expiration date of 30 May 1995, or the date upon which the new GATT Agreement on Government Procurement came into effect, whichever was earlier (the new EU-U.S. agreement came into force on 1 January 1996). Meanwhile, the provisions of the original memorandum of understanding had been extended, following signature of the new agreement at Marrakesh.[63]

Linked to the former bilateral agreement but with the character of an autonomous CCP measure, the action the EU took against the United States in 1993 when it chose to implement sanctions against U.S. contractors came in response to similar sanctions imposed on the Community by the U.S. government under the Title VII of the 1988 U.S. Omnibus Trade and Competitiveness Act.[64] The U.S. sanctions had targeted Community firms, preventing them from bidding for U.S. federal procurement contracts outside their scope, or below-threshold value of the 1988 threshold levels. The EU responded by extending similar punitive measures to all firms established in and operating from the United States on public supplies, public services, and public works contracts awarded by central government authorities. It became a dead letter following the further agreement that was reached in April 1994 between the EU and the United States in an attempt to resolve their differences and in the spirit of negotiations for the new Agreement on Government Procurement that has since entered into force.

Summary and Conclusions

The issue of competences in the external trade policy of the EU remains a difficult one for both the EC and the member states. Competence frequently is shared in vital international trade issues in the services area as well as in the field of intellectual property protection. This is in marked contrast to trade in goods, where the EC exercises exclusive competence on the international plane.

The importance of the competences issue is demonstrated in the institutional participation of the EC and the member states in the WTO. This extends to the legal and practical implications of various forms of participation, including voting and other forms of decisionmaking in WTO fora such as the ministerial conference, the WTO council, and the individual councils that have been established to oversee the main trade agreements, as well as the field of dispute settlement. The current status of EU-U.S. commercial relations in the WTO context in key areas such as financial services, intellectual property rights protection, and government procurement suggest the difficult path the EC and member states must tread in the WTO global trading system.

Notes

1. Text of the Final Act and the WTO Agreement can be found in *The Results of the Uruguay Round of Multilateral Trade Negotiations: The Legal Texts* (Geneva: GATT Secretariat, 1994) p. 2 ff.; also at 33 *International Legal Materials* 1144 ff. (1994).

2. Singapore Ministerial Declaration, adopted 13 December 1996 at the first meeting of the WTO at ministerial level, WT/MIN(96)/DEC, 18 December 1996.

3. Annex 4 to the WTO Agreement contains the plurilateral agreements (the Agreement on Government Procurement, the International Dairy Agreement, the Arrangement Regarding Bovine Meat, and the Agreement on Trade in Civil Aircraft), which have not been signed by the WTO's entire membership and thus are binding only on certain WTO members.

4. Annexes 2 and 3 to the WTO Agreement.

5. WTO Agreement, Article XI:1. I generally use the term "European Community" ("Communities"), or simply "Community," rather than "European Union," since it is the European Communities that are members of the WTO. As of 1 January 1995, the member states of the EC were Austria, Belgium, Denmark, Finland, France, Germany, Greece, Ireland, Italy, Luxembourg, the Netherlands, Portugal, Spain, Sweden, and the United Kingdom. Nevertheless, on occasion when referring to policy developments, I occasionally use the term "European Union."

6. For a review of the EC's participation in the Food and Agriculture Organization (FAO), see R. Frid, "The European Economic Community: A Member of a Specialized Agency of the United Nations," *European Journal of International Law* 4, 2 (1993): 239–255.

7. J. Groux and P. Manin, *The European Communities in the International Legal Order* (Brussels: European Perspectives, 1985), pp. 46–53; R. G. Sybesma-Knol, *The Status of Observers in the UN* (Brussels: Vrije Universiteil Brussel, Centrum voor de Studje van het Recht van de Verenidge naties en de Gespecialiseerde Organisaties, 1981), chapters 4 and 7, section c. On secondary legislation, see Opinion 2/91 of 19 March 1993 *Re Convention No. 170 of the International Labour Organization Concerning Safety in the Use of Chemicals at Work,* OJ 1993, C 109/1 [1993] *Common Market Law Review* 800; see also N. Emiliou, "Towards a Clearer Demarcation Line? The Division of External Relations Power Between the Community and Member States," *European Law Review* (1993): 76–86, and N. A. Neuwahl, case note in *Common Market Law Review* (1993): 1185–1195.

8. Article 228 sets out procedures for conclusion of agreements between the Community and other states or international organizations, including resort to an opinion from the European Court of Justice by any Community institutions or member states on the compatibility of the proposed accession with the Treaty of Rome under Article 228.6.

9. See, for example, Opinion 1/78 of 4 October 1979 *Re the Draft International Agreement on Natural Rubber* [1979], *European Court Reports* 2871; [1979] 3 *Common Market Law Review* 639.

10. M. Cremona, "The Common Foreign and Security Policy of the European Union and the External Relations Powers of the European Community," in D. O'Keeffe and P. M. Twomey (eds.), *Legal Issues of the Maastricht Treaty* (London: Wiley Chancery Law, 1994), p. 251; see also E. Stein, *External Relations of the European Community: Structure and Process,* vol. 1, book 1, of *Collected Courses of the Academy of European Law* (London: Kluwer, 1991), p. 179 ff., especially further literature on the subject in footnote 202. For a more recent appraisal of the CFSP, see E. Regelsberger and W. Wessels, "The CFSP Institutions and Procedures: A Third Way for the Second Pillar," *European Foreign Affairs Review* 1 (1996): 29–54.

11. The ECJ clarified the meaning of Article 228.2 in a case involving an agreement on competition that the Commission had entered into, on behalf of the Community, with the United States. The Court declared the agreement void; the exercise of powers vested in the Commission under Article 228 is an exception to the general rule that the Council is responsible for concluding international agreements; see Case C-327/91 France v. Commission, *European Court Reports* [1994] I-3641 at 3675, and J. Kingston, "External Relations of the European Community— External Capacity Versus Internal Competence," *International and Comparative Law Quarterly* 44, 3 (1995): 659–670.

12. Besides the large number of association agreements that the EC has entered into with Mediterranean countries, countries of the former East European bloc, and in the sphere of EEC-ACP (African Caribbean, Pacific) trade and cooperation agreements (successive Lomé conventions) an agreement such as that establishing the European Economic Area was also concluded on the basis of mixed competence under Article 238 EC, OJ 1994 L 1/1.

13. In advance of possible future Community accession to either the Berne convention for the Protection of Literary and Artistic Works and the Rome convention for the Protection of Performers, Producers of Phonograms, and Broadcasting Organizations, the Commission in 1991 put forward a proposal for Council decisions concerning the accession of the member states to both conventions on the basis of Articles 57.2, 66, 100a, and 113 EEC COM (90) 582 of 11 January 1991; see I. Govaere, "Intellectual Property Protection and Commercial Policy," in M. Maresceau (ed.), *The European Community's Commeuropean court reportsial Policy After 1992: The Legal Dimension* (Dordrecht: Martinus Nijhoff, 1993), p. 220.

On the environment, see Council Decision No. 88/540/EEC of 14 October 1988, OJ 1988, L 297/8 of 31 October 1988 implementing the 1985 Vienna convention for the Protection of the Ozone Layer, 26 *International Legal Materials* (1987) 1516 on the basis of Article 130s EC (entered into force for EC on 15 January 1989); similarly in the case of Council Decision No. 91/690/EEC of 12 December 1991, OJ 1991, L 377/28 of 31 December 1991 implementing the 1990 London Amendment to the Montreal on Substances that Deplete the Ozone Layer 26 *International Legal Materials* (1987) 1541 (entered into force for the EC on 10 August 1992); see P. Demaret, "Environmental Policy and Commercial Policy: The

Emergence of Trade-Related Environmental Measures (TREMs) in the External Relations of the European Community," in Maresceau, *The European Community's Commeuropean court reportsial Policy,* pp. 341–344, note 17, and pp. 346–349.

14. Previously EC Article 116, the provision was repealed and replaced under the Maastricht Treaty by Article J.2(3).

15. Request of 6 April 1994, OJ C 218/20 of 6 August 1994; see Opinion 1/94 of 15 November 1994 *On Community and Member States' Competences in Concluding the WTO Agreement,* [1994] *European Court Reports* I-5267; [1995] 1 *Common Market Law Review* 205, para. 24; see more recently Opinion 2/94 of 28 March 1996 *Re the Accession of the Community to the European Human Rights Convention* [1996] 2 *Common Market Law Review* 265.

16. The Court confirmed its earlier view in Opinion 1/78, para. 45.

17. Opinion 1/94, paras. 43–53.

18. The Court noted that part 3, section 4, of the TRIPs agreement has a counterpart in Council Regulation No. 3842/86 of 1 December 1968, laying down measures to prohibit the release for free circulation of counterfeit goods, OJ 1968, L 375/1: Opinion 1/94, paras. 55–57.

19. Community competence at the internal level is still largely restricted to harmonization of national regulations on the basis of Articles 100, 100a, and 235; see further Govaere, "Intellectual Property Protection," pp. 216–217.

20. C. Tomuschat, "Liability for Mixed Agreements," in D. O'Keeffe and H. Schermers (eds.), *Mixed Agreements* (Boston: Kluwer, 1983), pp. 125–132, and P. Allott, "Adherence to and Withdrawal from Mixed Agreements," in O'Keeffe and Schermers, *Mixed Agreements,* pp. 97–121.

21. See the related ECJ Opinion 1/78 of 14 November 1978 on the *Draft Convention of the International Atomic Energy Agency on the Physical Protection of Nuclear Materials, Facilities and Transports* [1978] *European Court Reports* 2151 at 2165, especially at p. 2180, para. 35; [1979] 1 *Common Market Law Review* 131, where the Court concluded that the subject matter fell partly under EC competence (physical protection) and partly under member states' competence (criminal jurisdiction and extradition). However, it considered the actual division of competences to be a purely "domestic question in which third parties have no need to intervene."

22. Articles 2, 4, and 5 in Annex IX to the 1982 Law of the Sea Convention and the EC declaration upon signing the Law of the Sea Convention, reprinted in *Common Market Law Review* (1986) p. 521 at p. 538; see K. Simmonds, "The Community's Participation in the UN Law of the Sea Convention," in D. O'Keeffe and H. Schermers (eds.), *Essays in European Law and Integration* (Boston: Kluwer, 1992), p. 179. Also, Article 13(3) of the 1985 Vienna convention for the Protection of the Ozone Layer, (also Annex II to the Council Decision No. 88/540/EEC of 14 October 1988, referred to therein); see J. Temple Lang, "The Ozone Layer Convention: A New Solution to the Question of Community Participation in 'Mixed' International Agreements," *Common Market Law Review* 23 (1986): 157–176.

23. WTO Agreement, Article IX.1 and footnote 2, see notes 32–34 below.

24. Joined Cases 21-24/72 *Third International Fruit Company N.V. v Produktschap voor Groenten en Fruit,* Preliminary Ruling of 12 December 1972, [1972] *European Court Reports* 1219; [1975] 2 *Common Market Law Review* 1 and Joined Cases 267-269/81 *Amministrazione delle Finanze dello Stato v. Società Petrolifera Italiana Spa* (SPI) *and SpA Michelin Italiana* (SAMI), Preliminary Ruling of 16 March 1983 [1983] *EUROPEAN COURT REPORTS* 801 at 823; [1984] *Common Market Law Review* 354; see M. Maresceau, "The GATT in the

Case-Law of the European Court of Justice," in M. Hilf, F. Jacobs, and E.-U. Petersmann, eds., *The European Community and the GATT* (Boston: Kluwer, 1986), pp. 102–126 and E.-U. Petersmann, "Application of GATT by the Court of Justice of the European Communities," *Common Market Law Review* 20 (1983): 397–437.

25. P. Pescatore, *The Law of Integration: Emergence of a New Phenomenon in International Relations, Based on the Experience of the European Communities* (Leiden: Sijthoff, 1974), p. 6; Sybesma-Knol, *The Status of Observers,* p. 158.

26. For an overview of mixed institutional participation in commodity agreements and the practice of decisionmaking in those bodies, see M. E. Footer, "Participation of the European Communities in the World Trade Organization," in S. V. Konstadinidis (ed.), *The Legal Regulation of the European Community's External Relations After the Completion of the Internal Market* (Aldershot: Dartmouth, 1996), pp. 83–85.

27. Articles C and J.8(3) of the TEU, in particular.

28. This article, Article XXIV, has been taken up in Annex 1A to the WTO Agreement in the GATT 1994, which comprises (1) the original GATT 1947 as rectified, amended, or modified; (2) the legal *acquis* of the GATT; (3) six understandings; and (4) the Marrakesh Protocol containing the market access concessions on goods agreed upon during the Uruguay Round.

29. WTO Agreement, Article IV.1. The first WTO ministerial conference was held in Singapore, 9–13 December 1996.

30. WTO Agreement, Article IV.2.

31. Ibid., Article IV.5.

32. Ibid., Article IX.1. See further on the use of consensus as a decisionmaking technique K. Zemanek, "Majority Rule and Consensus Technique in Law-Making Diplomacy," in R. St. J. McDonald and D. M. Johnston (eds.), *The Structure and Process of International Law: Essays in Legal Philosophy Doctrine and Theory* (Dordrecht: Martinus Nijhoff, 1986), pp. 871–877.

33. WTO Agreement, Article X *in extenso,* ibid., Article XII.2.

34. Article IXC.1. See also footnote 2 to that article, which makes clear that at no time shall the number of votes of the EC and their member states exceed the number of member states of the EC.

35. Opinion 1/94, para. K, Council's response to *Question 11.*

36. Opinion 2/91, paras. 12 and 36.

37. See response by the Council to *Question 11,* at I, pp. 98–102.

38. The so-called UNCTAD formula was used at the 1971 International Wheat Conference and provided for an EC delegation, chaired by a representative of the Commission, together with the member state representative that presided over the Council at the time, with both acting as spokesmen; see Footer, "Participation of the European Communities," p. 102, footnote 101.

39. N. March Hunnings (ed.), *Encylopedia of European Union Law: Constitutional Texts* (London: Sweet & Maxwell, 1996), vol. 1, 12.1422C.

40. *Results of the Uruguay Round,* pp. 404 ff. The DSB provision is in DSU, Article 2.1.

41. For example, Article XXII of the agreement specifically provides for dispute settlement under the DSU rather than by the Committee on Government Procurement, as under the 1988 agreement.

42. This is in line with general international law, which permits enforcement through self-help measures, more commonly known as reprisals or countermeasures, provided that the measure taken is preceded by a prior demand for reparation that has gone unheeded and the measure is in proportion to the harm caused. See *The Naulilaa Case (Portugal v. Germany)* 2 UNRIAA 1012 at 1026 (1928), and the *Air Services Agreement Case (France v. United States)* 18 UNRIAA 416, paras. 81–

98. See DSU, Article 22, paras. 1 and 2. DSU, Article 1.1, defines covered agreements as those listed in appendix 1 of DSU, that is, all of the multilateral trade agreements appended to the WTO Agreement, as well as the plurilateral agreements in Annex 4 thereto.

43. See XIV. *Effect of Question of Competence on How Views Are Expressed Within the WTO,* statement from the Commission, for the hearing in Opinion 1/94, I–63/64.

44. B. Hoekman, *Developing Countries and the Uruguay Round: Negotiating on Services,* World Bank Policy Research Working Paper (No. 1220 1993), p. 14.

45. S. Golt, *Trade Issues in the Mid-1980's* (New York: British–North America Committee, 1988), p. 47.

46. See M. E. Footer, "The International Regulation of Trade in Services Following Completion of the Uruguay Round," *International Lawyer* 29, 2 (Summer 1995): p. 458.

47. Golt, *Trade Issues.*

48. M. J. Gibbs, "Continuing the International Debate on Services," *Journal of World Trade Law* 19 (1985): 207.

49. Council Directive 89/646/EEC of 15 December 1989, OJ 1989 L 386/1.

50. At the request of the EC, the actual deadline was extended from 30 June to 28 July 1995 to afford the United States more time to try to negotiate satisfactory commitments.

51. *Second Protocol to the General Agreement on Trade in Services,* WTO Doc. S/L/11 (24 July 1995); reprinted in *International Legal Materials* 35 (1996) p. 203. Entry into force of this protocol was scheduled for 1 August 1996, contingent upon its acceptance by all participating countries. Failing this, a GATS council decision provided that all WTO members were free to modify their market access commitments and MFN undertakings over the next sixty days (*Decision on Commitments in Financial Services,* WTO Doc. S/L/8, para. 1, 24 July 1995), in ibid., p. 204.

52. *Second Decision on Financial Services,* WTO Doc. S/L/9 (24 July 1995), in ibid., p. 205.

53. B. Hoekman and M. Kostecki (eds.), *The Political Economy of the World Trading System: From GATT to WTO* (Oxford: Oxford University Press, 1996), pp. 144–146.

54. Ibid., pp 146–147.

55. Opinion 1/94, paras. 59–68.

56. Annex 4 to the WTO Agreement, *Results of the Uruguay Round,* p. 438; parties to the agreement include Canada, the EC and the fifteen members states, Israel, Japan, Korea, the Netherlands with respect to Aruba, Norway, Switzerland, and the United States. Six WTO members have observer status: Australia, Colombia, Iceland, Liechtenstein, Singapore, and Turkey. Two non-WTO members also enjoy observer status: Chinese Taipei and Latvia. On the earlier agreements, see GATT, *BISD,* 33S/190 (1987).

57. M. E. Footer, "Remedies Under the New GATT Agreement on Government Procurement," *Public Procurement Law Review* 4 (1995): 80–93.

58. Article III.

59. Articles VII and XIV.

60. Article IX.

61. See further M. E. Footer, "Public Procurement and EC External Relations: A Legal Framework," in N. Emiliou and D. O'Keeffe (eds.), *The European Union and World Trade Law* (Chichester, England: John Wiley & Sons, 1996), pp. 293–309.

62. The two decisions were Council Decision 93/323, O.J. (1993) L 125/1 of

10 May 1993, and Council Decision 93/324, O.J. (1993) L 125/54 of 20 May 1993. These have since been annulled by the ECJ in its decision of 7 March 1996 in Case C-360/93 *European Parliament v. Council of the European Union*; see M. E. Footer, "C-360/93 on the Community's External Powers in the Area of Public Procurement," *Public Procurement Law Review* 5 (1996), CS148-149. The utilities directive, Directive 90/531 on the procurement procedures of entities operating in the water, energy, transport, and telecommunications sectors, OJ 1990 L 297/1, has since been replaced by a consolidated version, Directive 93/38 coordinating the procurement procedures of entities operating in the water, energy, transport, and telecommunications sectors, OJ 1993, L 199/84.

63. See Council Decision 95/215/EC of 29 May 1995, [1995] OJ L 134/25.

64. The EU measure was Council Regulation 1461/93/EEC of 8 June 1993 concerning access to public contracts for tenderers from the United States OJ (1993) L 146/1. The U.S. measure was Pub. L. No. 100-418, 102 Stat. 1107 (enacted 23 August 1988); title VII relates to the "Buy America" legislation under the Buy America Act of 1988.

PART 6

CONCLUSION

18

The IGCs and the Renegotiation of European Order After the Cold War

Anthony Forster & William Wallace

The policy debate across the European Union in 1996 contained a central contradiction. The international context within which West European governments operated had fundamentally altered over the previous seven to eight years. Yet both the institutions through which they operated and the policy *acquis* on which their intricate patterns of multilateral negotiation rested remained substantially unchanged. Uneasy awareness of the tensions to which this contradiction gave rise was evident in the capitals of all the member states, although neither in Brussels nor in member states was there any coherent attempt to reconcile the two. As so often before in the evolution of European integration, it was easier to focus on the established agenda than to recast it, easier to agree on interim measures than on long-term packages, easier to postpone decisions than to face up to dilemmas that might be avoided until after the next national elections at least. In late 1996 the most confident prediction the observer might make about the outcome of the 1996–1997 IGC was that it would end by calling for a further IGC to consider the issues it had left to one side—as the Maastricht IGC had done five years before.

The Transformation of Europe

The institutions of West European integration had developed over nearly forty years within a stable, U.S.-led security framework and with a clear eastern boundary across the middle of pre-1945 Germany marked by the barbed wire of the iron curtain and the concentration of Soviet forces beyond. Idealist historians of European integration preferred to downplay the importance of this geopolitical framework, to focus attention instead on the farsightedness of Monnet and the creative role of the Commission in constructing a supranational "Europe." More recent scholarship, often drawing upon archive material from the 1940s and 1950s now accessible in Western Europe and the United States, has reemphasized the importance of U.S. influence—even pressure—and of the perceived external and internal threat of communist expansion in bringing together France and Germany (with the Low Countries and the then vulnerable Italy) into an institutional structure more tightly drawn than Britain or other Organization for European Economic Cooperation (OEEC) member states would accept.[1] Recent studies have similarly underlined the centrality of "the German question" in American thinking and in French and Benelux responses.[2] Within this broader security community, it was possible over subsequent decades for West European politicians and administrators to take political-military questions for granted, presenting the EC as a new type of "civilian power" alongside—rather than dependent upon—the United States.

The events of 1989–1991 thus represented a sharp break: transforming the geopolitical framework, undermining many of the assumptions on which "Europe" (necessarily again defined as Western Europe) had been built. Germany was reunited, against the strong initial preferences of the French and British governments, to emerge once again as the "central power" within the European region.[3] The Soviet threat first retreated and then disappeared, leaving the countries between Germany and Russia proclaiming their determination to "return to Europe" through rapid accession to the EC. The United States partly withdrew, running its forces in Europe down from over 300,000 to 100,000, telling its European allies in 1990–1991 that financial assistance and political responsibilities for East and Central Europe *and* the Balkans, including the former Yugoslavia, rested on West European shoulders. It seemed, as the Luxembourg presidency unwisely proclaimed while visiting a disintegrating Yugoslavia in June 1991, that "the hour of Europe [had] come" and that the EC/EU would emerge from the shadow of the United States to become the guarantor of regional order.

For Western Europe's citizens, however, there was little sense of radical transformation requiring a radical political response. For the populations of the former socialist states and their political leaders, the changes of 1989–1991 represented as rapid and fundamental a transformation of their lives as the years 1939–1949, which had witnessed the emergence of the order that was now collapsing. For West European voters, in contrast, the brief excitement of the demolition of the Berlin Wall and, for some, their later brief anxiety over the prospect of a reunited Germany disturbed a pattern of politics that in most other respects remained entirely familiar. Their political leaders continued their struggle to complete the "1992" program and to consider how to move on toward the goal of monetary union first declared twenty years before.

The Uruguay Round appeared to present challenges to the Community's *acquis* as awkward as the distant prospect of Eastern enlargement. The United States reasserted its leadership role in regional and global security, from James Baker's "New Atlantic Partnership" speech of December 1989 through the Bush administration's response to the Iraqi invasion of Kuwait to the reformulation of NATO's "strategic concept" in 1991 and the Clinton administration's proposals for a rebalanced alliance in 1994.[4] The unexpectedly high costs of German unification and the recessionary impact that rising German interest rates imposed on the whole EU economy reinforced the settled self-preoccupations of national politics across Western Europe: popular resistance both to high taxation and to cuts in welfare provision, widespread fears about unemployment and economic change, rising distrust for political elites. This was not a political climate within which it would have been easy to generate support for major changes in EU structures, spending patterns, or established policies in order to accommodate the needs of states that had for fifty years been excluded from the "Europe" with which the voters of the EU's member states were familiar.

IGCs as Negotiating Processes: The Lessons of Maastricht

Nearly thirty years passed between the three intergovernmental conferences of the 1950s that laid the foundations of West European integration and the convening of the IGC of 1985–1986. Once the Communities had achieved the immediate objectives set out in the treaties, heads of government convened to launch new initiatives, most successfully at The Hague summit of December 1969. From 1974 these were institutionalized in the European Council, with the "bicephalous presidency" of Council and Commission responding to the challenges of Mediterranean enlargement and sponsoring the creation of the EMS.[5] Recognition that a broader package of policy changes was needed led to the 1985 IGC and the 1986 Single European Act. The decade since then saw two further IGCs: first the twin monetary and political conferences of 1990–1991 and then the further conference (of 1996–1997) promised in Article N of the 1992 Maastricht Treaty on European Union. IGCs in the Community policy process seem to be following the path that meetings of heads of government took, from exceptional events to an increasingly institutionalized element in the negotiation of the major package deal—on what appears to be a five-year rather than a six-month cycle.[6]

The institutions of West European integration, it should be remembered, were designed to handle issues of low politics (market regulation and deregulation, sectoral common policies) on the basis of a permissive political consensus. The "supranational compromise" struck by national negotiators in the 1950s had transferred substantial powers to the new European institutions only in strictly limited fields, with the most sensitive issues associated with statehood and national identity left to one side.[7] Among the most deeply rooted characteristics of European policymaking have been settled preferences for incrementalism over strategic review, for agreement on immediate specific tasks moderated by commitment to loosely defined future objectives, and for the deferral of politically difficult decisions to a later stage—as in successive three-stage plans for monetary union. By the mid-1980s, however, the spillover effect of accumulated common policies, the unbalanced impact of the established *acquis* on a Community expanding from ten to twelve members, and the processes of informal economic and social integration had created demands for a renegotiated package of policy and institutional changes broader than even European Councils could manage.

The issues coming onto the European agenda, in addition to those questions of foreign policy and cooperation among ministries of justice and interior outside the competences of the EC that the Single European Act place under the European Council, included many of the most sensitive and symbolic areas of sovereignty and nationhood: diplomacy and defense, currency and fiscal transfers, citizenship, immigration, border control, justice, and police.[8] The relatively well prepared framework of the 1985 IGC, starting with the agenda-setting report of the Dooge Committee and moving through negotiation among senior officials and ministers to a concluding European Council, thus grappled with a political agenda intended to lead to substantial changes in the treaty framework and underlying policy and political balance.

Formally there were two IGCs in 1990–1991. Member governments had committed themselves to launch an IGC on economic and monetary union, to consider appropriate revision of the Treaty of Rome to achieve this objective, before the transformation of European order in the winter of 1989. This built on the success of the Single European Act and the progress achieved since then toward the achievement of a single market by 31 December 1992. It had been evident from the initiation of the EMU project twenty years earlier that "the realization of economic and monetary union demands the creation or the transformation of a certain number of Community organs to which powers until then exercised by the national authorities will have to be transferred."[9] The Werner Committee Report had therefore called for the convening of an intergovernmental conference before the conclusion of the first stage of this intended three-stage process, under Article 236 of the EEC treaty, since the changes required "presuppose a modification of the Treaties of Rome."[10]

The revolutions in Eastern Europe and the prospect of German unification unbalancing the internal equilibrium of the EC led President Mitterrand and Chancellor Kohl in April 1990 to propose a parallel intergovernmental conference on political union, citing the profound geopolitical changes occurring in Europe as justification. They specifically called for the formulation of a Common Foreign and Security Policy as a central feature of the transformation of the European Community into a European Union, alongside a strengthening of EC "legitimacy" and improvements in its decisionmaking mechanisms.[11] The focus of their preoccupation was on Germany itself and its future containment within a tighter European Union, to ensure—in the phrase of Thomas Mann that first Hans-Dietrich Genscher and then Chancellor Kohl "intoned many times like a blessing or a prayer"—"a European Germany, not a German Europe."[12] The wider question as to how the EC/EU might adapt to the emerging post–Cold War European order, on which French and German perspectives then differed sharply, was left to one side. Negotiators subsequently proceeded on the explicit assumption that they should not consider the implications of future enlargement of the European Union until the negotiations were closed. The Maastricht Treaty on European Union thus in many ways reflected the pre-1989 agenda marginally adapted rather than any proactive attempt to define a new strategic agenda.[13]

Yet the twin IGCs of 1991 were never separable from the international events taking place around them. Participating governments were constantly distracted by international developments, which fed back into the IGC negotiations, not least because they raised issues about the intentions and capabilities of European powers.[14] Foreign ministers who met to negotiate the details of their commitment to a CFSP in the course of 1990–1991 were waylaid first by the Gulf crisis and the U.S.-led reconquest of Kuwait, then by the worsening crisis in Yugoslavia, then by the Moscow coup; the Soviet Union disintegrated as heads of governments were preparing for their final meeting in December 1991. Parallel negotiations within NATO on the definition of a new "strategic concept," reconciling U.S. and French perspectives on "European identity" within the Western Alliance, had to be concluded before the IGC on political union could unblock the dossier on the role of the WEU.[15] Foreign ministers were also preoccupied with the final stages of the GATT Uruguay Round. Negotiations to create a European Economic Area, to bring the mostly neutral EFTA associates closer to the EC without full membership, were proceeding parallel to the Maastricht IGCs, only to be rendered redundant by the decision first of Austria and then of the governments of Sweden, Finland, Norway, and Switzerland that there was no viable alternative to membership—and no longer a geopolitical block to European neutrals' becoming full members. The scale of overload on policymakers in 1991 was exceptional by any standard. It led in the run-up to the Maastricht European Council in December 1991 to a desperate scramble to settle remaining differences among participants so that policymakers could turn their attention to more pressing issues.

Given the length and complexity of the IGC process, the outcome of the yearlong negotiations could scarcely be described as the product of rational actors pursuing defined national objectives. No governments had entirely coherent positions. Foreign ministries routinely differed from domestic ministries; when politicians were directly engaged, they often moved away from carefully crafted briefs prepared by officials. Governments struggled to make domestic trade-offs to satisfy various domestic groups while simultaneously bargaining with their partners to pursue specific policy objectives.[16] Policy was "made" through disjointed incrementalism, muddling through, and mutual adjustment rather than rational decisionmaking, and final agreements were satisficing rather than optimizing. As in more routine negotiations, bargaining skills were as important as formal positions.[17] The big four—Britain, France, Germany, and Spain, countries that were influential in terms of their size—did not always have their way, since observable power resources did not necessarily convert into bargaining leverage.[18] The Greek government's announcement in early December 1991 that it would link its approval of the TEU to its acceptance into membership of the Western European Union (until then resolutely opposed by the British and German governments because of the complications of the Greek-Turkish relationship) gained reluctant acquiescence in circumstances in which negotiators were anxious to complete and preoccupied with more central issues.[19]

The core executives of national governments remain the final arbiters in treaty negotiations; it is their responsibility to settle the final package, their signature on the treaty. But one should not exaggerate the autonomy of heads of government bargaining on the basis of perceived national interests.[20] Transborder economic and political networks have developed strong links; on a number of sectoral issues under discussion at Maastricht, these played a central role in shaping government positions. The social partners (ETUC and UNICE) and the social affairs directorate of the European Commission played an important role, for example, in crafting key aspects of its social policy clauses.[21] Neither should the intergovernmental nature of the process overshadow the significance of the other European institutions. The European Commission and its president were important players in the IGC-EMU, though Delors overplayed his hand at several crucial junctures in the political union negotiations.[22] The Secretariat of the Council of Ministers and its legal service, often overlooked as players, provided crucial support for the Luxembourg and Netherlands presidencies in drafting treaty articles. The European Parliament shaped the agenda for addressing the legitimacy gap of the European Union; while transnational party caucuses, particularly Christian democrat and socialist groups meeting at the level of heads of government, were significant for prebargaining agreements immediately prior to European summits.[23]

The difficulty in reaching agreement at Maastricht on issues of high politics—money and currency, defense and foreign policy, border controls and police, representation and accountability—reflect the problems posed by the transfer of central symbols of sovereignty for governments whose legitimacy rests upon the authority of the nation incorporated in the state. Yet the exact nature of each government's response and its willingness to relinquish autonomy in these areas varied considerably. Moreover, the complexity and range of issues under discussion at Maastricht limited the number of policy areas for which national governments could effectively hold the gate between national and international politics. All governments had to decide which issues they chose to define as key to the preservation of sovereignty and autonomy; different governments chose different issues.[24] Preoccupation with such crucial issues of national politics distracted them from the transformation of their international environment. Poland and Hungary were already pressing for EU membership while the Maastricht IGC was being negotiated. But it is characteristic of multilateral negotiations that hard bargaining around the table squeezes out the interests of those outside.

Incrementalism as Innovation: The EU and the Wider Europe, 1990–1996

From 1949 to 1989, East-West relations had been preeminently superpower relations, mediated therefore for West European governments through the Atlantic Alliance under U.S. leadership. The development of European Political Cooperation, in particular through its engagement in the Conference on Security and Cooperation in Europe, had given EC member governments some autonomous involvement in East-West relations from the early 1970s on, of particular value to West Germany as a multilateral framework for *Ostpolitik*.[25] The Soviet Union had refused to recognize the EC as an international body throughout the 1960s and 1970s; when Soviet policymakers attempted instead to present the CMEA as the equivalent of the EC, West European governments refused to accept the comparison. It was not until the summer of 1988, several years after perestroika had begun, that a joint EC-CMEA declaration was signed.[26] Western trade with Eastern Europe remained insignificant throughout the 1980s apart from rising imports of Soviet gas; within the Commission a handful of officials handled what economic relations there were, focusing for much of their time on antidumping measures.[27]

    The EC's first response to evidence of systemic change in East-Central Europe was necessarily incremental and ad hoc. The Commission and the major member states willingly accepted, at the G7 summit in July 1989, that responsibility for the coordination of aid from OECD states to countries in transition away from socialism should be assigned to the EC—perhaps not fully understanding that U.S. enthusiasm for transferring this task to the EC reflected a settled determination that Western Europe should shoulder the main financial burden. Technical and financial assistance for the first transition states began some months before the Berlin Wall came down, with the PHARE program later extended to almost all the countries between Germany and the former Soviet Union, as well as to the Baltic states. Commission staff transferred from other directorates-general or national governments or recruited on temporary contracts from elsewhere built up the PHARE program, negotiated trade and cooperation agreements with a succession of countries, and set up Commission delegations to manage the flow of assistance in the transitional states and to symbolize the Community's new commitment. Their clients grew from the two transitional states of the summer of 1989 to five (with Czechoslovakia, Romania, and Bulgaria) by the summer of 1990, and then exponentially to over twenty with the disintegration of the Soviet Union in late 1991, for which a separate program, TACIS, was established.

Strategic redirection was inhibited by the disjointed processes of change, rolling from one former socialist state to another, with each new regime looking for its own bilateral relationship with the West as it moved away from the forced cooperation of the CMEA era. But it was also inhibited by the structural weaknesses of the Community itself and by the absence of consensus among member states. The Commission's characteristically disjointed approach to external relations was exacerbated by rivalries within the college of commissioners and by the expansion post-Maastricht of the section within the Secretariat-General that had handled Commission relations with European Political Cooperation into a new directorate-general for external political relations, DG IA, paralleling and partly duplicating the work on external economic relations of DG I.[28] Detailed negotiations on trade brought in directorates-general on industry and agriculture, with their associated lobbies and sectoral interests within member governments sufficiently well entrenched to resist political direction through European Council communiqués. Negotiation of Europe agreements in 1990–1991, intended to put relations with the Central and East European states onto a track that implied eventual membership, was marked by effective resistance from national ministers of agriculture and their clients, from Beligan mushroom growers and sausage producers to Scottish jam makers. Initial hopes within postsocialist states that the EC would welcome them rapidly into membership were tempered by the sobering experience of sectorally focused negotiations on textile quotas, steel, and agriculture.[29]

Postsocialist governments, most of all the three Visegrád states of Poland, Hungary, and Czechoslovakia, attached the greatest importance to what they regarded as their return to the West. They found it difficult and disillusioning to learn that relations with the CEECs were only one among many preoccupations for the EC/EU and its member states from 1990 to 1993—even more difficult and disillusioning to discover how reluctant West European governments were to accept their pleas for a definite commitment to full membership within a clear and short timescale. But it was unlikely that a majority of member states could have been found at any point between 1989 and 1993 for any such commitment; the relevant sections of the Commission concerned with the CEECs could therefore move only incrementally, from proposal to proposal.

The German government was most strongly committed, beyond unification, to the integration of Poland into Western institutions; ministers regularly intoned that they did not wish the eastern boundary of the European Community to remain the eastern boundary of Germany. The French government was deeply resistant to full membership for the CEECs, fearing (correctly) that expansion to the east would lead to a more German-centered Europe in which France would play a less central role. French diplomatic initiatives therefore promoted alternatives, from the European Bank for Reconstruction and Development and the Mitterrand proposal for a European "Confederation" to the later Balladur proposals for a pact on stability in Europe.[30] The British government expressed enthusiasm for extensive enlargement, without apparently considering the institutional or financial implications, leaving its partners suspicious that its enthusiasm was fueled by hopes that enlargement would weaken the EU's supranational elements and destroy the common agricultural policy. The Spanish government's determination to entrench in the Maastricht TEU a stronger commitment to "cohesion"—increased financial transfers from richer to poorer member states—reflected its awareness that northern and Eastern enlargement would shift the future balance of the EU away from its Mediterranean members. Dutch concern at the lessening of U.S. commitment and the redefinition of its relationship with a stronger Germany made commitment to a "core Europe" a higher priority than the cost and complexities of admitting the CEECs.[31] Italian domestic politics, embedded in the Cold War from 1949 to 1989, were fundamentally destabilized by its end, with inexperienced ministers in new governments preoccupied with far more immediate issues than long-term European restructuring. Danish political leaders were rediscovering their historical ties with the Baltic states, looking to the accession of other Nordic states from EFTA to provide a strong counter-lobby to Germany's concentration on the Visegrád group.

Caught up in the populist backlash against ratifying the Maastricht Treaty, increasingly preoccupied by the worsening conflict in the former Yugoslavia, attempting at the same time to pull the West European economy out of recession and to hold to the agreed target of monetary union, the EU's member governments gave only intermittent attention to Europe's future institutional architecture. The United States continued to press them on security architecture, first developing through NATO the Partnership for Peace and then pushing for enlargement of NATO to Poland or beyond. The queue of potential members lengthened, as Slovakia divided from the Czech Republic, Slovenia successfully disengaged from Croatia and Serbia, and the three Baltic states separated from the CIS. Few EU members were enthusiastic about grappling with the complex implications of early enlargement, but it was politically difficult to deny the applicants' case.

So the EU gave way slowly, from European Council to European Council, responding to Commission proposals and pressure from applicant governments. The Copenhagen European Council in June 1993 set out a series of targets for applicants to meet before negotiations could open on full membership, thus conditionally accepting the goal of eventual accession without giving any promises on a timescale. The European Council in Essen in December 1994 declared a "preaccession strategy," including an upgraded multilateral "structured dialogue" and additional assistance with the process of adaptation. The communiqué at Corfu in June 1994 promised that negotiations with Cyprus and Malta would open "within six months of the conclusion of the forthcoming IGC," while that of Madrid in December 1995 added that negotiations with the ten European associates would open on the same timescale.

The 1996 IGC and Beyond

The TEU specified four areas to be reviewed by the 1996 IGC: the scope of the codecision procedure (Article 189b), security and defense (Articles J.4 and J.10); the hierarchy of Community acts (Declaration 16); and energy, tourism, and civil protection (Declaration 1). The agenda was extended in successive meetings of the European Council in 1993 and 1994 to include other institutional questions, in particular the weighting of majority votes and the threshold for qualified majority decisions (an issue that almost derailed the final stages of negotiation with the EFTA candidates in June 1994) and the number and selection of commissioners. Enlargement from twelve to fifteen in January 1995 (with the accession of Austria, Sweden, and Finland, a Norwegian referendum having again rejected membership, while an earlier Swiss referendum had blocked negotiations by rejecting the European Economic Area) had increased the EU's diversity and substantially extended its frontiers since the last IGC; the special problems of Arctic agriculture and Alpine agriculture and transit had been incorporated into the *acquis,* and the EU now had a long land frontier with Russia.

The European issues that most preoccupied member governments in 1996—monetary union, economic growth, the looming issues of EU and NATO enlargement, the management of the Bosnian conflict after the expiration of the twelve-month IFOR mandate—were not formally on the agenda. This follow-up conference to the Maastricht Treaty was intended to review the effectiveness of the procedures agreed in the TEU, and for some governments to reopen the question of integrating the issues handled under Maastricht's second and third pillars (CFSP and justice and home affairs)— into the tighter Community structure. The institutional issues to be discussed nevertheless reflect both the wider political and economic context and the response of the different member governments to them.[32]

The sobering experience of the long-drawn-out ratification process for the Maastricht Treaty, which had demonstrated that the permissive popular consensus on which West European had relied in the 1960s and 1970s no longer held, set further limits to the style and content of this IGC.[33] No national government had actively educated its public about the issues at stake and the implications of the treaty during the IGC negotiations of 1990–1991. By 1996–1997 there was an awareness among policymakers that treaty reforms must if possible be readily understandable, not least because the national press and national parliaments have become at once less trusting and more active in following the course of the negotiations. At least six member states (Denmark, Ireland, France, Sweden, Austria, and Finland) have indicated they will hold referenda, and a lengthy process of parliamentary ratification is in prospect in Britain and Germany. Finally, the economic backdrop of high unemployment and the recent experience of the longest recession since the war make for a difficult psychological context in which to negotiate treaty reforms and have encouraged some social democratic governments to raise the question of adding the promotion of employment to the treaty's economic and monetary objectives.[34]

As one well-informed commentator has remarked, there are in effect seventeen agendas for the 1996–1997 IGC: those of the fifteen member states and those that the EP and Commission bring to the negotiations.[35] In the light of the confusions and competing drafts of the 1991 IGC, a Reflection Group was established in 1994, on the model of the pre-1985-IGC Dooge Committee; chaired by the Spanish minister, Carlos Westendorp, it comprises personal representatives of EU foreign ministers plus two representatives of the EP.[36] Though its final report was, in the words of the (London) *Independent* of 13 November 1995, "tortuous and confused," it managed to agree that there should be only one IGC rather than a multistage process. The Madrid European Council in December 1995 approved the report and agreed that the IGC would start with a special European Council in Turin on 29 March 1996 "in order to establish the political and institutional conditions for adapting the European Union to present and future needs, particularly with a view to enlargement."[37] At the next European Council in Florence in June 1996, it was further agreed that an additional European Council in October would review progress, with a draft treaty expected to be ready for the Dublin European Council in December 1996.[38] Increasing exasperation among other major governments with the obstructive approach of the weak and internally divided British Conservative government had led to a lengthening of the anticipated timetable of the IGC, to postpone the concluding European Council—at which the final package would be tied up—until after the last possible date for a British general election, in May 1997. It seemed nevertheless likely that the momentum of the IGC and the midterm prospect (as in the Maastricht IGC) of a draft treaty text would have foreclosed many of the issues on the agenda before a new British government could take its seat at the table for the final session.

The agenda set out by the Westendorp Reflection Group is more cautious than the more integrationist member states had hoped. Its repeated references to dissent from a majority view most often referred to the British representative, the minister of state for European affairs in the Foreign Office, a Conservative Euroskeptic who brought the deep divisions within his own party into the Reflection Group. But there was only a limited consensus among the other sixteen. Hardly surprisingly, therefore, the report envisages a relatively limited IGC.[39] The institutional items on the agenda, however, relate to underlying questions about the character of the European Union and the balance among its member states: confederal versus intergovernmental structures, uniformity versus diversity, large states versus small, effectiveness versus representativeness, legitimation through Community-level representation versus greater involvement of national parliaments.

The issue of enlargement hovers over all of these. Even if another IGC were to be anticipated within five years (i.e., in 2001–2002), the drift of European Council concessions, the vigor with which the most advanced of the Europe associates are pursuing the targets marked out in the preaccession strategy, and the sustained pressures exerted by Poland and Hungary in particular make it likely that entry negotiations will by then have moved a long way, possibly even as far as accession for a first group. Institutions designed for a Community of six member states, since stretched to accommodate nine, then ten, then twelve, and now fifteen, must somehow be adapted to incorporate twenty to twenty-five—perhaps even as many as twenty-seven to thirty—within the next five to fifteen years. The Community method has depended on the generation of consensus, at multiple levels from official working groups to European Councils and on multiple issues: a style of policymaking well suited to small groups, with their informal style and implicit understandings. The larger the group, the more necessarily formal the procedures, the greater the demand for a firm and consistent chair, for formal votes instead of consensual compromise, for smaller groups to caucus beforehand to promote their own agendas.[40] Except for Poland, all twelve candidate members are in Community terms small states, five of them (Malta, Cyprus, and the Baltic states) ministates. All, including Poland, will be net beneficiaries of the Community budget, net consumers of extended security guarantees.

The Maastricht compromise on institutional structure was an agreement to disagree on the management of foreign and security policy and on the extensive network of cooperation that had grown up on cross-border policing, border control, immigration and visas, asylum and refugees, and measures against drugs and terrorism (justice and home affairs).[41] Experience since then of the hard choices involved in post–Cold War strategy and diplomacy has reduced expectations on CFSP and diminished still further most governments' willingness to assign such responsibilities to the Commission within a supranational Community framework. There appears to be an emerging consensus that the EU requires a strengthened planning, analysis, and forecasting unit, with weaker support for the French proposal for a CFSP "high representative" to coordinate the dispersed activities of different European organizations and governments.[42] As during the Maastricht IGC, negotiations over further integration of European foreign and defense policies intertwine with developments within NATO. The French reintegration into NATO, balancing moves toward greater European autonomy within the alliance, the management of the Bosnian conflict after IFOR, and above all the issue of how NATO's proposed Eastern enlargement relates to EU enlargement and to a future institutionalized European order, all set the terms within which the CFSP dossier will be negotiated. Justice and home affairs is a more contested area, in which the political sensitivity of the issues covered is balanced by increasing concern in many countries at the absence of effective political accountability and judicial review, with consequent demands to transfer some dossiers from the third pillar to the Community, as allowed for in Article K.9 of the TEU.[43]

Uniformity versus diversity in Community rights and obligations has been debated since the first enlargement, under such labels as variable geometry, flexibility, and multitier or multispeed Europe.[44] Three concerns intersect here: insistence by French, German, and Dutch political leaders that the commitment to monetary union among a smaller qualified group must be maintained; irritation in some "core" countries at maverick behavior among current members; and awareness that enlargement will bring in further divergent interests and demands. The parameters of the debate on a "core Europe" were set by a German CDU/CSU parliamentary group policy paper in the summer of 1994 that envisaged a small group of five or maybe six states (France, Germany, the Benelux countries, and perhaps Spain) moving ahead on monetary union and defense.[45] The British prime minister countered the following year with a plea for a more flexible framework of institutionalized cooperation and integration within an expanding EU.[46] In December 1995 Chancellor Kohl and President Chirac redefined the core Europe idea by proposing an avant-garde group of governments: both a more tightly integrated core and a caucus that could define the agenda and provide collective leadership for a more diverse and less coherent EU.

Enlargement raises a number of delicate issues about weighted voting, the calculation of qualified majorities, the size and representativeness of the Commission, the European Court of Justice, and the European Parliament.[47] The specter of coalitions of small states, *demandeurs* on the

Community budget, outvoting the large member states that are also the largest net contributors has encouraged the Germans, French, and British to press for a rebalancing: for a "double-majority" (weighted by assigned votes and by population) requirement in the Council of Ministers, a closer correlation between national electorates and allocated seats in the EP, even (on the part of France) an abandonment of the principle of at least one commissioner and judge per member state. But for the Swedes and Finns, and behind them the Czechs, Estonians, and others, the symbolic representation provided by "their" commissioner in Brussels (and their judge in Luxembourg) weighs more heavily than the threat such an expansion poses to the effectiveness of Community policymaking.

Conclusions

In a world of rational actors and coherent governments, strategic objectives would be set and institutions molded to serve them. In a world of democratic political leaders, coalition governments, and ministries with their own client groups and interests and with extensive transgovernmental links, incremental change and an indirect approach to underlying issues may be the only path available in handling the contradictions between domestic and international politics, between popular perceptions and governmental necessity. West European leaders, both individually and collectively through the EU, have compounded the contradictions by the heady rhetoric they employed in the years before and immediately after the revolutions of 1989–1991, arousing in Central and Eastern Europe expectations they were unable and unwilling to meet.[48] But confederal politics is messy and incoherent, moving from one unsatisfactory compromise to another. The foreign policy of the federal United States, with its far stronger central institutions, has also characteristically relied on excessive rhetoric, barely disguising the congressional compromises needed to deliver some proportion of what the rhetoric promises.[49]

As with so much in the history of European integration, the observer is struck at once by the fragility of the moving consensus and by the recognition that it nevertheless continues to move. With deep reluctance on the part of a great many member governments, in the face of impatience and frustration from the CEECs, the EU has nevertheless over the past five years moved in its usual crabwise fashion a long way toward accepting these applicant states as future members within a not-too-distant future. It has resisted reexamining its own internal bargains while setting out repeated targets for adjustments it expects the applicants to make before negotiations for entry may formally open. Yet there is a widespread but rarely voiced recognition within member governments that the *acquis* (even the Common

Agricultural Policy) will have to adjust and that the budgetary balance must again be altered in the five-year package to be negotiated before 1999.

It would be neater and braver to address the long-term issues of the construction of a stable post–Cold War European order in one grand inter-governmental congress. But great uncertainties still intervene to inhibit a grand design: over the extent of U.S. continuing commitment, over the pace of transition in different CEECs, over the future orientation of Russia and the management of instability in southeast Europe. The voters of Western Europe do not want grand designs, let alone designs that imply higher taxation or extended foreign commitments; governments across Western Europe have painfully learned that their citizens want them to concentrate their attention, and their tax revenues, on domestic concerns. Their political leaders struggle to reconcile the contradictions, addressing some of the most sensitive issues of state sovereignty as well as the underlying problem of reconstructing a stable European order. They struggle from European Council to European Council and from IGC to IGC. One may predict that they will reconvene another IGC before they have resolved those contradictions; but one may also hesitantly predict that the EU *will* enlarge eastward, perhaps also southward, and will somehow adapt its institutions and working practices to meet that need. By the time of the next IGC, it may have become clear whether such an incremental approach is sufficient or whether the transformation of European geopolitics requires a more radical transformation of institutions designed to serve only its Western countries.

Notes

1. Thomas A. Schwartz, *America's Germany: John J. McCloy and the Federal Republic of Germany* (Cambridge: Harvard University Press, 1991); François Duchêne, *Jean Monnet: The First Statesman of Interdependence* (New York: Norton, 1994); David W. Ellwood, *Rebuilding Europe: Western Europe, America and Postwar Reconstruction* (London: Longman, 1992); Pascaline Winand, *Eisenhower, Kennedy and the United States of Europe* (New York: St. Martin's Press, 1993). See also Max Beloff, *The United States and the Unity of Europe* (Washington, DC: Brookings Institution, 1963). One of the strongest impressions left by Duchêne's biography of Monnet is how much of Monnet's influence in France and beyond after the war flowed from his superb contacts in Washington.

2. Dirk Spierenburg and Raymond Poidevin, *The History of the High Authority of the European Coal and Steel Community* (London: Weidenfeld, 1994), especially chapter 1; Edward Fursdon, *The European Defence Community: A History* (London: Macmillan, 1980).

3. Hans-Peter Schwarz, *Deutschland als Zentralmacht Europas* (Berlin: Siedler, 1994).

4. William Wallace, *Regional Integration: The West European Experience*

(Washington, DC: Brookings Institution, 1994); Anand Menon, Anthony Forster, and William Wallace, "A Common European Defence?" *Survival* 34, 3 (Autumn 1992): 98–118.

5. Fiona Hayes-Renshaw and Helen Wallace, *The Council of Ministers* (London: Macmillan, 1996).

6. Stephen Genco, "Integration Theory and System Change in Western Europe: The Neglected Role of System Transformation Episodes," in Ole Holsti, Randolph Siverson, and Alexander George (eds.), *Change in the International System* (Boulder: Westview, 1980) p. 55.

7. Leon N. Lindberg and Stuart A. Sheingold, *Europe's Would-be Polity: Patterns of Change in the European Community* (Englewood Cliffs, NJ: Prentice-Hall, 1970), p. 295.

8. William Wallace (ed.), *The Dynamics of European Integration* (London: Pinter, 1990), especially chapter 1.

9. Report of the Werner Committee, *The Achievement of Economic and Monetary Union* (Brussels: Bulletin of the European Communities, 1970).

10. Ibid., p. 24. See also William Wallace, "The Administrative Implications of Economic and Monetary Union Within the European Community," *Journal of Common Market Studies* 12, 4 (1974): 410–445.

11. Richard Corbett, "The Intergovernmental Conference on Political Union," *Journal of Common Market Studies* 30, 3 (September 1992): 271–298. Philippe de Schoutheete, "The Negotiations Concerning Chapter V of the Treaty of Maastricht," paper presented at the Centre for Higher Defence Studies, January 1994, Palazzo Salviati, Rome.

12. Timothy Garton Ash, *In Europe's Name: Germany and the Divided Continent* (London: Jonathan Cape, 1993), p. 386.

13. Helen Wallace, "European Governance in Turbulent Times," *Journal of Common Market Studies* 31, 3 (1993): 293–303.

14. Anne Deighton, "On the Cusp? Britain, Maastricht and European Security," paper presented to the European Institute, May 1996, Florence, p. 2.

15. Anthony Forster and William Wallace, "Common Foreign and Security Policy: A New Policy or Just a New Name?" in Helen Wallace and William Wallace (eds.), *Policy-Making in the European Union* (Oxford: Oxford University Press, 1996), p. 422.

16. Peter Evans, Harold Jacobson, and Robert Putnam (eds.), *Double-Edged Diplomacy: International Bargaining and Domestic Policy* (Berkeley: University of California Press, 1993).

17. Helen Wallace, "Making Multilateral Negotiations Work," in Wallace, *Dynamics of European Integration*, p. 217.

18. Wayne Sandholz, "Choosing Union: Monetary Politics and Maastricht," *International Organization* 47, 3 (Winter 1993): 1–40.

19. Arthur den Hartog, "Greece and European Political Union," in Finn Laursen and Sophie Vanhoonacker (eds.), *The Intergovernmental Conference on Political Union: Institutional Reforms, New Policies and International Identity of the European Community* (Maastricht: European Institute of Public Administration, 1992), pp. 79–98.

20. Andrew Moravcsik, "Negotiating the Single European Act," in Robert O. Keohane and Stanley Hoffmann (eds.), *The New European Community* (Boulder: Westview, 1991), chapter 2.

21. Anthony Forster, "Empowerment and Constraint: Britain and the Negotiation of the Treaty on European Union," Ph.D. diss., Oxford University, 1996, chapter 3.

22. Ken Endo, "Political Leadership in the European Community: The Role of the President of the Commission," Ph.D. diss., Oxford University, 1996; G. Ross, *Jacques Delors and European Integration* (Cambridge: Polity Press, 1995).

23. George Tsebelis, "The Power of the European Parliament as a Conditional Agenda-Setter," *American Political Science Review* 88, 1 (1994): 213–228; Simon Hix, "The Emerging Party System? The European Party Federations in the Intergovernmental Conference," *Politics* 13, 2 (1993): 38–46.

24. William Wallace, "Government Without Statehood," in Wallace and Wallace, *Policy-Making in the European Union,* pp. 452–454.

25. Philippe de Schoutheete, *La Coopération Politique Européene* (Brussels: Editions Labor, 1986).

26. John Pinder, *The European Community and Eastern Europe* (London: Pinter, 1991).

27. Marc Maresceau (ed.), *The Political and Legal Framework of Trade Relations Between the European Community and Eastern Europe* (Dordrecht: Martinus Nijhoff, 1989). In the paragraphs that follow, we draw closely on Ulrich Sedelmeier and Helen Wallace, "Policies Towards Central and Eastern Europe," in Wallace and Wallace, *Policy-Making in the European Union,* chapter 14.

28. Simon Nuttall, *European Political Cooperation* (Oxford: Clarendon Press, 1992); Michael Smith, "The Commission and External Relations," and Simon Nuttall, "The Commission and Foreign Policy-making," in Geoffrey Edwards and David Spence (eds.), *The European Commission* (London: Longman, 1994).

29. Heinz Kramer, "The European Community's Response to the 'New Eastern Europe,'" *Journal of Common Market Studies* 31, 2 (1993): 213–244; Jacek Saryusz-Wolski, "The Reintegration of the 'Old Continent': Avoiding the Costs of 'Half-Europe,'" in Simon Bulmer and Andrew Scott (eds.), *Economic and Political Integration in Europe: International Dynamics and Global Context* (Oxford: Blackwell, 1994), chapter 2.

30. Steven Weber, "Origins of the European Bank for Reconstruction and Development," *International Organization* 48, 1 (1994): 1–38; Sedelmeier and Wallace, "Policies Towards Central and Eastern Europe."

31. Netherlands Scientific Council for Government Policy, *Stability and Security in Europe: The Changing Foreign Policy Arena* (The Hague: Netherlands Scientific Council for Government Policy, 1995).

32. Kirsty Hughes, "The 1996 IGC and EU Enlargement," *International Affairs* 72, 1 (January 1996): 2.

33. William Wallace and Julie Smith, "Democracy or Technocracy? European Integration and the Problem of Popular Consent," *West European Politics* 18, 3 (1995): 137–157.

34. J. Lipsius (pseudonym), "The 1996 Intergovernmental Conference," *European Law Review* (June 1995): 238.

35. Ibid., p. 242. See also *Report of the Council on the Functioning of the Treaty on European Union* (Brussels: Council of Ministers, 1995). For the Commission Opinion, see "Reinforcing Political Union and Preparing for Enlargement, 28 February 1996, *Europe Documents,* no. 1978, 8 March 1996. For the EP Opinion, see "Resolution on the Functioning of the Treaty on European Union with a View to the 1996 Intergovernmental Conference—Implementation and Development of the Union," *Europe Documents,* no. 1936/37, 25 May 1995; and European Parliament Resolution on the 1996 Intergovernmental Conference, *European Documents,* no. 1982, 13 April 1996.

36. The Westendorp Report is discussed in *Agence Europe,* 6 December 1995, p. 2.

37. Presidency Conclusion of the Madrid European Council, *European Documents* no. 6629, 17 December 1995.

38. Presidency Conclusion of the Florence European Council, *European Documents* no. 6755, 23 June 1996.

39. Reflection Group, "Reflection Group's Report on the 1996 Intergovernmental Conference," SN 519/95 (Reflex 20), 5 December 1995.

40. Defenders of an intergovernmental approach sometimes point out that the sixteen-member North Atlantic Treaty Organization manages an integrated military alliance on the consensus principle. But NATO is a U.S.-led organization; it is a central and underlying principle of the EU that there should not be a dominant European power providing such leadership.

41. Monica den Boer, "Justice and Home Affairs: Cooperation Without Integration," in Wallace and Wallace, *Policy-Making in the European Union,* chapter 15; Joerg Monar and Roger Morgan (eds.), *The Third Pillar of the European Union: Cooperation in the Fields of Justice and Home Affairs* (Brussels: European Interuniversity Press, 1995).

42. Reflection Group's Report on the 1996 Intergovernmental Conference, section VIII.

43. See *Memorandum de la Belgique, Pay-Bas et du Luxembourg en vue de la CIG 1996.* For the British view of the IGC, see Stephen George, "The Approach of the British Government to the 1996 Intergovernmental Conference of the European Union," *Journal of European Public Policy* 3, 1 (March 1996): 45–62. For the French approach, see Anand Menon, "France and the IGC of 1996," *Journal of European Public Policy* 3, 2 (June 1996): 231–252.

44. Helen Wallace and William Wallace, *Flying Together in a Larger and More Diverse European Union* (The Hague: Netherlands Scientific Council for Government Policy, 1995).

4. 5CDU/CSU-Fraktion des Deutschen Bundestages, *Reflections on European Policy* (colloquially labeled the Schäuble-Lamers paper) (Bonn: CDU/CSU, 1994). The paper was aimed at an Italian target as well as at the "awkward" group of Britain, Greece, and Denmark; the CDU was signaling that Germany was not prepared to underwrite an uncontrolled fiscal deficit resulting from the weak economic leadership of successive Italian governments.

46. John Major, "Europe: A Future That Works," the second William and Mary lecture, Leiden, the Netherlands, 7 September 1994 (FCO Verbatim Service).

47. Anthony Teasdale, "The Politics of Majority Voting in Europe," *Political Quarterly* 66, 2 (1995): 101–115; Martin Westlake, "The European Parliament, National Parliaments and the 1996 IGC," *Political Quarterly* 66, 1 (1995): 59–73.

48. Christopher Hill, "The Capability-Expectations Gap, or Conceptualizing Europe's International Role," *Journal of Common Market Studies* 31, 3 (September 1993): 305–328.

49. Theodore Lowi, "Making Democracy Safe for the World," in James Rosenau (ed.), *Domestic Sources of Foreign Policy* (New York: Free Press, 1967), pp. 295–331.

Acronyms

ACE	Action by the Community Relating to the Environment
ACP	African, Caribbean, and Pacific
AFSOUTH	Armed Forces South
ARF	ASEAN Regional Security Forum
ARRC	Allied Rapid Reaction Corps
ASEAN	Association of Southeast Asian Nations
CAP	Common Agricultural Policy
CBI	Confederation of British Industries
CCP	Common Commercial Policy
CDU	Christian Democrat Union
CEC	Commission of the European Communities
CEECs	Central and Eastern European Countries
CEFTA	Central European Free Trade Agreement
CFCs	chlorofluorocarbons
CFSP	Common Foreign and Security Policy
CIS	Commonwealth of Independent States
CJTF	Combined Joint Task Force
CMEA	Council for Mutual Economic Assistance
COE	Community Operations Concerning the Environment
COREPER	Committee of Permanent Representatives
CORINE	Coordinating Information on the Environment
CSCE	Conference on Security and Cooperation in Europe
CSU	Christian Social Union (Germany)
DG	Directorate-General
DSB	Dispute Settlement Body
DSU	Dispute Settlement Understanding
EAGGF	European Acquisitional Guidance and Guarantee Fund
EAP	Environmental Action Program
EC	European Community

ECB	European Central Bank
ECJ	European Court of Justice
ECSA	European Community Studies Association
ECSC	European Coal and Steel Community
EEA	European Economic Area
EEB	European Environmental Bureau
EEC	European Economic Community
EFTA	European Free Trade Area
EIONET	European Information and Observation Network
EMI	European Monetary Institute
EMS	European Monetary System
EMU	Economic and Monetary Union
EP	European Parliament
EPC	European Political Cooperation
EPU	European Political Union
ERDF	European Regional Development Fund
ERM	exchange rate mechanism
ESCB	European System of Central Banks
ESDI	European Security and Defense Identity
ESF	European Seasonal Fund
ETUC	European Trade Union Confederation
EU	European Union
Euratom	European Atomic Energy Community
Eureka	European Research Cooperation Agency
Eurochambres	European Association of the Chambers of Commerce
Eurofor	European Force
Euromarfor	European Marine Force
Europol	European Police
EWC	European Works Councils
FAO	Food and Agriculture Organization
FAWEUs	Forces Answerable to the WEU
FDI	foreign direct investment
FN	National Front (France)
FPÖ	Austrian Freedom Party
GATS	General Agreement on Trade in Services
GATT	General Agreement on Tariffs and Trade
GDP	gross domestic product
GNP	gross national product
IFOR	Implementation Force
IGC	Intergovernmental Conference
ILO	International Labor Organization
IMPEL	Network for the Implementation and Enforcement of Environmental Law
JHA	Justice and Home Affairs

KEDO	Korean Energy Development Organization
LIFE	L'Instrument Financier pour l'Environnement
MFN	most-favored nation
MOVE	Management, Organization, Vision, Environment
MRAs	mutual recognition accords
MTNs	multilateral trade negotiations
NAC	North Atlantic Council
NATO	North Atlantic Treaty Organization
NGO	nongovernmental organization
NTA	New Transatlantic Agenda
NTM	New Transatlantic Marketplace
OAU	Organization for African Unity
OECD	Organization for Economic Cooperation and Development
OEEC	Organization for European Economic Cooperation
OSCE	Organization for Security and Cooperation in Europe
PCF	French Communist Party
PFP	Partnership for Peace
PHARE	Poland and Hungary Assistance for Economic Restructuring
PoCo	Political Committee
QMV	qualified majority voting
SCA	Special Committee on Agriculture
SDRs	special drawing rights
SEA	Single European Act 1
SPD	Social Democratic Party (Germany)
TABD	Transatlantic Business Dialogue
TACIS	Technical Assistance to the Commonwealth of Independent States
TAD	Transatlantic Declaration
TEU	Treaty on European Union
TGWU	Transport and General Workers Union
TRIPs	Trade-Related Aspects of Intellectual Property Rights
TUC	Trades Union Congress
UNCTAD	UN Conference on Trade and Development
UNICE	Union of Industries of the European Community
USDAW	Union of Shop, Distributive, and Allied Workers
WEAG	Western European Armaments Group
WEC	Western European Council
WEU	Western European Union
WHO	World Health Organization
WTO	World Trade Organization

Contributors

Stephanie B. ANDERSON	Assistant Professor Department of Political Science Bentley College Waltham, MA, USA
Peter BALAZS	Ambassador Embassy of Hungary Bonn, Germany
Elizabeth BOMBERG	Lecturer Department of Politics University of Stirling Stirling, United Kingdom
Joseph I. COFFEY	Interdisciplinary Research Associate Princeton University Princeton, NJ, USA
Desmond DINAN	Associate Professor Department of History George Mason University Fairfax, VA, USA
R. Amy ELMAN	Assistant Professor Department of Political Science Kalamazoo College Kalamazoo, MI, USA

Mary E. FOOTER	Program Legal Counsel International Development Law Institute Rome, Italy
Anthony FORSTER	Lecturer in Politics Department of Politics University of Nottingham Nottingham, United Kingdom
Robert GEYER	Lecturer Department of Politics University of Liverpool Liverpool, United Kingdom
Roy H. GINSBERG	Associate Professor Department of Government Skidmore College Saratoga Springs, NY, USA
Dorothee HEISENBERG	Lecturer Department of Economics Yale University New Haven, CT, USA
Bart KERREMANS	Assistant Professor International Relations Catholic University Leuven Leuven, Belgium
Pierre-Henri LAURENT	Professor Department of History Tufts University Medford, MA, USA
Peter H. LOEDEL	Assistant Professor Department of Political Science West Chester University West Chester, PA, USA
Marc MARESCEAU	Professor and Director European Institute University of Ghent Ghent, Belgium

John McCORMICK	Assistant Professor Department of Political Science Indiana University, Purdue University at Indianapolis Indianapolis, IN, USA
John PETERSON	Jean Monnet Senior Lecturer Department of Politics University of Glasgow Glasgow, United Kingdom
Michael E. SMITH	Teaching Fellow Department of Society and Politics University of California Irvine, CA, USA
Beverly SPRINGER	Professor Department of International Studies American Graduate School of International Management Glendale, AZ, USA
Ronald TIERSKY	Professor Department of Political Science Amherst College Amherst, MA, USA
William WALLACE	Reader Department of International Relations London School of Economics and Political Science London, United Kingdom
Alison M. S. WATSON	Lecturer Department of International Relations University of St. Andrews St. Andrews, United Kingdom

Index

About the Book

The struggle between those who seek a more integrated and even a federal Europe and those proposing a looser confederation was once again highlighted at the 1996–1997 Intergovernmental Conference and reflected in the IGC's decisions. This fourth volume in the European Community Studies Association's biennial series examines the divisions within the EU in the key areas of the Common Foreign and Security Policy, European monetary Union, enlargement,and structural reform.

Pierre-Henri Laurent is professor of history at Tufts University. *Marc Maresceau* is professor of European Community law and director of the European Institute at the University of Ghent, where he also holds the Jean Monnet Chair.